CHINA'S
PUBLISHING
INDUSTRY

CHINA'S PUBLISHING INDUSTRY

From Mao to the Market

QIDONG YUN

Cheung Kong School of Journalism and
Communication, Shantou University,
Guangdong, China

CP

CHANDOS
PUBLISHING

An imprint of Elsevier

Chandos Publishing is an imprint of Elsevier
50 Hampshire Street, 5th Floor, Cambridge, MA 02139, United States
The Boulevard, Langford Lane, Kidlington, OX5 1GB, United Kingdom

Notices
Knowledge and best practice in this field are constantly changing. As new research and experience broaden our understanding, changes in research methods, professional practices, or medical treatment may become necessary.

Practitioners and researchers must always rely on their own experience and knowledge in evaluating and using any information, methods, compounds, or experiments described herein. In using such information or methods they should be mindful of their own safety and the safety of others, including parties for whom they have a professional responsibility.

To the fullest extent of the law, neither the Publisher nor the authors, contributors, or editors, assume any liability for any injury and/or damage to persons or property as a matter of products liability, negligence or otherwise, or from any use or operation of any methods, products, instructions, or ideas contained in the material herein.

British Library Cataloguing-in-Publication Data
A catalogue record for this book is available from the British Library

Library of Congress Cataloging-in-Publication Data
A catalog record for this book is available from the Library of Congress

ISBN: 978-0-08-100919-2 (print)

ISBN: 978-0-08-101003-7 (online)

For information on all Chandos Publishing publications
visit our website at https://www.elsevier.com/books-and-journals

  Working together
to grow libraries in
developing countries

www.elsevier.com • www.bookaid.org

Publisher: Glyn Jones
Acquisition Editor: Glyn Jones
Editorial Project Manager: Katie Chan
Production Project Manager: Debasish Ghosh
Cover Designer: Alan Studholme

Typeset by MPS Limited, Chennai, India

CONTENTS

List of Figures   *ix*

List of Tables   *xi*

Acknowledgments   *xiii*

List of Abbreviations   *xv*

1. Introduction   **1**

    1.1 Media Transformation in China   3

    1.2 Focus and Approach   9

    1.3 Organization of the Book   13

    Endnotes   15

    References   16

2. Mapping Book Publishing in China   **19**

    2.1 Publishing as a Business   19

    2.2 Regulation, Administration, and Control   24

    2.3 Decentralization in Book Publishing   33

    2.4 Privatization and Internationalization   43

    2.5 Booksellers and the Supply Chain   50

    2.6 Problems of Chinese Book Publishing   53

    2.7 Recent State Policies   58

    2.8 Summary   61

    Endnotes   62

    References   63

3. From Communization to Commercialization: China's Publishing From 1949 to 1992   **67**

    3.1 Communization of Publishing: 1949—56   70

    3.2 Operation of Planned Book Publishing: 1956—79   87

    3.3 Commercialization of Book Publishing: 1979—92   97

    3.4 Summary   103

    Endnotes   104

    References   105

4. Ideology and the Commercialization of Book Publishing in China   **109**

    4.1 China's Shaky Ideology Before the Economic Reform   111

    4.2 China's Ideology in Flux   113

4.3 Ideology and Publications   115
4.4 Commercialization of Publishing and Ideology   118
4.5 Ideology, Intellectuals, and Politics   120
4.6 Summary   122
Endnotes   123
References   123

5. Conglomeration: The Formation of Publishing Groups   **129**

5.1 The Different Stages of the Conglomeration of Publishing   130
5.2 Institutional Organization   137
5.3 Economic Advantages   143
5.4 Globalization and Publishing Groups   150
5.5 Summary   154
Endnotes   155
References   156

6. Corporatization: The Transition to Enterprises   **161**

6.1 Introduction   162
6.2 The Status of Publishing Houses   165
6.3 The Reform of Public Service Units and the Transformation
        of Publishing Houses   168
6.4 Economic Sustainability and the Corporatization of Publishing Houses   177
6.5 The Reform of State-Owned Enterprises and the Commercialization
        of Publishing Houses   186
6.6 Summary   188
Endnotes   189
References   191

7. Digital Publishing: Challenges and Opportunities   **197**

7.1 Overview   198
7.2 e-Books in Trade Publishing   200
7.3 Online Fiction Publishing   210
7.4 Summary   216
Endnotes   216
References   217

**8. Politics, Profit and Digital Prospect: Guangdong Provincial
    Publishing Group as a Case**   **221**

8.1 Background   221
8.2 The Conglomeration of GDPG   223

8.3 The Corporatization of GDPG 232
8.4 Persistent Powers: GDPG and Party Politics 235
8.5 Digital Publishing: New Technology, Old Business Model 249
8.6 Summary 254
Endnotes 254
References 255

Conclusion **257**
Appendix 1: GDPG Activities in 2005 *261*
Appendix 2: Intervention of the Party-State in the Activities of GDPG (2005) *275*
Index *289*

LIST OF FIGURES

Figure 2.1   Copublishing supply chain in China's trade publishing.   52

LIST OF TABLES

Table 2.1   Overview of China's book publishing industry (1950−2016)   21

Table 2.2   Book consumption per person in China   21

Table 2.3   Number of book publishers   34

Table 2.4   Annual retail sales of top 20 publishers in 2015   36

Table 2.5   Top 10 publishing groups in the retail market: January to October 2015   37

Table 2.6   Top 10 Publishers by Sales Revenue in 2013   37

Table 2.7   Total number of publishing houses in different provincial regions (collated in January of 2010)   39

Table 2.8   Title output by regions (2015)   40

Table 2.9   Regional book sales from state-owned booksellers (2013)   41

Table 2.10   Book imports in China (by value and volume): 2011−2016   47

Table 2.11   Rights licensing of books acquired by Chinese publishers: 2011−2016   48

Table 2.12   Export of licensed rights by Chinese publishers (2009−2016)   50

Table 2.13   Percentage of school books in China's book market (2012−16)   56

Table 2.14   Total inventory and total annual sales (by volume and value)   57

Table 2.15   Top ten publishing groups in term of economic strength (2015)   60

Table 3.1   Periods of publishing history during the People's Republic (1949−92)   68

Table 3.2   Number of publishers (1950−56)   75

Table 3.3   Title output of China's book publishing (1947−54)   82

Table 3.4   Output of machine-made paper and paperboard (1955−62)   90

Table 3.5   Title output of China's book publishing (1965−76)   92

Table 3.6   Number of publishers (1971−79)   96

Table 3.7   Number of publishers (1979−92)   99

Table 3.8   Title output of publishers (1979−89)   101

Table 5.1   Key events in the process of conglomeration and corporatization   130

Table 5.2   List of publishing groups in China   135

Table 6.1   Numbers of students and schools during the stage of compulsory education (2006−11)   180

Table 7.1   Sales of digital publications (including e-books): 2012−16   202

Table 7.2   Annual revenue of national digital publishing parks in China in 2015 (billion yuan)   209

Table 8.1   Business areas of GDPG and its member firms   224

Table 8.2   Annual revenue and profit of SPM (million yuan)   248

ACKNOWLEDGMENTS

This book stems from my research at Loughborough University a few years ago. In order to keep up with the developments in China's publishing industry and to verify the conclusions of my research, I have followed up with regular visits to the main site of my research in Guangdong, and found that the main arguments of my earlier research appear to have sustained the test of time. I would like to express my deep gratitude to Professor Graham Murdock at Loughborough University. Without his generous support and inspiration, this book would not have been possible. I am also grateful to Professor James Stanyer and Professor Chris Berry for offering me invaluable advice on an earlier version of this research. Professor Paul Richardson and Angus Phillips from the Oxford International Centre for Publishing Studies at Oxford Brookes University also read earlier drafts of some chapters, and I sincerely thank them for their comments and feedback.

I am extremely grateful to all my friends, particularly Sanguo Cheng and Yanhong Kong, in the publishing industry in China. They have generously shared their views with me and sometimes helped me to get in touch with other professionals in the industry. However, I have to protect the anonymity of most of them either because they wanted to stay anonymous or because they may have touched on sensitive topics. My gratitude also goes to my colleagues at Shantou University, especially Dongsheng Fan, Jing Bai, Dharma N. Adhikari, John H. Noonan, and Linjun Fan, for their assistance and moral support. Three postgraduate students, Haimian Huang, Xining Yin, and Xingyu Zhang, provided assistance in checking the references in the book.

I am deeply indebted to Shaolin, Zhiya, Liuli, and Lutian. Without their love and support, I could not have completed this book.

Earlier versions of parts of this book have been published previously in the Journal of Scholarly Publishing 45. 2 (2014): 142–171 (doi: 10.3138/jsp.45.2.003) and LOGOS: Journal of the World Publishing Community 24. 1 (2013): 19–29. I thank the University of Toronto Press (www.utpjournals.com) and Brill (www.brill.com) for their permission to reuse parts of my own articles.

Finally, I would like to thank Glyn Jones, Katie Chan, Debasish Ghosh, and George Knott at Elsevier for their patience and flexibility.

LIST OF ABBREVIATIONS

APP	Administration of Press and Publication
APPRFT	Administration of Press, Publication, Radio, Film, and Television
AR	Augmented Reality
B2C	Business-to-Consumer
BAT	Baidu, Alibaba, and Tencent
CAC	Cyberspace Administration of China
CCP	Chinese Communist Party
CD	Compact Disc
CEPIEC	China Educational Publications Import & Export Corporation
CNNIC	China Internet Network Information Centre
CNKI	China National Knowledge Infrastructure
CNPIEC	China National Publications Imports and Exports Corporation
ELT	English Language Teaching
GAPP	General Administration of Press and Publication
GDPG	Guangdong Provincial Publishing Group
GPPH	Guangdong People's Publishing House
IPO	Initial Public Offering
ISBN	International Standard Book Number
KDP	Kindle Direct Publishing
MPR	Multimedia Print Reader
NCAC	National Copyright Administration of China
NDRC	National Development and Reform Commission
NRI	Network Readiness Index
OECD	Organisation for Economic Cooperation and Development
PEP	People's Education Press
PPP	Purchase Parity Power
PPB	Press and Publishing Bureau
SAPPRFT	State Administration of Press, Publication, Radio, Film, and Television
SARS	Severe Acute Respiratory Syndrome
SOE	State-Owned Enterprise
SPPA	State Press and Publication Administration
STM	Science, Technology, and Medicine
SPM	Southern Publishing and Media Company
WTO	World Trade Organization

CHAPTER 1

Introduction

This book is a study of the transformation of China's contemporary book publishing industry, but it also contributes to the understanding of media transformation in China as a whole. Chinese media, including book publishing, has undergone significant changes since the start of economic reforms at the end of the 1970s. Much research has been carried out to understand the commercialization of the media industry in China and its possible political implications. Scholars interested in Chinese creative industries have also explored the compatibility of the concept of creativity with the rigid regulatory regimes in China's media industry (Keane, 2013; Wang, 2004). However, book publishing appears to have generally been ignored by researchers.

Despite the fact that books have played an essential role in our cultural lives for centuries, publishing has been much less studied in comparison with other, more publicly visible sectors, such as the press and broadcasting. Research by Thompson (2005, 2012) is among the handful of recent scholarly contributions to the understanding of the publishing industry in Western countries, Britain and the United States in particular. Concerning contemporary book publishing in China, the collection edited by Baensch (2003) and the book by Xin (2010) provided some industry information in English. But some of the industry information contained in these two books is now a bit dated. More importantly, both books hardly go beyond providing descriptive information, leaving deep questions unanswered, such as how the publishing industry in China, under the dual pressures of market competition and the state control, is structured and what the dynamics behind the daily operations of publishers are.

It is quite unfortunate that the book publishing in China has not been well studied. Although the publishing industry in China is a relatively small sector in the cultural industries, it is "a major source of content for other media and cultural industries" (Thompson, 2005: 3). In addition, research on the transformation of China's book publishing can not only fill a gap in our present knowledge, but also enrich our understanding of China's media as a whole for a couple of reasons. First, treating "the

China's Publishing Industry
DOI: https://doi.org/10.1016/B978-0-08-100919-2.00001-2

media" as a single system is seriously misleading in developing our understanding of the impact of transition since different media sectors face different political and economic situations in China. Detailed studies of particular sectors are essential. Second, book publishing, as a print media, is a well-established industry with a much longer history than the development of broadcasting or the Internet in China. It therefore offers us an extended period in which to investigate its relationship with the party-state. Last but not least, book publishing is arguably less immediately politically sensitive than the major popular news media of press and broadcasting, and its commercialization has been pushed further than other print and broadcasting media sectors. This is exemplified in the fact that several publishing groups have been listed on China's stock market, something that has rarely happened in the press and broadcasting media sectors.

As Tsou (1986: xli) has rightly suggested, the change in the relationship between the party-state and society is uneven in different social sectors. Reform of the media system, due to its ideological sensitivity, has generally lagged behind other industries. Within the media industry, different sectors also exhibit different levels of ideological sensitivity. The more closely a media sector affects the exercise of power in society, the stronger the motive for scrutiny or control from interest groups (McQuail, 2000: 31). As book publishing is less ideologically sensitive, it could be commercialized further than other media sectors, which makes it a unique arena for understanding the media commercialization in China. Pei (1994: 161) has also argued that book publishing was ideologically "the (media) industry that experienced the highest level of pluralization and liberalization in China during reform." The party-state, being cautious about the reform of the media system, appears to be using book publishing as a test field for its reform policies before extending them to other media sectors. An example is the newspaper publishing. Most market-oriented newspaper publishers had been transformed from public institutions (or public service units) (*shiye danwei*) into enterprises (*qiye*) by the end of 2012, following exactly the route of corporatization in the book publishing industry.

Book publishing is less politically sensitive because of its more culture-oriented content, long production process, and usually limited numbers of readers. Books in China were traditionally used to preserve officially sanctioned wisdom or knowledge of the natural and social worlds. Although modern printing technology and the expansion of basic literacy extended their role, the rise of modern audio visual media marginalized them as a means of mass communication. Consequently, preservation of knowledge and the use in education are still the major roles of the state book publishing in China. Due to this intrinsic role, book publishing touches on current political affairs less frequently than news media. On top of that, the production process is much longer than most other media. The party-state, since it could intervene much more easily in this process, may feel less obliged to subjugate publishing houses to stringent daily control. Consequently book publishing could enjoy slightly more operational autonomy. More importantly, readers of a book are usually limited in numbers in comparison with other media sectors. If we accept that "educational" or "serious" media do not usually reach large numbers of receivers and so are "marginal to power relations" (Mcquail, 2000: 31), it is entirely plausible to argue that book publishing is likely to be less ideologically sensitive because of its limited readership.

1.1 MEDIA TRANSFORMATION IN CHINA

China's publishing industry is very different from that in Western countries in the sense that it is still not fully market-driven. Like other sectors of the media in China, the state control features prominently in the operation of the industry. Any attempt to understand China's publishing industry has to take this into account and to situate the discussion in a broad social context.

China is still a party-state ruled by the Chinese Communist Party (CCP) and claims to be upholding the "socialism with Chinese characteristics." However, as the economic reforms over the past four decades have changed nearly every aspect of the society, China has departed so radically from the planned system of the Maoist period that some scholars argued that it is better defined as "capitalism with Chinese characteristics" (Huang, 2008). With the economy becoming increasingly integrated into the world capitalist system, many have wondered whether the Party could maintain a tight control over the cultural life, which is crucial for its monopoly of political power. The constitution and transformation of China's media system is central to this debate because, uniquely among economic sectors, the media and cultural industries, not only play an increasingly important role in sustaining economic growth, but also provide the major symbolic sites on which public culture is constituted.

China's media have been defined as the "mouthpiece" of the Party and have played an instrumental role in supporting the Party's grip of power. The Party's early struggle for political power and its subsequent political mass campaigns after the establishment of the People's Republic relied heavily on ideological propaganda. Disseminating this was the central role of the Party controlled media. As the party-state after Mao has increasingly relied on economic performance as its source of legitimacy however, the role of the media has been shifted from being a state-sponsored propaganda "mouthpiece" into a hybrid system marked by commercialization. The media and cultural industries now not only play an important role in fostering the development of other industries, but have been themselves classified by the Chinese government as a "pillar" industry in its 12th five-year plan.

The potential political implications of this transformation have attracted increasing comment and speculation. Because the media continue to follow political dynamics due to its ideological role but are also increasingly shaped by market dynamics, the conflict and compromise between these two dynamics makes them a potent vantage point for understanding the paradox of China's transformation. Although much research on China's media has centered on the political implications of media commercialization (e.g., Stockmann, 2013; Lee, 2000; Zhao, 1998), comparatively little effort has been expended on understanding how the media have been commercialized. It seems to be taken for granted that the commercialization of the media system is inevitable as the whole society is changing under the impact of economic reforms. Although this is true, it does not help us much in developing a more in-depth understanding of the institutional transformation of China's media. Since media institutions are part of the overall structure of society (McQuail, 2000: 61), we need to take into account the impact of broad social transformation on media institutions. The main task is not just to state the linkage between media commercialization and the social transformation, but to illustrate how it operates in practice. In developing a fuller understanding of media commercialization, overemphasis either on a monolithic and all-powerful state or an emancipating market force should be avoided. China's media system is full of contradictions, and different forces and players have to operate under constraints. Murdock and Golding (2005: 63), when discussing the contradictions within capitalist media systems, argued that the key players "cannot always do as they would wish" and it is important to analyze "the nature and sources of these limits." It is also an important task to understand the contradictions and structural limits within China's media system. As we will see, the commercialization of book publishing has been marked by tensions and contradictions, between local and central government, between different branches of central government, and between the hoped for outcomes of particular policies introduced by the party-state and their unintended consequences.

To avoid potential confusion between the two related terms of "marketization (*shichang hua*)" and "commercialization (*shangye hua*)," which are often used interchangeably, I incline to use "commercialization" to describe the transformation of China's media in this book. It has been noticed that there is a convolution of the state and capital (Lee et al., 2007; Winfield and Peng, 2005) during the commercialization of Chinese media, while the "marketization level" is still very low (Wang, 2004: 16). This is why I would like to differentiate these two terms. For me, "marketization" implies an exposure to market forces at institutional level, while "commercialization" may just point to the business restructuring at the organizational level even though the progress toward a market mechanism is stagnating. In a critique of the marketization of media in the West, Murdock and Golding (1999: 8) defined marketization to be "policy interventions designed to increase the freedom of action of private corporations and to institute corporate goals and organizational procedures as the yardsticks against which the performance of all forms of cultural enterprise are judged." Four dimensions to this main process have been identified, including privatization, liberalization, deregulation, and corporatization (Hardy, 2014: 58). Some of these processes may have happened to a limited extent during the media transformation in China, but certainly not all.

In contrast, we can identify the process of commercialization as a major force for change at both the institutional and content level of China's media. Before the economic reforms, the operation of media organizations was tightly controlled by the Party and the "political indoctrination and mass mobilization" was their predominant task (Zhao, 1998: 4), though their precise role varied according to the political strategy of the Party during different periods. This political task waned after the economic reforms. The party-state became less intrusive in content production, and media organizations were given more operational autonomy. In addition, the media, formerly mainly or fully sponsored by the party-state, were initially allowed and later encouraged to make profits in line with the new emphasis on economic growth as the prime task of the party-state. With direct state bursaries being gradually reduced to nearly nonexistent, media were entrusted with the double role of "mouthpiece and money-spinner" (Zhao, 1999). This institutional commercialization, however, could not move on without changes in the ideological context. Before the economic reforms, media were permeated by political ideology, with class struggle becoming the primary focus during periods of upheaval such as the Cultural Revolution. As this role faded after the economic reforms, media organizations and products proliferated, bringing about a more plural cultural realm. Although it would now be difficult to reverse these changes as a different socioeconomic foundation has been created by the economic reforms (Chu, 1994: 17), the predominant control of the party-state over the media continues. Media organizations are still officially owned by the state and coercive power is constantly resorted to when the media seems to be transgressing the boundary set by the party-state.

Commercialization is the central but not the only important dynamics underlying the transformation in China's media. Stockmann (2013: 8) referred the different aspects of Chinese "media marketization" as deregulation, commercialization, and privatization, intentionally choosing the term of deregulation rather than decentralization to "stress its link" to a global trend toward deregulation. However, I found decentralization is much more pertinent in China's case. The defining features of China's institutional economic reform, according to Chung (2001: 46), "may be epitomized as the changes toward decentralization, marketization, and privatization." These changes are certainly reflected in the transformation of China's media but if we also take into account the impact of globalization, the transformation of China's media might be summarized as commercialization, decentralization, privatization, and internationalization. Privatization and internationalization are simply derivatives of the process of commercialization, and their impact is still largely restricted by the party-state. Decentralization, however, has emerged as another dynamics which can hardly be neglected in any discussion of the commercialization.

Decentralization is one of those terms which are widely but loosely used with a fluid boundary. Yu (2009: 17) has used it to describe not only the diversified media outlets affiliated to ministries and local governments, but also the emergence of "non-state media content providers." Zhao (2008: 96) has described this key change as "market fragmentation along territorial and sectoral boundaries." In the context of this book I use the term of decentralization in a way similar to Zhao's "market fragmentation," referring to the rise of regional media and media diversification at the central level. But "market fragmentation" is only capable of describing the changes since the economic reforms. Assuming that decentralization as a transformation process started only after the economic reforms would be far from the fact. Schurmann (1968: 175), when discussing China's economic policy during the Maoist period, distinguished two forms of decentralization, calling them "decentralization I" and "decentralization II," which means delegating decision-making power to "production units themselves" or to lower level "regional administration," respectively, and argued that the second of these was Mao's strategy of decentralization. Eckstein (1977: 131) has used the terms "market decentralization" and "bureaucratic decentralization," which are more self-explanatory, to describe the increased autonomy of individual enterprises or devolution of power to local authorities. Clearly "market decentralization," a central aspect of commercialization, was seldom considered under Mao. Mao's China oscillated between a "centralized command" system and a "decentralized command" (ibid: 93) system, because centralization led to rigidity while decentralization led to disorder of the command system. Since most of China's media sectors under Mao were either not well developed (such as television broadcasting) or limited in numbers and restricted in content coverage to regional levels (such as local Party newspapers), they were not fully subject to cycles of centralization and decentralization. But this cycle was clearly manifested in book distribution, as we will see in more detail in a later chapter.

Although bureaucratic decentralization occurred several times during the Maoist period, it gathered a new momentum and expanded its scope after the economic reforms, for several reasons. First, there was a political consideration. The reformers encouraged the decentralization of economic issues in order to undermine "the power of conservative central planners" (Breslin, 1996: 51). Second, China's economic reforms adopted a gradualist approach as the party-state did not have a clear overall blueprint for change. It was an essential part of this approach to allow regional governments to initiate reform policies on a trial basis before the central government decided to adopt or ban them. Third, given that the pervasive power of the state still predominates in economic and social life, decentralization becomes an important way of promoting economic development by encouraging the initiatives of regional governments. Further, the fiscal decentralization started in 1980 greatly increased the economic power of local governments. As a result, the party-state, according to Gries and Rosen (2004), is better called "states." The political implication of economic decentralization, however, is limited. Despite the changes since the reform, China "remains a communist party state" and the central party-state "still controls the appointment of senior local leaders (Goodman, 1994: 4). The center may tolerate local deviations on economic issues "as long as they promote growth at the system level," but "political and organizational realms" are regulated by political reasoning and deviation in these issues are rarely allowed (Chung, 2001: 65). China's media, now both an industry for profit and also a cultural arena with ideological implications, are inevitably caught up in these dynamics.

The commercialization of China's media is therefore intertwined with decentralization. As the commercialization turned the media into profit sources, local authorities and other central ministries were eager to establish media outlets for financial interests, and the profit accumulated in commercialized media provided financial resources for their further expansion. It is the proliferation of media outlets especially those affiliated to local authorities that is the main driving force of decentralization of media. Competition among the increasing number of media outlets has also fostered commercialization. However, local governments tend to impose trade barriers to protect their affiliated media organizations, and this has hindered further commercialization of the media.

However, there are debates among researchers on the impact of decentralization. While Wu (2000) argued that the party-state "still exercises tight control" over the media despite decentralization, Tong (2010) declared that the "centralized media control theory" is in crisis due to the rise of local power. Tong's argument, although interesting, is less persuasive. Conceptually, Tong confused the interests of local bureaucrats with local interests. Empirically, the cases that Tong mentioned, in which local authorities controlled the coverage of local media on certain events despite "the central government's will" (ibid: 925), can be seen as cases of local bureaucrats trying to conceal their policy failures or wrongdoings. This kind of case is not unusual even in a centralized system and not strong enough to demonstrate a decline in ideological control by the central party-state. Tong's presumption that any will of the central party-state in a centralized system should be implemented smoothly by its local agents is flawed. This was not the case even during the Maoist period.[1] By providing a detailed account of the transformation of the state publishing sector this study hopes to contribute to the more general debate on the decentralization of media system.

Commercialization and decentralization can be regarded as two differ-ent ways in which the party-state is adjusting its relationship with the society. Decentralization is more of a realignment of power relationships within the elites of the party-state, while commercialization is a conces-sion of the control to the society (Breslin, 1996: 7). If market dynamics is fully introduced, decentralization will lose its ground for existence. China's transformation after the economic reforms then can be summa-rized as a gradual retreat of the state from its penetration into the society, although with "definite limits" (Tsou, 1986: xxxix). If we take into account this broad transformation of the society and its impact on media institutions, commercialization clearly should be treated as the main theme of this transformation.

1.2 FOCUS AND APPROACH

This study attempts to understand the transition dynamics of the com-mercialization of the publishing industry in China. The main question this study tries to address is how the commercialization of China's book publishing has been marked by the interplay of the party-state and the market. Selecting this as the prime research question has largely predeter-mined that the focus of this study is on the institutional dimension, with-out much space left for normative appraisal. This is certainly not to deny the importance of measuring the progress of media commercialization in China from a moral perspective, but this task has already been embarked on by many researchers, who have diverged sharply on the question of whether the market should be further fostered from a liberal-democratic perspective (Lee, 2000) or criticized for its "failure" from a critical politi-cal economy perspective (Zhao, 1998 and 2008).

The state and the market, as the major political and economic institu-tions (Clark, 1998: 18), are the two most important forces media institu-tions have to negotiate. In China's case, the continuing role of the predominant party-state and the growing force of market dynamics raised a number of questions. To what extent have market forces, touted by many as a would-be challenging force against the Party control, been shaping the commercialization of China's book publishing? As regards the party-state, which has been undergoing many changes, such as the decen-tralization, the renovation of the Party ideology, and the adjustment of relationships of the Party to the state and the state to the enterprises, we can ask what the implications of these adjustments are for the commercialization of China's book publishing.

The first question regarding market forces is relevant to normative debates over the political economy of Chinese media. There are two main approaches to the political economy of media, the liberal and the critical (Murdock and Golding, 2005: 62). Lee (2000), although slightly changing the terms, has discussed the applicability of these different approaches. He has argued that the "liberal-pluralist" approach focuses on the critique of the state, while the "radical-Marxist" approach focuses on the critique of the capital. According to him, neither approach should "be regarded as universal," and "crucial contextual differences" need to be taken into account for an appropriate approach (ibid: 28). He maintains that, the "radical-Marxist" approach is "most powerful in criticizing liberal-capitalist media systems" when the "state control of the media is more benign in advanced capitalism" (ibid: 36) and the liberal-democratic state could be the guardian of the public interest. In contrast, the "liberal-pluralist approach may apply to authoritarian media system" (ibid: 28) where state control continues to be the major obstacle to a democratic media. While Lee has argued that the "radical-Marxist approach throws little light" on the media in the authoritarian state like China (ibid), Zhao (2008: 7) has placed "the tradition of critical communication scholarship" at the center of her analysis. Situating her analysis in a broad social context which she believes to be characterized by the implementation of "neoliberalism with Chinese characteristics," she has tried to illustrate the "mutual constitution between the communication system, the party-state, and Chinese society" (ibid: 4–5), and argued that the voices of leftists and workers have been marginalized by the pro-market media.

The discussion on the interplay of the party-state and market forces in China's book publishing in this study may have implications for this debate. If market forces are proved to be still weak, then it would be hardly feasible to lay the blame on them as the main forces for manipulating symbolic resources. To do so would be like warning a starving orphan of the harm of obesity, which is not wrong in content but inappropriate in context. Calling for public intervention to address market failures, mainly from the state, is also unlikely to be viable in China, as the party-state has always employed the notion of "public interest" as an ideological device, just as McQuail (1992: 3) warned, to "cloak unjustified regulatory ambitions."

Nobody can afford to neglect the dominant power of the party-state in any understanding of China's transition. According to Tsou (1986: 221), "political power continues to dominate society and is the ultimate, unchallengeable arbiter of China's fate." During the economic reforms, the party-state gave more autonomy to individuals and other social organizations, but also set its own political bottom line. The Party never intended to release its grip on political power and has set limits to the liberalization of the society with "four fundamental principles"[2] (ibid: 250). The duality of media organizations, which is manifested in their being "both similar to and different from other industries" (Murdock and Golding, 2005: 60), may mean that media commercialization might follow the route of other industries, but will also face particular control from the party-state. In the process of media transformation, the Party also set limits to the commercialization. These limits are known as the principle of "four unchangeables" reiterated by the Party constantly, which means that under no circumstances can the core principles of "media as the mouthpiece of the Party and the people, Party's control over the media, Party's control over the media cadres and media's role in correctly guiding the public opinion" be changed (*xinwen meiti zuowei dang he renmin houshe de xingzhi bunengbian, dang guan meiti bunengbian, dang guan ganbu bunengbian, jianchi zhengque de yulun daoxiang bunengbian*).[3] However, the operations of political institution have been adjusted since the economic reforms, and this has had important impact on media institutions.

After the disastrous Cultural Revolution, the Party realized that the political institution had to be reformed, not only to facilitate economic reforms, but also to prevent another political turmoil from arising. As White (1993: 44) summarized, this led to separations "between politics and administration, between politics and economics and between administration and the economy." First, the Party readjusted its relationship with the state. Due to the self-limitation of the Party, there was a separation between the Party and the government (Tsou, 1986: 314). The Party, although assuming political, ideological, and organizational leadership over the government, avoids interfering with the day-to-day decisions of government departments. Legalization was also pursued by the party-state to promote predictability in the political and economic life of the society. Second, the impact of ideology faded in economic activities, which allowed for pragmatic economic policies. Third, the government has substantially reduced its involvement in the daily operation of enterprises. Last, the party-state was decentralized and local government acquired more power, particularly over local economic activities.

All these transformations have had a profound impact on media institutions. Media researchers have certainly realized this. According to Chan (2002: 31), as the party-state shifted its policy from class struggle to economic development, the loosening of ideological control was "crucial to reform in the media industry." The subsequent increase in media autonomy was accompanied by increased government regulations (Chan, 2002: 38). Focusing on book publishing, this study set out to explore the detailed linkage between the transformation of political institutions and the ongoing process of media commercialization in China.

Most studies of book publishing divide it into different areas, such as trade publishing, educational publishing, academic publishing, and so on, which raises the question of what area of book publishing this study should focus on. However, posing the question in this way presumes that the book publishing structure in China is similar to that of Western countries. The classification of the book publishing business in Western countries is consumer-oriented and largely the result of market competition. China's publishing houses, however, have been allocated "subject areas" (chushu fanwei) for their publishing business by the state. A publishing house in China could engage in educational publishing, trade publishing, and also academic publishing, as long as the books fall within its "subject areas." For example, a provincial Science and Technology Publishing House could publish school textbooks on science subjects, books for medical professionals, academic books on scientific researches, and trade books on gardening or family medical guides. The focus of this study is on the institutional changes of state-owned publishers, which could engage in a couple of areas of the business. Private publishers, however, are excluded from this study. Although, as we will see, they could not operate without the cooperation of state-owned publishers, they require detailed study on their own account.

Two main methods of data collection are employed in this study: documentary research and a field study mainly in Guangdong province. As mentioned earlier, book publishing has a long history in China and one of the main aims of this study has been to place recent changes in the context of longer trends in order to arrive at a more comprehensive account of continuities and breaks. In pursuit of this aim the early chapters (outlined below) mainly draw on a wide range of documentary sources in an effort to construct a more comprehensive picture, with semistructured interviews being carried out to provide additional information. Published books are a good starting point for sketching out the contours of the book publishing industry in China. Books of collected archives or memoirs provided essential resources for the description of the history of China's book publishing. Trade journals are another important source of secondary data about China's publishing industry. Articles in trade journals, based on the authors' personal experience, provided invaluable data about the industry.

This historical and contextual work is complemented by original research on the current situation of book publishing based on a case study of the Guangdong Provincial Publishing Group (GDPG). This publishing group is located in Guangdong province, a leading province in China's economic reform, and is one of the first two publishing groups approved by the central party-state. There are two reasons for focusing on one provincial publishing group. First, provincial publishers constitute the majority of China's publishing houses. Second, they provide an opportunity to investigate the interaction of local governments and central government departments and its consequences for both the process of commercialization and the exercise of political control.

By doing an internship in two of the member firms of GDPG from November 2006 to January 2007, I was able to experience how Chinese publishers are actually operating and to collect some first-hand primary data through observations and informal interviews. More formal semistructured interviews followed after the internship. A corporate monthly publication, which recorded all the important events within GDPG, provided more information about the daily operation of GDPG. Published articles on the local publishing industry were also consulted. As relevant information comes from a variety of sources, including observation, formal and informal interviews, corporate publications and documents, and published articles, I was able to develop techniques of triangulation, which greatly enhanced the reliability of the data. More recent visits to GDPG and informal interviews have also been carried out in order to keep up with its development.

1.3 ORGANIZATION OF THE BOOK

The book starts with the introduction in this chapter, giving a contour of the broad social context and media transformation in China. Whilst the media transformation in China can be summarized as the processes of commercialization, decentralization, privatization, and internationalization, commercialization and decentralization are the two major ones. This chapter also explains the focus and theoretical framework of this study in examining the dynamics of China's publishing industry.

Chapter 2, Mapping Book Publishing in China, offers an overview of China's contemporary publishing industry, which provides a foundation for further discussion. By examining the structure and operation of the industry, it reveals that a hybrid state-and-market system is the main feature of China's publishing industry and has led to some endemic problems.

Following this chapter are two chapters mapping out the institutional and ideological contexts of the current publishing industry. Chapter 3, From Communization to Commercialization: China's Publishing From 1949 to 1992, presents a history of book publishing, from the establishment of the People's Republic to the beginning of the 1990s. The formation of a planned publishing industry in the first half of the 1950s and the disintegration of this planned system at the beginning of the 1980s appear to be two opposite processes. This chapter details the institutional changes over this period, and also explores how these changes happened. Chapter 4, Ideology and the Commercialization of Book Publishing in China, moves on to discuss the impact of ideological renovation on the commercialization of book publishing, arguing that a changed ideological context is essential for the commercialization of book publishing. Restoring this context redresses the overly mediacentric tendency apparent in some analyses of China's changing media. Contrary to the argument that market forces are the source of cycles of liberalization and retrenchment in the ideological control of the party-state, this chapter argues that the ideological renovation was initiated by the Party and the ideological cycles have their own logic.

Conglomeration (the formation of publishing groups) and corporatization (the transformation of publishing houses into enterprises), the two major policies pursued by the party-state in restructuring the book publishing, are discussed in the next two chapters. Chapter 5, Conglomeration: The Formation of Publishing Groups, discusses the rationale of conglomeration, looking at the impact on the publishing industry of changes to political institutions on the one hand and business trends in other industries on the other. Chapter 6, Corporatization: The Transition to Enterprises, discusses the policy of corporatization, demonstrating the impact of the broader reform of public service units and the state-owned companies on the transformation of publishing industry. The growing concern of the party-state over the economic sustainability of the industry also made the corporatization inevitable.

Chapter 7, Digital Publishing: Challenges and Opportunities, explores the impact of the interplay of the party-state, market forces, and the new technology on the digital transformation of trade publishing in China. Due to the institutional and structural problems in China's trade publishing and strict regulations, the e-book publishing business has been underperforming. However, as a result of the inability of the e-book business to tap into the trade market, the wide adoption of digital technologies and relatively relaxed regulations led to the self-publishing opportunities for serialized web fiction. The online fiction business, dominated by private capital, has achieved a unique commercial success, but the tightening up of government regulations may pose problems for the business.

Chapter 8, Politics, Profit and Digital Prospect: Guangdong Provincial Publishing Group as a Case, anchors the general processes of commercialization and decentralization in concrete experience, employing the case of GDPG to examine the conclusions reached in the previous three chapters on the conglomeration, corporatization, and digitization of China's publishing. The roles of the party-state and market forces on the operation of GDPG are examined by analyzing its daily activities. The political and economic functions of this publishing group are also explored.

A concluding chapter sums up the tasks and findings of this study.

ENDNOTES

1. There was a case that Peng Zhen, the Mayor of Beijing, instructed the local paper in 1965 not to publish an article criticizing Wu Han, the deputy Mayor, despite Mao's will. Although Mao instructed a book of collected articles criticizing Wu Han to be published, the Beijing Xinhua Bookstore refused to distribute this book (see Tian, 2002).
2. The Four Fundamental Principles or Four Cardinal Principles were stated by the former leader Deng Xiaoping. They include: the principle of upholding socialist path; the principle of upholding people's democratic dictatorship; the principle of upholding the leadership of Communist Party; the principle of upholding Marxist–Leninist–Mao Zedong Thought.
3. These "four unchangeables" are sometimes paraphrased as "the Party's control over the media cannot be changed (*dang guan meiti bunengbian*), the Party's control over top media personnel cannot be changed (*dang guan ganbu bunengbian*), the Party's control over the ideological direction of media cannot be changed (*dang guan daoxiang bunengbian*) and the Party's control over the asset structure of the media cannot be changed (*dang guan zichan bunengbian*).

REFERENCES

Baensch, R.E. (Ed.), 2003. The Publishing Industry in China. Routledge, Abingdon, Oxon.

Breslin, S.G., 1996. China in the 1980s: Centre-Province Relations in a Reforming Socialist State. Macmillan, Basingstoke.

Chan, J.M., 2002. China: media liberalization under authoritarianism. In: Price, M.E., et al., (Eds.), Media Reform: Democratizing the Media, Democratizing the State. Routledge, London, pp. 27—46.

Chu, L.L., 1994. Continuity and change in China's media reform. Journal of Communication 44 (3), 4—21.

Chung, J.H., 2001. Reappraising central—local relations in Deng's China. In: Chao, C.M., Dickson, B.J. (Eds.), Remaking the Chinese State: Strategies, Society, and Security. Routledge, London, pp. 46—75.

Clark, B., 1998. Political Economy: A Comparative Approach. Praeger, Westport, CT.

Eckstein, A., 1977. China's Economic Revolution. Cambridge University Press, Cambridge.

Goodman, D.S.G., 1994. The politics of regionalism: economic development, conflict and negotiation. In: Goodman, D.S.G., Segal, G. (Eds.), China Deconstructs: Politics, Trade and Regionalism. Routledge, London, pp. 1—20.

Gries, P., Rosen, S., 2004. Popular protest and state legitimation in 21st-century China. In: Gries, P., Rosen, S. (Eds.), State and Society in 21st-Century China: Crisis, Contention, and Legitimation. Routledge Curzon, London, pp. 1—23.

Hardy, J., 2014. Critical Political Economy of the Media: An Introduction. Routledge, London.

Huang, Y., 2008. Capitalism with Chinese Characteristics: Entrepreneurship and the State. Cambridge University Press, Cambridge.

Keane, M., 2013. Creative Industries in China: Art, Design and Media. Polity, Cambridge.

Lee, C.C., 2000. Chinese communication: prisms, trajectories, and modes of understanding. In: Lee, C.C. (Ed.), Power, Money, and Media: Communication Patterns and Bureaucratic Control in Cultural China. Northwestern University Press, Evanston, IL, pp. 3—44.

Lee, C.C., He, Z., Huang, Y., 2007. Party-market corporatism, clientelism, and media in Shanghai. The International Journal of Press/Politics 12 (3), 21—42.

McQuail, D., 1992. Media Performance: Mass Communication and the Public Interest. SAGE, London.

McQuail, D., 2000. McQuail's Mass Communication Theory, fourth ed. Sage, London.

Murdock, G., Golding, P., 1999. Common markets: corporate ambitions and communication trends in the UK and Europe. The Journal of Media Economics 12 (2), 117—132.

Murdock, G., Golding, P., 2005. Culture, communications and political economy. In: Curran, J., Gurevitch, M. (Eds.), Mass Media and Society, fourth ed. Hodder Arnold, London, pp. 60—83.

Pei, M., 1994. From Reform to Revolution: The Demise of Communism in China and the Soviet Union. Harvard University Press, Cambridge, MA.

Schurmann, F., 1968. Ideology and Organization in Communist China. University of California Press, Berkeley, CA.

Stockmann, D., 2013. Media Commercialization and Authoritarian Rule in China. Cambridge University Press, Cambridge.

Thompson, J.B., 2005. Books in the Digital Age: The Transformation of Academic and Higher Education Publishing in Britain and the United States. Polity, Cambridge.

Thompson, J.B., 2012. Merchants of Culture: the Publishing Business in the Twenty-First Century, second ed. Polity, Cambridge.

Tian, S., 2002. Truth: 80 Historical Questions about Mao (Zhen xiang: Mao Zedong shishi 80 wen). China Youth Publishing House, Beijing.

Tong, J., 2010. The crisis of the centralized media control theory: how local power controls media in China. Media, Culture & Society 32 (6), 925–942.

Tsou, T., 1986. The Cultural Revolution and Post-Mao Reforms: A Historical Perspective. University of Chicago Press, Chicago.

Wang, J., 2004. The global reach of a new discourse: how far can 'creative industries' travel? International Journal of Cultural Studies 7 (1), 9–19.

White, G., 1993. Riding the Tiger: The Politics of Economic Reform in Post-Mao China. Macmillan, Basingstoke.

Winfield, B., Peng, Z., 2005. Market or party controls? Chinese media in transition. Gazette: The International Journal for Communication Studies 67 (3), 255–270.

Wu, G., 2000. One head, many mouths: diversifying press structures in reform China. In: Lee, C.-C. (Ed.), Power, Money, and Media: Communication Patterns and Bureaucratic Control in Cultural China. Northwestern University Press, Evanston, IL, pp. 45–67.

Xin, G., 2010. Publishing in China, second ed. Cengage Learning, Singapore.

Yu, H., 2009. Media and Cultural Transformation in China. Routledge, London.

Zhao, B., 1999. Mouthpiece or money-spinner? The double life of Chinese television in the late 1990s. International Journal of Cultural Studies 2 (3), 291–305.

Zhao, Y., 1998. Media, Market, and Democracy: Between the Party Line and Bottom Line in China. University of Illinois Press, Urbana, IL.

Zhao, Y., 2008. Communication in China: Political Economy, Power, and Conflict. Rowman & Littlefield, Lanham, MD.

CHAPTER 2

Mapping Book Publishing in China

This chapter aims at providing some essential background information about China's book publishing for the discussion in this book. The publishing industry in China has undergone significant changes in the past four decades, while the recent mass adoption of digital technology is also bringing new opportunities and challenges for publishers. However, publishers are just one player in the business, and they are inevitably susceptible to pressures from other players, especially booksellers. This chapter, although focusing primarily on book publishing, will therefore try to give a broad view of the whole book business.

The transformation of China's book publishing can be summarized as the result of a combination of commercialization, decentralization, privatization, and internationalization, with commercialization being the main theme intertwined with decentralization. This chapter will map China's book publishing by covering all these themes. It places particular emphasis on the role of state control in the industry. Although this is a well worked theme in accounts of the communications system under communism, particularly in areas such as the press and broadcasting with a direct relationship to the organization of Party propaganda, it has generally not been well discussed in the relevant literature on China's publishing. Through a close reading of the regulations issued by the government and by reviewing the unique practices prevalent within publishing, it demonstrates that the state control permeates nearly all areas of the industry.

2.1 PUBLISHING AS A BUSINESS

Book publishing in China used to be predominantly a political propaganda tool of the party-state, but has now been commercialized, with profit-seeking emerging as a predominant feature. Publishers are given more operational autonomy in deciding what to publish (although still within the ideological boundary of the Party), and they compete fiercely in the marketplace for profit if not for survival. The commercialization of

China's Publishing Industry
DOI: https://doi.org/10.1016/B978-0-08-100919-2.00002-4

book publishing has brought about significant improvements to the industry since the economic reform. Compared with the limited number of titles during the Maoist period (a significant proportion of which were propaganda books), Chinese publishers now produce huge amounts of books in terms of annual title output. It has recently overtaken the USA and UK as the world's largest publisher of new titles and new editions (Richardson and Chu, 2015: 1), producing 262,415 new book titles in 2016.

The huge number of titles may well be applauded as a signal of cultural plurality and the success of market forces in book publishing. However, it would be misleading to think of China's book publishing as a business fully driven by free market forces in the Western sense. Book publishing in China, to a large extent, is still subordinate to politics and its transformation is highly susceptible to shifts in the political situation. The term of "hybrid creations of government and business" (Chu, 2003: 98) is therefore more accurate in defining the role of China's publishing houses.

2.1.1 Market Overview

China's book publishing industry not only issues a large number of titles annually, but also in volume. It is said that China is the largest book market by volume and the second largest by value on the basis of purchase parity power (PPP) (Richardson and Chu, 2015). According to the official statistics, total sales increased to RMB85.25 billion yuan (about US $13.38 billion[1]) in 2016 (SAPPRFT, 2017). As the official figure for total sales only includes those from state-owned book distributors, the actual sales must be even higher.

As Table 2.1 shows, the whole industry has developed rapidly since the economic reform started in the late 1970s. Although the total print run sometimes stagnated, such as in 2014 and especially in the first decade of the 21st century, overall the figures show a trend of steady increase, largely in line with the economic growth. However, according to the official statistics, the total value of list prices has increased much faster than the total print run, and the total sales is also growing much faster than the units sold (see Table 2.2), which implies that the steady increase of book price is a major booster for the expansion of the book market.

2.1.2 Book Consumption

Despite the expansion of book publishing, book consumption per person in China still falls well behind developed countries when taking into

Table 2.1 Overview of China's book publishing industry (1950–2016)

Year	Output of titles	Output of new titles	Total print run (billion copies)	Total value of list prices (RMB billion yuan)	Total sales (RMB billion yuan)
2016	499,884	262,415	9.037	158.096	85.249
2015	475,768	260,426	8.662	147.609	78.142
2014	448,431	255,890	8.185	136.347	77.799
2013	444,427	255,981	8.310	128.928	73.563
2012	414,005	241,986	7.925	118.337	71.258
2011	369,523	207,506	7.705	106.306	65.359
2010	328,387	189,295	7.171	93.601	59.988
2009	301,719	168,296	7.037	84.804	58.099
2005	222,473	128,578	6.466	63.228	49.322
2000	143,376	84,235	6.274	43.010	37.686
1999	141,831	83,095	7.316	43.633	35.503
1990	80,224	55,254	5.636	7.664	(not available)
1980	21,621	17,660	4.593	(not available)	(not available)
1970	4889	3870	1.786	(not available)	(not available)
1960	30,797	19,670	1.801	(not available)	(not available)
1950	12,153	7049	0.275	(not available)	(not available)

Source: SAPPRFT[2].

Table 2.2 Book consumption per person in China

Year	Population (million)	Total units sold (billion)	Total value of sales (RMB billion yuan)	Average book consumption (units)	Average book consumption (RMB yuan)
2016	1,382.71	7.025	85.249	5.08	61.65
2015	1,374.62	6.742	78.142	4.90	56.85
2014	1,367.82	6.986	77.799	5.11	56.88
2013	1,360.72	6.808	73.563	5.00	54.06
2012	1,354.04	6.832	71.258	5.05	52.63
2011	1,347.35	6.578	65.359	4.88	48.51
2010	1,341.00	6.462	59.988	4.82	44.73
2005	1,307.56	6.336	49.322	4.85	37.72
2001	1,276.27	6.925	40.849	5.43	32.01

Source: Figures of population are from National Bureau of Statistics of China. Total volumes of sales are from SAPPRFT.

account the huge population. Looking at Table 2.2, the stagnation of total units sold and the average book consumption per person confirms a saturated book market. Average annual book purchase per person staggers along at about 5 books, and average spending was RMB61.65 yuan (about US$9.68) in 2016. However, as the figures listed here included sales to libraries and other organizations, and school books usually account for a majority of the total value of sales (as will be discussed later in this chapter), the actual consumer expenditure on books must be significantly lower. In contrast, the average number of books bought by UK customers in 2008 was 12 and the average spending was £83 (about US $111) (The Booksellers Association, ca. 2010). China's book market, therefore, is huge but "to some extent underdeveloped" (Richardson and Chu, 2015: 24). Certainly the figures from the official source did not take into account the market of serialized web fiction, known commonly as "internet literature" (*wangluo wenxue*) in China (it will be discussed in Chapter 7: Digital Publishing: Challenges and Opportunities). A huge amount of online novels are now read as web series on mobile phones for free or at an extremely low price rather than as sold e-books. They have become a big business, but mainly for technology companies rather than publishers and the statistics of the publishing industry rarely take them into account.

Although Chinese people have traditionally appreciated the importance of education, the reading culture is relatively weak in comparison with major developed countries (Gao, 2013). According to the recent National Reading Survey published by the Chinese Academy of Press and Publication, Chinese adults (over 18 years old) read 7.86 books per capita in 2016, including 4.65 physical books and 3.12 e-books (but this survey appears to have counted online novels and treated them as e-books). In the United States, the average number of books read by adults was 12 in 2015 (Pew Research Center, 2016). If we take into account the fact that many people in China mainly read test preparation books or textbooks, the reading culture is not very strong. The Chinese government has been aware of this and drafted the National Reading Promotion Decree in 2017 to encourage reading among the population.

Income disparity, especially between urban and rural residents, has been a persistent social problem in China. This is also reflected in the book business. Urban areas are much more important than rural areas for book sales. According to the official statistics from the State Administration of Press, Publication, Radio, Film, and Television

(SAPPRFT) (2017), sales through the urban state-owned outlets is 5.73 times of that through the rural ones. Although the huge income disparity between them is probably the major culprit, the different levels of average education and literacy may contribute.

2.1.3 Market Share of Book Categories

The market share of different book categories usually provides very useful information in understanding a book market. In Western countries, book publishing is usually divided into consumer publishing (or trade publishing) and nonconsumer publishing. According to Clark and Phillips (2008), consumer books are aimed mainly at the indefinable "general reader" and are prominently displayed in high street bookshops, while nonconsumer books have more defined markets and the customers can be reached through their place of work. These two categories are then broken down into subcategories, such as fiction, nonfiction/reference, children's, school/ELT, and academic/professional. This classification is customer-oriented and suits the needs of a market-driven publishing industry. In China, however, the industry lacks sales statistics based on these categories, as official statistics use fairly detailed subject categories, such as philosophy, economics, and literature, etc., to report book production. In the official statistical report from SAPPRFT on the book retail business, books are categorized into philosophy and social science, culture and education (mainly school textbooks and supplementary learning materials), literature and arts, science and technology, children's books, higher education and vocational education textbooks, school textbooks, and the so-called general books (mainly reference books). Chinese publishers adopt a similar classification and divide books into roughly eight categories: social sciences, natural sciences and technology, literature and arts, children's books, Chinese classics, education/pedagogy, academic books, and reference books (Richardson and Chu, 2015: 44; Xin, 2010: 43).

According to the annual report from SAPPRFT (2017), philosophy and social sciences books accounted for 6.8% of the sales of state-owned bookshops in 2016, culture and education (mainly school textbooks and supplementary learning materials) 69.83%, literature and arts 6.63%, science and technology 4.33%, and other books 7.90%. Clearly, educational publishing is the most important sector of the industry. For the retail market, more accurate data would be from Beijing OpenBook, a specialist book sales monitoring company. A recent report from OpenBook shows that social sciences books accounted for 23.09% of the retail sales in 2016, children's 23.51%, supplementary learning materials 15.31%, literature 13.28%, science and technology 8.03%, languages 6.82%, lifestyle 3.95%, arts 3.89%, biographies 1.42%, and others 0.72% (OpenBook, 2017). However, as textbooks are sold directly to schools, their sales are not recorded by the system of Beijing OpenBook.

2.2 REGULATION, ADMINISTRATION, AND CONTROL

The Party redefined its relationship with the state, as part and parcel of the economic reform. Zheng (1997: 18), distinguishing the Party from the state, confined the state mainly to "legislative, judicial, administrative, and military institutions." To foster the economic growth, the Party initiated a process of state-building during the economic reform (ibid: 17). Government departments, although under the guidance and control of the Party, have become predominant in the daily administration of the society. In the publishing industry, whilst publishing houses obtained more operational autonomy after the commercialization, government administration and regulation have been strengthened to curtail the impact of market forces (Chan, 2002: 38).

2.2.1 Administration Authority

The State Administration of Press, Publication, Radio, Film, and Television (SAPPRFT), under the leadership of the State Council, is now the central government department responsible for the administration of book publishing and other media industries in China. It came into being when the State Council merged the General Administration of Press and Publication (GAPP) and the State Administration of Radio, Film, and Television into one in 2013. GAPP was the dedicated government department responsible for the administration of book, periodical, and newspaper publishing. This dedicated administration system can be traced back to 1987 when the State Press and Publication Administration (SPPA) was established in January that year. To strengthen its authority in the administration of publishing, SPPA was promoted to a bureaucratic position of ministry level in the government hierarchy and was renamed the GAPP in 2001. GAPP used to control directly some affiliated national publishers, but it handed over its affiliated publishing businesses to the China Publishing Group, in order to separate its government administration duties from its business operations. At local levels, corresponding administration departments are also established. There are local Administration of Press, Publication, Radio, Film, and Television (APPRFT) in every province. However, the local APPRFT, although subject to the guidance of SAPPRFT, is mainly under the supervision of its local government and Party propaganda department.

The main administrative responsibilities of SAPPRFT focus on the control of the industry, through licensing the publishers, guiding the ideological direction, supervising the printing industry, controlling the importation of publications, supervising book distribution, and fighting against illegal publishing/piracy. The National Copyright Administration of China (NCAC) and SAPPRFT are in effect "two operations within the same apparatus" (Richardson and Chu, 2015). SAPPRFT is also responsible for making plans for the development and reform of the publishing industry, and supervising the burgeoning digital publishing business (mainly online and mobile publishing). But the trend of media convergence means that other government departments are also involved in the administration of digital publishing, especially the Ministry of Industry and Information Technology and the increasingly powerful Cyberspace Administration of China (CAC). CAC is effectively also the overarching Internet governance body of the central Party, which is titled the Office of the Central Leading Group for Cyberspace Affairs (*zhongyang wangxin ban*). This central leading group was established in 2014 and is currently chaired by the central Party leader.

The Party propaganda department also plays a significant role in the control and administration of book publishing. Strictly speaking, it is not a government administration department. Nonetheless, as the Party controls the government, it can easily exert pressure on the industry. There is a hierarchical Party propaganda system, with the Central Party Propaganda Department at the top and different levels of local Party propaganda departments being established along the hierarchical line. The operation of the Party propaganda department remains somewhat elusive as few documents are publicly available. The responsibilities of the Central Propaganda Department were briefly described in a party-affiliated website (see People's Daily, ca. 2009). Brady (2008), in her discussion of the power of the Central Propaganda Department, cited a directive of the Party in 1977 about the reestablishment of this organization. Although the wordings from these two sources are different, it can be inferred that the Central Propaganda Department is in charge of the propaganda and the ideological control across the whole cultural arena (including media, art, and even social sciences research). It not only controls some important news organizations, such as the People's Daily and Xinhua News Agency, but also guides the operation of SAPPRFT, the Ministry of Culture and the Chinese Academy of Social Sciences. The Central Party Propaganda Department enjoys the privilege of deciding or suggesting senior appointments to all these aforementioned organizations and to provincial Party propaganda departments. Clearly, it can easily wield its power over book publishing by exerting pressure on SAPPRFT. The Central Party Propaganda Department also took over direct control of the China Publishing Group from the GAPP when GAPP as a government department was stripped of its affiliated publishing businesses. In the same vein, local Party propaganda departments control corresponding local APPRFTs and local publishing houses. Book publishing then, like other media sectors, is under the dual "disciplinary systems" of "the State and the CCP (Chinese Communist Party)" (Brady, 2008: 16).

The Publishers Association of China and the Books and Periodicals Distribution Association of China are not independent trade associations. They are normally headed by retired directors of the government publishing administration department. Being controlled in fact by SAPPRFT, these associations can help the government department with its administration tasks. Some of the government administrative duties, such as the assessment and rating of publishers, were handed over to these associations when SAPPRFT was launched in 2013.

2.2.2 Regulations and Laws

To maintain the state control over book publishing and also to alleviate some endemic problems arising from a crippled market mechanism, GAPP, the previous government administration department, assumed many regulatory duties which resulted in it promulgating a large number of decrees covering nearly every aspect of book publishing, such as editor's qualification, royalty to authors, book distribution, establishment of publishers, editing process and quality, printing, book importing and exporting. In addition, the government administration department constantly promulgates new decrees or modifies old ones to deal with new issues arising in book publishing. For example, a new regulation promulgated in February 2017 requires licensed publications importers to exercise censorship over the books to be imported and report a list of them to the government for approval. This regulation applies to electronic databases as well, which would require continual censorship. The operation of a few international publishers was affected as a consequence, including the prestigious Cambridge University Press (The Economist, 2017).

The most important regulation is probably the *Regulations on the Administration of Publication* (*chuban guanli tiaoli*), which was promulgated by the State Council in 2001 and was modified slightly in 2016. It is more authoritative than other decrees issued by SAPPRFT. According to this regulation, the establishment of any publishing company has to undergo a procedure of approval by SAPPRFT. SAPPRFT is authorized by the State Council in this regulation to design the overall plan on the "total amount (*zongliang*), structure (*jiegou*) and geographic layout (*buju*)" of publishers. This means that SAPPRFT can control the total number of publishers, the number of publishers allowed to publish in certain subject areas, and the number of publishers in a particular region. This regulation listed the requirements for the establishment of a publishing house, but it also stated that the establishment should be in accordance with the overall plan of SAPPRFT, which put the approval completely under the discretion of SAPPRFT. Currently it is extremely difficult for a new publishing company to be approved, which is manifested in the rather static total number of publishers over the past decade (see Table 2.3).

Another regulation on printing businesses also has implications for book publishing. The *Regulations on Administration of Printing Industry* was promulgated in 2001 and was slightly revised in 2017 by the State Council. Apart from state-owned printers, private capital and foreign capital are allowed to enter the printing industry. However, book printing is strictly controlled by the government. According to this regulation, printers entering the book printing business have to be licensed by the provincial government administration departments and printers are not allowed to "print (those) publications explicitly prohibited by the State or published by nonpublishing units." Printers are also required to verify the commissioning letter of publishers before accepting a printing task and also to send a copy to local APPRFTs before they start the printing. As the format of this commissioning letter is designed by SAPPRFT and produced by provincial APPRFTs, only state-owned publishers are able to obtain these forms. As a consequence, the commissioning letter actually functions as a printing license for each book. A recent revision in 2017 included an article that printers seriously breaching the regulation could even face criminal charges.

Copyright law is the cornerstone of modern publishing industry. Following the establishment of the People's Republic in 1949, all laws promulgated by the former government, including the copyright law, were abolished (Shen, 2008: 12). This left China without a copyright law for about 40 years. Some may have found this to be astonishing. A couple of researchers attributed this to "a lack of cultural and legal traditions for dealing with cultural materials as property" (Bates and Liu, 2010: 7–8). However, it is worth pointing out that there was institutionally no need for a copyright law during the period of the planned economy, as authors had little economic right over their works and publishers were not under pressure to generate profits. Piracy was very unlikely as all publishers, booksellers, and printers were owned and strictly controlled by the state. Shortly after the economic reform, the Ministry of Culture issued a regulation in 1984 on copyright protection (Shen, 2008: 14), which provided a loose protection for authors in the new social context. But it was not until 1990 that China promulgated its copyright law (ibid: 14), subscribing two years later to the Berne Convention and the Universal Copyright Convention in 1992. To meet the requirements of the entry into the World Trade Organization (WTO), China amended its copyright law in October 2001. In 2010 the copyright law was revised again.

Interestingly, the current publishing administration and regulation system is to some extent similar to the system before 1949. Under the rule of Kuomintang (or the Nationalist Party), the major rival to the Communists, the Central Propaganda Department of Nationalist Party played an important role in the control of media, and there was also a hierarchical party and government system in place to censor publications (see Wu et al., 1997: 141–145). Some of the regulations, such as the *Decree on Censoring Books and Magazines*,[3] seem to be able to find their contemporary counterparts.[4]

2.2.3 Sponsoring System

According to the *Regulation on Management of Publishing*, there has to be a sponsoring organization (*zhuguan bumen*) and a managing organization (*zhuban bumen*) for each and every publishing house in China. This sponsoring system also applies to newspaper and magazine publishing. The sponsoring organization usually owns the publishing house and has the predominant control over it. The sponsoring organization (*zhuguan bumen*) could set up a separate managing organization (*zhuban bumen*) dedicated to managing the operation of the subsidiary publishing house, or it could assume the role of the managing organization itself. This sponsoring organization has to be a state agency or a state-controlled organization with a qualified position in the bureaucratic hierarchy. In book publishing, there are several kinds of sponsoring organizations. They include ministries of central government, local Press and Publication Administration Bureaus and other government departments, universities, important research institutes, national "people's mass organizations",[5] the army (Song, 2003), and the Party Committee.[6] Although the *Regulation on Management of Publishing* does not openly prohibit the establishment of private publishing houses, the requirement for sponsoring and managing organizations in fact excludes the possibility of independent private publishers. The sponsoring system effectively puts all publishing houses under the hierarchical control of the party-state, which can issue directives to the sponsoring organizations to control their affiliated publishing houses whenever necessary. However, a potential problem with this system is that the sponsoring organizations could resort to their bureaucratic power to pursue economic interests for their affiliated publishing business. This problem was so serious in newspaper and magazine publishing that the central Party and government had to wage a campaign in 2003 against the compulsory subscription of magazines and newspapers.

2.2.4 Censorship and Self-Censorship

There are two kinds of censorship for Chinese publishers, prepublication censorship and the post-publication censorship. According to the *Administrative Provisions on Book Publishing* (*tushu chuban guanli guiding*), all publishers have to prepare an annual publishing plan (*niandu xuanti*) in advance. This includes an overall report and a list of book proposals, and it has to be approved by a state agency, which will be the local APPRFT for local publishers or the relevant sponsoring organization for national publishers. The local APPRFTs or other sponsoring organizations then have to submit an analysis report of the publishing plans with an attached list of publishing proposals to SAPPRFT. All books have to be approved before their publication. Publishers may add new book proposals to their annual publishing plan, but these extra book proposals also have to be approved. Publishers used to be able to apply for their extra proposals to be approved quarterly (Zhejiang Provincial PPB, 2002) or monthly. Those quarterly added book proposals were known as quarterly publishing plans (*jidu xuanti*). Although this gave publishers some flexibility, there was normally a limit on how many extra book proposals could be approved. For other urgent publishing proposals, publishers were expected to give strong reasons to support their application for approval. These restrictions would make it difficult for publishers to respond quickly to changes in the market. In 2009, SAPPRFT introduced a new policy and publishers can now apply online to the government at any time to have their extra publishing plans approved.

SAPPRFT normally issues a notice in the autumn of every year requesting the annual publishing plans of publishers for the next year. In this notice, SAPPRFT would suggest some "important topics," depending on contemporaneous political tasks, for publishers to choose, and also warn publishers off some topics. During the prepublication censorship, book drafts are normally not required for scrutiny. But the government administration department does list a few sensitive topics, and publishing proposals on these topics have to submit book drafts for scrutiny.[7]

Post-publication censorship is organized by the government. In a decree issued in 1994,[8] SAPPRFT required local APPRFTs or the sponsoring organization to organize post-publication "scrutiny readings" (*shendu*) for published books. An analysis report is also required to be submitted to SAPPRFT every three months following these "scrutiny readings."

Self-censorship is probably more important in China's book publishing however. After all, prepublication censorship does not censor the detailed content of books and post-publication censorship could not change the fact that many copies may have already been sold. Recognizing this, the government devolves most of the censorship duties to publishers themselves. All senior staff of publishing houses are aware of the prevailing ideological boundary in book publishing through frequent "political studies" (*zhengzhi xuexi*). SAPPRFT requires manuscripts to undergo three stages of scrutiny (*sanshen*) within the publishing house before its publication.[9] Normally, the executive editor is responsible for the first stage of scrutiny reading, a senior editor in charge of a specific subject area is responsible for the second stage, and the editorial director of the publishing house makes the final judgement. As a wrong decision to publish a politically unacceptable book would incur penalties for relevant decision-makers and publishing houses, publishers are under strong pressure for self-censorship.

2.2.5 Other Control Measures Over Publishers

Publishing houses are allocated specific subject areas (*chushu fanwei*) for their publishing business. The main subject area of a publisher is often reflected in its title. For most provinces, there is a people's publishing house, a literature and art publishing house, an educational publishing house, a fine arts publishing house, and a children's publishing house. Local people's publishing houses are intended as the key publisher in serving the propaganda tasks of its local Party and government, and publish books mainly in the area of social sciences. At the same time publishing in some subject areas might be more profitable than others. So to help those publishers assigned unprofitable or less profitable subject areas to survive, the restriction on subject areas is fluid. But there is still a rough boundary for each publisher. Books published outside the allocated subject areas normally should not exceed a certain percentage in the annual publishing plan of a publisher.[10]

Book publishers have to apply for International Standard Book Numbers (ISBNs) for their books before the publication. ISBN was originally created in the 1960s as a unique book identifier to be used in book distribution, but was adopted in China as the sole legal identity of books. Acquiring an ISBN for a book is like obtaining a license for a specific book to be published and distributed. SAPPRFT controls the issuing of ISBNs, and by so doing, has great leverage on publishing houses. The past practice used to be that a qualified editor would be allocated five ISBNs annually (Liu, 2006). A publisher, depending on its number of qualified editors, could then be licensed a block of ISBNs each year. However, some state-owned publishers illegally sold their allocated ISBNs to private publishers to make a profit. In order to curtail this problem, the government introduced a policy called real-name registration system (*shiming zhi*) in 2009, under which ISBNs are now only issued to specific publishing proposals with exact book titles and other detailed product information. SAPPRFT, by controlling the total amount of ISBNs licensed, effectively controls the total title output of the industry.

The performance of publishers was assessed a couple of times by GAPP and the Central Party Propaganda Department in 1990s. This assessment was formalized into a complex points system in 2008 which quantified all the factors that the party-state thought should guide the operation of publishers into the system.[11] A wide range of factors, such as the book prizes received, honors awarded to publishers, book production quality, copyrights exported, record of upholding the party-line, business performance, and editor's qualification, contribute to an overall possible total of 1000 point. An extra factor, activities of "social public interest" (*shehui gongyi*), was worth another 30 points. These "social public interest" activities normally refer to donations to schools or libraries and support for the development of rural villages. Based on the points a publisher scores, it would be rated according to a scale of four grades. However, this point system seems to have been scrapped and replaced by another scheme called China Publishing Governmental Awards, which still serves as a guide for the operation of publishers. Publishers normally enter the competition for this award every three years.

As should already be clear, SAPPRFT exercises considerable influence over publishers. The establishment of a publishing house has to be approved by SAPPRFT. In addition, every publisher has to report to SAPPRFT biennially for an assessment (known as *nianjian*). Failing to pass this assessment will result in the suspension of its publishing business or even the withdrawal of its license to publish. All editors have to acquire a professional qualification. Although this general requirement applies to many other industries and services, keeping to the ideological line of the Party is a prerequisite for editors to progress in this qualification system. SAPPRFT also holds sway over what books should or should not be published. It announces a list of sensitive topics (*zhongda xuanti*) and requires publishing plans on these topics to be approved by relevant Party or government departments and be reported to itself and the Central Party Propaganda Department. The Central Party Propaganda Department and SAPPRFT issues an annual notice of "important topics" (*zhongdian xuanti*) according to the central topic of propaganda tasks. Publishers are then required to propose a certain percentage of books on "important topics" in their annual publishing plans.[12] When they submit their plans for approval, they are also required to report how many books on "important topics" have been published during the previous year. Publishing projects on these topics are known as "theme publishing" (*zhuti chuban*) in the industry. In addition, SAPPRFT and the Central Party Propaganda Department intermittently issue notices on currently sensitive topics or important topics to publishers.

As can be seen, book publishers in China are institutionally and administratively controlled by the party-state through a variety of mechanisms. SAPPRFT, as the top government administration department, decides who can publish, what should be published, what kinds of publications are prohibited and how many titles can be published. Hence, although book publishers have to survive on their profit, they still have to publish a certain number of books on "important topics" to fulfill their propaganda tasks.

2.3 DECENTRALIZATION IN BOOK PUBLISHING

Decentralization is another major aspect of the transformation of book publishing. To understand it, we have to discuss the so-called "tiao and kuai" bureaucratic system. As mentioned earlier, local APPRFTs are under the supervision of SAPPRFT as well as the local government, forming a matrix-like system. This matrix, is not confined to book publishing, but is a general feature of the Chinese bureaucratic system and is known as the "tiao (vertical line) and kuai (horizontal piece)" system. As Lin (2001: 126) has explained, the administrative units within the government are usually under two sets of commands. Commands from central government ministries traveling down to the relevant administrative units of local governments along the hierarchy line formed a vertical command system, known as "tiao." The other set of commands, from local Party or government to subsidiary government departments or other organizations form a horizontal command system, known as "kuai." The balance of control between "tiao" and "kuai" varies depending on the political context of concentration or decentralization. According to the sponsoring system book publishers have to be affiliated to their sponsoring organizations within this "tiao and kuai" matrix. At the same time, the Party itself is also organized in a matrix, with the central Party departments as the "tiao" and the local Party committee as the "kuai." The relevant position within the government matrix is usually supervised by a corresponding Party department in the Party matrix. In book publishing, the local APPRFTs are supervised by local Party propaganda departments. Publishers, under the supervision of these dual matrices and their sponsoring organizations, therefore, have many bosses whose interests may conflict.

2.3.1 National and Regional Publishers

According to the *General Information of National Press and Publishing Industry in 2016* produced by SAPPRFT (2017), there were a total of 584 state-owned book publishers[13] (including 33 imprints of publishers) in 2016 in mainland China. Although this number varies in different years, it has been fairly stable over the past decade, staying at around 580. This is because the establishment of publishing houses is tightly controlled by SAPPRFT, and, partly thanks to this control over the entry of new competitors, few publishers went bust. Publishers are defined as either national or local according to their affiliated sponsoring organizations. Publishers affiliated to central Party or state agencies are national publishers, while those affiliated to local Party or state agencies are local publishers. After the economic reform, publishers affiliated to local state agencies have increased rapidly and as the figures in Table 2.3 show, have become the majority of publishers. This development has accelerated the decentralization of publishing.

The situation for university presses however is different. All universities in China have their sponsoring organizations, which could be the Ministry of Education, other government ministries, or corresponding local education bureaus. The sponsoring organization of a university would also be the sponsoring organization of the university press, with the university being the managing organization of the press. However, it appears that university presses affiliated to the Ministry of Education are only defined as national publishers if they are located in Beijing and as

Table 2.3 Number of book publishers

Year	National publishers	Regional publishers	Total
2016	219	365	584
2015	219	365	584
2014	221	362	583
2013	221	361	582
2012	220	360	580
2011	220	360	580
2010	221	360	581
2009	221	359	580
2008	220	359	579
2007	220	358	578
2006	220	353	573
2005	220	353	573
2004	220	353	573
2003	220	350	570
1976	40	35	75
1966	38	49	87
1956	54	47	101

Source: The data from 2003 to 2016 are from SAPPRFT[14] and the data from 1956 to 1976 are from Song et al. (1999: 163–191).

local publishers if they are located elsewhere (see the list of national and local publishers in Pan et al., 2005). This is probably for administrative convenience, as publishers normally have to submit their publishing proposals to, or sort out many other administrative issues with, local APPRFTs or their sponsoring organizations. It would be more difficult for many university presses affiliated to the Ministry of Education but based outside Beijing to communicate with the Ministry of Education.

As Table 2.3 shows, the number of national publishers, which are mainly affiliated to central state agencies, has also increased, quintupling between 1976 (at the end of the Cultural Revolution) and 2016. By and large, every government ministry has one or more affiliated publishing house. Many central state agencies, such as the army, the Supreme People's Court, and the Supreme People's Procuratorate, also have affiliated publishing houses. Although some ministries were terminated in the reshuffle of government departments, their affiliated publishing companies normally continue to exist with an appropriate new sponsoring organization. China Electric Power Press, which used to be sponsored by the Ministry of Electrical Power for example, is now affiliated to the State Grid Corporation of China, which is a state-owned company supervised directly by the State Council. Many of these state agencies are much more powerful than SAPPRFT in the state bureaucracy, which weakens the control of SAPPRFT. Some nongovernment or semigovernment organizations also have affiliated publishing houses. The *Writers Association* owns the Writer's Publishing House, and the *Women's Federation* owns China Women's Publishing House.

2.3.2 Market Share of Publishers

If the above discussion on decentralization is mainly from an administrative perspective, the following discussion will be from a commercial perspective. By looking at the market share of different publishers, we can find out if the market is concentrated in a few publishers. In terms of sales revenue in the retail market in 2015, the prestigious Commercial Press topped the list (see Table 2.4). Statistics from Beijing OpenBook suggested a change of ranking in 2016. Beijing United Publishing Company became the top player in the retail market, accounting for 2.49%, followed by CITIC Press with a figure of 2.13%. It was also reported by Beijing OpenBook that more than half of the publishers had a miniscule presence in the market, with less than 0.1% share of the retail

Table 2.4 Annual retail sales of top 20 publishers in 2015

Rank	Publisher	Market share (%)
1	Commercial Press	2.61
2	People's Publishing House	2.51
3	China Machine Press	1.89
4	People's Post and Telecommunications Press	1.65
5	Hunan Literature and Art Publishing House	1.64
6	Beijing United Publishing Company	1.59
7	Zhejiang Juvenile & Children's Publishing House	1.59
8	CITIC Press	1.58
9	Chemical Industry Press	1.55
10	Foreign Language Teaching and Research Press	1.54
11	Electronic Industry Press	1.54
12	Shaanxi People's Education Press	1.41
13	Changjiang Literature and Art Publishing House	1.40
14	Chinese Overseas Publishing Company	1.35
15	People's Literature Publishing House	1.20
16	Educational Science Publishing House	1.16
17	Foreign Language Press	1.13
18	Party Construction Reading Materials Press	1.07
19	China Children's Press and Publication Group	1.04
20	21st Century Publishing House	1.03

Source: Liu, B., Wu, S., 2016. China Publishing Yearbook 2016 (*zhongguo chuban nianjian 2016*). China Publishing Yearbook Publishing Company (*zhongguo chuban nianjian zazhishe youxian gongsi*), Beijing (in Chinese).

sales during the first half of 2017 (Jia, 2017). Overall the retail market in China has seen little concentration. However, concentration might be considerably higher in some subject areas, such as the English language teaching (ELT) market. The Foreign Language Teaching and Research Press takes over 20% of the whole ELT market, including 10% of the school ELT textbook market and 50% of the tertiary ELT market (Richardson and Chu, 2015).

Publishing conglomerates, known as the publishing groups, have been established in China, and many publishers in China are now members of them. The concentration level in the retail market is still low even if the market share is calculated based on publishing groups. In the retail market for the first 10 months in 2015, China Publishing Group was the top player, accounting for 6.8% of the market (see Table 2.5).

However, these two rankings did not take into account the sales of textbooks, which do not go through the retail channel. In terms of total annual sales revenue in 2013, leading publishers in China are mainly

Table 2.5 Top 10 publishing groups in the retail market: January to October 2015

Rank	Publishing groups	Market share (%)
1	China Publishing Group	6.80
2	Shanghai Century Publishing Group	4.00
3	Jiangsu Phoenix Publishing and Media Group	3.17
4	China South Publishing and Media Group (Hunan)	2.85
5	Hubei Changjiang Publishing and Media Group	2.82
6	Zhejiang Publishing United Group	2.81
7	Jilin Publishing Group	2.73
8	China International Publishing Group	2.70
9	Beijing Publishing Group	2.10
10	Shaanxi Xinhua Publishing and Media Group	1.94

Source: China Publishing and Media Journal (*zhongguo chuban chuanmei shangbao*), 2015. Analysis of the market share of publishing groups in the retail market January to October (*1–10 yue quanguo chuban jituan lingshou shichang bantu fenxi*). <http://www.600757.com.cn/show-22-9071-1.html> (accessed 30.09.17) (in Chinese).

Table 2.6 Top 10 Publishers by Sales Revenue in 2013

Rank	Publisher	Sale revenue (RMB billion yuan)
1	People's Education Press	3.46
2	Higher Education Press	3.03
3	Commercial Press	2.44
4	Science Press	1.77
5	Foreign Language Teaching and Research Press	1.73
6	Beijing Normal University Publishing House	1.66
7	Jiangsu Education Publishing House	1.51
8	Guangxi Normal University Press	1.44
9	Hunan Education Press	1.44
10	People's Medical Press	1.42

Source: Richardson, P., Chu, X., 2015. PA Market Report China. The Publishers Association, London.

educational publishers (see Table 2.6). Although the top two players are now both members of the gigantic China Education Publishing and Media Group and their total sales were nearly RMB6.5 billion yuan, it can still be inferred from the figures that the concentration level of the book market is relatively low, considering the fact that the total sales in 2013 were over RMB73.56 billion yuan.

2.3.3 The Provincial Publishing Industry

China is a vast country with a huge population, with many of its provinces having a population larger than the UK. As a result, apart from a couple of remote or less populous areas, such as Tibet and Hainan, most provincial book markets could sustain a sizable local publishing industry.

Beijing, as the capital city accommodating nearly all national publishers, is the center of China's book publishing. According to data collected in 2003 (Sun and Wei, 2005), of the 570 publishing houses in China in that year, 235 were based in Beijing (including 218 national publishers and 17 local publishers affiliated to Beijing municipal government). Shanghai, which used to be the center of China's publishing industry before 1949, is now the second most important center with about 40 publishers. Apart from these two centers, the remaining publishing houses tend to be spread more evenly across the country. In order to acquire accurate data on the number of publishers in different regions, I collated a list from the website of China Book Publishing (*zhongguo tushu chuban wang*) (www.bkpcn.com), which was affiliated to GAPP and provided a list of book publishers. The original address for this website was www.chinabook.gapp.gov.cn, which clearly revealed that it was administered by GAPP. By excluding three electronic publishers from its list, a total number of 578 book publishers were found and a table of the number of publishers for each provincial region was produced (see Table 2.7).

National publishers used to produce nearly half of the total title output of China's publishing industry. In 2003 they published 81,828 titles, accounting for about 42.98% of the total title output of that year (Sun and Wei, 2005). However, local publishers have increased their output rapidly. According to the China Publishing Yearbook 2016, national publishers produced 194,085 titles (a total of 2,220.43 million copies) in 2015, while the output of local publishers reached 281,683 (a total of 6,441.90 million copies) (Liu and Wu, 2016). In term of the title output by regions, Beijing is leading the league as most national publishers are based there. Jiangsu province has overtaken Shanghai as the second most prolific region, producing 26,503 titles in 2015 (see Table 2.8).

It is not very easy to assess the book sales in individual provinces. The statistics published by the China Book Business Report (*zhongguo tushu shangbao*), a trade paper, provide a useful reference. Although it is claimed that the data are collected by the SAPPRFT, caution should be exercised as only the sales from state-owned booksellers are included and there is

Table 2.7 Total number of publishing houses in different provincial regions (collated in January of 2010)

Rank	Region	Publishing houses
1	Beijing	236
2	Shanghai	39
3	Guangdong	19
4	Liaoning	18
	Jiangsu	18
6	Shandong	17
	Shaanxi	17
8	Sichuan	16
9	Jilin	14
	Zhejiang	14
	Hubei	14
12	Tianjin	13
	Heilongjiang	13
	Hunan	13
15	Henan	12
16	Fujian	11
	Xinjiang	11
18	Anhai	10
19	Gansu	9
20	Shanxi	8
	Guangxi	8
	Yunnan	8
23	Inner Mongolia	7
	Jiangxi	7
	Hebei	7
26	Guizhou	5
27	Hainan	4
28	Chongqing	3
	Ningxia	3
30	Qinghai	2
	Tibet	2
	Total	578

Source: www.bkpcn.com.

also a lack of transparency in the way these data are reported to SAPPRFT. According to these data, Jiangsu province led the league in 2013 (see Table 2.9). Sales of national book distributors,[15] which were not included in the data of any province and were likely to be institutional sales or sales to private booksellers, were listed separately.

Table 2.8 Title output by regions (2015)

Rank	Region	Titles	Percentage of titles output (%)
1	Beijing (including national publishers)	125,412	43.3
2	Jiangsu	26,503	5.6
3	Shanghai	24,492	5.1
4	Jilin	23,823	5.0
5	Hubei	15,543	3.3
6	Shandong	14,760	3.1
7	Zhejiang	13,701	2.9
8	Hunan	11,815	2.5
9	Xinjiang	11,278	2.4
10	Liaoning	10,964	2.3
11	Shaanxi	10,459	2.2
12	Guangdong	10,088	2.1
13	Sichuan	10,038	2.1
14	Anhui	8902	1.9
14	Yunnan	8465	1.8
16	Guangxi	7532	1.6
17	Henan	7410	1.6
18	Hebei	6817	1.4
19	Jiangxi	6729	1.4
20	Tianjin	6421	1.3
21	Chongqing	6156	1.3
22	Heilongjiang	6087	1.3
23	Shanxi	3812	0.8
24	Gansu	3412	0.7
25	Fujian	3395	0.7
26	Hainan	3198	0.7
27	Inner Mongolia	3125	0.7
28	Ningxia	2686	0.6
29	Qinghai	779	0.2
30	Guizhou	738	0.2
31	Tibet	648	0.1

Source: Liu, B., Wu, S., 2016. China Publishing Yearbook 2016 (*zhongguo chuban nianjian 2016*). China Publishing Yearbook Publishing Company (*zhongguo chuban nianjian zazhishe youxian gongsi*), Beijing (in Chinese).

SAPPRFT also established another system to evaluate the size of the publishing industry in different provinces based on a matrix of financial measures, and Guangdong, Beijing, Jiangsu, Zhejiang, and Shandong were the top five regions in this ranking (SAPPRFT, 2014). Although the pictures presented by these two rankings are slightly different, overall wealthy or populous provinces have more vibrant book trade business.

Table 2.9 Regional book sales from state-owned booksellers (2013)

Rank	Region	Book sales (RMB million yuan)	Percentage of national sales (%)
1	Jiangsu	5819	7.91
2	Hunan	5796	7.88
3	Zhejiang	5226	7.10
4	Shandong	4936	6.71
5	Sichuan	4310	5.86
6	Anhui	3975	5.40
7	Henan	3839	5.22
8	Jiangxi	3278	4.46
9	Guangdong	2961	4.03
10	Shanxi	2852	3.88
11	Hebei	2427	3.30
12	Shaanxi	2323	3.16
13	Yunnan	1973	2.68
14	Guangxi	1950	2.65
15	Hubei	1871	2.54
16	Xinjiang	1864	2.53
17	Shanghai	1850	2.51
18	Chongqing	1810	2.46
19	Fujian	1792	2.44
20	Guizhou	1574	2.14
21	Beijing	1357	1.84
22	Gansu	1247	1.70
23	Heilongjiang	1064	1.45
24	Liaoning	1054	1.43
25	Inner Mongolia	843	1.15
26	Jilin	576	0.78
27	Tianjin	428	0.58
28	Hainan	136	0.18
29	Qinghai	102	0.14
30	Tibet	84	0.11
31	Ningxia	25	0.03
	National distributors	4223	5.74

Source: *China Book Business Report* (Wen, D., 2016. The change of economic weight in China's book trade (*zhonguo shuye geju tuxian shili yanbian*). <http://www.cbbr.com.cn/article/46819.html> (accessed 09.01.17) (in Chinese)).

2.3.4 A Fragmented Market

Alongside the geographical decentralization of publishing, we also see a fragmentation of the book market. The sponsoring system, although helpful for the party-state to exercise its control over publishing houses through the "tiao and kuai" bureaucratic hierarchy, has created a fragmented industry structure. As different media sectors are affiliated to different state agencies, it is difficult to develop cross-media mergers or cooperation.

As discussed before, many central state agencies own affiliated publishing business and act as their sponsoring organizations. These central state agencies had strong economic interests in their affiliated publishing businesses and normally required them to hand over some of the profits until the recent reform of corporatization, not to mention other hidden economic benefits they could ask for. In return, these publishers relied on their sponsoring organizations for publishing resources or even for market share. The Law Press, affiliated to the Ministry of Justice for example, publishes the authoritative test preparation books for the Qualification Test of Lawyers every year, because this test is organized by the Ministry of Justice. Other publishers may rely on administrative power for their market share. China Electric Power Press, which used to be affiliated to the Ministry of Electric Power Industry, enjoyed a monopoly in the publishing and distribution of technical standards in the electric power industry. After this ministry was canceled by the government, the publisher turned to the China Electricity Council (*zhongguo dianli qiye lianhehui*), a trade association responsible for technical standards, for support. The Council duly issued a notice to its members, which stated that China Electric Power Press had the exclusive rights to publishing technical standards of the industry and requested its members not to purchase any collection of standards produced by other publishers (China Electricity Council, 2006).

Although regional publishers do not have these kinds of influential connections, they mainly rely on their local sponsoring state agencies to achieve a certain market share in their local textbooks or supplementary learning materials market. The structures of provincial publishing industries are very similar. Most provinces have established their own publishing groups, which usually consist of a people's publishing house, a science and technology publishing house, an education publishing house, a children's publishing house, etc., and also control most of their local Xinhua bookstores. As publishers in different provinces produce many similar titles, provincial publishing groups could force the local Xinhua bookstores to prioritize their local titles, leading to local protectionism.

As a result of regional trade barriers and the monopoly in many sectors of the industry, the national book market, like a sliced cake, remains both fragmented and also relatively static. It is hard for stronger publishers to expand and for weak publishers to disappear. The same situation also prevails in book distribution, with local protectionism throwing up major barriers to the development of an efficient national distribution channel.

2.4 PRIVATIZATION AND INTERNATIONALIZATION

2.4.1 Private Publishers

Private publishers, according to the regulations of the government, are not allowed to exist. However, private capital has been active in publishing since the 1980s by collaborating with state-owned publishers through various back doors. Although China's private publishers do nearly all the tasks officially approved state-owned publishers do, they have to rely on state-owned publishers to apply for ISBNs and printing permissions for their books.

Private publishers, lacking the publishing license to do their business, normally register as a "cultural studio (*wenhua gongzuoshi*)" or "cultural company (*wenhua gongsi*)." It is not possible to get the exact figures for how many there are, but it was once estimated that there are more than 10,000 private publishers in the industry, half of which are in Beijing (Xie, 2010). Most of these are very small in scale with probably just a couple of employees. But a few have developed into large companies. The gross sales of Beijing Republic Publishing (*Gonghe Liandong*), a private publisher, was said to be about RMB300 million yuan (about US $47.10 million) in 2008 (Zhou, 2009). Several other private publishers also reported a total turnover between RMB200 million and RMB500 million yuan (Hexun, 2009). Compared with state-owned publishers facing institutional and administrative constraints, profit-oriented private publishers run much more efficiently. It is believed that most bestsellers in the consumer market are produced by private publishers (ibid). Supplementary learning materials are the other main business area for private publishers. Some of the largest private publishers have established their brand in this business, such as the well-known King & Key Education Group (or *zhihong jiaoyu*) in Shandong province, which was just listed in the domestic stock market in 2017, and the Chunyu Education Group in Jiangsu province.

However, it would be over simple to see this private sector solely as a competitor to state approved enterprises. Private publishers have developed a symbiotic relationship with state-owned publishers in the industry. Many state-owned publishers rely on private publishers for profitable publishing projects, while private publishers have to rely on state-owned partners for ISBNs. On the other hand, private publishers, by prospering in the industry, have squeezed the market share and the profit margin of state-owned publishers. Some state-owned publishers, by surviving like parasites on private publishers, gradually lost their competitiveness in book publishing, leading some professionals to regard private publishers as "gravediggers" of the state-owned publishers (Xu, 2009). The government administration department has been fully aware of the existence of private publishers but tacitly allowed their development to a certain extent. Officially the government prohibits the "trading of ISBNs" (*maimai shuhao*), but it tends to only crack down on those books which have transgressed its ideological tolerance.

There are different ways of cooperation between the private and state-owned publishers, depending on the relative bargaining powers of the two sides. Private publishers may run as book packagers for the state-owned publishers and only leave the printing and distribution tasks to the latter. Sharing the risk and cost with the state-owned publishers, they may receive royalty from their state-owned partner as their income. Small private publishers usually collaborate with the state-owned ones in this way. But stronger private publishers usually prefer to control more of the process, and many small state-owned publishers merely sell ISBNs to their private partners, leaving the whole project and all risks to the latter. State-owned publishers could sell their allocated ISBNs at a price falling between RMB10,000 and RMB30,000 yuan (about US$1570 to US $4710) for each ISBN (All-China Federation of Industry and Commerce, 2009). A state-owned publisher with 200 licensed ISBNs could easily earn RMB3 million yuan (about US$471,000) without doing any publishing business (ibid). Another way of cooperation works like copublishing, with both sides sharing the production cost and making profit through their own distribution channels.

China's book industry has been criticized by many readers and professionals for the poor average quality of books. This problem can be at least partially attributed to the size and the business strategies of private publishers. Most private publishers are very small in scale and may not have enough resources to produce quality books. Although some of them may have enough resources, most private publishers tend to focus on books which yield short-term gains and quick profits for several reasons. First, private publishers, without legal status, did not have strong interest in publishing quality books to establish an enduring brand. Second, although quality backlists are crucial assets for publishers, private publishers could hardly benefit from them even if they have published them, for they might someday be cracked down on by the government[16] and the copyrights of their books may be owned by their state-owned partners. Third, they are particularly prone to piracy, for not being qualified publishers they cannot resort to legal action. In addition, they may have to rely on a former state-owned partner for the permission to reprint if a book still sells. Price wars in the book trade have also been partially attributed to the vulnerability of private publishers, as it might be difficult for them to resort to legal actions to control their book distributors.[17]

Recognizing the growing centrality of private operators in the general consumer market, SAPPRFT has launched an initiative to assimilate private publishers into the state-controlled publishing industry in recent years. In April 2009, SAPPRFT officially announced its policy of "encouraging and supporting private capital to enter permissible areas (of publishing business)." The aim was to incorporate them into the existing structure of "industry planning and administration" in order to regulate them more effectively (GAPP, 2009). This move ratified the existing practice of some state-owned publishers forming joint-venture companies with private publishers (for example, Yangtze River Art and Literature Publishing House and a couple of prominent private publishers formed a joint venture in 2006), but the government insists that these joint-ventures be controlled by the state-owned publishers, and they still have to rely on ISBNs from the state-owned publishers for their business. A notable case following this move was a joint venture formed by Jiangsu Phoenix Publishing Group and Beijing Republic Publishing in 2009. However, the new measure was probably also a response to the destabilizing impact of private publishers. The government may have restricted the subject areas open to private publishers. A notice issued by the government in 2010 (GAPP, 2010) listed science and technology, finance and economics, supplementary learning materials, music and arts, and children's books as permissible subject areas for private publishers, while intentionally leaving out possibly more sensitive areas such as social science and literature. Since state-owned publishers would only be interested in a few successful private publishers for joint ventures, the majority of private publishers will remain in the private sector.

Another tentative effort of the government toward private publishers was the launch of Beijing Publishing Creative Industry Park in 2010. Some major private publishers, such as Beijing Motie Book and

Thinkingdom Media Group (also known as *Xinjingdian Wenhua*), have established their operations in this park. Beijing United Publishing Company (formerly Jinhua Publishing House), as the sole state-owned partner in the park, by charging a fee, provides scrutiny reading services of the manuscripts from these private publishers and then authorizes them to printers. In this kind of cooperation, private publishers can apply for ISBNs for free through this state-owned partner, and they have more rights over their books and usually exercise complete control over the distribution. Private publishers in the park seem to be getting more confident about this cooperation and have increased their title output. This is probably why Beijing United Publishing Company became the top player in the book retail market in 2016. Essentially Beijing United Publishing Company acts as a state agency to control the ideological direction of the publishing projects from private publishers while it provides some services to the latter to facilitate their operations within a state-controlled system.

The business environment has recently become more friendly for private publishers. In 2013, the central Party issued the *Decision of the Central Committee of the Communist Party of China on Some Major Issues Concerning Comprehensively Deepening the Reform*, announcing a wide range of reform programs. Regarding the publishing industry, this document suggested the "separation of publishing and printing" (*zhiban fenli*). It basically means that private publishers can now pay the printers directly rather than pay through their state-owned partners, although it insisted that the printing work still be commissioned by state-owned publishers. A few provincial regions, including Jiangsu, Hubei, and Beijing, started to pilot this policy in 2016. This policy significantly facilitated the smooth operation of private publishers, especially in terms of accounting and taxation.

As a result of the more lenient policies from the government, private publishers seem to have gained more legal rights over their books, and can now leave their logo or brand on the copyright page of their books. A couple of them, such as the Thinkingdom Media Group, recently even managed to get listed on the domestic stock market.

But however amiable the government may have become toward private publishers, it is unlikely that SAPPRFT will grant them publishing licenses. As a private publisher commented, the government is unlikely to issue publishing licenses to private publishers because it is such a small industry in the economy that the state might not think it is worthwhile to risk its "cultural safety" (Hou, 2009). It is clear that the full development of private publishers will endanger the survival of many state-owned publishers, which, in turn, would weaken the control of the government. As a result, the new policies of the government are most usefully interpreted as an effort to take advantage of the commercial and creative acumen of private publishers while maintaining the supremacy of the economic and political interest of the party-state.

2.4.2 Foreign Books and Capital in China's Publishing

The importation of books is strictly controlled by the government for ideological reasons. Companies have to apply for a license to import any kinds of publications, and no private book distributors are allowed to enter the book import business. There are about 40 book import companies (Xin, 2005: 162), but only a couple of nationwide book importers. The China National Publications Imports and Exports Corporation (CNPIEC), a member firm of the China Publishing Group, is the largest and accounts for over 60% of the market share (see CNPIEC, c2015). China Educational Publications Import and Export Corporation (CEPIEC), a member of the China Education Publishing and Media Group, is another major importer and mainly provides services to educational institutions. Their main customers are libraries. Book import of China has been increasing steadily (see Table 2.10), but the monopoly of state-owned book importers helps the state to control the inflow of books. As mentioned earlier, licensed book importers are responsible for censoring the books they import and they have to get their lists approved by the government in advance. Unacceptable books should not be listed in their catalogue for customers. In addition, a regulation[18] issued by the State Science and Technology Commission and the Central Party Propaganda Department seems to have restricted the purchase of "social science (including culture and arts) publications" to a limited number of state-controlled organizations.

Table 2.10 Book imports in China (by value and volume): 2011–2016

Year	2016	2015	2014	2013	2012	2011
Value (million US$)	144.22	144.99	125.88	120.55	137.08	116.67
Volume (million copies)	15.52	14.19	9.78	8.58	7.44	7.55

Source: SAPPRFT.

As the price of imported books is prohibitively high for ordinary Chinese readers and language is also a problem, book imports are unlikely to increase rapidly in the short term. However, foreign books can also enter China's book market through licensing the translation or reprint rights.

Foreign books used to be strictly controlled during the Maoist period. The change on the political and ideological climate after the economic reform however made it possible for western titles to be extensively translated and introduced into China, especially in the first half of 1980s when most books were translated without permission from Western publishing companies or authors. But since China promulgated the copyright law in 1990 and joined the *Berne Convention for the Protection of Literacy and Artistic Works* and the *Universal Copyright Convention* in 1992, rights trading between Chinese and Western publishers has increased rapidly. In 1996, 2915 copyrights were bought by Chinese publishers, but this number has now more than quintupled (see Table 2.11). Rights trading is also under the control of the government. Chinese publishers have to register their rights licensing contract with a copyright administration department, which is located either within SAPPRFT or a local APPRFT.[19] After the registration, Chinese publishers still have to apply for approval to publish, and also for a quota of foreign currency in order to pay royalties to foreign publishers. Foreign books, although providing a source of income for Chinese publishers, have also squeezed the market share of domestic publishers.

Following the conditions of China's entry into the WTO, foreign capital has been allowed to enter the publications retail business since 2003 and the wholesale business since 2004. However, although the book distribution business is open to foreign capital, there is no significant presence of foreign capital in this sector. The most prominent attempt at market entry was the book club that Bertelsmann set up in Shanghai in 1997 with a Chinese partner, long before China officially opened its publication distribution market to foreign capital. However, more than 10

Table 2.11 Rights licensing of books acquired by Chinese publishers: 2011–2016

Year	2016	2015	2014	2013	2012	2011
Rights acquired	16,587	15,458	15,542	16,625	16,115	14,708

Source: SAPPRFT.

years of activity failed to generate profit and in 2008 its book club, online bookstore, and chain bookstores were closed, signaling the harsh market environment in book distribution.

Foreign capital has been more successful in online bookselling. Both of the two most famous online bookstores, Dangdang.com and Amazon.cn, involve foreign investors.

Foreign capital, like private capital, is theoretically prohibited from entering the publishing business. However, a couple of foreign companies have established joint ventures with China partners. Tongqu (or Children's Fun Publishing Co. Ltd.) was set up in 1994 by Egmont, a Danish company, and People's Posts and Telecommunication Press. Beijing Huazhang Graphics and Information Company was set up in 1995 by China Machine Press and Multi-Lingua Publishing International, an American company, to publish computing and business titles. But these joint ventures have to publish under the brand of their Chinese partners.

The entry of foreign books into China's book market has undoubtedly helped to create a more plural cultural arena, but as can be seen from the above discussion, the impact of foreign books, as well as foreign capital, remains strictly constrained by the party-state.

2.4.3 Going Out

The party-state has also encouraged publishers to "go out" (*zou chuqu*), by exporting or licensing books to foreign countries. The government has long been aware of the deficit in its trade in cultural products with Western countries. Impressed by the role of American culture in bolstering its global reach and power, the Chinese government has become increasingly interested in exporting more Chinese cultural products, not only to reduce the deficit in the trade of cultural products, but also to enhance the "soft power of the nation," a task put forward by the Party in its 17th National Party Congress in 2007. For the Party, book publishing is not only a "mouthpiece" for political propaganda, but also a business for profit and a channel for 'soft power." SAPPRFT and the Central Party Propaganda Department have been supporting this last aim by encouraging publishers to attend international book fairs and providing subsidies for the translation of Chinese books into other languages. From Table 2.12, it can be seen that the export of licensed rights of Chinese books did increase rapidly between 2009 and 2016. However, this increase is mainly the result of the "going out" policy rather than the

Table 2.12 Export of licensed rights by Chinese publishers (2009–2016)

Year	2016	2015	2014	2013	2012	2011	2010	2009
Total	8328	7998	8088	7305	7568	5922	3880	3103

Source: SAPPRFT.

commercial success. Chinese publishers are more intent on fulfilling SAPPRFT's export quotas than "making any money on the export licenses," and "have frequently been signing very advantageous contracts for their export partners" in order to push up their number of exported titles "at any price" (Richardson, 2010: 135). Although the statistics from SAPPRFT suggested that 1,483 book titles were licensed to the United States and another 353 to Britain in 2016, many of them "probably never will" appear in the markets (ibid).

2.5 BOOKSELLERS AND THE SUPPLY CHAIN

The book distribution business is now fully opened to private companies, but the state-owned Xinhua bookstores continue to dominate the business. Xinhua Bookstore was a nationwide distribution system during the period of planned economy. It ran rather like a hierarchical government bureaucracy, following both the ideology and the dominant management style. The General Store of Xinhua Bookstore (*xinhua shudian zongdian*) in Beijing coordinated the operation of the Xinhua Bookstore system, and the provincial Xinhua bookstores worked as wholesalers within their provinces distributing publications to their subordinate Xinhua bookstores. Following economic decentralization however, the General Store of Xinhua Bookstore lost its control over provincial bookstores. Majoring in the book wholesaling business, it is now a member of the China Publishing Group. At the regional level, three features characterize the present system. First, the distribution of school textbooks remains the monopoly of the Xinhua bookstores and is their major source of profit due to the huge number of textbooks needed in schools. Second, many provincial Xinhua bookstores have been merged with local publishers into provincial publishing groups. Third, although provincial Xinhua bookstores have usually managed to maintain a degree of control over many lower-level Xinhua bookstores, municipal level Xinhua bookstores in big cities are often out of the control of provincial Xinhua bookstores. The main reason is that they are affiliated to powerful municipal governments and could resist the control of provincial Xinhua bookstores. In addition, municipal Xinhua bookstores benefit from the large wealthier population in big cities and may also receive indirect subsidies from the municipal governments. As a result, the financial clout of some municipal Xinhua bookstores is strong and may exceed that of their provincial counterparts.

In contrast to the main Xinhua Bookstore channel, private booksellers, known as the "second channel" (*er qudao*) of distribution, developed quickly after the economic reform, overtaking the number of Xinhua bookstores. Of a total 163,102 bookstores in 2016, 105,872 were privately owned (see SAPPRFT, 2017), but most of them are very small in scale. Shortly after China's entry into the WTO, the government removed all restrictions on private distributors in the book wholesale business in 2003.[20] However, facing the competition from Xinhua Bookstores and the increasingly powerful online booksellers, lots of private physical bookstores have closed down. Although the government extended a tax break enjoyed by Xinhua to all book distributors in 2013, it has not changed the fact that many private booksellers are in financial difficulty.

It is widely acknowledged that the lack of a national distribution network has made the book distribution business less efficient and added unnecessary cost to publishers. As noted above, Xinhua Bookstore as a nationwide system was decentralized during the economic reform. The local protectionism of provincial governments protecting their affiliated Xinhua bookstores throws up major barriers to the development of an efficient national distribution channel. The recent conglomeration often saw mergers between provincial Xinhua bookstores and provincial publishing groups, which have enhanced the control of provincial publishing groups over their local markets. Private booksellers, being refused the "general distribution right (*zong faxingquan*)" for a long time and still refused entry into the profitable area of textbook distribution, are in a disadvantaged position. The restrictions faced by private book distributors, and their resulting difficulties in doing business, have excluded the possibility of an efficient national distribution channel being established by means of private capital. Consequently, in order to promote their book sales, publishing houses, often have to deal with book distribution themselves, which is known as "house distribution" (*sheban faxing*). They may sell books not only to different regional Xinhua wholesalers, but also to second channel wholesalers, other state-own wholesalers, and even retailers (Sun, 2003). Many lower level wholesalers and retailers also have to deal with many different publishers and wholesalers. This inefficient distribution system has increased business cost for both publishers and booksellers. In addition, house distribution may put publishers in competition with wholesalers, who are their distribution agents.

The state-owned channel and the private channel do interact in different ways, depending on the publisher of the book. If the book is published solely by a private or a state-owned publisher, both channels would be used for the distribution of the book. If a book is published by a private publisher with the cooperation of a state-owned one, the private publisher may take full control of the book distribution through both channels if the state-owned publisher merely sells the ISBNs to its private partner. The more common practice is for both sides to distribute the books through their own channels separately. In this case, there will normally be a clear cleavage between the two channels. For this more common copublishing practice in the trade publishing, the general features of the present supply chain can be shown in Fig. 2.1. The actual practice is

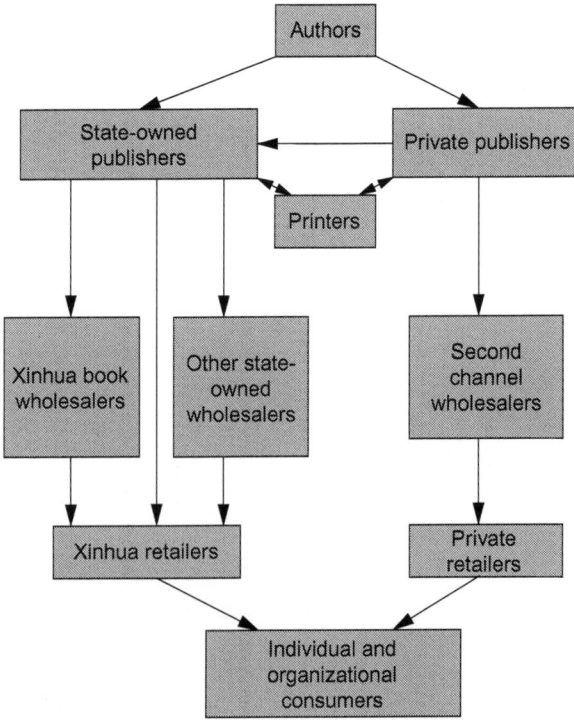

Figure 2.1 Copublishing supply chain in China's trade publishing.

more complex than this schematic chart. First, book distribution to libraries is not included in the chart, and the suppliers are diverse in this area. Second, as mentioned earlier, either private publishers or a state-owned partner could distribute through both channels depending on their way of cooperation.

The rise of online book retailers has posed serious threat to brick-and-mortar bookstores, especially to private booksellers. In 2016 the sales revenue of online retailers surpassed that of the brick-and-mortar bookstores for the first time. Dangdang, Jingdong, and Amazon are the three leading online retailers (Yang, 2017). But as Dangdang and Amazon also sell their books via Alibaba's Tmall, the largest business-to-consumer (B2C) online retail platform in China, Tmall is in fact an important player as well. In order to support the physical bookstores, the government now provides subsidies for them to apply, although these are usually not a significant amount.

2.6 PROBLEMS OF CHINESE BOOK PUBLISHING

Book publishing in China, despite its progress from both a business and cultural perspective, still faces many problems, some of which have already been touched on earlier.

2.6.1 Piracy

Rampant piracy has been a serious problem for China's book publishing. It was estimated by the government in 2007 that pirates produce about 500 million books a year (see The Bookseller, 2008). There are a couple of sources of pirated books (see Successwbj, 2006). The first source comes from unauthorized printing from printers. Some printers may print a few extra copies and sell them to book retailers for a profit. Occasionally, publishers may also request printers to produce more copies than stipulated in the printing contract to evade tax or royalties. These extra illegal copies are also regarded by professionals as pirated copies, although they originate from the publishers themselves. But the major source of piracy is pirates. The causes for the rampant piracy are complex, but a few can be mentioned here.

First, some regional governments are not effective in fighting piracy. As local governments benefit from a prosperous printing industry and book distribution within the region, some may not have strong incentive to control piracy. In addition, the corruption of some government officials may inhibit the effort of fighting piracy. There have been cases of local officials colluding with booksellers and printers in the production and sale of pirated books (ibid).

Second, some printers are willing to take risk for pirates. Although book printing is strictly regulated by the government, the expansion of the printing industry in China has led to the rapid expansion of printers across the country. Intense competition among them drives some printers to take risk in order to survive (ibid).

Third, the current situation of book distribution also makes the distribution of pirated books possible. The lack of an efficient national distribution system may leave some time for pirated copies to grab market share. In addition, the "second channel" in book distribution provides an efficient distribution network for pirated books. The "second channel" was developed by private booksellers and private publishers in the 1980s. As private publishers were forbidden by the government, their business was in a gray area and the "second channel" was beyond the reach of effective government supervision. However, this distribution network could also be used as an ideal channel for pirated books.

Last, the rise of digital technologies and the Internet has also made it harder to control piracy. Many pirated e-books are available online for download. In addition, the online retailing platforms also make it easier for small online retailers to sell pirated copies.

Massive piracy has caused major problems for the publishing business. For publishers, especially trade publishers, most books might not make much profit or are even money-losing while a few books are extremely profitable, such as the bestsellers and reference books. Hence the profits from bestsellers are extremely important for publishers to compensate their losses in other publishing projects. However, bestsellers and reference books are the primary target of pirates. As a result, piracy greatly squeezes the profit margins of publishers, and may force some to price their books higher in order to recoup their investment.

2.6.2 Reliance on School Books

School books in this discussion include both school textbooks and supplementary learning materials. As mentioned earlier, school books account for the largest share of the book market, although the weight of school textbooks has been declining due mainly to the decline in student numbers and the government price control over textbooks.

Detailed sales figures for school books and supplementary learning materials are now available in the annual industry report from the government. According to the *General Information of the National Press and Publishing Industry in 2016* from SAPPRFT, textbooks accounted for about 26.77% of the total book sales and supplementary learning materials about 27.95%. Put together they accounted for over half of the sales of the industry (see Table 2.13). In addition, many supplementary learning materials are produced by private publishers and then sold directly to schools. As their sales are not recorded by SAPPRFT, the actual weight of school books in the whole book trade must be much higher. The actual sales of supplementary learning materials was said to be between RMB40 and RMB60 billion yuan, double the official figure (Zhu, 2016). School books play a crucial role in China's book publishing, as they are not only important for publishers, but also for printers and booksellers. It was estimated that 70%–80% of the profit of most Xinhua bookstores comes from the distribution of school books (China Publishing Today, 2008). The preponderance of school books implies a weak trade book publishing industry, since the market for trade books will be relatively small.

There have been a lot of complaints from school teachers and parents about the market of supplementary learning materials. One common complaint is that the market has been suffering from oversupply of supplementary learning materials, with the editorial quality of many books being very poor (Zhu, 2016). For those books with good quality, piracy becomes the biggest threat. Another complaint is that many schools and local education bureaus may force their students to buy specific supplementary learning materials, even if the quality of these books is poor. Bribery from booksellers (especially private booksellers because they have full control over their funds) to these gatekeepers is rampant. Prices of those books are usually set high and then they are sold at heavy discount through the distribution channel, which leaves space for corruption.

In response to these complaints, the government has taken a few measures to regulate the market. SAPPRFT and the Ministry of Education issued a decree in 2001 to restrict compulsory book distribution to school students,[21] but this could hardly prevent it from happening. Another measure taken by SAPPRFT was to control the total output. It required the number of supplementary learning materials titles to be no more than 10% of the annual publishing plans of publishers.[22] In addition, it launched an annual campaign of "quality checks" on supplementary

Table 2.13 Percentage of school books in China's book market (2012–16)

Year	Total sales (RMB billion yuan)	Textbook	Percentage of textbook (%)	Supplementary learning materials	Percentage of supplementary learning materials (%)	Total percentage of school books (%)
2016	85.249	22.820	26.77	23.827	27.95	54.72
2015	78.142	21.755	27.84	19.914	25.48	53.32
2014	77.799	22.740	29.23	16.656	21.41	50.64
2013	73.563	22.388	30.43	16.170	21.98	52.41
2012	71.258	22.849	32.07	14.217	19.95	52.02

Source: SAPPRFT.

learning materials. In 2008, several publishers were asked to recall some of their learning materials and were fined a nominal amount of RMB10,000 yuan (about US$1570) due to the poor quality of their books (China Press and Publishing Journal, 2008). But the problems persisted and, starting from 2011, the government had to issue a new set of regulations to counter the problems (as will be discussed later). These measures may lessen the problems to a certain extent, but they cannot solve them as long as there is no real competition among publishers and students are subject to the pressure of schools and governments in their purchase of learning materials.

2.6.3 Excess Inventory

Another problem with China's book publishing is the excess inventory of the industry (see Table 2.14). This seems to be an inevitable problem as long as publishers have to produce some propaganda books with little possibility to sell in the market. Most professionals within the industry agree that excess inventory signals that many books produced by publishers are unsalable in the market (Li, 2007). As a result, many publishers may find themselves in a precarious financial situation.

It can be seen from the above table that the total inventory of publishers and Xinhua bookstores has been increasing steadily, especially in terms of total list price. Substantial inventories indicate serious problems of the industry. Although inventories are not necessarily made up entirely of returned books from booksellers due to the fact that some books may take longer to sell, a steady increase of inventory is a sure sign of a mounting number of returned unsalable books. As can be seen from the

Table 2.14 Total inventory and total annual sales (by volume and value)

Year	Volume (billion copies)		Value (RMB billion yuan)	
	Inventory	Annual sales	Inventory (total list price)	Annual sales
2016	6.575	7.025	114.301	85.249
2015	6.783	6.742	108.244	78.142
2014	6.639	6.986	101.011	77.799
2013	6.519	6.808	96.44	73.563
2012	5.600	6.832	84.188	71.258
2011	5.586	6.578	80.405	85.249

Source: SAPPRFT.

table, the total list price of inventory has exceeded annual sales since 2012, which meant that it may take more than a year for the market to absorb the total inventory even if the industry were not to produce any new books. More importantly, as textbook sales accounts for a large percentage of total sales, and most books in the inventory are likely to be nontextbooks, the ratio between real market sales (after deducting the sales of textbooks) and the inventory (predominantly nontextbooks) is a major cause for concern. The excess inventory of book publishing implies serious problems for the industry.

2.7 RECENT STATE POLICIES

Recent state intervention in the book publishing industry has been marked by two major policies: conglomeration and corporatization. We will examine both in more detail in later chapters so we will simply outline the basic contours of each here.

2.7.1 Conglomeration

The party-state invested considerable effort in establishing publishing groups, which are to some extent similar to Western media conglomerates. After the central party-state approved the establishment of the Shanghai Century Publishing Group and the Guangdong Provincial Publishing Group in December 1998, publishing groups have been established across the country. As discussed earlier, publishing houses are affiliated to specific sponsoring organizations, which are embedded within the "tiao and kuai" bureaucratic matrix. Publishing groups have been formed either along the vertical line of a central state organization or the horizontal line of the local Party/government. The Science Publishing Group and China Publishing Group are examples of the first kind, while provincial publishing groups are examples of the second kind. The Science Publishing Group includes all publishing related businesses affiliated to the Chinese Academy of Sciences. When it was formed in 2000, it consisted of a core publisher, the Science Press, together with the University of Science and Technology of China Press, Beijing Hope Computer Company, China Science Magazine, China Scientific Publication Imports and Exports Company, and Beijing Kehai Hi-tech Company. The China Publishing Group, now affiliated to the Central Party Propaganda Department, is one of the strongest publishing groups in China. Its core member firms consist of a few important national publishers and two national publication wholesalers, including the prestigious Commercial Press, Zhonghua Book Company, Xinhua Bookstore General Store (*xinhua shudian zongdian*), and China National Publications Import & Export Corporation (CNPIEC). All these publishers and distributors were formerly affiliated to the central government administration department, and the first Director of the group, Yang Muzhi, was a former Deputy Minister of GAPP. This reflected the continuing control of the state over the group.

The establishment of publishing groups started initially as a tentative policy, but was later endorsed as a state policy by the central government. Although doubts and problems accompanied the process of conglomeration in book publishing, most provinces, except for a couple of remote areas, have established their provincial publishing groups. As noted before, the size of the publishing industry in remote areas is much smaller and might not be very profitable. This is probably the reason why cross-regional cooperation among publishing groups only happened in these areas, for their local governments have much less economic incentives to protect their regional book publishing. In Hainan province, the smallest province in China with a population of less than 9 million in 2010, the local Xinhua bookstores were acquired by the Jiangsu Phoenix Publishing and Media Group in 2008. In another remote provincial region, Ningxia, the provincial publishing group was also acquired in December 2009 by the China Publishing Group.

Provincial publishing groups usually enjoy the monopolistic profit in textbook publishing business in their provinces, and may receive some subsidies from their local governments. Consequently, although the China Publishing Group consists of some prestigious publishers and is the top player in the retail market, its economic clout is dwarfed by many provincial publishing groups according to a ranking based on a matrix of financial measures from SAPPRFT (see Table 2.15).

2.7.2 Corporatization

The second major reform in China's book publishing is the transformation of most state-owned publishers into business enterprises, a process which can be called corporatization. The party-state started to push forward this conversion at the end of 2003, and only a couple of publishers charged with providing a "public service," such as the People's Publishing House and Braille Publishing House, are allowed to remain as "public

Table 2.15 Top ten publishing groups in term of economic strength (2015)

Rank	Publisher	Evaluation score
1	Jiangsu Phoenix Publishing and Media Group	3.0965
2	Hunan Publishing Investment Holding Group	1.8193
3	Jiangxi Provincial Publishing Group	1.6457
4	China Education Publishing and Media Group	1.4274
5	Zhejiang Publishing United Group	1.0451
6	Anhui Publishing Group	1.0228
7	Hebei Publishing and Media Group	0.9976
8	China Publishing Group	0.9033
9	Shandong Publishing Group	0.6376
10	Hubei Changjiang Publishing and Media Group	0.5570

Source: SAPPRFT, 2016. Analysis of press and publishing industry in 2015 (*2015 nian xinwen chuban chanye fenxi baogao*). <http://www.sapprft.gov.cn/upload/files/2016/8/9153448117.pdf> (accessed 06.12.17) (in Chinese).

service units." Most publishing houses are now registered as business entities. After the corporatization, a few publishing groups got listed on the domestic stock market.

2.7.3 Village Libraries

As mentioned earlier, income disparity among Chinese residents, particularly between urban residents and rural residents, has been a serious social problem in China. The so-called "three-rurals" (or "*sannong*") problem, which is the problem with peasants, villages, and agriculture in rural areas,[23] has become a major issue for the central government. Some policies, such as reducing taxes for farmers and providing subsidies to education and medical services in rural areas, have been adopted. Following the Party's guideline, SAPPRFT has aimed at helping the development of rural areas by building large number of "village libraries (*nongjia shuwu*)." Normally the central government and local governments share the cost of establishing village libraries. The government also requires each village library to hold at least 2000 volumes of books. It was reported that by the end of 2009, nearly 300,000 village libraries had been established and the total investment from the government reached RMB5 billion yuan (about US$785 million) (see China Central Television, 2010). The policy of establishing "village libraries" not only helps enhance the image of the Party, but also boosts the size of book market.

2.7.4 Licensing and Price Control in Supplementary Learning Materials Publishing

As mentioned earlier, the government has issued a series of rigid regulations since 2011 to counter the endemic problems in the business of supplementary learning materials. It is now required that publishers engaged in this business have to be licensed by the government first. Licensed publishers are then required to get the permission of the copyright owners of the textbooks if they plan to publish supplementary materials to support the learning of particular textbooks. After these books are published, although they can be sold at the retail market, they are usually not allowed to be sold directly to schools unless they are listed in a local catalogue of recommended books. It is the responsibility of provincial education administration bureaus to maintain their local catalogues and they usually select just one supplementary book for each subject to be included in the catalogue. If a book is fortunate enough to be included in a local catalogue, it still has to be priced according to a guideline set by the provincial government based on the book length, usually the number of its signatures. Finally these books can only be sold by "qualified distributors." Although it is not clarified what "qualified distributors" exactly means, they tend to be the state-owned Xinhua bookstores in practice. As a result of these policies, many private publishers suffered loss of market share, but the state-owned publishing groups and Xinhua bookstores increased their monopolistic profits.

These regulations may have relieved some problems in the business of supplementary learning materials, but they also created new ones. The recommended books in local catalogues have effectively become compulsory for students. In addition, as provincial governments tend to include the books from local publishing groups in their catalogues, local protectionism becomes more entrenched.

2.8 SUMMARY

China's book publishing industry has expanded rapidly after the partial introduction of market forces but, despite its development since commercialization, it remains marked by major problems. If the central theme in the reform of book publishing is the introduction of market forces, then the persistence of control from the party-state poses a stubborn hindrance to this process. State control is pervasive in its control over who can publish, what can and cannot be published, how many titles can be published, and sometimes even who should buy what (as seen in the compulsory distribution of supplementary learning materials). Consequently, a real publishing market driven by competition and consumer demand remains elusive. Further, since allowing the market to take full control of book publishing is not a feasible option for the party-state, problems in book publishing have to be addressed by state intervention, but as we have noted, and as we shall see in more detail in later chapters, the forms this has taken have often generated new tensions and difficulties.

ENDNOTES

1. Exchange rate used in the conversion is 1:6.37.
2. The data from 2000 to 2008 are from the official annual report of "General information of the national press and publishing industry (quanguo xinwen chuban ye jiben qingkuang)" by SAPPRFT. The data from 1950 to 1990 are from Fang (1993: 688–691).
3. Decree on Censoring Books and Magazines (tushu zazhi shencha banfa) was issued by the Kuomintang government in 1934.
4. GAPP issued a couple of decrees on censoring the book publications, such as the Notice on Strengthening the Scrutiny Reading of Books (jiaqiang tushu shendu gongzuo de tongzhi) in 1994 and Decisions on Improving further the Scrutiny Reading of Books (guanyu jinyibu jiaqiang tushu shendu gongzuo de yijian) in 2004
5. The so-called "people's mass organizations" are usually other political organizations, such as the so-called democratic parties, labor union, etc., which are actually controlled by the party-state.
6. Song (2003) did not mention the Party committee for publishing houses, but the Party committee (mainly the propaganda department) can be the sponsoring organization of publishing houses, such as the Wuhan Publishing House (with the sponsoring organization being the Wuhan Municipal Party Propaganda Department).
7. See Administration on the publishing of books, periodicals, audio–video products and electronic publications on sensitive topics (tushu qikan yinxiang zhipin dianzi chubanwu zhongda xuanti beian banfa), which was issued by SPPA in 1997).
8. See Notice on Strengthening the Scrutiny Reading of Books (guanyu jiaqiang tushu shendu gongzuo de tongzhi), which was issued by SPPA in 1994.
9. See Administrative Provisions on Book Publishing (tushu chuban guanli guiding) issued by GAPP in 2008.
10. There is no clear rule from SAPPRFT about this percentage and it may vary depending on the decision of SAPPRFT, but it tends to be at around 10%. The Yunnan Provincial Press and Publication Bureau (PPB) stipulated this percentage to be 10% in a provincial regulation issued in 1995 for local publishers (Yunnan Provincial PPB, 1995). A publishing group in Guangdong also stipulated this percentage to be 10%.
11. See Regulation on Grading and Assessing Business-oriented Publishing Houses (jingying xing tushu chuban danwei dengji pinggu banfa), which was issued by GAPP in 2008.
12. The Jiangsu Provincial Press and Publication Bureau required that its regional publishers "should guarantee more than 10%" of their publishing plans on "important topics" (Jiangsu Provincial PPB, 2003).

13. Publishers specializing in audio, video, and electronic publishing are not included in this number.
14. SAPPRFT publishes the General Information of National Press and Publishing Industry (quanguo xinwen chuban ye jiben qingkuang) annually.
15. The sales of national book distributors included house sales of national publishers, sales from the General Store of Xinhua and several other national book import and export companies.
16. In a notice issued by the Central Party Propaganda Department and GAPP in 1993, which was titled Notice on prohibiting the trading of ISBN (guanyu jinzhi maimai shuhao de tongzhi), private publishers engaged in trading ISBNs could face confiscation of books, financial fines, and termination of business license as cultural companies.
17. A private publisher sued an online bookseller for selling its books at extremely low price, but was refuted by the court for not being the right business entity to launch the lawsuit (see Mo, 2010).
18. This regulation, titled CNPIEC approval procedure for the import of books and periodicals (zhongguo tushu jinchukou zong gongsi jinkou shukan ziliao shenpin guanli guiding), was issued in 1984).
19. See a regulation titled Notice on the Registration of Licensing Contract of Foreign Books (guanyu dui chuban waiguo tushu jinxing hetong dengji de tongzhi), which was issued by National Copyright Administration of China in 1995.
20. Only after that were private distributors allowed to have the "general distribution right" (zong faxingquan), which means the right of being the sole wholesaler of a book for publishers.
21. See Regulation on School Ancillary Study Aids (zhongxiaoxue jiaofu cailiao guanli banfa).
22. See Implementation of Regulation on School Ancillary Study Aids (guanyu zhongxiaoxue jiaofu cailiao ganli banfa de shishi yijian) issued by SAPPRFT in 2001).
23. "Sannong" problem refers to the hardship of farmers, the poverty of villages and the precarious agriculture.

REFERENCES

All-China Federation of Industry and Commerce, 2009. Suggestions on opening publishing business to some qualified private publishers (*dui bufen youtiaojian de minying shushang geiyu chubanquan shidian de ti'an*). <http://www.cbpa.cn/Html/NewsView.asp?ID=204&SortID=28> (accessed 17.01.10) (in Chinese).

Bates, B.J., Liu, T., 2010. A cultural approach to DRM implementation in China. Westminster Paper in Communication and Culture 7 (1), 7−26.

Brady, A.-M., 2008. Marketing Dictatorship: Propaganda and Thought Work in Contemporary China. Rowman and Littlefield, Lanham, MD.

Chan, J.M., 2002. China: media liberalization under authoritarianism. In: Price, M.E., et al., (Eds.), Media Reform: Democratizing the Media, Democratizing the State. Routledge, London, pp. 27−46.

China Central Television, 2010. 300,000 village libraries established (*woguo yi jiancheng 300,000 nongjia shuwu*). <http://www.fumuqin.com/InfoFiles/007027002/104234-43199.html> (accessed 20.01.10) (in Chinese).

China Electricity Council, 2006. Notice on the publishing and distribution of technical standards in electricity industry (*guanyu dianli biaozhun chuban faxing deng youguan shixiang de tongzhi*). <http://dls.cec.org.cn/news/deptnews.asp?id=110> (accessed 23.01.10) (in Chinese).

China Press and Publishing Journal (*zhongguo xinwen chuban bao*), 2008. GAPP cracking down on poor quality study aids, 19 publishers being punished (*chuban zongshu yancha buhege jiaofu duwu, 19 chubanshe shou chufa*). <http://news.sohu.com/20080226/n255367434.shtml> (accessed 27.01.07) (in Chinese).

China Publishing and Media Journal (*zhongguo chuban chuanmei shangbao*), 2015. Analysis of the market share of publishing groups in the retail market January to October (*1—10 yue quanguo chuban jituan lingshou shichang bantu fenxi*). <http://www.600757.com.cn/show-22-9071-1.html> (accessed 30.09.17) (in Chinese).

China Publishing Today (*chuban shangwu zhoukan*), 2008. 70% to 80% of the profit of most Xinhua bookstores comes from the distribution of textbooks and supplementary learning materials (*duoshu xinhua shudian 70%—80% de lirun laiyuanyu jiaocai jiaofu*). <http://news.xinhuanet.com/edu/2008-03/25/content_7855872.htm> (accessed 21.01.10) (in Chinese).

Chu, X., 2003. 'Crossing the river by feeling the pebbles': WTO membership spurs reforms in Chinese publishing. LOGOS 14 (2), 95—100.

Clark, G., Phillips, A., 2008. Inside Book Publishing, fourth ed. Routledge, London.

CNPIEC, c2015. Brief introduction. <http://group.cnpeak.com/h/en/ComJianJie1/> (accessed 10.03.10).

Fang, H. (Ed.), 1993. China Publishing Yearbook 1990—1991 (*zhongguo chuban nianjian 1990—1991*). China Publishing Yearbook Publishing Company (*zhongguo chuban nianjian zazhishe youxian gongsi*), Beijing (in Chinese).

Gao, H., 2013. Why aren't Chinese people reading books anymore? <https://www.theatlantic.com/china/archive/2013/08/why-arent-chinese-people-reading-books-anymore/278729/> (accessed 28.09/17).

GAPP, 2009. Guiding principles on pushing forward the reform of press and publications system (*guanyu jinyibu tuijin xinwen chuban tizhi gaige de zhidao yijian*). <http://news.xinhuanet.com/newscenter/2009-04/06/content_11137354_1.htm> (accessed 16.01.10) (in Chinese).

GAPP, 2010. Guiding principles on pushing forward the development of publishing industry (*guanyu jinyibu tuidong xinwen chuban chanye fazhan de zhidao yijian*). <http://www.gapp.gov.cn/cms/html/21/508/201001/695926.html> (accessed 17.01.10) (in Chinese).

Hexun, 2009. Private publishers monopolised the market of bestsellers, a long way for state-owned publishers to reform (*minying chuban longduan changxiaoshu, guoyou chubanye gaizhi renzhong daoyuan*). <http://news.hexun.vnet.cn/2009-12-11/121992947.html> (accessed 17.01.10) (in Chinese).

Hou, Y., 2009. How will Chinese private publisher's dream fit the reality after the implementation of a new policy (*xinzheng zhixia minying shushang de mengxiang ruhe zhaojin xianshi*). <http://finance.jrj.com.cn/book/2009/07/0214115402619-2.shtml> (accessed 17.01.10) (in Chinese).

Jia, Z., 2017. Low concentration level in China's book market: not a single publisher accounts for over 5% of the market share (*zhongguo tushu shichang jizhongdu bugao, shang weiyou qiangshi chubanshe zhanbi chaoguo 5%*). <http://www.bookdao.com/article/400757/> (accessed 30.10.17) (in Chinese).

Jiangsu Provincial PPB, 2003. Regulation of Jiangsu Provincial PPB on book proposals (*jiangsu sheng xinwen chuban ju tushu xuanti guanli guiding*). <http://www.jsxwcbj.gov.cn/ReadNews.asp?NewsID=5023> (accessed 15.01.10) (in Chinese).

Li, J., 2007. Excess book inventory needs to be reduced (*tushu kucun jidai jianfei*). <http://www.dushu.com/news/2007/07-10/11190.html> (accessed 25.01.10) (in Chinese).

Lin, Y., 2001. Between Politics and Markets: Firms, Competition, and Institutional Change in Post-Mao China. Cambridge University Press, Cambridge.

Liu, B., 2006. On the reform of publishing industry (*xinwen chuban zhongshu fushuzhang liu binjie: tan chuban tizhi gage*). <http://news.sina.com.cn/c/2006-05-19/19189911418.shtml> (accessed 05.12.08) (in Chinese).

Liu, B., Wu, S., 2016. China Publishing Yearbook 2016 (*zhongguo chuban nianjian 2016*). China Publishing Yearbook Publishing Company (*zhongguo chuban nianjian zazhishe youxian gongsi*), Beijing (in Chinese).

Mo, Z., 2010. Publishing industry does not need the help of book distribution business (*chubanye yongbuzhao faxingye laidang leifeng*). Southern Metropolitan Daily (*nanfang doushibao*), 12 January. <http://epaper.nddaily.com/A/html/2010-01/12/content_989932.htm> (accessed 24.01.10) (in Chinese).

OpenBook, 2017. Retail market report of the book trade in 2016 (*2016 nian quanguo tushu lingshou shichang baogao*). <http://www.cptoday.cn/news/detail/2670> (accessed 20.12.2017) (in Chinese).

Pan, G., et al., 2005. China Publishing Yearbook 2005 (*zhongguo chuban nianjian 2005*). China Publishing Yearbook Publishing House, Beijing (in Chinese).

People's Daily, ca. 2009. Main duties of Central Propaganda Department of CCP (*zhonggong zhongyang xuanchuanbu zhuyao zhize*). <http://cpc.people.com.cn/GB/64114/75332/5230610.html> (accessed 10.01.10) (in Chinese).

Pew Research Center, 2016. Mean and median number of books read per year 2011−2015. <http://www.pewinternet.org/2016/09/01/book-reading-2016/pi_2016-09-01_book-reading_a-02/> (accessed 10.01.10).

Richardson, P., 2010. Book review: publishing in China—an essential guide second ed. LOGOS 21 (1−2), 133−136.

Richardson, P., Chu, X., 2015. PA Market Report China. The Publishers Association, London.

SAPPRFT, 2014. Analysis of press and publishing industry in 2013 (*2013 nian xinwen chuban chanye fenxi baogao*). <http://www.sapprft.gov.cn/sapprft/upload/files/2016/5/23144742848.pdf> (accessed 05.12.17) (in Chinese).

SAPPRFT, 2016. Analysis of press and publishing industry in 2015 (*2015 nian xinwen chuban chanye fenxi baogao*). <http://www.sapprft.gov.cn/upload/files/2016/8/9153448117.pdf> (accessed 06.12.17) (in Chinese).

SAPPRFT, 2017. General information of the national press and publishing industry in 2016 (*2016 nian quanguo xinwen chuban ye jiben qingkuang*). <http://www.sapprft.gov.cn/sapprft/govpublic/6677/1633.shtml> (accessed 05.12.17) (in Chinese).

Shen, R., 2008. Difficulties, happiness and expectations—legislation of the Copyright Law during the economic reform (*jianxin, xiyue yu qipan—gaige kaifang zhong de zhuzuoquan lifa*). China Publishing Journal (zhongguo chuban) 10, 12−14.

Song, M., 2003. Investigation into the evolvement and adjustment of sponsoring unit system in book publishing (*chuban danwei zhuguan zhuban zhidu de youlai yu tiaozheng de tansuo*). <http://www.cbkx.com/2003-4/475_2.shtml> (accessed 03.10.08) (in Chinese).

Song, Y. et al. (Eds.), 1999. Archives of Contemporary China's Publishing, vol. 8 (zhongguo dangdai chuban shiliao dibajuan). Da Xiang Publishing House, Zhengzhou (in Chinese).

Successwbj, 2006. Investigation into China's pirated book market—the astounding experience of a fake book pirate (*zhongguo daoban tushu shichang diaocha—yiming wei daoban shushang de zhenhan licheng*). <http://hi.baidu.com/wsxz/blog/item/ac263ad8-be73d73733fa1c1f.html> (accessed 21.07.07) (in Chinese).

Sun, Q., 2003. The market positioning of wholesalers in China's future book business (*zhongguo shuye weilai pifashang fenxiaoshang de shengcun weizhi*). <http://www.openbook.com.cn/Information/0/196_1.html> (accessed 28.07.10) (in Chinese).

Sun, B., Wei, Y., 2005. Report on the development of China book industry in 2004 (*2004 nian chubanye fazhan baogao*). In: Cui, B. (Ed.), Media Industry Bluebook: China media

2004–2005 (*2004–2005 nian zhongguo chuanmei chanye fazhan baogao*). Social Science Documents Press, Beijing (in Chinese).

The Bookseller, 2008. China produces 500 m pirated books a year. <http://www.thebookseller.com/news/35825-china-produces-500m-pirated-books-a-year.html> (accessed 20.01.10).

The Booksellers Association, ca. 2010. UK book buyers 2004–2009. <http://www.booksellers.org.uk/Industry-Info/Industry-Reports/Book-Industry-Statistics/UK-Book-Buyers-2004-2008.aspx> (accessed 09.02.11).

The Economist, 2017. Cambridge University Press battles censorship in China. <https://www.economist.com/news/china/21727100-tense-political-year-communist-party-wants-no-dissent-cambridge-university-press-battles> (accessed 05.12.17).

Wen, D., 2016. The change of economic weight in China's book trade (*zhongguo shuye geju tuxian shili yanbian*). <http://www.cbbr.com.cn/article/46819.html> (accessed 09.01.17) (in Chinese).

Wu, Z., et al., 1997. Archives of Guangdong Province: Publishing (*guangdong shengzhi: chubanzhi*). Guangdong People's Publishing House, Guangzhou (in Chinese).

Xie, X., 2010. The No. 1 government document in publishing industry opened the door for private capital (*xinwen chuban yihao wenjian rang minying ziben zoushang qiantai*). Daily Business News (meiri jingji xinwen) 2010.1.06. <http://www.nbd.com.cn/newshtml/20100106/20100106043909346.html> (accessed 15.01.10) (in Chinese).

Xin, G., 2005. Publishing in China: An Essential Guide. Thomson Learning, Singapore.

Xin, G., 2010. Publishing in China: An Essential Guide, second ed. Cengage Learning, Singapore.

Xu, N., 2009. Private capital is attracted by the opportunity of taking control of the troubled state-owned publishers (*minying ziben yueyueyushi, xiang jie zhuanqi gaizhi chaodi guoyou chubanshe*). <http://media.people.com.cn/GB/22114/176694/176701/10555258.html> (accessed 15.01.10) (in Chinese).

Yang, Y., 2017. China's online bookselling business in 2016: online retailers overtaking the bookstores in sales (*2016 nian zhongguo tushu wangshang xiaoshou geju, wangdian shouchao shitidian*). <http://www.ce.cn/culture/gd/201703/24/t20170324_21371887.shtml> (accessed 06.12.17) (in Chinese).

Yunnan Provincial PPB, 1995. Provisional regulation on strengthening the administration of publishing plans (*guanyu jiaqiang xuanti guanli de zanxing banfa*). <http://www.zffz.yn.gov.cn/ynxwcbbqj/5261615038187175936/20081210/189807.html> (accessed 14.01.10) (in Chinese).

Zhejiang Provincial PPB, 2002. Provisional regulation of Zhejiang Province on the publishing plans of books, audio–video products and electronic publications (*zhejiang sheng tushu yinxiang zhipin dianzi chubanwu xuanti guanli banfa shixing*). <http://www.zjxwcb.gov.cn/Html/zcfg_bjgfxwj/2011-03/16/a32a00fb070b4f4fafec0bb41dbd10fb.html> (accessed 11.01.10) (in Chinese).

Zheng, S., 1997. Party vs State in Post-1949 China: The Institutional Dilemma. Cambridge University Press, Cambridge.

Zhou, W., 2009. New wealth game of private publishers (*minying shushang de xin caifu youxi*). Southern Weekly (nanfang zhoumo) 13 May. <http://www.infzm.com/content/28352> (accessed 17.01.10) (in Chinese).

Zhu, Y., 2016. The dark tricks in the school supplementary learning materials business (*zhongxiaoxue jiaofu shichang taolu shen*). <http://society.people.com.cn/n1/2016/1103/c1008-28832847.html> (accessed 06.12.17) (in Chinese).

CHAPTER 3

From Communization to Commercialization: China's Publishing From 1949 to 1992

Understanding Chinese publishing history during the period of the People's Republic is essential for a full understanding of China's publishing industry. First, despite profound changes since the start of economic reform, the industry is still imbued with legacies inherited from the old system under the planned economy. Contextualizing current changes historically helps us understand the continuities as well as the breaks. Second, an historical account explains why and how the significant institutional change in book publishing was initiated. There are, however, few serious studies on this topic and this chapter sets out to fill this gap.

This chapter tries to offer a brief account of the period from the establishment of the communist regime in 1949 to China's full embrace of a socialist market economy in 1992. However, trying to provide in just one chapter even a brief account of such a long and tumultuous period is a difficult task, and many details have to be left out. There are already abundant archives and memoirs available from mainly Chinese sources about specific issues in the industry or specific publishers (such as the prestigious Commercial Press). But what is lacking in our knowledge about this period of publishing history is an overall picture of its changes along with analysis that explains the interactions between different sectors of the industry and between the industry and the broader social and political context. This is what I try to address here.

Book publishing under communist leadership has seen two major transitions: first, the subjugation of book publishing to the Party's total control by eliminating market forces and private publishing businesses, and, second, the reversal of this process brought on by the economic reform. The period in-between saw the operation and adjustment of "communized" book publishing within a planned economy (see Table 3.1 for an overview).

China's Publishing Industry
DOI: https://doi.org/10.1016/B978-0-08-100919-2.00003-6

Table 3.1 Periods of publishing history during the People's Republic (1949–92)

Periods	Publishing	Book distribution
Period one (1949–56): communization and centralization.	Private publishing industry was eliminated, and state-owned publishing industry was subjugated to the control of central planning.	A national hierarchical Xinhua Bookstore system enjoyed a monopoly after private book distribution business was eliminated.
Period two (1956–79): oscillation between decentralization and recentralization under the planned economy.	A period of decentralization with overproduction occurred during the Great Leap Forward, followed by a period of recentralization. The Cultural Revolution saw another period of decentralization with extreme politicization and decline of output. A brief period of recentralization followed before the introduction of market reform.	Xinhua Bookstore system underwent cycles of decentralization followed by recentralization.
Period three (1979–92): commercialization and decentralization.	Publishers gradually became more market-oriented. The number of local publishers increased rapidly and they acquired more operational autonomy. Private publishing emerged as a gray business.	Xinhua Bookstore was decentralized and commercialized; The monopoly was broken by the emergence of private distribution business.

This chapter argues two pivotal points in the interpretation of China's publishing history. First, it systematically demonstrates that the planned publishing industry was from the outset characterized by inherent contradictions. Second, it shows that the transition to a commercialized system became inevitable given the changes in the general operating environment after the introduction of economic reforms.

Following the establishment of the People's Republic in 1949, the party-state embarked on an initial process of economic recovery and political consolidation. As its political and economic control across the country was reinforced, the Party became confident enough to launch the socialist transformation (*shehui zhuyi gaizao*) in 1953. Although the original "general line for the transition to socialism" promulgated by the Party adopted a gradualist approach and allowed for a fairly long period of transformation, estimated to be about 15 years or even longer, the process was actually completed by the end of 1956. Initially, a centrally planned economy modeled after the Soviet Union was established but it soon came under critical scrutiny. Impatience among the Party leaders about the pace of economic growth gradually prevailed. In addition, the Party started to examine the disadvantages of the Soviet model, such as the rigidity of the plan, the increased tendency to bureaucratism, and the inequalities arising from the bureaucratic hierarchy and material incentives. To overcome these perceived faults in the system, the Party leaders, particularly Mao, launched a mild rectification campaign within the Party, and encouraged non-Party intellectuals to speak out in a movement known as the "Hundred Flowers." However, this plan backfired and a lot of criticism was directed at even socialism and the Party itself. Mao quickly launched a counterattack on the critics and many intellectuals, dubbed as "rightists," were suppressed in the "Anti-Rightist Campaign" in 1957.

Mao pushed through the idea of the Great Leap Forward in 1957 as an alternative development strategy different from the Soviet model. Considerable power was delegated from the central government bureaucracy to local Party committees and governments, and many People's Communes (*renming gongshe*) were established. The campaign of the Great Leap Forward, however, not only led to disastrous famine and other economic problems, but also contributed to the Sino-Soviet split. Although the economy gradually recovered from 1961, deep fissures among the Party leaders arising from the Great Leap Forward campaign developed, which planted the seeds of Cultural Revolution (Lieberthal, 1987).

Mao officially launched the Cultural Revolution in 1966 to attack the Party establishment. The initial stage, from 1966 to 1969, was extremely chaotic, as Mao "failed to design a viable and enduring alternative political order to replace the one he sought to overthrow" (Harding, 1997: 239).

Efforts were made to rebuild the state structure from 1970, but the Cultural Revolution was only formally brought to a halt after Mao's death in 1976. The economy suffered far less from the Cultural Revolution than from the Great Leap Forward, but the consequences for cultural and educational affairs were far greater (ibid). Universities were shut down for several years and middle schools sometimes suspended their instruction. Many intellectuals were persecuted during this period. Paradoxically, however, the chaos of the Cultural Revolution can also be seen as "an important condition" for the post-Mao reforms (ibid: 246–247).

The post-Mao era started with moves to rehabilitate the centrally planned system and initiated another economic "leap" (Naughton, 1995). After this failed, the Party made a significant shift in 1978 toward economic reforms centered on the gradual introduction of market forces. This move, although achieving rapid economic growth, was not free from opposition from conservatives. The Chinese leader, Deng Xiaoping, made another effort in early 1992 to revive the reform after the Tiananmen Square incident in 1989, but it was not until October 1992 that the party-state officially embraced the "socialist market economy." All these events had an impact on China's book publishing.

3.1 COMMUNIZATION OF PUBLISHING: 1949–56

By 1949, a party-controlled Xinhua Bookstore publishing and distribution system had already been established in areas controlled by the Party. A similar operation also existed in areas not controlled by the Party, such as Shanghai and Hong Kong, although they were often concealed as private businesses (Xu, 2001). When the print media still dominated—before the development of broadcast media in China—books, because of their portability, durability, and length, were seen by the Party as an important "mouthpiece" for political propaganda in its struggle for political power. The Xinhua Bookstore, although it appeared to be a business organization, was actually a Party organ and was responsible for the distribution of Party publications. The Central Party Press Commission (*zhongyang dangbao weiyuanhui*) of the Chinese Communist Party (CCP), consisting of a publishing section and a distribution section, was established in 1937. These sections also used the titles of Liberation Press (*jiefang she*) and Xinhua Bookstore, respectively. The Xinhua Bookstore was merged into the CCP Propaganda Department as its Distribution Section in 1946. The Distribution Section of CCP Propaganda Department used the designation of General Store of Xinhua Bookstore (*xinhua shudian zongdian*) when distributing books in the marketplace, but styled itself as the Distribution Section of CCP Propaganda Department when distributing books within the Party system. As the Party gradually controlled more areas, many local Party propaganda departments established their own book publishing and distribution businesses, which usually but not always used the title of Xinhua bookstore. Local Xinhua bookstores engaged in publishing, printing, and distribution, which was similar to other publishers at that time that operated under the title of "bookstore" while conducting multiple activities. The publishing and distribution system of the Party was decentralized, a system, according to Hu Yuzhi, the first Director of General Bureau of Publications (*chuban zongshu*), that had grown out of the imperatives imposed by the period of civil war (see Wang, 2001: 78). The books published and distributed by the Xinhua bookstores before 1949 mainly fulfilled the propaganda tasks of the Party in its struggle for the state power.

The Chinese publishing industry had undergone great difficulties due to the disruption of a few years of war against an invading Japan and the following civil war. When the Party came into power in 1949, all publishers affiliated with or in support of the previous Nationalist (*Guomingdang*) government were immediately confiscated. But a large number of private publishers and booksellers, mainly in Shanghai, which was the center of China's publishing industry at that time, were allowed to continue their business, and they coexisted alongside a party-controlled publishing system, of which most parts were controlled by local Party propaganda departments. For ideological reasons and also to establish a centrally planned economy, these private publishing businesses had to be subdued and the decentralized party-controlled publishing system assimilated into a national planned system. The Soviet publishing industry became the model for the transformation of China's publishing industry, and many Soviet practices, such as price control over books, restrictions on the subject areas addressed by publishers, and government control over payments to authors (Walker, 1995), would all be adopted in China.

From 1949 to 1956, the Party engaged in a process of reorganizing the party-controlled publishing industry and eliminating private publishing business, a process that can be termed "communization." A government administration department, the General Bureau of Publications (*chuban zongshu*), was launched in 1949 to take over the publishers and booksellers affiliated with the Party propaganda departments and also to deal with private publishing businesses. The Party realized that moving the Xinhua Bookstore from a Party organ to a state-owned organization would have far-reaching implications for its operation, and reminded Xinhua that in its new role it would have to deal with private publishing businesses and non-Party authors rather than the Party-affiliated organizations only (Yuan et al., 1995: 295). The double requirements of "running as an enterprise (*qiye hua*)" and publishing propaganda books became a key topic in Party meetings about the Xinhua Bookstore in 1949 (Yuan et al., 1996: 267–296, 333). The General Bureau of Publications, which controlled some state-owned publishing business, was not only a national administration bureau. It also had an editorial branch engaged directly in the publishing of some publications, such as the Xinhua Monthly Magazine (*xinhua yuebao*) and the Book Review (*tushu pinglun*). The editorial branch was terminated in late 1950 in order to "separate enterprises and government administration" and streamline the bureaucracy of the General Bureau of Publications (ibid: 106). The intricate relationship between the Party, the government administration department, and publishing houses established at that time was a key characteristic of China's book publishing industry under Communism, and has remained largely so till now.

3.1.1 Unification and Specialization

The General Bureau of Publications proposed the dual policies of unification (*tongyi*) and specialization (*zhuanyehua*) as the key planks in the reorganization of state-owned publishing industry. A nationwide hierarchical Xinhua Bookstore system was formed with the General Administration of Xinhua Bookstore (*xinhua shudian zong guanlichu*) being established as the headquarters. This headquarters, although nominally a business organization, was also the Publishing Branch (*chuban ju*) of the General Bureau of Publications and assumed government administrative responsibilities. This was then probably a sensible arrangement during the planned economy when the government had an intricate relationship with the state-owned publishing industry. As this headquarters was funded by the Xinhua Bookstore system, it helped the central government to control its budget. Similar arrangements for provincial publishing administration departments were terminated only recently. The publishing administration department in Guangdong province, for example, was funded by local publishing industry until October 2001 (Ding et al., 2004).

According to the principle of specialization, a unified Xinhua Bookstore system, which combined publishing, distribution, and printing businesses, was required to be divided into three separate enterprises. As a consequence, the General Administration of Xinhua Bookstore was divided into the General Store of Xinhua Bookstore (*xinhua shudian zongdian*) which specialized in book distribution; the People's Publishing House (*renmin chubanshe*) which specialized in publishing; and the General Administration of Xinhua Printer (*xinhua yinshuachang zong guanlichu*) which specialized in printing. These three organizations also assumed government administration responsibilities in their business sectors and their leaders all held positions in relevant government or Party departments.

Local Xinhua bookstores were divided accordingly into local people's publishing houses, local Xinhua bookstores, and local Xinhua printers. These local activities were formally subject to the dual control of both the central government and local governments. But the Xinhua Bookstore system, which now retained only the book distribution business, was mainly a centralized hierarchical system, with the General Store of Xinhua Bookstore serving as the headquarters to facilitate the nationwide distribution of books. In contrast, the local people's publishing houses, like local Party papers, were mainly intended to serve local governments and local readerships; therefore, they were controlled mainly by local governments while also being subject to the guidance of the central government. Local people's publishing houses under the planned economy had a strong incentive to control local Xinhua printers in order to guarantee the production of their books (Wang, 1982). As a result, it was hardly feasible to establish a centralized printing industry, and the central government department only provided guidance to local printers.

The decentralized nature of the printing industry led to a unique practice known as "plate-renting" among the state-owned publishers. As textbooks and influential propaganda books were published by national publishers in Beijing, the government felt it more economical to send printing plates to local publishers for production than to have printing paper transported to Beijing and then the printed books transported across the country (ibid). To save the cost and delay of transport and also to utilize local printing capacity, national publishers rented the plates of some books to local publishers who would then arrange local production and distribution.

Among publishers, local people's publishing houses were required to "specialize" in the local market and national publishers were required to "specialize" in particular subject areas in order to avoid "duplication and waste" (*chongfu langfei*) of publications. As a subject area usually fell within the responsibility of a particular government department, national publishers were assigned an affiliated government department which acted as the "sponsoring organization" and controlled their publishing plans. For example, the People's Education Press was "led" by the Ministry of Education and the People's Literature Publishing House by the Ministry of Culture. As a result, most national publishers were under the dual control of their sponsoring organization and the General Bureau of Publications, with the sponsoring organization being responsible for the editorial issues and publishing plans. This arrangement finally evolved into what is known in the industry as the "sponsoring system" (*zhuguan zhuban zhidu*).

There were, however, some problems in operating a control system divided between the publishers on the one hand and the Xinhua bookstores on the other. Since the bookstores were part of a centralized system, they did not have an automatic interest in distributing the books of local publishers. In addition, in the dual control system, Xinhua bookstores could play the two bosses against each other. It was reported that a few Xinhua bookstores sometimes used local government as an excuse to counter the instructions from their superior Xinhua bookstores, and vice versa (Yuan et al., 1996: 287–288). At the same time, some publishers were affiliated to powerful local governments or central state agencies, which could pose challenges to the authority of the General Bureau of Publications (ibid: 255–256).

A unified and centralized Xinhua Bookstore system was, according to the first Director of the General Bureau of Publications, instrumental in creating China's first nationwide book distribution system. Only a unified system could, through cross-subsidy, afford to expand into every part of the country, including particularly remote and poorer areas (see Zheng, 1987: 16). For the Xinhua Bookstore system, profit-seeking was never its primary goal, although it was not completely absent from its business calculations. The unified control was also intended as a way of restricting profit-seeking so that "valuable but unpopular books" (a euphemism for propaganda books) could be distributed across the country (ibid: 16).

This institutional structure, as can be expected, would certainly lead to economic problems at a later stage.

The unification of the Xinhua Bookstore system was not achieved without resistance from local governments. Since local governments had initially invested in the establishment of their local Xinhua bookstores, many of them tried to protect their interests by delaying the handover of control or diverting assets and staff before the unification. Directives from the central party-state had to be issued to prohibit these kinds of resistance (Qian et al., 1991: 13−14).

3.1.2 The Elimination of Private Publishing Businesses

In hindsight, it is not surprising that the party-state was determined to build a socialist planned economy as soon as it could and little room would be left for private publishing businesses. What the mass media, including book publishing, produced, according to the Party, was not "normal goods" but "mainly propaganda products for thought (work) and politics" (Yuan et al., 1999: 465). To ensure that this aim was pursued as vigorously as possible, eliminating private publishing businesses became a priority in achieving the "socialist transformation." Although private newspaper publishing had already been eliminated by 1952, private book publishing business, probably due to the fact that it was seen as less immediately politically sensitive, was not eliminated until the end of 1956 (see Table 3.2).

Already in 1951, the party-state made a firm decision that private publishing business should be eliminated within 5 years (see Yuan et al., 1996: 496).[1] This policy was not publicly circulated and many private

Table 3.2 Number of publishers (1950−56)

Year	Total publishers	National (state) publishers	Local (state) publishers	Private publishers
1956	101	54	47	0
1955	96	37	40	19
1954	167	30	40	97
1953	352	21	41	290
1952	426	16	54	356
1951	385	13	51	321
1950	211	6	21	184

Source: Song, Y., et al. (Eds.), 1999. Archives of contemporary China's publishing, vol. 8 (*zhongguo dangdai chuban shiliao*). Da Xiang Publishing House, Zhengzhou, pp. 163−234 (in Chinese).

entrepreneurs at the time did not expect this transformation to start just a couple of years after the establishment of the People's Republic, as the Party had originally talked about allowing a transition period of 10–15 years (Wu, 2005: 32).

Having decided to nationalize the publishing business, the party-state adopted a gradualist approach and tried different ways to eliminate private operators rather than rely solely on political suppression. There were probably several reasons for this. First, the party-state tried to minimize both the opposition from private entrepreneurs and the risk of social unrest arising from unemployment during the initial stage of regime consolidation. Second, the Party was still locked in a struggle with the Nationalist regime that had retreated to Taiwan, and blatant confiscation would not help to win hearts and minds and would damage the Party's attempts to promote positive publicity. Third, since the state-owned publishers were still weak, the party-state had to rely on the cooperation of private publishers for textbook publishing and tolerate private publishers to a certain extent so that the industry could produce a wide range of books during the process of transformation. The government was fully aware of the deficiencies of the state-controlled publishers—especially in the publishing of maps, reference books, picture story books, and other popular books—and acknowledged that they needed to be expanded gradually while simultaneously reducing the number of private publishing businesses (see Fang and Wei, 2008: 56–57).

The party-state adopted a general policy of "utilization, restriction, and transformation" (*liyong, xianzhi, gaizao*) toward private entrepreneurs, including private publishing businesses. Utilization was the main strategy pursued at the beginning of regime consolidation. Although censorship against old publications was inevitable, the Party allowed most private publishers and booksellers to carry on with their businesses but aimed to "gradually strengthen the control (over) and restriction (on private publishers) in order to make them serve the Party" (Yuan et al., 1995: 119). When the Party first came into power, it faced an immediate task of providing enough textbooks for schools. As the state-controlled publishing industry at the time did not have enough capable staff, paper supplies, printing capacity, and financial capital to meet this challenge, the party-state sought the cooperation of private publishing businesses. To achieve this end, two party-controlled publishers, Xinhua Bookstore and SDX Joint Publishing House, formed joint venture companies with major private publishers in Beijing and Shanghai, respectively, in 1949 to publish textbooks. Many textbooks owned by these private publishers were either adopted directly or adopted after adaptation. However, as the state-controlled publishing industry became stronger, private publishers were forced to withdraw from these joint ventures. By the end of 1950, the state-owned People's Education Press achieved a monopoly on textbook publishing.

After this initial period of utilization, the party-state embarked on a process of "restriction and transformation" which built on and extended policy initiatives that had already expanded the reach of the party-state. At the end of 1949, the state council established a paper supply commission to ration printing paper to all publishers, a move which endangered the operation of private printers.[2] In addition, according to the policy of specialization, many private publishers were forced to focus only on publishing, distribution, or printing—a restriction that substantially weakened their ability to exercise vertical control over the supply chain. When the party-state started to restrict and gradually eliminate the private publishing businesses, it did so by adopting a combination of political and economic measures.

One major administrative measure designed to restrict private publishing businesses was the control over business licenses. In 1952, all private publishers, booksellers, and printers were required to register with the government in order to be licensed. However, many of them failed to obtain a license, because the government administration departments had been instructed not to grant licenses to those private publishing businesses that were not following the party line. In the meantime, the government managed to collect enough business information about all private publishers in the process of registration, so that appropriate strategies could be designed against them at a later stage (Yuan et al., 1996: 496). In addition, all private publishers were required to establish a dedicated "editorial branch" (*bianji bu*) in order to be licensed, a requirement that effectively made it impossible for many small private publishers that could not afford such a branch to obtain a license. Although the government issued temporary licenses to some private publishers on the condition that an editorial branch would be established later, it had no intention of allowing them to continue in business. According to the General Bureau of Publications, the issuing of temporary licenses was just a "struggle strategy" in order to minimize the opposition from private publishing businesses, and local governments were instructed not to envisage issuing long-term licenses to private publishers even after their establishment of an "editorial branch" (see Yuan et al., 1999: 75).

Administrative restriction was also imposed on the business areas of private publishers. When textbook publishing became monopolized by the state-owned People's Education Press, a couple of major private publishers which had relied heavily on textbook publishing, such as the prestigious Commercial Press (*shangwu yinshuguan*) and Zhonghua Book Company (*zhonghua shuju*),[3] were immediately in trouble. Private publishers were not only excluded from textbook publishing, but also prohibited from publishing other popular categories at that time, including the following: biographies or posters of communist leaders, study aids of laws or state regulations, dictionaries, maps, children's books, and translated foreign books. Even Party documents were not allowed to be published by private publishers.[4] According to the principle of specialization, the state also restricted private publishers to particular subject areas (*zhuanye fangxiang*) in order to prevent them from "ranging" across different subject areas and "exploiting loopholes" (*zuan kongzi*) (Yuan et al., 1999: 75).

The party-state also imposed controls over book prices. Private publishers used to vary their book prices according to the different distribution costs in different regions. But in January 1951, the government ordered all published books to use a fixed price, a move which substantially reduced the profit margins of private publishers. The Xinhua Bookstore system was also instructed to help the state to control the book prices charged by private publishers (Yuan et al., 1999: 78 and 89). As Xinhua gained predominance, they could refuse to distribute a book if the price was deemed "too high."

In addition to implementing direct administrative measures, the party-state also sought to control the general business environment that private publishers relied on for their survival. In order to restrict private publishing business, the state-owned Xinhua bookstores initially did not sell books for private publishers (Yuan et al., 1996: 105). Private publishing businesses, facing the problem in distribution and pressure from censorship, were in difficult situation in early 1950 and their relationship with the state-owned publishing businesses was abrasive. However, in order to reduce the problem of unemployment[5] and win the support of private publishing business, Xinhua bookstores started to sell books for private publishers in October 1950. This immediately had a positive impact on private publishing businesses, and private publishers and printers greatly expanded their businesses (ibid). The Xinhua Bookstore system was also requested to focus mainly on book wholesaling, and to reduce its competition with private book retailers by cutting promotions and suspending its sale of stationery (see Fang, 2001: 114). Private booksellers took this opportunity to expand, which in turn provided an opportunity for private publishers. This was the main reason for the expansion of private publishers in 1950 and 1951 (see Table 3.2).

The party-state saw achieving control over book wholesaling as a crucial step toward eliminating private booksellers and publishers. According to the principle of specialization, the book distribution businesses of several major private publishers were merged into a specialized book distributor, the "China Book Distribution Company," in 1951. This immediately established another nationwide book distributor second only to the Xinhua Bookstore system. Although this company was formally a joint public—private enterprise, it was effectively controlled by the party-state. A couple of years later, the government forced private publishers to withdraw their shares from the joint venture and merged it into the Xinhua Bookstore system. By the end of 1954, the Xinhua Bookstore system controlled 98% of the book distribution business by value (Fang and Wei, 2008: 61), and book wholesaling was completely under the control of the party-state. The state-controlled book wholesalers, by taking advantage of its monopolistic control over the distribution network, became the only distribution agents for many private publishers, and forced many private book retailers to rely on state-controlled wholesalers. This process of "gradually severing the links between private publishers, book wholesalers and retailers" (see Yuan et al., 1999: 462) planned by the party-state laid the foundation for the final elimination of the private publishing business. In addition, printers were forbidden to print books for unlicensed private publishers or self-publishing authors (ibid: 339). Private printers, with their printing capacity being assimilated to the planned economy in 1953, came under the control of the government (Gu and Gao, 1984).

Once the party-state gained full control over the book wholesaling business, private publishers and booksellers were completely at its mercy. But even with this unassailable advantage, the party-state continued to pursue a gradualist policy to eliminate private publishing businesses. The state-controlled book distributors were allowed to sell books from some private publishers in order to "placate" them and avoid "making too many enemies at the same time" (ibid, 471) at the beginning of the "socialist transformation." But when the party-state felt confident enough to undermine private publishing businesses, state-owned distributors were often instructed to restrict their services to private publishers. In 1954, the Xinhua Bookstore system's wholesaling to private book retailers slumped, forcing many private book retailers into bankruptcy. However, social and political realities intervened to force a change of policy. Faced with the problem of unemployment, in 1955 the party-state instructed the Xinhua Bookstore system to alleviate the problems of private booksellers. This resulted in Xinhua Bookstore as a wholesaler offering preferential discounts to private booksellers—even though these caused losses for Xinhua—and reducing the operating hours of its retail stores to leave more customers for private booksellers. Gullible private booksellers would only later realize that these concessions, however amiable they appeared to be, turned out to be just a temporary "struggle strategy" (*douzheng celue*) of the Party.

In order to eliminate private publishers altogether, the party-state systematically restricted access to essential business resources. It instructed state-controlled publishers to compete with private publishers for author resources and required those potential authors employed by state-owned organizations to prioritize state-controlled publishers as outlets for their books. After private banks were eliminated by the end of 1952, state-owned banks were instructed to restrict their loans to private publishers. Book advertising from private publishers and distributors was also restricted in state-controlled newspapers and magazines. As the party-state controlled paper supplies, it demanded that private publishers used state-owned book distributors as their sole distribution agent as a condition of obtaining rationed paper supplies, a restriction that also helped to eliminate private book distributors.

Poaching capable personnel from private publishers was another important strategy. As state-owned publishing houses were often short of specialists, such as map experts and picture book artists, they were instructed by the party-state to "absorb" capable editorial, drawing, and production specialists from private publishers "in order to gradually weaken" them, even though these specialists might be regarded as "politically backward" (see Yuan et al., 1999: 77). Since state-owned publishers did not have to worry about generating profits and their staff enjoyed higher political status, it was difficult for private publishers to retain their gifted staff.

These administrative and economic measures were accompanied and backed by political pressure. The Three and Five Antis campaigns (*sanfan wufan yundong*)[6] that started at the end of 1951 exerted substantial political pressure on private publishing business. Private printers were criticized for the "poor" production quality of the books they delivered to state-owned publishers.[7] As admitted by the then director of the General Bureau of Publications, nit-picking (*zhao mafan*) from the government at private publishers was also common (Yuan et al., 1996: 255). Many private publishers were forced to close or had to restrict their publishing plans to avoid the ideological crackdown (Yuan et al., 1998: 432 and 162).

Censorship toward private publishers was gradually tightened up as the Party's grip on power became more secure. An in-house system of self-censorship at state-owned publishers was formally established in 1952. This required a book manuscript to be scrutinized at least by the author, the executive editor, a senior editor in charge of the relevant subject area, and the editorial director before the approval of the director of the publishing house could be given. It worked as a kind of prepublication censorship and has continued to the present. There was no formal prepublication censorship system for private publishers but, ironically, this placed them in a worse situation since the post-publication censorship of the party-state was completely unpredictable and it was difficult for private publishers to avoid confiscation or prohibition of their books in response to political vagaries. Although some private publishers applied for their books to be censored before the publication to avoid prohibition, these requests were refused by the party-state. This was probably because formal prepublication censorship might place the party-state in an embarrassing position if publications they had initially approved became unacceptable at a later stage. The uncertainty surrounding the boundaries of censorship was to the Party's advantage since they could pounce upon and confiscate books entirely at their discretion.

Party-endorsed book reviews played an important role in the censorship. In addition to the book reviews published by the General Bureau of Publications, newspapers and magazines were frequently asked to publish book reviews. Government departments often imposed prohibition or confiscation after a book was criticized in book reviews.[8] State-controlled book distributors were also instructed to censor books according to the guidance provided by book reviews (Yuan et al., 1996: 497). In this way, book reviews operated as a kind of post-publication censorship, and played an important role in the "socialist transformation of private publishing business" (Fang and Wei, 2008: 41).

Trade unions were also strengthened and Party branches were set up in many private publishers, which weakened the control of private entrepreneurs over their businesses. In this hostile political environment, the party-state easily "persuaded" some private publishers to close down. At the beginning of 1952, the prestigious Commercial Press was not even able to find a manager to represent it in its negotiations with the government because of the threatening political environment (Yang, 2000: 155). Faced with this situation, a number of large private publishers applied to be transformed into joint public—private enterprises, in which they could at least earn a dividend according to the size of their shareholding. However, private publishers were gradually edged out of these joint ventures and eventually eliminated altogether.

3.1.3 Problems of Communized Book Publishing

The publishing industry at this stage initially benefited from the economic recovery and the success of a 5-year industrialization plan. Some accounts of Chinese publishing history tend to interpret this period as a golden age with "a great progress" (Fang and Wei, 2008: 3) as measured by the increased output of both titles and volumes. This view, however, is not supported by the data shown in Table 3.3, which shows the title output in the years after 1951 actually decreased. These figures point to intrinsic institutional problems within this ideology-dominated planned system, problems which laid the foundation for the situation during the period of the Cultural Revolution.

Extreme politicization in book publishing was already apparent. The Xinhua Bookstore was instructed as early as 1951 to improve its "sense of political responsibility" (*zhengzhi xing*) in the distribution of books. According to this instruction, books with significant importance as propaganda were not allowed to be returned to publishers and should instead be distributed in large numbers (Yuan et al., 1996: 448—457). Although state-owned publishers and distributors were required to operate with the "spirit of enterprises" for profit (Yuan et al., 1995: 292—295), profit-oriented operations were usually criticized and subordinated to the

Table 3.3 Title output of China's book publishing (1947—54)

Year	1947	1949	1950	1951	1952	1953	1954
Output	1569	8000	12,153	18,300	13,692	17,819	17,760

Source: Wu, Y., 2011. China's Publishing History During the Republican Period (*minguo chuban shi*). Fujian People's Publishing House, Fuzhou (in Chinese) and Fang, H., 1996. Book publishing statistics in People's Republic of China (*zhonhua renmin gongheguo tushu chuban tongji*) (1949.10—1989.12). In: Song, Y., et al. (Eds.), 1999. Archives of Contemporary China's Publishing (*zhongguo dangdai chuban shiliao*), vol. 2. Da Xiang Publishing House, Zhengzhou, pp. 100—104 (in Chinese).

political need for propaganda (Yuan et al., 1996: 327–329). The General Bureau of Publications also started to require all books, including those for children's literacy education, to be imbued with "Marxism, Leninism and Mao Zedong Thought" (ibid: 311). Publishers were also warned to be vigilant in ensuring the "class nature" of books on natural sciences, and these books were required to be ideologically censored by people who had "good political consciousness" (*zhengzhi xiuyang hao*) (ibid: 414–415) even though they might not be capable of understanding the specialized content of the books.

Once the party-state had acquired total dominance over the society and book publishing was oriented toward political propaganda, compulsory distribution (*qiangpo tanpai*) became unavoidable. Since Xinhua Bookstore was simultaneously required to serve massive propaganda tasks and also to run as a profit-seeking enterprise, compulsory distribution was the only way to achieve both targets. In early 1951, the central party-state already recognized that there were serious problems of compulsory distribution and asked local governments to redress them. However, as long as propaganda was the paramount task, this proved impossible. To serve the political needs of different campaigns, huge numbers of books were "sold" with the assistance of compulsory distribution. For example, one propaganda book was recorded as having "sold" over nine million copies (ibid: 219). Political threats were often used as part of compulsory distribution (Lai, 2003). Xinhua bookstores even forced some people to sell their precious editions of ancient books to paper mills as waste paper in order to pay for compulsorily distributed propaganda books and also to wipe out the "poisonous feudal legacy" (*fengjian yidu*) (Qian et al., 1991: 89; Liu and Shi, 1999: 25). Compulsory distribution aroused massive resentment among poor peasants. When the party-state realized that compulsory distribution seriously damaged its legitimacy, it started to crack down on it in the beginning of 1953, ignoring the fact that its own institutional design and massive political propaganda had led to the problem. Although the problem of predatory compulsory distribution may have been alleviated to a certain extent due to the self-restriction of the party-state, it could never be rooted out completely and recurred frequently.

As Xinhua Bookstore was instructed to provide spiritual "food" rather than just sell books for profit and as political propaganda was its prime task, financial losses were inevitable. Book prices were usually set at a low level in order to promote propaganda books. But despite the assistance of compulsory distribution, there was often a large amount of unsold stock.

The value of unsold stock by June 1952, for example, was over half of the total liquidity of the Xinhua Bookstore.[9] After compulsory distribution was forbidden in 1953, unsold book stock inevitably increased even more quickly. This generated huge financial problems for Xinhua Bookstore and some branches financially collapsed (Lai, 2003). The ensuing shortage of cash flow forced Xinhua Bookstore to reduce its purchase of new books from publishers. As a result, customers were often unable to find the books they intended to buy, leading to the so-called "book drought" (*shuhuang*) acknowledged by the government. Eventually the financial losses in the state-owned publishing industry had to be reimbursed from government funds.

The book drought, however, was caused not only by the economic problems of Xinhua Bookstore. When the ideological censorship gradually tightened up and the whole industry had to chant the Party mantras, the range of available books inevitably plummeted. The General Bureau of Publications instructed in February 1952 that a stricter censorship should be applied in publishing. Local government administration departments, in order to avoid political risks, adopted even tougher ideological lines in their own censorship (see Yuan et al., 1998: 15–18 and 25–27 for example). The General Bureau of Publications was later criticized by the central Party propaganda department for the overly strict censorship carried out across the country (ibid: 82) and admitted in July 1952 that its censorship of many books was unreasonable (ibid: 77–81). Censorship was applied not only to publishers and booksellers, but also to book-renting stands. Most of the books owned by these stands were picture story books, such as fantasy and detective stories. The censorship carried out by the government confiscated many of the books they held as they were designated as ideologically unacceptable (Yuan et al., 1996: 478). The strict censorship, by eliminating reading alternatives, helped to promote the propaganda books. Many capable authors refrained from taking up writing due to the fear of harsh ideological pressure. As private publishing was diminishing, professional authors gradually lost the business environment which had sustained them, hence the inevitable decrease of independent creative talents.

The dearth of new books was also exacerbated by the inefficiency of the state-controlled publishing system. The state-owned publishers, due to their monopolistic privileges, had little incentive to contact authors for new publishing projects. The principle of specialization restricted local publishers to publishing "accessible books" (*tongsu duwu*) for the local market—most of which were actually propaganda books—giving national publishers a monopoly in their designated subject areas. Authors therefore had no choice but to go to a particular state-owned publisher. As a result, editors often had a condescending attitude toward their authors and were usually sluggish in responding to them. In addition, in the prevailing atmosphere of extreme politicization, editors tended to reject manuscripts if there was any ideological risk.

The changed relationship between state-owned publishers and Xinhua Bookstore also had adverse impacts on both sides. According to the principle of "planned distribution," Xinhua Bookstore subscribed to a total number of copies before a book was published. Books would then be produced and sent directly to them by printers. As none of these orders were allowed to be returned, publishers did not need a warehouse to keep book stock and did not need to worry about financial risks. However, because state-owned publishers were required to use Xinhua Bookstore as their sole distribution agent, it left them little room to maneuver if Xinhua refused to subscribe to enough copies of a book. Consequently, even if publishers wanted to be a bit more enterprising, they tended to play safe and publish titles to which the bookstores would fully subscribe.

The planned control of paper supply also imposed an additional constraint on publishers. Shortages of paper were common during the period of the socialist planned economy, which was also known as the shortage economy (Kornai, 1980). Problems with the supply of paper were inevitable in book publishing as long as the party-state insisted on more propaganda books and publishers did not need to worry about their financial losses. As a result, paper supply imposed a major material constraint on the expansion of the planned publishing industry. Limited paper supplies, which were devoted first to the production of textbooks and propaganda books, often forced the party-state to impose restrictions on the publishing of other new books and led to complaints from publishers. This also contributed to the sluggish operation of publishers.

In addition, since the state-owned publishers were not profit-oriented, they had little incentive or pressure to introduce or promote their books. Xinhua Bookstore had difficulty in deciding the size of any particular subscription, as the information available on a book was usually limited to the 200 or so words of description in the publisher's catalogue (Qian et al., 1991: 48). Consequently, in an effort to avoid problems with unsold book stock, Xinhua Bookstore tended to restrict their numbers of subscription quantities, especially after the crackdown on compulsory distribution. Xinhua Bookstore would usually contact organizations for book orders before they sent their subscription numbers to publishers, and would then order only a limited number of extra copies for retail.

The state-owned book distributors were also very sluggish in providing services. As long as the Xinhua Bookstore distributed enough copies of propaganda books to meet its political obligations and the huge number of textbooks that constituted its major source of income, it had little interest in meeting the demand in its retail service. Consequently, many customers found the books they wanted to buy were out of stock in local Xinhua bookstores. Within the bookstore system, then, large stocks of unsold propaganda books coexisted with a permanent shortage of books that met market demand. This mismatch inevitably accentuated the problem of the book drought.

In 1951, books on science and technology subjects accounted for only 2.23% of the total published books in terms of copies printed, and 69.7% of them were published by private publishers (Yuan et al., 1998: 204−205). Children's books, reference books, literary books, social science books, and ancient classics were also in serious shortage. The party-state acknowledged that the book drought would have serious repercussion on culture and education and would hinder the improvement of technology. But since the drought was an intrinsic problem of ideological control and central planning in the publishing industry, the party-state could only alleviate it by relaxing its ideological grip. In 1954, the central Party instructed that the censorship standard could be slightly loosened in order to improve the output of titles. In addition, as the publishing industry under the Party control produced few creative books, the General Bureau of Publications was obliged to organize the reprint of books published before 1949 in order to relieve the book drought.

The state-owned printers also operated with low-efficiency. Their printing costs were usually higher than—sometimes even double—those of private printers (Yuan et al., 1995: 139 and 294). In addition, the relatively few new titles issued and the large print runs of single propaganda books also had an impact. A printing industry that had been developed to produce a large number of titles with relatively small print runs was now required by the General Bureau of Publications to upgrade its equipment in order to meet the new demands of a transformed publishing industry where very large print runs of few books were normal. This focus had to be reversed again after the commercialization of the publishing industry at the beginning of the 1980s, when again there were problems of adjustment, as we will see later.

3.2 OPERATION OF PLANNED BOOK PUBLISHING: 1956–79

Economically, the communized book publishing operated as a centrally planned system. Politically, it was oriented toward ideological propaganda. Consequently, it was vulnerable to changes in political and economic policies. Two political initiatives in particular, the Great Leap Forward and the Cultural Revolution, had a great impact. But even in these highly disruptive circumstances the fundamental political and economic characteristics of book publishing did not change significantly. So the period from 1956 to 1979 can still be usefully characterized as a period of adjustment and operation of a planned publishing industry.

3.2.1 The Great Leap Forward and the Following Adjustment: 1956–66

The campaign of the Great Leap Forward, which lasted from 1958 to 1960 and led to disastrous consequences, was rooted in an overambitious plan for economic growth. The establishment of a centrally-planned economy had placed "enormous power in the central government ministries" (Lieberthal, 1987: 301), which relied heavily on the skills of experts. Mao, who was discontented with the "unhealthy tendencies in the Party and government bureaucracies" (ibid, 293) inherent in the centrally-planned system and with the slow pace of economic growth delivered by an earlier economic plan, decided to accelerate growth through mass mobilization. To facilitate this, considerable powers held by the central government were devolved to local Party branches and local governments.

Book publishing was inevitably caught up in the ensuing political upheaval. In the "Hundred Flowers" movement in 1957, which encouraged open discussion of party-state policies, much criticism against the centrally-planned publishing industry was raised in meetings convened by the Ministry of Culture. Some suggestions for change touched on the fundamental problems of the centrally-planned system. They included: loosening the publishing restrictions on subject areas, removing the constraints on local publishers and permitting free competition among publishers, allowing the establishment of editors-owned cooperative publishers (*tongren chubanshe*), removing the government administration department of publishing industry, devolving more operational decisions in publishing plans and financial control to publishers, and breaking the monopoly of the centralized Xinhua Bookstore system. However, the party-state had no intention of loosening its grip over book publishing or abandoning the planned system, and many of the suggestions put forward were later dismissed as "rightist attacks." Once suggestions for significant institutional change were taken off the agenda for debate, the only option left was to pursue a more radical approach to adjusting the centrally-planned system. This was the option pursued during the Great Leap Forward campaign.

Book publishing, along with every other economic sector, was encouraged to greatly increase its output during the period of the Great Leap Forward. In 1958, publishers started to compete with each other in their output of new titles. Many books were published in an extremely short period of time. It was said that the Commercial Press produced 11 new books in just 5 days and Shanghai People's Publishing House produced 15 new books in 6 days (see Fang and Wei, 2008: 103). Nearly every county-level Party branch and government either established their own publishing houses or simply edited and printed books without the designation of a publishing house. Consequently, in 1958, the output of book publishing increased by more than 65% as measured by the number of titles, 87% by copies printed, and 45% by paper consumption over the previous year (Fang, 2006: 839). However, since publishers were required by the party-state to put "politics in command," many "published" books were just collections of propaganda articles. Because the number of manuscripts produced by experts or professional authors had always been insufficient, publishing houses looked to the "masses" (*qunzhong*) as the main source of authors, but the quality of those manuscripts was usually poor.

As the average print run of books increased, the Ministry of Culture envisaged an increase in the profits of publishers and instructed them to lower their book prices in order to facilitate propaganda.

There was a need to adjust the regulation governing payment to authors. State-owned publishers after 1949 had adopted an author payment system based on the length of a manuscript, its quality and subject area, and its print run. According to this practice, some propaganda books with huge print runs generated much higher payment to authors than quality books with small print runs. In response to this problem, the Ministry of Culture issued a regulation in 1958 to reduce the weight of the print run in the calculation for payment. In 1960, it replaced this system with a one-off payment system based only on the length and quality of the manuscript.

The centralized Xinhua Bookstore system, after acquiring the status of a monopoly, was already considered by the government as "too centralized" (*jizhong guodu*) and "too inflexible" (*guanli guosi*). In accordance with the general trend toward decentralization that characterized the Great Leap Forward, control over Xinhua bookstores was completely devolved to provincial Party branches and governments. Control was then further devolved to lower-level Party branches and governments.

A decentralized Xinhua Bookstore system was essential for the "Great Leap Forward" as the books of local publishers needed to be distributed. With the establishment of People's Communes in rural areas, many "commune bookstore" (*gongshe shudian*), under the dual control of the local Party and local Xinhua bookstores, sprouted up across the country to facilitate the distribution of much increased output of the industry. A few printing factories controlled by the Ministry of Culture were also handed over to local Party committees and governments in 1958 (see Zhang et al., 1999).

Publishers were also granted more autonomy as a result of a government directive issued in August 1957 giving them the power to seek preferential contract terms with the Xinhua Bookstore system. Publishers could decide the number of copies of a book to be dispatched to a Xinhua bookstore (although extra copies not subscribed to by the Xinhua bookstore were allowed to be returned to publishers) or chose to ask the Xinhua Bookstore distributor to pay at least 60% of the cost of the print runs as decided by the publishers. This policy, which enabled publishers to fix print runs of their books while forcing Xinhua Bookstore to partly share the financial risks, was expressly designed by the party-state to facilitate the Great Leap Forward in publishing. The Xinhua Bookstore also embarked on its own Great Leap Forward, setting a target of achieving a 40% increase in distribution volume for 1958 over the previous year (Yuan et al., 2004: 397). As a result, compulsory distribution inevitably recurred.

The radical approach in the Great Leap Forward only aggravated the existing problems of the planned publishing industry. Many so-called books were just propaganda pamphlets. Unsold book stock held by the Xinhua Bookstore increased rapidly. In 1958, the unsold book stock in Shanghai Municipal Xinhua Bookstore reached as high as 41.1 million copies (Fang and Wei, 2008: 107). By the time when the Great Leap Forward was formally brought to a halt at the beginning of 1961, Xinhua bookstores across the country, with huge unsold book stock, were inevitably having cash-flow problems and were in financial difficulties. Most commune bookstores were closed down, but the cost of their unsold book stock had to be borne by Xinhua bookstores. There was no alternative but for the central government to reimburse Xinhua's financial losses. More than RMB70 million yuan was pumped into Xinhua Bookstore in 1962 in order to get the system up and running again (see Zheng, 1987: 31). Considering that the total sales by Xinhua Bookstore in 1962 were about RMB284 million yuan[10] and its net profit would be much less than this figure, this financial subsidy from the government was huge.

During the Great Leap Forward, paper demand surged due to the rapid increase in the output of the publishing industry. Although the paper output was said to have increased (see Table 3.4) as paper mills also started the competition in increasing their output, the quality was often poor as paper mills simplified their production process in order to increase the amount of output (Yu, 2009; Li, 2009). Consequently, the supply of paper suitable for book printing actually declined (see Yuan et al., 2004: 522−524). To support the "leap" in book publishing, the paper reserves held by the Ministry of Culture were depleted to a point that "it could hardly sustain the normal publishing of newspapers, books and magazines of national publishers" (ibid: 527). Due to the paper supply shortage, the paper available for nontextbook publishing in 1961 plummeted to the level of 1951 (see Fang and Wei, 2008: 112). The government could not even provide enough textbooks for schools and had to encourage the recycling of used textbooks. There was also a serious

Table 3.4 Output of machine-made paper and paperboard (1955−62)

Year	Output (thousand tonnes)
1955	575
1956	729
1957	913
1958	1218
1959	1700
1960	1802
1961	1101
1962	1116

Source: Wang, W., et al. (Eds.), 1987. Almanac of China's Paper Industry (*zhongguo zaozhi nianjian*) 1986. China Light Industry Press, Beijing (in Chinese).

shortage of new books in bookstores, and a book drought as a cultural problem recurred.

After the period of the Great Leap Forward ended, the central party-state started to redress the problems in book publishing. Many publishing houses were closed or merged. In order to control the output of book publishing, publishers were required to seek the approval of relevant government departments if the print run of a book exceeded a certain amount. To relieve the problem of the book drought, Xinhua Bookstore was instructed to make available used books for resale and also to provide a book rental service. In addition, more than 260 books, many of them classic literary works and reference books, were reprinted by the Xinhua Bookstore according to the feedback of lower level Xinhua bookstores (Zheng, 1987: 31). The old author payment system, based on the combination of book length and print run, was restored in May 1962 (see Liu and Shi, 1999: 80). The decentralized Xinhua Bookstore system was also changed. Although a unified national Xinhua Bookstore system was not restored, provincial Xinhua bookstores regained control over lower-level Xinhua bookstores within their provinces, and the General Store of the Xinhua Bookstore regained its authority to issue regulations to lower-level Xinhua bookstores.

3.2.2 The Cultural Revolution and the Following Adjustment: 1966–79

Mao's radical approach, having only temporarily receded after the Great Leap Forward, returned during the decade-long Cultural Revolution (1966–76). Rather than try to push through another campaign of economic leaps in the Party and state bureaucracies, the Cultural Revolution attacked their supposed failings. Book publishing, together with other cultural sectors, was severely affected during this period as "culture" became an arena of ideological and political struggle (see Table 3.5). Before the Cultural Revolution was officially launched in 1966, Mao had already initiated a "rectification" campaign in 1964 directed against the cultural bureaucracy. However, the scale of this campaign was restricted by the Party bureaucracy, and "the rectification faded away" (Goldman, 1987: 475) by the beginning of 1965. It did, however, have impact on the publishing industry, including the termination of the author payment system based on the combination of book length and print run and the restoration of the one-off payment based on book length in November 1964 (see Liu and Shi, 1999: 92).

Table 3.5 Title output of China's book publishing (1965—76)

Year	Total amount	Amount of new titles
1976	12,842	9727
1975	13,716	10,633
1974	11,812	8738
1973	10,372	8107
1972	8829	7395
1971	7771	6473
1970	4889	3870
1969	3964	3093
1968	3694	2677
1967	2925	2231
1966	11,055	6790
1965	20,143	12,352

Source: Fang, H., 1996. Book publishing statistics in People's Republic of China (*zhonhua renmin gongheguo tushu chuban tongji*) (1949.10—1989.12). In: Song, Y., et al. (Eds.), 1999. Archives of Contemporary China's Publishing (*zhongguo dangdai chuban shiliao*), vol. 2. Da Xiang Publishing House, Zhengzhou, pp. 100—104 (in Chinese).

The attack against the Party and the state bureaucracy initiated by Mao in the first phase of the Cultural Revolution led to extensive social disorder and economic disruption. During this initial stage, many publishers were merged or closed, and many employees in the publishing industry were sent to a cadre school for reeducation. Before the Cultural Revolution, there were 87 publishers across the country employing a total of 4570 qualified editors. But the number dropped to 53 publishers with 1355 qualified editors (Fang and Wei, 2008: 123). In addition, some of these publishers could not operate properly due to the political turmoil. The Ministry of Culture, as the government administration department responsible at the time for publishing and other cultural issues, was paralyzed after the Red Guards took control of it. In its place, the "Publishing Office of Chairman Mao's Works" (*mao zhuxi zhuzuo chuban bangongshi*) was established in May 1967 and assumed the responsibilities of government administration. Xinhua Bookstore was also controlled by the Red Guards. Nearly all employees of the General Store of Xinhua Bookstore were sent to a cadre school in April 1969 (Li et al., 1996: 46). Provincial Xinhua bookstores faced a similar fate and many were merged with local branches of the "Publishing Office of Chairman Mao's Works" or the local people's publishing houses. Payment to authors was terminated due to the extreme leftist ideology during that period. It is not surprising that a full concept of copyright, which is based on the recognition of property rights and market operation, faced conditions hostile to its existence at that time.

If a communized book publishing had always revolved around political tasks, during the Cultural Revolution this focus superseded all others. The fundamentalist ideology fueling the Revolution led to the extensive censorship of books, and many published titled were prohibited. By the end of 1970, 7870 titles amounting to more than 80.3 million copies published by national publishers were prohibited for sale and had to be locked away in a warehouse in Beijing. A total of 338.04 million copies were forbidden to be sold in local Xinhua bookstores (see Fang and Wei, 2008: 127). On the other hand, the consolidation and promotion of the personality cult surrounding Mao meant that publishing Mao's works and portrait posters of him became a central task of publishers. This concerted focus on the "beloved leader" was the main reason why the "Publishing Office of Chairman Mao's Works" could assume the responsibility of government administration. A stunning volume of copies of Mao's works began to appear. It has been said that during the period of Cultural Revolution, 10.8 billion copies of Mao's works and portrait posters of him were printed, accounting for 36% of the period's total 30,017 publisher items (Fang and Wei, 2008: 131). The print run of one single book, the *Quotations from Chairman Mao* (*maozhuxi yulu*)—popularly known as "*The Little Red Book*" because of its red cover and handy pocket size—ran to 1.027 billion copies (ibid). From 1970, the publishing of model plays became another central task of book publishing. In less than 2 years, the total copies of six model plays produced by publishers in Beijing had reached as high as 31.15 million (ibid: 142). The publishing of other books was often restricted in order to save the paper for Mao's works.

The extreme politicization of book publishing led to economic and cultural problems. To facilitate the propaganda task, the prices of Mao's works, portrait posters, and model plays were usually set very low, often below even the production cost. In addition, despite the assistance of compulsory distribution, there were still huge unsold stocks of propaganda books. All the financial losses had to be reimbursed by the government. Clearly, the greater the output of propaganda books was, the heavier the financial burden the government had to bear.

During the initial stage of the Cultural Revolution, the publishing of Mao's works was facilitated by a series of preferential policies. The transportation or postage costs involved in their distribution were waived by the government, together with business tax and interest on bank loans that publishers were normally expected to pay (Wang, 1996: 184–185). The distribution of these huge volumes of propaganda books seldom relied on voluntary purchasing by individual customers. Instead, they were usually sold to state-controlled organizations, involved in different kinds of hierarchical "systems," who then distributed copies to individual members (see Fang and Wei, 2008: 135 and 168). This so-called "system distribution (*xitong faxing*)" needed to "rely on the leading organs of the Party or government" (Wang, 1996: 196) and was in fact a form of compulsory distribution.

Despite the assistance of the coercive power of the party-state, there were still huge unsold stocks of propaganda books. By June of 1979, there were 450 million volumes of unsold Mao's and Marx–Lenin works in the warehouses of Xinhua Bookstore, accounting for 27% of the total unsold book stock (Wang, 1996: 187). These stocks, which were published by using bank loans, caused huge economic problems for Xinhua Bookstore in 1979 when it was required to pay interest on the loans (ibid). Even before this crisis the government had been obliged to bail Xinhua out with substantial financial subsidies amounting to RMB230 million yuan in 1972 and another RMB80 million yuan in 1976 (Liu, 1996: 159). Considering that the total sales of Xinhua Bookstore in 1972 were about RMB401 million yuan,[11] the Xinhua Bookstore System technically went bankrupt.

The problem of a book drought was inevitable. New title output slumped from 12,352 in 1965 to 2231 in 1967, of which more than half were textbooks and many others were propaganda books. The publishing of children's books was nearly nonexistence from 1967 to 1969. Output of STM (science, technology, and medicine) titles also plummeted. Although books in this category were less politically sensitive, the shortage of paper supply and printing capacity forced a slump in production in 1966 when the party-state ordered publishers to suspend the reprinting of STM books and reduce new STM titles as much as possible in order to save the paper and printing capacity for the production of Mao's works. As nearly all reference books were censored, there was not even a comprehensive dictionary available for school students. Interestingly however, even during this period of extreme book drought and political pressure, the state control over literature was not complete. Underground hand-copied fictions were written and circulated amongst the urban population and the "educated youth" (*zhiqing*) who had been sent to labor in the countryside (Link, 1989).

The extreme politicization of book publishing endangered both the economic sustainability of the industry and its ability to contribute to general cultural reproduction. After the most chaotic stage of the Cultural Revolution, initial attempts to redress the serious problems in book publishing were started in 1971. A few publishers were reestablished and many editors were able to resume work in the industry. The General Store of Xinhua Bookstore resumed its operations in 1973 and the National Publishing Administration Bureau was established as the responsible government administration department in the same year. These measures represented efforts to partially restore the institutions of a centralized planned book publishing, which had been seriously disrupted at the beginning of the Cultural Revolution. Efforts to relieve the book drought were also made. The imposition of an extreme version of the official ideology had proved to be a serious hindrance as it led to strict censorship. After the prime minister intervened a couple of times, attacking the extreme censorship, a new reference book called the *Xinhua Dictionary* was finally published in 1971 (Liu and Shi, 1999: 124–127). Some ancient Chinese history texts and classic novels were also reprinted.

Further adjustment however was only possible after the end of the Cultural Revolution. After Mao's death, the initial response of the party-state to the administrative chaos and economic problems "was to emphasize the rehabilitation of the command economic system" and to rebuild the central planning institutions (Naughton, 1995: 64). Moves back toward a centrally planned publishing system were an integral part of this restoration. More editors were called back from the cadre schools to prepare for the publication of new national school textbooks, which needed to purge the ideological legacy of the Cultural Revolution. To encourage authors to increase their output, the one-off payment system was resumed in October 1977. A couple of years later, the calculation of payment to authors based on book length and print run was restored in May 1980, although the proportion of payment based on print run was restricted (see Fang, 2000). More publishers were reestablished and some new publishers were launched (Fang and Wei, 2008: 214) (see Table 3.6). The decentralized Xinhua Bookstore system was ordered by the central government in December 1978 to return to the practice from before the Cultural Revolution. Within each province, the provincial Xinhua bookstore regained control over lower-level Xinhua bookstores. The slight relaxation of ideology after the Cultural Revolution allowed space for the planned publishing system to slightly relieve the book drought. A few

Table 3.6 Number of publishers (1971–79)

Year	Total amount	National	Regional
1979	129	63	66
1978	105	53	52
1977	82	41	41
1976	75	40	35
1975	75	39	36
1974	67	33	34
1973	65	29	36
1972	51	22	29
1971	46	17	29

Source: Song, Y. et al. (Eds.), 1999. Archives of Contemporary China's Publishing Vol. 8 (zhongguo dangdai chuban shiliao dibajuan). Da Xiang Publishing House, Zhengzhou (in Chinese).

classic Chinese and Western literary works that had been prohibited during the Cultural Revolution were reprinted in 1978. These books usually sold out quickly due to the long suppressed hunger for books. The government instructed publishers to increase their publishing of children's books, reference books, and STM books. The National Publishing Administration Bureau also organized the reprinting of 32 million copies of children's books, reference books, and STM books, and they too quickly sold out (ibid: 203–204).

The restoration of the national higher education entrance examination[12] created a huge demand for examination preparation textbooks and higher education textbooks, but continuing shortages of paper were a major problem and there was even not enough paper to publish basic textbooks (Liu and Shi, 1999: 165–166). These shortages were accentuated by the "serious waste of paper" (ibid: 170 and 172–173) arising from the large volumes of propaganda books that were still being published. The fifth volume of *Selected Works of Mao Zedong* was published in April 1977. 220 million copies of this book were printed, but were pulped in 1982 due to the gradual change of Party ideology (ibid: 165). Paper was still reserved for publishing Mao's works (ibid: 181). Many books published during the Cultural Revolution, including the *Quotations from Chairman Mao*, had to be prohibited and pulped (ibid: 180–181). The financial losses had to be borne by the central government (ibid: 166) so that the planned publishing system could operate properly again.

Book publishing in China during this period, like publishing in the early periods of the Soviet Union, oscillated "between centralization and decentralization" (Kenez, 1985: 241). Economically, the Maoist approach during the period of the Great Leap Forward and the Cultural Revolution created a "decentralized planned economy" (Wu, 2005: 56). Politically, it ushered in extreme politicization and strict censorship. However, this radical approach had only aggravated the existing problems. Despite the delegation of administrative power to lower-level Party branches and governments, the central party-state had retained overall control over book publishing, which was manifested in the relative ease with which it implemented recentralization. The major adjustments were focused on the rehabilitation of a centralized publishing system and the relaxation of ideology. Although these measures could relieve the intrinsic problems in the system to a certain extent, they could never resolve them completely.

3.3 COMMERCIALIZATION OF BOOK PUBLISHING: 1979–92

The initial effort of the party-state to boost economic development after the Cultural Revolution, by reestablishing the main institutions of the centrally planned economy immediately faced problems. An overambitious economic plan led to another economic crisis (Naughton, 1995). In order to right an economy that had swung between "stagnancy in a centralized planned economy and disorder in a decentralized planned economy" (Wu, 2005: 56) for nearly three decades, a new set of economic reform proposals, based on market-oriented reforms, was finally introduced. This new political and economic context facilitated the commercialization of book publishing.

When the economic reform was started in 1978, economic growth replaced "class struggle" as the key focus of the party-state. Following this significant shift, political propaganda ceased to be the primary task of book publishing. It was only after this depoliticization that the party-state was willing to relax its grip slightly to allow the introduction of market forces into the publishing industry. Yet the reform of book publishing, although initiated by the party-state, was not completely under its control. The reform policy introduced into book publishing mainly followed the pattern established for state-owned enterprises. At the same time, the changed economic context forced the party-state to reform the old institutions of book publishing. It was this push-and-pull effect that resulted in the collapse of a planned publishing system.

3.3.1 The Expansion of Autonomy

Expanding operational autonomy, which was the initial aim of enterprises reform, was also implemented in book publishing. Xinhua bookstores were given more freedom in disposing of unsold book stock, starting from November 1978. Restrictions on the operation of local publishers were challenged. Local publishers had been required to specialize in their local markets and also to commission only authors resident within their region in order to avoid competition. Due to this restriction, the scope of regional publishers was quite limited. Local publishers, understandably, had always been resentful toward this restriction. As the mindset of economy reform began to prevail, the publishers in Hunan province started to challenge this restriction in 1978 (see Zheng, 2002). A few other regional publishers also challenged it in a conference held in April 1979. These challenges were fostered by a profound institutional change.

As Naughton (1995: 43) has argued, ideology was a crucial weapon wielded by the central party-state in its efforts to exert control over local governments during the Maoist period of administrative decentralization. After the revision of the Party ideology in 1978, however, the imposition of extreme ideological guidelines backed by possible political persecution faded away, enhancing the relative power of local governments. As there had always been intricate relationships between local publishers and local publishing administration departments, the latter tended to defend the interests of local publishers wherever possible. This symbiotic relation continued into the reform period. The Hunan People's Publishing House offers an example. After the Hunan Provincial Publishing Administration Bureau (*hunan sheng chuban shiye guanli ju*) was established in March 1978, the Hunan People's Publishing House also became the Editorial Branch (*bianjibu*) of the provincial Publishing Administration Bureau (Hu et al., 1991: 292). Following the significant changes in the political and ideological environment, local publishing administration departments could challenge the restrictions imposed by "specialization" without worrying too much about possible political persecution. For the National Publishing Administration Bureau, there was also a need to boost the title output of book publishing in order to relieve the book drought. Increasing the output of regional publishers was an ideal option. In addition, initial economic growth after the Cultural Revolution had boosted book sales: sales in 1978 showed an increase of 39% over sales in 1976. The expanding book market alleviated the worries of the National Publishing

Administration Bureau about competition among publishers, and the restriction on local people's publishing houses was loosened.

Local people's publishing houses were allowed to publish on any subjects and to compete in the national market. Due to the expansion of the local publishing industry, a few editorial branches of provincial people's publishing houses were spun off into separate publishing houses—such as provincial science and technology publishing houses and provincial education publishing houses—though they were still required to specialize in their assigned subject areas. Many central state agencies also applied to establish affiliated publishing houses. However, regional publishers expanded more rapidly and soon outnumbered national publishers (see Table 3.7). The proliferation of publishers affiliated to local and central state agencies gradually intensified the competition in the book market. As book publishing in some subject areas, such as education, is much more profitable than other subject areas, some publishers were in a disadvantaged position in the competition because of the subject restriction imposed on them. The resentments and financial difficulties of these publishers forced the government administration department to loosen the subject restrictions and allowed publishers to publish a certain percentage of books outside of their subject areas. However, in an effort to

Table 3.7 Number of publishers (1979—92)

Year	Total amount	National	Regional
1992	480	183	297
1991	465	178	287
1990	462	176	286
1989	462	176	286
1988	448	173	275
1987	415	160	255
1986	395	148	247
1985	371	143	228
1984	295	125	170
1983	260	120	140
1982	214	109	105
1981	191	100	91
1980	169	89	80
1979	129	63	66

The imprints of publishers were not included.
Source: Fang, H., Wei, Y., 2008. General History of Chinese Publishing: Volume on People's Republic of China (*zhongguo chuban tongshi: zhonghua renmin gongheguo juan*). China Books Publishing House, Beijing (in Chinese).

regulate the competition among publishers, this restriction as a principle is still in place.

Financial autonomy was also increased for publishers and bookstores. Publishers and Xinhua bookstores used to hand over all their profits to the government in return for having their overhead costs reimbursed (see Yuan, 2008).[13] Profit retention as a general reform policy for state-owned enterprises was introduced into Xinhua bookstores in 1979. Profit retention for publishers was carried out more cautiously. Publishers were initially required in November 1979 to be financially self-sufficient, but a couple of regional publishers in Jiangsu province had already started profit retention at the end of 1979 (see Hu et al., 1996: 578). However, it was not until December 1981 that publishers controlled by the National Publishing Administration Bureau (*guojia chuban ju*) were allowed to retain part of their profit. As part of this policy, publishers and Xinhua bookstores started to pay bonuses as material incentives to their employees. A few years later, the contract responsibility system, which became a new reform policy for state-owned enterprises in 1988, was also implemented in book publishing. Publishers and Xinhua bookstores could retain all their profits after submitting a fixed amount of profit and tax to governments. These reform policies gradually turned publishers and Xinhua bookstores into profit-seeking business entities. Not surprisingly, in this changed context "specialization" as a principle of the planned publishing system would be challenged by publishers.

Due to the increased number of publishers, the relaxation of restrictions on subject areas, and rapid economic growth, book publishing became more vibrant and, as the figures reported in Table 3.8 show, title output increased rapidly, from just over 17,000 in 1979 to just under 75,000 in 1989. However, this upsurge meant increased competition which endangered the survival of some publishers so, in an effort to control the overall title output, the central government administration department issued a regulation in 1994 limiting the amount of ISBN (International Standard Book Number) numbers issued to publishers.

3.3.2 Dismantling the Monopoly in Book Distribution

As showed earlier, a monopolized Xinhua Bookstore system had a great impact on the operation of publishers. Publishers, after they became profit-seeking entities, were increasingly resentful of the monopoly of the Xinhua Bookstore, which they saw as a bottleneck in the distribution of

Table 3.8 Title output of publishers (1979—89)

Year	Total amount	New titles
1989	74,973	55,475
1988	65,962	46,774
1987	60,193	42,854
1986	51,789	39,426
1985	45,603	33,743
1984	40,072	28,794
1983	35,700	25,826
1982	31,784	23,445
1981	25,601	19,854
1980	21,621	17,660
1979	17,212	14,007

Source: Fang, H., 1996. Book publishing statistics in People's Republic of China (*zhonhua renmin gongheguo tushu chuban tongji*) (1949.10—1989.12). In: Song, Y., et al. (Eds.), 1999. Archives of Contemporary China's Publishing (*zhongguo dangdai chuban shiliao*), vol. 2. Da Xiang Publishing House, Zhengzhou, pp. 100—104 (in Chinese).

their books. To facilitate book distribution, publishers were permitted to open local bookstores or sell books to customers by post, and the book distribution business was also gradually opened to other state-owned capitals and private capitals. As a result, non-Xinhua retail outlets sprung up across the country. It was estimated that there were 28,000 non-Xinhua bookstores and 13,000 book stands by 1987 (Fang and Wei, 2008: 290). The provincial Xinhua Bookstore systems were also broken down in 1988 in order to improve the efficiency of book distribution, and lower level Xinhua bookstores were turned into independent business entities. As market forces came to play an increasingly important role in the book distribution business, the General Store of Xinhua Bookstore lost its raison d'être of providing guidance to lower-level Xinhua bookstores and was thus turned into a pure business entity in 1987.

The increase in private and other non-Xinhua bookstores and the emergence of a large number of independent county-level Xinhua bookstores opened up opportunities for publishers to choose their wholesalers and also led to the emergence of private wholesalers. Private wholesalers and retailers gradually formed another distribution channel, which, in contrast with the Xinhua Bookstore distribution system, came to be known as the "second channel." The increasing competition from private booksellers in turn exerted economic pressure on Xinhua bookstores and forced them to become further commercialized.

The rising private book distributors, after accumulating enough capital, started to edge into book publishing. The printing and paper supply industries were also commercialized and opened to private capital. Taken together, commercialized book distribution, book printing, and paper supply provided essential resources for the rise of private publishers. They were also aided from an unexpected quarter. Faced with intensified competition in book market generated by the increased number of publishers and increased title output, many state-owned publishers were willing to sell their allotted ISBN numbers to more market-oriented private publishers in order to ensure their own continued profit or survival. As a result, the private publishing sector, which had been eliminated in the 1950s during the process of "communization," gradually reemerged. The competition from private publishers also forced state-owned publishers to be more market-oriented.

3.3.3 Price Controls and Author Payment

Under the planned publishing system, book prices were controlled by the government and set at a low level to facilitate the widest possible circulation of Party propaganda and to encourage the spread of practical knowledge. Continuing this low-price policy and price control over books was hardly feasible in the new economic situation. Paper price started to rise in 1978 and the government had to subsidize the publishers to compensate for this increased cost. In addition, increased title output at the beginning of 1980s led to a shortage in printing capacity. The low-price policy may have impeded the improvement of printing technology and papermaking technology, as publishers, faced with the price control on their books, had needed to exercise stringent control over their production costs. Since the paper quality was usually not good enough, the technology of lithographic printing had hardly been adopted (Tian, 1982). Letterpress and hand composition of movable type were still dominant at the beginning of the 1980s.

During the Cultural Revolution, new-title output was usually limited while the print runs of propaganda books were often huge. As a result, typesetting capacity remained underdeveloped and high speed rotary letterpress machines, which were more suitable for long-run book printing, were prevalent. The increase in book titles at the beginning of the 1980s immediately exposed the shortage of typesetting capacity. For science and technology books, which usually entailed more complex composition, the problem was even more serious. As the average print run declined and title output increased, printers faced more short-run or medium-run printing tasks. But because of the price control imposed by the government, printers equipped with high speed rotary letterpress machine preferred book titles with large print runs in order to maximize their profits. The production of many short-run and medium-run books was therefore greatly delayed.[14] Academic books and STM books, which were usually short-run titles, were hit the hardest and remained difficult to get published (Meng, 1984). The delays in production could make books quickly obsolete after their publication, which would create further economic problems for publishers, leading them to prefer popular books printed in large numbers, which delivered larger profits, rather than high quality short-run titles.

Price control over book production relied on the price control over raw materials, "such as paper, steel, oil, and cotton" (Ze, 1995: 453), and labor costs. Any increase in the price of these elements would exert pressure on the price control over book production. The government had to raise the standard production fees printers could charge publishers, especially for short-run printing. Operational costs of publishers, including payment to authors and other overheads, also increased rapidly. Private publishers, which ran much more efficiently and were out of the control of government regulation, were usually willing to offer much greater payment in order to attract talented authors. Publishers had to "break government regulations and pay under-the-table fees" (ibid) to authors in order to acquire their book drafts. In this environment, government control over payment to authors became unsustainable. This control was finally scrapped in 1999 and the practice of royalties began to prevail.

Increased production and overhead costs in turn forced the government to allow publishers to increase gradually their book prices. As a first move, in August 1988, publishers were given the freedom to set the price of academic books or professional books with small print runs, although they were still required to restrict their profit margins to between 5% and 10% (Liu and Shi, 1999: 247−248). Price control over books except textbooks was finally abolished in 1993.

3.4 SUMMARY

The media are not only political institutions, but also business and cultural institutions (Hallin and Mancini, 2004: 47), and book publishing is particularly so. Before the economic reform, book publishing revolved around the production of propaganda. At the same time, the party-state, powerful as it was during the Maoist period, was forced to adjust its control over book publishing to allow for the economic reproduction of the industry and for cultural reproduction more generally, generating a central contradiction at the heart of the planned publishing system. Although decentralization during the Maoist period was an attempt to devolve administrative control to local Party committees and governments, it did not change the fundamental relationship between the party-state and the publishing industry. It was only after the economic reform that book publishing acquired autonomy to a certain extent. The commercialization of publishing, although initiated by the party-state, was not completely under its control. The complicated interaction of publishers, book distributors, and printers, and the interaction of book publishing industry with the broader social and economic context brought about the inevitable collapse of the old system.

ENDNOTES

1. Although this archive did not show any date and issuing authority, it was likely to be the General Bureau of Publications, as it was mentioned that the General Bureau of Publications discussed this drafted plan in a meeting (see Yuan et al., 1998: 356). The General Bureau of Publications reiterated in 1952 that private publishing business had to be controlled by the party-state in 5 years (Yuan et al., 1998: 441). It seems that this policy was drafted by the General Bureau of Publications after it was instructed by the Propaganda Department of CPC in autumn 1951 to restrict private publishing business (Yuan et al., 1999: 468)
2. As different government departments, such as the Ministry of Light Industry and Ministry of Commerce, sometimes sold their extra stock of paper in the market, private publishers could purchase some printing paper from the market. This, to a certain extent, weakened the control of party-state over paper supply (Yuan et al., 1999: 177).
3. Textbook publishing accounted for over 70% of the business of several big private publishers, including the Commercial Press and Zhonghua Book Company (Yuan et al., 1995: 256).
4. The central Party propaganda department explained in an instruction the rationale for the monopoly of state-owned publishers over the publishing of party documents, which was not only to ensure the "accuracy," but also to ensure these documents could be withdrawn from distribution or modified when they became "inappropriate for propaganda" after the change of political situations (Yuan et al., 1995: 219).
5. In a later report by the General Bureau of Publications, it argued for a gradualist approach to avoid aggravating the problem of unemployment (Yuan et al., 1999: 255).
6. The so-called Three Antis Campaign was a mass campaign launched at the end of 1951, which targeted urban cadres on charges of corruption, waste, and bureaucracy, and the so-called Five Antis Campaign targeted capitalists on charges of bribery, theft of state property, tax evasion, cheating on government contracts, and stealing state economic information. It was widely agreed that many victims committed suicide during the campaigns.

7. As private printers were often forced to make public apologies in newspapers, the government issued an instruction to restrict the numbers of public apologies in newspapers in order to avoid the impression of nit-picking by state-owned publishers (Yuan et al., 1998: 83).
8. The General Bureau of Publications admitted the problem of widespread prohibition imposed by the government, and had to instruct local government departments not to always link negative book reviews to the prohibition of books (Yuan et al., 1998: 79).
9. According the General Bureau of Publications, it was said that the total value of unsold book stock by June 1952 reached RMB84 billion yuan in old currency (see Yuan et al., 1998: 273). The value of total assets of Xinhua Bookstore was RMB21.75 million yuan and the total liquidity was RMB 15.56 million yuan in new currency by August 1952 (see Zheng, 1987: 18–19). As one yuan in new currency equals 10,000 yuan in old currency, the total value of Xinhua's unsold book stock was RMB8.4 million yuan in new currency, which was over half of its total liquidity. Although we do not know if the total value meant total list price or total discounted price from publishers, heavy unsold book stock was clearly a serious financial problem for Xinhua Bookstore).
10. Calculated on the data from Li (1996: 121–122).
11. Calculated on the data from Li (1996: 121–122).
12. During the Cultural Revolution, the selection of students for tertiary education was based mainly on political and family background of students rather than academic performance.
13. It seemed that profit retention had been carried out in Jiangsu provincial Xinhua bookstores for several years before 1979. However, the profit had only been allowed to improve their book stores and warehouses (Hu et al., 1996: 578).
14. At the beginning of the 1980s, it could take up to 300 days for a printer to finish the production of a printing order commissioned by a publisher. The average production time was only shortened to 130 days in 1990 (see Fang and Wei, 2008: 277).

REFERENCES

Ding, G. et al., 2004. Provincial publishing group to be transformed into an enterprise, government department ceased its role of player (*sheng chuban jituan jiang zhuanzhi wei qiye, zhengfu buzai dang yundongyun*). Southern Daily (*nanfang ribao*), 3 September 2004. <http://www.southcn.com/news/gdnews/hotspot/qhch/tz/200409030098. htm> (accessed 07.04.09) (in Chinese).

Fang, H., 1996. Book publishing statistics in People's Republic of China (*zhonhua renmin gongheguo tushu chuban tongji*) (1949.10–1989.12). In: Song, Y. et al. (Eds.), 1999. Archives of Contemporary China's Publishing (*zhongguo dangdai chuban shiliao*), vol. 2. Da Xiang Publishing House, Zhengzhou, pp. 100–104 (in Chinese).

Fang, H., 2000. Authors' Payment System in New China 1949–99 (*xinzhongguo gaochou zhidu jishi 1949–99*). In: Fang, H. (Ed.), 2001. Archives of Publishing in China: Modern China, vol. 3, part 2 (*zhongguo chuban shiliao: xiandai bufen di san juan shang*). Shandong Education Publishing House, Jinan, pp. 261–292 (in Chinese).

Fang, H. (Ed.), 2001. Archives of Publishing in China: Modern China, vol. 3, part 1 (*zhongguo chuban shiliao: xiandai bufen di san juan shang*). Shandong Education Publishing House, Jinan (in Chinese).

Fang, H., 2006. Publishing industry during the period of Great Leap Forward (*dayuejin niandai de chuban gongzuo*). In: Song, Y., et al., (Eds.), Archives of China's Publishing: Modern Period Supplementary Volume (*zhongguo chuban shiliao xiandai bufen bujuan*). Shandong Education Publishing House, Jinan, pp. 826—849. (in Chinese).

Fang, H., Wei, Y., 2008. General History of Chinese Publishing: Volume on People's Republic of China (*zhongguo chuban tongshi: zhonghua renmin gongheguo juan*). China Books Publishing House, Beijing (in Chinese).

Goldman, M., 1987. The party and the intellectuals: phase two. In: MacFarquhar, R., Fairbank, J. (Eds.), The Cambridge History of China. Cambridge University Press, Cambridge, pp. 432—477.

Gu, Z., Gao, Q., 1984. The socialist transformation of private printing industry in Shanghai (*shanghai shi siying yinshua gongye de shehui zhuyi gaizao*). In: China Printing Technology Association (Ed.), Chinese Printing Industry Yearbook (*zhongguo yinshua nianjian*) 1982—83. Printing Industry Press, Beijing, pp. 218—224. (in Chinese).

Hallin, D., Mancini, P., 2004. Comparing Media Systems: Three Models of Media and Politics. Cambridge University Press, Cambridge.

Harding, H., 1997. The Chinese state in crisis, 1966—69. In: MacFarquhar, R. (Ed.), The Politics of China: The Eras of Mao and Deng, second ed. Cambridge University Press, Cambridge, pp. 148—247.

Hu, F., et al., (Eds.), 1996. Historical Documents of Jiangsu Province: Publishing (*jiangsu shengzhi: chubanzhi*). Jiangsu People's Publishing House, Nanjing (in Chinese).

Hu, Z., et al., (Eds.), 1991. Historical Document of Hunan Province, vol. 20. Press and Publication: Publishing (*hunan shengzhi di ershi juan xinwen chubanzhi chuban*). Hunan Publishing House, Changsha (in Chinese).

Kenez, P., 1985. The Birth of the Propaganda State: Soviet Methods of Mass Mobilization, 1917—29. Cambridge University Press, Cambridge.

Kornai, J., 1980. Economics of Shortage. North-Holland, Amsterdam.

Lai, H., 2003. Official publishing and forced distribution—a study of publication policy in early People's Republic of China (*zhongdian faxing yu qiangpo tanpai—zhonggong jianguo chuqi chuban zhengce yanjiu*). Bulletin of the Institute of Modern History Academia Sinica (zhongyang yanjiuyuan jindaishi yanjiusuo jikan) 40, 141—188 (in Chinese).

Li, J., 2009. The past is not like smoke: listening to the old stories (*wangshi bing bu ruyan: ting tamen jiang na guoqu de gushi*). China Pulp and Paper Industry (zhongguo zhiye) 21, 122—129 (in Chinese).

Li, T., 1996. Book distribution for the construction of a new socialist countryside (*wei jianshe shehuizhuyi xinnongcun fuwu de tushu faxing gongzuo*). In: Wang, D., et al., (Eds.), History of the General Store of Xinhua Bookstore (*xinhua shudian zhongdian shi*). Xinhua Bookstore, Beijing, pp. 106—122. (in Chinese).

Li, J., et al., 1996. The change of continuity in the system and institution of the General Store of Xinhua Bookstore (*xinhua shudian zhongdian tizhi jigou yange*). In: Wang, D., et al., (Eds.), History of the General Store of Xinhua Bookstore (*xinhua shudian zhongdian shi*). Xinhua Bookstore, Beijing, pp. 41—50. (in Chinese).

Lieberthal, K., 1987. The Great Leap Forward and the split in the Yenan leadership. In: MacFarquhar, R., Fairbank, J. (Eds.), The Cambridge History of China, vol. 14. The People's Republic, Part 1: The Emergence of Revolutionary China 1949—65. Cambridge University Press, Cambridge, pp. 291—359.

Link, P., 1989. Hand-copied entertainment fiction from the Cultural Revolution. In: Link, P., et al., (Eds.), Unofficial China: Popular Culture and Thought in the People's Republic. Westview Press, Boulder, pp. 17—36.

Liu, Q., 1996. Evolution of the Finance Administration System of Xinhua Bookstore (*xinhua shudian caiwu guanli tizhi de yanbian*). In: Wang, D., et al., (Eds.), History of the General Store of Xinhua Bookstore (xinhua shudian zhongdian shi). Xinhua Bookstore, Beijing, pp. 156—162. (in Chinese).

Liu, G., Shi, F. (Eds.), 1999. 50 Years Events of New China's Publishing (*xinzhongguo chuban wushinian jishi*). Xinhua Publishing House, Beijing (in Chinese).

Meng, Z., 1984. Printing of books and magazines in 1981 and 1982 (*1981—82 nian shukan yinshua huigu*). In: China Printing Technology Association (Ed.), China Graphic Arts Annual (*zhongguo yinshua nianjian*): 1982—83. Printing Industry Publishing House, Beijing, pp. 3—8. (in Chinese).

Naughton, B., 1995. Growing Out of the Plan: Chinese Economic Reform, 1978—93. Cambridge University Press, Cambridge.

Qian, P., et al., (Eds.), 1991. History of Central-South District Xinhua Bookstore (*zhongyuan zhongnan xinhua shudian shi*). Hubei People's Publishing House, Wuhan (in Chinese).

Song, Y., et al., (Eds.), 1999. Archives of Contemporary China's Publishing, vol. 8 (*zhongguo dangdai chuban shiliao*). Da Xiang Publishing House, Zhengzhou (in Chinese).

Tian, M., 1982. Development of lithographic printing in publishing industry (*jiaoyin yinshu de huigu he zhanwang*). In: China Printing Technology Association (Ed.), China Graphic Arts Annual (*zhongguo yinshua nianjian*): 1981. Printing Industry Publishing House, Beijing, pp. 42—46. (in Chinese).

Walker, G., 1995. Russia and the former USSR. In: Altbach, P., Hoshino, E. (Eds.), International Book Publishing: An Encyclopedia. Garland Publishing, New York, pp. 559—565.

Wang, D., 1996. The book distribution of Selected Works of Mao Zedong and Mao's other works (*Maozedong xuanji deng maozedong zhuzuo de faxing gongzuo*). In: Song, Y., et al. (Eds.), 1999. Archives of Contemporary China's Publishing (*zhongguo dangdai chuban shiliao*), vol. 4. Da Xiang Publishing House, Zhengzhou, pp. 171—198 (in Chinese).

Wang, F., 2001. Recollection of the general administration of Xinhua Bookstore (*huiyi Xinhua shudian zhong guanlichu*). In: Fang, H. (Ed.), Archives of Contemporary China's Publishing, vol. 3, part 1 (*zhongguo chuban shiliao: xiandai bufen di san juan shang*). Shandong Education Publishing House, Jinan (in Chinese).

Wang, Y., 1982. The administration of printing industry (*yinshua gongye de guanli tizhi wenti*). In: China Printing Technology Association (Ed.), China Graphic Arts Annual (*zhongguo yinshua nianjian*): 1981. Printing Industry Publishing House, Beijing, pp. 15—20. (in Chinese).

Wang, W., et al., (Eds.), 1987. Almanac of China's Paper Industry (*zhongguo zaozhi nianjian*) 1986. China Light Industry Press, Beijing (in Chinese).

Wu, J., 2005. Understanding and Interpreting Chinese Economic Reform. Thomson Texere, New York.

Wu, Y., 2011. China's Publishing History During the Republican Period (*minguo chuban shi*). Fujian People's Publishing House, Fuzhou in Chinese.

Xu, X., 2001. On China Press (*guanyu zhongguo chubanshe*). In: Wu, D. (Ed.), Archives of China's Publishing: Modern Period (*zhongguo chuban shiliao: xiandai bufen*), vol. 2. Shandong Education Publishing House, Jinan (in Chinese).

Yang, Y., 2000. Commercial Press: The Rise and Fall of Private Publishing (*shangwu yinshuguan: minjian chubanye de xinshuai*). Shanghai Educational Publishing House, Shanghai (in Chinese).

Yu, Y., 2009. An indelible journey of life: the memoirs of Yu Yi-Ji (*nanwang suiyue yu yi-ji huiyilu*). China Pulp and Paper Industry (zhonghua zhiye) 30 (17), 89—99 (in Chinese).

Yuan, L., 2008. The first reform of publishing administration system: my memoir of the reform of financial system of publishing industry (*shouci gaige chuban guanli tizhi shimo—wo qinli de chuban caizheng guanli zhidu gaige*). Publishing Research (chuban faxing yanjiu) 2008 (11), 12—17 (in Chinese).

Yuan, L., et al., (Eds.), 1995. Archives of Publishing in thePeople's Republic of China (*zhonghua renmin gongheguo chuban shiliao*): 1949. China Books Publishing House, Beijing (in Chinese).

Yuan, L., et al., (Eds.), 1996. Archives of Publishing in the People's Republic of China (*zhonghua renmin gongheguo chuban shiliao*): 1951. China Books Publishing House, Beijing (in Chinese).

Yuan, L., et al., (Eds.), 1998. Archives of Publishing in the People's Republic of China (*zhonghua renmin gongheguo chuban shiliao*): 1952. China Books Publishing House, Beijing (in Chinese).

Yuan, L., et al., (Eds.), 1999. Archives of Publishing in the People's Republic of China (*zhonghua renmin gongheguo chuban shiliao*): 1954. China Books Publishing House, Beijing (in Chinese).

Yuan, L., et al., (Eds.), 2004. Archives of Publishing in the People's Republic of China (*zhonghua renmin gongheguo chuban shiliao*): 1957−58. China Books Publishing House, Beijing (in Chinese).

Ze, D., 1995. China. In: Altbach, P., Hoshino, E. (Eds.), International Book Publishing: An Encyclopedia. Garland Publishing, New York, pp. 447−461.

Zhang, S., et al., 1999. General History of Chinese Printing (*zhongguo yinshua tongshi*). Printing Industry Publishing House, Beijing (in Chinese).

Zheng, Q., 2002. Huzhen and his thoughts on publishing (*huzhen he ta de chuban guan*). Publishing Science (chuban kexue) 38, 70−71 (in Chinese).

Zheng, S., 1987. History of general store of Xinhua Bookstore (*wushi chunqiu hua xinhua: xinhua shudian zhongdian jianshi*). In: Zheng, S. (Ed.), 50 Years History of Xinhua Bookstore (*xinhua shudian wushi chunqiu*). Xinhua Bookstore, Beijing, pp. 1−42.

CHAPTER 4

Ideology and the Commercialization of Book Publishing in China

The previous chapter explored the institutional changes in China's book publishing over four decades. But institutional change in cultural production cannot be separated from the changes in cultural space.

It is generally accepted that although no or little political freedom has been achieved, individuals now enjoy more personal and cultural freedom than during the Maoist period (Goldman and MacFarquhar, 1999: 23). Many researchers attributed the rise of this relatively relaxed cultural space to the declining capability of the party-state to maintain its ideological grip due to the changing media scene, such as the cultural influence from the outside world (ibid), the administrative decentralization (or fragmentation) of the state (Lynch, 1999; Tong, 2010), the recent rise of Internet and mobile communication, journalistic professionalism (Hallin and Mancini, 2004: 279; Polumbaum, 2008; Qian and Bandurski, 2011; Wang, 2010), and more importantly the tension between control and media commercialization (Hallin and Mancini, 2004: 279; Wu, 2000). However, ideological control underwent spells of relative relaxation even during the Maoist period and at the beginning of economic reform (Goldman, 1987), when the aforementioned factors played no role at all. Hardly any impact of the cultural influence from the outside world and modern communication technology was seen at that time. In addition, administrative decentralization in the current form and media commercialization had not even started. Moreover, the further incorporation of China's economy into the global capitalist system after its entry into the World Trade Organization (WTO) in 2001 and another tide of commercialization of media at the beginning of this century did not necessarily lead to another period of ideological relaxation, and there has in recent years even been "an increase in political control" alongside "a continuation of marketization" (Sparks, 2008: 17).

Consequently, some more nuanced counter arguments have been developed. It has been argued that, the Internet is probably better

China's Publishing Industry
DOI: https://doi.org/10.1016/B978-0-08-100919-2.00004-8

understood as a new arena for constant struggle between the state and the society (Yang, 2009a; Zheng, 2008), and the control over it has been implemented quite successfully in China (Brady, 2008; Wacker, 2010). The simplistic view of the systemic conflicts between the media commercialization and the Party control has been challenged (Sparks, 2012; Zhao, 2012; Hadland and Zhang, 2012). Both Stockmann (2013) and Zhao (2012) pointed out that, in spite of the process of commercialization, there exist two distinct press sectors, a market-based press sector and an official Party organ press sector, fulfilling different tasks. As regards the cultural space tolerated by the Party for negotiation, Zhang (2011) adopted the concepts of Hallin (1986) and demonstrated that there are three different spheres, which are the sphere of consensus, the sphere of legitimate controversy, and the sphere of illegitimate controversy, for Chinese media workers. In the sphere of consensus, which encompasses the Party ideology, and the sphere of illegitimate controversy, which contains some taboo topics, the Party allows no challenge or opposition, while the sphere of legitimate controversy is an area open for negotiation or even encouraging criticism. But she also added that the boundaries between these spheres are "in no way fixed" (Zhang, 2011: 141).

All these discussions are very illuminating, but still leave a couple of questions unanswered. If the arguments presented at the beginning of this chapter are not adequate to explain the emergence of a relatively more relaxed cultural sphere, what could be the other factors contributing to the ebb and flow of the ideological control? What has led to the shifting of boundaries between negotiable and nonnegotiable spheres? This chapter turns to the Party's ideology itself as an additional dimension in our understanding of the changing media scene in China. Chan (2002) and Akhavan-Majid (2004) mentioned respectively the impact of the declining ideological control from the Party and the "deideologization" of society on the media reform in China, however they did not go on to elaborate on this process and the argument of a declining ideological control is also questionable. Focusing on book publishing, this chapter argues that the role and content of the Party ideology has shifted during the economic reform, and this shift paved the way for media commercialization as it not only created a relatively freer cultural space for media content but also facilitated institutional change of media organizations. In addition, by placing ideological evolution firmly in the context of Party politics, it offers a possible way of understanding the ideological prospects for the near future.

4.1 CHINA'S SHAKY IDEOLOGY BEFORE THE ECONOMIC REFORM

Ideology, as many have demonstrated (Freeden, 2007; Eagleton, 1991; Griffin, 2007), is a difficult word to define. It is beyond the scope of this chapter to review this definitional debate in detail, but it is important to have a working definition of this controversial concept before any sensible discussion about it could proceed. Thompson's critical conceptualization of ideology as a symbolic form which "serves to establish and sustain relations of domination" (Thompson, 1990: 58) is a good starting point in the present context. Ideology, in the case of communist countries, often refers to the explicit and systemic political and economic doctrines officially upheld by the Party to legitimize its political domination and causes. Although this narrower approach may have the weakness of not being able to imply that implicit ideological propaganda is also carried out by the Party (and there may well be an increasing use of it), and ordinary, everyday media content often performs an ideological role unwittingly, I adopt this approach in this discussion for two reasons. First, despite all the transformations that have happened in China, the Party still upholds some explicit and systemic doctrines as its guiding principles, which this approach reflects well in this context. Second, my focus here is not on what exactly the Party ideology is, but rather on the shift of the official ideology and the impact of this shift on media commercialization. This approach has a relatively clear boundary, which minimizes possible confusions in this discussion.

Ideology usually played a crucially important role in the politics of communist regimes, and political systems like these were even called "ideocracy" (White, 1999). Communist ideology can be regarded as a "totalistic" ideology (Schwarzmantel, 2008: 7) as it is "all encompassing and prescribes a 'politically correct' view about everything from the origin of the universe to hairstyles" (Fu, 1994: 180). As a consequence it left only a narrow space for the Party to adapt its policies according to different political situations. The resulting inflexibility can be seen as an inherent weakness of communist ideology. In addition, the personality cult common in communist countries invested the predominant Party figure with the status of paramount ideological leader. This also contributed to the inflexibility of communist ideology, since ideological divergence may endanger the personal authority of the Party leader, a factor which partly explains the endemic purges within the Party on ideological grounds in many communist countries.

As communist states usually derive their policy legitimacy from the official ideology, variations or shifts of policy are usually manifested first in ideological debates. If the communist ideology was convincing to many people within and without the Party at the beginning of the People's Republic, it gradually became shaky even during the Maoist period. There were several reasons for this.

First, as it was usually unavoidable for the party-state to adjust its domestic policies in response to changed circumstances, it was difficult for the party-state to maintain a consistent official ideology to justify completely different policies. Before the economic reform, there were already ideological debates and policy shifts in the economic field in China. The Maoist radical model of economic development differed from the orthodox Leninist model favored by other Party leaders (Schram, 1974: 43). The disastrous Great Leap Forward initiated by Mao became a focus of dispute among the higher echelons of the Party resulting in purges as Mao struggled to maintain his authority. However, following the Great Leap Forward, there were series of policy adaptations aimed at resolving the economic crisis it had created, which "led to a widening gulf between Maoist ideology and Party practice in policy implementation" (Ahn, 1973: 300). The reassertion of Maoist policy in the chaotic Cultural Revolution resulted in massive purges within the Party on ideological grounds. Economic policies such as "(m)aterial incentives, autonomy for enterprises, the encouragement of competition, pricing goods according to the real cost of production" were all judged unacceptable on ideological grounds and terminated (Gittings, 1989: 107). The vacillations of Party policies and the constant purges on ideological grounds during the Cultural Revolution weakened the credibility of the Party ideology.

Second, communist countries often diverged in their economic and political policies, especially foreign policies, which made it nearly impossible to maintain a coherent ideology across the communist bloc. This was clearly manifested in the Sino-Soviet split and the ensuing ideological debates between these two core members of the bloc. For example, Mao did not altogether approve of Khrushchev's denunciation of Stalin because he saw it as potentially endangering his own personality cult in China and as repudiating "aspects of Soviet past" which he regarded as worthy of celebration (Schram, 1974: 38). The divergence of foreign policy between the Soviet Union and China was another example of ideological conflict. While the Soviet Union in the 1960s promoted peaceful coexistence between the communist bloc and capitalist states, China under Mao opposed this policy and called for revolutionary struggle in the Third World (Schurmann, 1968). The Sino-Soviet split created an ideological dilemma for the Chinese Communist Party (CCP) since it had previously praised the Soviet Union as the first socialist state (ibid: 43). These disagreements between communist states, coupled with the vacillations of Party policies and the constant purges on ideological grounds during the Cultural Revolution, eventually brought the infallibility of the Party ideology into question.

4.2 CHINA'S IDEOLOGY IN FLUX

After Mao's death, the severe social and economic crisis caused by the Cultural Revolution forced the Party to break away from Maoist policy. The initial move was marked by a shift in emphasis from Maoist "class struggle" to "the rehabilitation of the command economic system" (Naughton, 1995: 59). However, this attempt failed and a different reform strategy had to be explored. As all policies in China "require an ideological discourse as justification" (Zhang, 1996: 2) however, China's official ideology had to be renovated to justify economic reform. Hence the process of economic reform was inevitably also a process of ideological renovation.

The first major ideological debate in the run up to reform was the debate on "criterion of truth" in 1978. After the Cultural Revolution, Hua Guofeng, Mao's successor, implemented the policy of the "Two Whatevers" ("upholding resolutely whatever policy decisions Chairman Mao made, and following unswervingly whatever instructions Chairman Mao gave"). This is probably unavoidable as Hua derived his legitimacy from Mao (Chen, 1995: 36). The debate on the "criterion of truth" (zhenli biaozhun) ended with reformist thinking and practice displacing Mao's doctrines as "the sole criterion of truth," opening the door for the implementation of pragmatic reform policies. It was only after this debate that economic reform policies such as profit retention could be widely introduced.

Throughout the subsequent process of economic reform, there have been renovations in many different aspects of the orthodox economic ideology, but they can be summarized as mainly a process of gradual acceptance of market mechanism and private ownership. The role of markets in the Chinese economy was the crux of the matter in its gradual ideological renovation. Initially, in 1982, the Party congress agreed that market mechanism could be used to supplement state planning. A couple of years later, when the idea of a "market economy" was still an ideological taboo, the Party declared in 1984 that the Chinese economy was a "planned commodity economy." It was not until Deng Xiaoping's speeches in south China in 1992 that the establishment of a "socialist market economy" was endorsed by the central Party as the official doctrine. During the process of ideological renovation, private ownership was gradually accepted and different forms of public ownership in agriculture and in industrial enterprises were explored, such as the contract responsibility system and shareholding.

Economic reforms would not have been possible without the prior renovation of official ideology. Deng Xiaoping's slogan of "socialism with Chinese characteristics," proposed in 1982, left enough fuzziness and flexibility to accommodate a range of policy options. However, the Party has gradually come into its ideological crisis. Many studies of communist ideology have employed a two-dimension framework, utilizing distinctions between pure ideology versus practical ideology (Schurmann, 1968), fundamental ideology versus operative ideology (Guo, 2012; Seliger, 1976), fundamental principles versus instrumental principles (Chen, 1995), or ideology of ends and ideology of means (Moore, 1950). The CCP has attempted to maintain a balance between these two dimensions during the reform period, upholding the fundamental principles of its defining ideology rhetorically but renovating its instrumental principles (Chen, 1995). As a result, it managed to maintain, to a certain extent, the ideological consistency essential for legitimacy while allowing flexibility in the adoption of pragmatic reforms designed to improve economic efficiency. However, the renovation of official ideology has gradually led to a "fundamental—instrumental discrepancy" (ibid: 17) and this balancing act has become unsustainable. The Party ideology overall lost its force and credibility (Bell, 2008; Weatherley, 2006; White, 1999) during the process of ideological renovation. Although a new potential base for legitimacy, based on economic success, stability, and nationalism/national greatness, has emerged (Balzer, 2004: 235), and the role of ideology as a source of legitimacy has declined, the Party still requires ideological rationale to justify economic and social changes, and a great deal of effort has been expended by the Party in publicizing its ideological innovations (Dickson, 2010: 23). Since the Party has to uphold its ideological legacy in order to justify its continuing monopoly of political power, the resulting gap between official ideology and everyday practice has generated pervasive cynicism and apathy (ibid: 5; Sparks, 2012: 62) among the general population. This hollowing out of official ideology has led the Party to change its propaganda strategy. An example is that the Party has been reviving Confucianism to a certain extent to replace communism in its ideological propaganda (Bell, 2008), reinventing itself as a guarantor of the Chinese tradition rather than an exterminator of the old feudal ideas during the Cultural Revolution.

4.3 IDEOLOGY AND PUBLICATIONS

Ideological variations have had great impact on publications and cultural production in general. Although cultural space during the Maoist period was generally limited, the political climate for cultural creativity was "relatively favorable" before the period of Cultural Revolution (Fokkema, 1991: 594) and publishing houses still had some scope to publish books in the intervals between political campaigns.

Following a brief period of ideological relaxation encouraged by the party-state in 1956 and early 1957, a massive political persecution was initiated by the "anti-rightist campaign" in 1957. This wave of persecution excluded any possibility of open criticism against Mao and the Party. In response, some intellectuals resorted to a traditional form of dissent employing the "indirect, figurative analogies used in discussions of history, literature, philosophy, art, and the theater" (Goldman, 1987: 219). However, censorship was rapidly extended into these cultural arenas and peaked during the Cultural Revolution.

The Cultural Revolution saw a period of extreme censorship of publications and other cultural products, arising from their comprehensive politicization and their definition as weapons of "class struggle." Most Chinese classics were criticized as feudal, and many foreign works were forbidden. Even books purely on Chinese bonsai or gardens or flower art could be criticized as promoting the cultural tastes of the "feudal literati" (Song, 1996). Massive censorship was not only implemented in book publishing, all cultural production suffered. In addition, keeping away from political issues was not possible. As Goldman (1987: 219) commented, Chinese intellectuals at that time lacked the privilege of their Confucian predecessors to "withdraw to their study or to a hilltop to pursue the life of an honorable scholar or to artist," and "had to participate in the system" in the People's Republic. This situation certainly applied to book publishing and other areas of cultural production. It was common for Mao's words to appear in a science or technology book to avoid being criticized as having the tendency of depoliticization. More generally, since book publishing mainly revolved around the needs of political campaigns the scope left for publishing houses "was very limited" (Song, 1999: 32). Although book publishing was subjugated totally to political needs, there were still political risks as the party line changed rapidly during that period. Fokkema (1991: 605) recorded how a novel, *The song of Ouyang Hai*, had to undergo a series of continual revisions from its first publishing in 1965 until 1979 due to changes in the political situation. Publications faced a dilemma of having the obligation of promoting the party line but also running "the risk that the party line will have been changed" (ibid) by the time they were ready for printing. Publishing of Mao's works and pictures became the dominant task of book publishing. There were, however, still political risks entailed in publishing Mao's works. Mao's own ideas "were constantly changing in the course of their implementation vacillation" (Schram, 1989: 1) and his works were subject to his own manipulations driven by "his very immediate preoccupations" (Schwartz, 1989: 21). Due to the fact that Mao "continued to develop his ideas" and "modified, adapted, and elaborated positions he had adopted earlier" (Schram, 1991: 1), his earlier published works or speeches often had to be censored, modified, or completely altered due to the change of political situation. Meisner (1999: 180) offers an example on how Mao at a later stage modified his original unpublished speech of "*On the Correct Handling of Contradictions among the People.*" Mao initially had encouraged criticism of Party bureaucracy in this speech. But after he shifted the policy from encouraging free speech in the "hundred flowers" campaign to repressing it in the "anti-rightist" campaign, the original version was altered and then published in People's Daily to justify the repression. In addition, after Mao purged many other Party leaders, their names which were cited in the original version of Mao's work had to be removed in revised versions (see Zhang, 2008 for examples). This need to tailor Mao's words to the vagaries of the political situation produced the paradoxical situation during the Cultural Revolution that the ardent Red Guards, who "were eager to preserve his every word unchanged" (Cheek, 1989: 76), assiduously edited various selections of his works. It was these unchanged versions that were severely censored and prohibited by Mao and the Party (Li, 2002). As can be seen, extreme politicization, rapid changes in political and economic situation, frequent political persecution of authors and editors for ideological deviation, and extensive censorship, made the operation of publishing houses and other cultural production extremely difficult.

When the Party nominated economic development as its paramount task after the "Cultural Revolution," depoliticization gradually replaced "class struggle" in the cultural sphere allowing publishers more room for maneuver in the choice of what to publish. Literary works prohibited during the period of "Cultural Revolution" were published and sold out quickly. The party-state reversed Maoist anti-intellectualism. Intellectuals, formerly attacked as "bourgeois specialists" during the Cultural Revolution because of their potential challenge to Party ideologues and Mao's thought (Tsou, 1986: 32), were now acclaimed by the party-state, and the publishing of science and technology books was encouraged as essential supports for economic growth.

Apart from depoliticization, there was another favorable political condition for more liberal thinking in the cultural sphere. As many members of the new power elites in the government, including Deng Xiaoping, had themselves been victims of the harsh oppression of the Cultural Revolution, they were willing to criticize many Maoist policies or allow those criticisms to be published, not only to justify their own legitimacy but also to support their power struggles against the remnants of the Maoists. When the "scar literature" (or "literature of the wounded"), in which the suffering of ordinary people under the Cultural Revolution was exposed, was popular at the end of the 1970s and the beginning of the 1980s, it "served a political end" and "strengthened the faction of Teng Hsiao-p'ing (Deng Xiaoping), who wanted to erase totally the effects of the Cultural Revolution" (Fokkema, 1991: 615). These changes in combination greatly expanded the scope for book publishing and ushered in a short period of prosperity.

At the start of the reform process, as Misra (1998: 193) has argued, the erosion of the ruling doctrine "undermined simultaneously its utility as an analytical tool, and the legitimacy of those who sought to enforce it." In order to achieve the goal of ideological renovation to pave the way for economic reforms, intellectuals, allied with reformist leaders, were encouraged to break through the constraints of an outdated ideology. Deng Xiaoping, by then rising to power, instructed the People's Publishing House in 1978 to translate and publish a series of Western academic books on political thought (Liu and Shi, 1999: 155). This process provided a much more relaxed sphere for the introduction of political and economic ideas from the West, which then further expanded the scope of book publishing.

Although the Party had to discard or revitalize many of the creeds of orthodox ideology in order to implement its reform policies, it had no intention of abandoning the official ideology altogether because that would endanger its ideological legitimacy. It therefore faced a dilemma. It needed to "allow a considerable degree of intellectual freedom throughout China, without having that freedom upsetting the familiar ideological patterns to the point of complete destruction" (Fokkema, 1991: 614). Consequently, whenever the legitimacy of the party-state seemed to be endangered, the Party would tighten up its control over the cultural sphere, and then relax it again when the perceived threat had receded. This oscillation resulted in a couple of rounds of ideological rectification, which included the first campaign against "bourgeois liberalization" roughly started in 1981, the campaign against "spiritual pollution" started in 1983, the second campaign against "bourgeois liberalization" started in 1986, and the campaign against "peaceful evolution" started in 1989.

Despite this incessant process of ideological rectification, which manifests exactly the persistent power of the Party, overall the cultural sphere after economic reform became more "lively and diversified" (Fokkema, 1991: 615). Although the ideological renovation of the Party mainly happened in the field of economic ideology, the official ideology as a whole inevitably became more flexible. It was the ideological shift and the expanded flexibility in the cultural sphere, I would argue, that created the business climate that has facilitated the market-oriented operation of publishing houses. Without this relaxed cultural space for market-oriented operation, the commercialization of publishing would hardly be possible.

4.4 COMMERCIALIZATION OF PUBLISHING AND IDEOLOGY

The shift of publishing from a predominantly ideological role toward an increasingly economic role after the start of economic reform inevitably entailed institutional changes, which is the process of commercialization. The Party was well aware of the unavoidable institutional changes in publishing due to this shift of role. It was acknowledged in an official directive issued in 1988 on the reform of publishing houses that, "in order to adapt to the change (of the role of publishing houses), the old institutions for publishing houses, including the control system (*lingdao tizhi*), operation system (*jingying tizhi*), management system (*guanli tizhi*), personnel system (*renshi tizhi*) and income distribution system (*fenpei tizhi*), etc., have to be actively while cautiously reformed".[1]

If economic reform is only possible after ideological renovation has first taken place, commercialization of publishing was also preceded by ideological breakthroughs. A prominent one concerned the issue of books as commodities. According to Yuan (1999: 106), from the late 1950s to the end of Cultural Revolution, proclaiming books to be a kind of commodity was ideologically unacceptable, and a former leader in the national publishing administration bureau was severely criticized as having "capitalist thinking" for espousing this view during the Cultural Revolution (ibid). It was only in 1979 that it became acceptable to refer to books as a kind of commodity and to argue that the operation of publishing houses should follow the new economic rules (ibid). Following the general acceptance of this view, the party-state renovated its operational guideline for publishing houses. In a directive promulgated by the party-state in 1983, publishing houses were required not only to "pursue the social benefit of publications" but also to "pursue the economic benefit of publications as commodities",[2] a formulation which pointed to the importance of profit in the operation of publishing houses. In pursuit of this goal, in a meeting held in 1984, the national publishing administration bureau required publishing houses to shift their operations from a production-orientation to a production-and-profit-orientation (Song, 2006: 11). It was only after the economic reform that publishing has gradually been acknowledged as not only "an ideological arena (*yishi xingtai shuxing*)," but also "a cultural establishment (*wenhua shuxing*)" and "an economic sector (*chanye shuxing*)" (Yang, 2009b).

Another ideological debate that impacted on the publishing industry concerned the legal status of publishing houses, which is the core issue of the corporatization of publishing houses. Due to the ideological guidelines of the Party, most publishers were not legally independent business entities, but so-called "public service units managed as enterprises (*shiye danwei, qiyehua guanli*)." If the term of "public service units" carries connotations of ideological control in the Chinese context, "managed as enterprises" points to the state's commercial ambitions for publishers after the economic reform. Although profit-seeking became accepted in the publishing industry, its relative weight in comparison with publishing's continuing political role was still debated. There were discussions in professional journals from the end of the 1990s to the beginning of the 2000s on whether publishing houses should be defined as public service units or business enterprises (see Wang, 1999; Song, 2004 for examples). As part of the effort to reform the "cultural system" in order to develop the cultural industries, the central government selected a few publishing groups and publishing houses in 2003 as pilot "cultural units" for the new policy of corporatization. In 2004, the central government transformed China Publishing Group into a business entity, kick-starting the process of corporatization in the publishing industry.

After the initial stage of commercialization, the party-state gradually realized that media are not just the "mouthpiece" (*houshe*) of the Party, but also play an increasingly important role in sustaining economic growth. It started to treat the cultural sector, including the media industries, as a new site for economic growth. The recognition of the economic role of the cultural sector culminated in the acceptance of the concept of "cultural industries" by the Party, which is a significant ideological breakthrough in its media policy. Although the term of "cultural industries" had been mentioned on different occasions at the end of the 1990s (Zhao, 2008: 109), it was, for the first time, officially endorsed by the Party in 2000 and in that year, the Party proposed to "push forward the development of cultural industries" in the national 10th five-year plan. Cultural industries were classified by the Party as a "pillar" industry in its 12th national five-year plan in 2010, which implies that the Party has increasingly viewed cultural industries as one of the key industry sectors to propel future economic growth (Liu, 2006) as well as boost its soft power. Once the concept of "cultural industries" was ideologically endorsed by the Party, more recent commercialization of book publishing, which could be summarized as the processes of conglomeration and corporatization, was carried out by the party-state.

4.5 IDEOLOGY, INTELLECTUALS, AND POLITICS

To better understand the impact of politics on the Party's ideological renovation, Merle Goldman's research on the relationship between the Party and the intellectuals offers a useful starting point. Goldman (1987) has traced cycles of repression and relaxation toward intellectuals back to the early period of the People's Republic. She argues that the Party held "a contradictory policy towards the intellectuals" right from the beginning of the People's Republic of China (PRC), in that the Party imposed the official ideology on the intellectuals on the one hand but also "tried to stimulate the intellectuals to be productive" (ibid: 218) on the other. This policy resulted in oscillations between "periods of repression" and "periods of relative relaxation" (ibid). In addition, these cycles were "also determined by political factors, particularly factional maneuvering and power struggles in top leadership" (Goldman, 1993: 287) when intellectuals were used by political factions in power struggles. Although these cycles happened under Mao as well as under Deng, the ideological relaxation under Deng were "more far reaching" and energized by a significant "cultural pluralism and political discourse" (Goldman, 1996: 37 and 48) because there was an ideological divergence among the top leaders. Goldman (1994) clearly demonstrated how the press was used by both the reformists and the remnant Maoists in their ideological and power struggles during the Deng Xiaoping era.

Putting politics into the center of our analysis of the Party's ideological policy has important implications, as it offers us a way of understanding trends in ideological control in the cultural sphere more fully. During most of the 1980s, the task of ideological renovation was devolved by the Party to "a broad base of theoretical workers" (Misra, 1998: 183) due to the fact that the reformists within the Party were still fumbling for their reform policy. This broad base resulted in a period of "intellectual pluralism" (ibid), which "was enhanced by the divisions within the leadership" regarding the extent and direction of further reform (ibid). If China's economic reform can be summarized as a gradual process toward marketization and was accompanied with ideological cycles, the market-oriented reform gained a final victory after the aim of creating a "socialist market economy" was adopted as the guiding principle of the Party in 1992. Once this was achieved, the ideological pluralism, which the reformists had needed to explore the options for economic reform, may have come to an end. Although factional struggles may still exist, there is no significant ideological divergence between different factions. Unless a faction within the Party is willing to renovate its political ideology, which is very unlikely in the near future, the need to engage intellectuals and other social groups in ideological debates between Party factions may not exist anymore, and so there is less likelihood of another major ideological liberation. In addition, "power at the top was much less fragmented" (Naughton, 2008: 92) after 1993. This argument is certainly more tenable since president Xi Jinping took power in 2012 and embarked on a significant anticorruption campaign. The recent concentration of power within the Party tends to lead to a further intensified ideological control. The internal "Document No. 9" (*jiuhao wenjian*) released by the Party in 2013 singled out seven topics, including universal values, press freedom, civil society, civic rights, and independent judiciary, to be banned from public discussion, which is clearly an effort to tighten its ideological grip.

Although ideological divergences at the top may have largely disappeared, the debates at the bottom still exist however. The embrace of marketization by the party-state has created a social base of bureaucratic capitalists, which "makes it vulnerable to attacks from both the left and the right for deviating from socialism and for a less than thorough accommodation of capitalism" (Misra, 1998: 16). The Party not only needs to suppress the political demands from proponents of liberal democracy, but also to counter attacks from the leftists based on the Maoist egalitarian principle. If the challenge to the Party ideology in the 1980s mainly came from the demand for liberal democracy, the attack from the egalitarian leftists has become increasingly prominent since the 1990s. When Jiang Zemin, the former Party leader, promoted "The Three Represents" as the new ideology and tried to bring the "emerging entrepreneurial and middle class" (Gu and Goldman, 2004: 13) into the Party, he suppressed the old Maoists who had ideologically attacked this policy (ibid). As the political demand for liberal democracy has always been vigilantly suppressed, the Maoist egalitarian principle, which is still nominally upheld by the Party ideology, becomes a handy and powerful symbolic resource for challenging the status quo. This partly explains the rise of the so-called "new left" (Li, 2015; Fewsmith, 2008) in China. As for the continued ideological "fundamental—instrumental discrepancy" faced by the Party, President Xi Jinping tried to address this ideological discrepancy by formulating his theory of "two irrefutables," which says that the accomplishments of Maoism cannot be refuted in the name of accomplishments of reform, and vice versa. This formulation is pretty much in line with Deng Xiaoping's earlier theory of "no debates" in settling the capitalism or socialism debate at the beginning of the economic reform, and is likely to remain as the Party's guiding principle in handling its ideological matters.

4.6 SUMMARY

Understanding the impact of ideological shift is essential to a full understanding of the commercialization of publishing in China but has been largely unexplored in research to date. The ideological shift following the start of economic reform not only facilitated the institutional changes involved in the commercialization of publishing industry, but also created more cultural scope for the commercial operation of publishing houses. Although the media has been subject to dual pressures from the Party and the market since its commercialization, ideological shift has helped ameliorate the pressure exerted by the Party ideology, and expanded the overlaps between the economics of "bottom line" and the tolerance of the "party line." Without this expanded cultural scope, the commercialization of book publishing and other media would not have been possible. However, as critical views usually fall outside the tolerance of the Party, plurality within the cultural field is limited. As a consequence, market dynamics may have encouraged mediocrity, obscenity, and tabloidization in China's cultural sphere as cultural producers look for products that are popular but politically relatively uncontentious. In addition, as the renovation of the official ideology may have come to an end and there is also a concentration of power within the Party recently, the Party's ideological control over media content and institutions is likely to remain tight. This control, however, may vary across different media sectors as well as across different media organizations within the same sector. It has been noticed that in the press industry, for example, the less ideological role a newspaper assumes, such as evening papers, the more "active and appealing it is to readers" (Pan, 2000: 77). This variation of ideological role that different media organizations assumed has had implications on the uneven process of commercialization among different media sectors and different media organizations.

ENDNOTES

1. See Decisions on the Current Reform of Publishing Houses (*guanyu dangqian chubanshe gaige de ruogan yijian*), which was promulgated in May 1988.
2. See Decisions on Improving the Performance of Publishing Undertakings (*zhonggong zhongyang guanyu jiaqiang chuban gongzuo de jueding*), which was promulgated by the Central Party Committee and State Council on June 6th, 1983.

REFERENCES

Ahn, B., 1973. Adjustments in the great leap forward and their ideological legacy, 1959–62. In: Johnson, C. (Ed.), Ideology and Politics in Contemporary China. University of Washington Press, Seattle, pp. 257–300.

Akhavan-Majid, R., 2004. Mass media reform in China: toward a new analytical framework. Gazette: The International Journal for Communication Studies 66 (6), 553–565.

Balzer, H., 2004. State and society in transitions from communism: China in comparative perspective. In: Gries, P., Rosen, S. (Eds.), State and Society in 21st-Century China: Crisis, Contention, and Legitimation. Routledge Curzon, New York, pp. 235–256.

Bell, D., 2008. China's New Confucianism: Politics and Everyday Life in a Changing Society. Princeton University Press, Princeton.

Brady, A., 2008. Marketing Dictatorship: Propaganda and Thought Work in Contemporary China. Rowman & Littlefield, Lanham, MD.

Chan, J., 2002. China: media liberalization under authoritarianism. In: Price, M., et al., (Eds.), Media Reform: Democratizing the Media, Democratizing the State. Routledge, London, pp. 27—46.

Cheek, T., 1989. Textually speaking: an assessment of newly available Mao texts. In: MacFarquhar, R., et al., (Eds.), The Secret Speeches of Chairman Mao: From the Hundred Flowers to the Great Leap Forward. Harvard University Press, Cambridge, Mass., pp. 75—103.

Chen, F., 1995. Economic Transition and Political Legitimacy in Post-Mao China: Ideology and Reform. State University of New York Press, New York.

Dickson, B.J., 2010. Dilemmas of party adaptation: the CCP's strategy for survival. In: Gries, P.H., Rosen, S. (Eds.), Chinese Politics: State, Society and the Market. Routledge, New York, pp. 22—40.

Eagleton, T., 1991. Ideology: An Introduction. Verso, London.

Fokkema, D., 1991. Creativity and politics. In: MacFarquhar, R., Fairbank, J.K. (Eds.), The Cambridge History of China Volume 15: The People's Republic, Part 2: Revolutions Within the Chinese Revolution 1966—82. Cambridge University Press, Cambridge, pp. 305—401.

Fewsmith, J., 2008. China Since Tiananmen: From Deng Xiaoping to Hu Jintao. Cambridge University Press, Cambridge.

Freeden, M., 2007. Ideology and political theory. In: Freeden, M. (Ed.), The Meaning of Ideology: Cross-disciplinary Perspectives. Routledge, London.

Fu, Z., 1994. Autocratic Tradition and Chinese Politics. Cambridge University Press, Cambridge.

Gittings, J., 1989. China Changes Face. Oxford University Press, Oxford.

Goldman, M., 1987. The party and the intellectuals. In: MacFarquhar, R., Fairbank, J.K. (Eds.), The Cambridge History of China Volume 14: The People's Republic, Part 1: The Emergence of Revolutionary China 1949—65. Cambridge University Press, Cambridge, pp. 218—258 and pp. 432—477.

Goldman, M., 1993. The intellectuals in the Deng era. In: Kau, M., Marsh, S. (Eds.), China in the Era of Deng Xiaoping: A Decade of Reform. M.E. Sharpe, London, pp. 285—326.

Goldman, M., 1994. The role of the press in post-Mao political struggles. In: Lee, C.C. (Ed.), China's Media, Media's China. Westview, Boulder, pp. 23—35.

Goldman, M., 1996. Politically-engaged intellectuals in the Deng—Jiang era: a changing relationship with the party-state. The China Quarterly 145, 35—52.

Goldman, M., MacFarquhar, R., 1999. Dynamic economy, declining party-state. In: Goldman, M., MacFarquhar, R. (Eds.), The Paradox of China's Post-Mao Reforms. Harvard University Press, Cambridge, Mass., pp. 3—29.

Griffin, R., 2007. Ideology and culture. In: Freeden, M. (Ed.), The Meaning of Ideology: Cross-Disciplinary Perspectives. Routledge, London, pp. 75—97.

Gu, E., Goldman, M., 2004. The transformation of the relationship between Chinese intellectuals and the state. In: Gu, E., Goldman, M. (Eds.), Chinese Intellectuals Between State and Market. RoutledgeCurzon, London, pp. 1—18.

Guo, S., 2012. Chinese Politics and Government: Power, Ideology and Organization. Routledge, London.

Hadland, A., Zhang, S., 2012. The 'paradox of commercialization' and its impact on media—state relations in China and South Africa. Chinese Journal of Communication 5 (3), 316—335.

Hallin, D., 1986. The 'Uncensored War': The Media and Vietnam. Oxford University Press, Oxford.

Hallin, D., Mancini, P., 2004. Comparing Media Systems: Three Models of Media and Politics. Cambridge University Press, Cambridge.

Li, H., 2015. Political Thought and China's Transformation: Ideas Shaping Reform in Post-Mao China. Palgrave Macmillan, Basingstoke.

Li, X., 2002. Edited book of long live Mao Zedong thought by mass organizations during the period of cultural revolution (*wenge shiqi qunzhong bianyin de maozedong sixiang wansui kaolue*). Research Documents on Party History (*dangshi yanjiu ziliao*) 4. <http://cpc.people.com.cn/GB/69112/70190/70194/5236740.html> (accessed 09.07.09) (in Chinese).

Liu, B., 2006. Cultural Industries are a New Sector Propelling Economic Development (*wenhua chanye shi zhongguo jingji de xin zengzhang dian*). China Press Industry (zhongguo baoye), <http://media.people.com.cn/GB/22114/88454/5977181.html> (accessed 08.10.08) (in Chinese).

Liu, G., Shi, F., 1999. 50 Years Events in New China's Publishing (*xin zhongguo chuban wushinian jishi*). Xinhua Publishing House, Beijing (in Chinese).

Lynch, D., 1999. After the Propaganda State: Media, Politics and "Thought Work" in Reformed China. Stanford University Press, Stanford, CA.

Meisner, M., 1999. Mao's China and After: A History of the People's Republic. Free Press, New York.

Misra, K., 1998. From Post-Maoist to Post-Marxism: The Erosion of Official Ideology in Deng's China. Routledge, New York.

Moore, B., 1950. Soviet Politics—The Dilemma of Power. Harvard University Press, Cambridge, Mass.

Naughton, B., 1995. Growing Out of the Plan: Chinese Economic Reform, 1978—93. Cambridge University Press, Cambridge.

Naughton, B., 2008. A political economy of china's economic transition. In: Brandt, L., Rawski, T.G. (Eds.), China's Great Economic Transformation. Cambridge University Press, Cambridge, pp. 91—135.

Pan, Z., 2000. Improvising reform activities: the changing reality of journalistic practice in China. In: Lee, C.C. (Ed.), Power, Money, and Media: Communication Patterns and Bureaucratic Control in Cultural China. Northwestern University Press, Evanston, IL, pp. 68—111.

Polumbaum, J., 2008. China Ink: The Changing Face of Chinese Journalism. Rowman & Littlefield, Lanham, MD.

Qian, G., Bandurski, D., 2011. China's emerging public sphere: the impact of media commercialization, professionalism, and the internet in an era of transition. In: Shirk, S. (Ed.), Changing Media, Changing China. Oxford University Press, Oxford, pp. 38—76.

Schram, S., 1974. Mao Tse-Tung Unrehearsed: Talks and Letters, 1956—71. Penguin, Harmondsworth.

Schram, S., 1989. The Thought of Mao Tse-Tung. Cambridge University Press, Cambridge.

Schram, S., 1991. Mao Tse-Tung's thought from 1949 to 1976. In: MacFarquhar, R., Fairbank, J.K. (Eds.), The Cambridge history of China Volume 15: The People's Republic, Part 2: Revolutions Within the Chinese Revolution 1966—82. Cambridge University Press, Cambridge, pp. 1—106.

Schurmann, F., 1968. Ideology and Organization in Communist China. University of California Press, Berkeley.

Schwartz, B.I., 1989. Thoughts on the late Mao—between total redemption and utter frustration. In: MacFarquhar, R., et al., (Eds.), The Secret Speeches of Chairman Mao: from the Hundred Flowers to the Great Leap Forward. Harvard University Press, Cambridge, Mass, pp. 19—38.

Schwarzmantel, J., 2008. Ideology and Politics. SAGE, London.

Seliger, M., 1976. Ideology and Politics. Allen & Unwin, London.

Song, M., 1996. Manifestation of ultra-leftism in book publishing (*jizuo sichao zai chuban gongzuo zhong de yixie biaoxian*). In: Song, Y., et al., (Eds.), Archives of Contemporary China's Publishing (*zhongguo dangdai chuban shiliao*), vol. 6. Da Xiang Publishing House, Zhengzhou, pp. 92−100. (in Chinese).

Song, M., 1999. From curbing the chaos and resuming order to the prosperity of publishing: 20 years great achievements of the development and reform of China's publishing (*cong boluanfanzheng dao fanrong chuban: zhongguo chuban gaige fazhan 20 nian de jubian*). In: Song, Y., et al., (Eds.), Archives of Contemporary China's Publishing (*zhongguo dangdai chuban shiliao*), vol. 8. Da Xiang Publishing House, Zhengzhou, pp. 29−39. (in Chinese).

Song, M., 2004. Letters on the essence of publishing houses as enterprises (*guanyu chubanshe qiye shuxing wenti de tongxin*). Publishing Science (chuban kexue) 2004 (2), <http://www.cbkx.com/2004-2/548.shtml> (accessed 09/08/09) (in Chinese).

Song, M., 2006. Historical Retrospection on the Reform of Book Publishing (*chuban tizhi gaige de lishi huigu*) Part 1. China Publishing Journal (zhongguo chuban) 2006 (5), 12−16 (in Chinese).

Sparks, C., 2008. Media systems in transition: Poland, Russia, China. Chinese Journal of Communication 1 (1), 7−24.

Sparks, C., 2012. Beyond political communication: towards a broader perspective on the Chinese press. Chinese Journal of Communication 5 (1), 61−67.

Stockmann, D., 2013. Media Commercialization and Authoritarian Rule in China. Cambridge University Press, Cambridge.

Thompson, J.B., 1990. Ideology and Modern Culture: Critical Social Theory in the Era of Mass Communication. Polity, Cambridge.

Tong, J., 2010. The crisis of the centralized media control theory: how local power controls media in China. Media, Culture & Society 32 (6), 925−942.

Tsou, T., 1986. The Cultural Revolution and Post-Mao Reforms: A Historical Perspective. University of Chicago Press, Chicago.

Wacker, G., 2010. Resistance is futile: control and censorship of the internet in China. In: Brokaw, C., Reed, C.A. (Eds.), From Woodblocks to the Internet: Chinese Publishing and Print Culture in Transition, c. 1800−2000. Brill, Leiden, pp. 353−381.

Wang, H., 2010. How big is the cage? An examination of local press autonomy in China. Westminster Papers in Communication and Culture 7 (1), 56−72.

Wang, Y., 1999. Public service units? or enterprises? (*shiye hu? qiye hu?*). Publishing Research (chuban faxing yanjiu) 1999 (1), 5−9 (in Chinese).

Weatherley, R., 2006. Politics in China Since 1949. Routledge, London.

White, G., 1999. The decline of ideocracy. In: Benewick, R., Wingrove, P. (Eds.), China in the 1990s. Macmillan, Basingstoke, pp. 21−33.

Wu, G., 2000. One head, many mouths—diversifying press structures in reform China. In: Lee, C.C. (Ed.), Power, Money and Media: Communication Patterns and Bureaucratic Control in Cultural China. Northwestern University Press, Evanston, IL, pp. 4−45.

Yang, G., 2009a. The Power of the Internet in China: Citizen Activism Online. Columbia University Press, New York, NY.

Yang, J., 2009b. An exploration on the evolution of the role of publishing in the People's Republic (*xinzhonguo dui chuban xingzhi renshi de lishi guiji tanjiu*). Publishing Research (Chuban Faxing Yanjiu) 2009 (9), 33−37 (in Chinese).

Yuan, L., 1999. The process and effect of confirming the status of books as commodity (*1ueren tushu shi shangpin de jingguo he zuoyong*). In: Song, Y., et al., (Eds.), Archives of Contemporary China's Publishing (*zhongguo dangdai chuban shiliao*), vol. 7. Da Xiang Publishing House, Zhengzhou, pp. 105—112. (in Chinese).

Zhang, S., 2008. Overview of the publishing of selected works of Mao Tse-Tung in New China (*xin zhongguo chengli hou mao zedong xuanji chuban gaikuang*). Panorama of Party History (dangshi bolan) 2008 (11), <http://cpc.people.com.cn/GB/85037/8474358.html> (accessed 09.06.09) (in Chinese).

Zhang, W., 1996. Ideology and Economic Reform Under Deng Xiaoping: 1978—93. Kegan Paul International, London.

Zhang, X., 2011. The Transformation of Political Communication in China: From Propaganda to Hegemony. World Scientific Publishing Company, Singapore.

Zhao, Y., 2008. Communication in China: Political Economy, Power, and Conflict. Rowman & Littlefield, Lanham, MD.

Zhao, Y., 2012. Understanding China's media system in a world historical context. In: Hallin, D., Mancini, P. (Eds.), Comparing Media Systems Beyond the Western World. Cambridge University Press, Cambridge, pp. 143—173.

Zheng, Y., 2008. Technological Empowerment: The Internet, State, and Society in China. Stanford University Press, Stanford, CA.

CHAPTER 5

Conglomeration: The Formation of Publishing Groups

Conglomeration, or the establishment of publishing groups, gradually became a major plank in the party-state's strategy for restructuring the book publishing industry from the late 1990s onwards. This process was mainly completed by 2009, with regional publishing groups being established in most provinces, although a couple of more national publishing groups were launched afterwards. Following the accomplishment of conglomeration, the focus of reform shifted to corporatization which involved converting most publishing houses and publishing groups from "public service units (*shiye danwei*)" into independent business entities. A few publishing groups have even managed to get listed on the domestic stock market (see Table 5.1 for key events in the process of conglomeration and corporatization). On the face of it then, propelled by these two major policy interventions, commercialization has been progressing rapidly in the book publishing industry. This chapter, and the next, questions this easy assumption by examining these dual processes of conglomeration and corporatization in detail. We begin with conglomeration.

Little serious research has been done to date on the conglomeration of publishing in China. Most articles in Chinese professional journals argued, more or less uncritically, in favor of creating larger publishing groups on the grounds that they enhance economies of scale and aid China in facing threats from Western media conglomerates (Zhu, 2005; Wei, 2001). Academic articles in English journals on the other hand, with the privilege of being free from the pressure of censorship, have incorporated a discussion of the implications of conglomeration for political control in their discussions of China's media groups. Focusing on the conglomeration of newspaper publishing for example, Zhao (2000: 16) argued that press managers "view conglomeration as a way to realize their political and business ambitions," while Party and government authorities "see it as a means to enhance press control" and to support unprofitable but socially and culturally important papers by cross-subsidizing them from the returns on profitable titles. In this view, it was

China's Publishing Industry
DOI: https://doi.org/10.1016/B978-0-08-100919-2.00005-X

Table 5.1 Key events in the process of conglomeration and corporatization

Time	Event
Apr/1992	The Shandong provincial government launched the first provincial publishing group
Dec/1998	The central government ratified the establishment of Guangdong Provincial Publishing Group and Shanghai Century Publishing Group
Apr/2002	The central government launched China Publishing Group
Nov/2002	The central Party proposed the development of cultural industries
Dec/2003	Corporatization was encouraged by the central party-state in some pilot cultural organizations
Mar/2004	China Publishing Group was corporatized
Dec/2007	Liaoning Publishing Group was listed on the domestic stock market
Aug/2017	China Publishing Group was listed on the domestic stock market

the "collusion between party authorities and newspaper managers" (ibid: 15) that led to conglomeration. Hu (2003: 22) endorsed this view arguing that the priority of the party-state in media conglomeration "is to strengthen its political control in the context of increasing marketization" and globalization. But as Lee et al. (2006: 585) pointed out, it was "the internal diversification of media organizations" that already laid the original base for conglomeration.

These arguments, although developed in relation to the newspaper industry, provide a solid starting point for analysis, but this chapter attempts to take them further by offering a more fine-grained account of the rationale behind the conglomeration of book publishing. First, it argues that conglomeration was an evolving and uneven process and was not completely led by the central party-state. Second, it offers detailed arguments and evidence in support of those commentators and industry observers who have expressed a skeptical view of the claimed economic benefits of conglomeration.

5.1 THE DIFFERENT STAGES OF THE CONGLOMERATION OF PUBLISHING

Before we start our discussion, we need to define the scope of the media groups we are looking at here, in this case, publishing groups. Interestingly, this has not been done in the literature mentioned above. In its literal meaning, the word group (*jituan*) just means an aggregation of a reasonable number of business firms, but in the commentary on conglomeration it has acquired additional meanings. Keister (2000, 2009) for example, in her research on China's business groups, though not giving a clear definition of a business group, laid out some essential characteristics. These include: undertaking transactions in "several markets rather than focusing on a single product or market," and member firms being characteristically "connected through a variety of social, legal, and economic ties" and "nearly always bound by ongoing social relations" (Keister, 2000: 27–28). Adopting Keister's view in this present discussion on China's book publishing produced a working definition of a "publishing group" as a group of publishing houses clustered under the control of a dominant firm or organization, with other member firms diversifying into different branches of business.

Some discussions of the evolution of China's publishing groups trace the process back to 1988, when several provincial arts and literature publishing houses established an organization named the "United Distribution Group of Provincial Arts and Literature Publishing Houses" (*difang wenyi chubanshe lianhe faxing jituan*) (Wei, 2001: 7). However, this was more like a short-term coalition concentrating on the mutual promotion and distribution of books rather than a conglomerate, though the word "group" was used. The *Guangzhou Daily* Group, a press grouping, which was launched in 1996, has been regarded by some as "the first conglomerate" (Lee et al., 2006) in China's media industry. But if we look at book publishing, we see that several provincial publishing groups which met the essential requirements for being considered a group had already been established a few years earlier, in 1992 and 1993. They included the Shandong Publishing General House (Group), the Sichuan Publishing Group Company, and the Jiangxi Publishing Group (see Wei, 2001). This elongated time perspective allows us to view conglomeration as an evolving process rather than a clear goal of the party-state.

China's media groups have usually been considered media conglomerates (Zhao, 2000; Hu, 2003; Lee et al., 2006). However, Keister (2000) argued that China's business groups, although similar to Western conglomerates in their organizational form, differ from them and more strongly resemble the Japanese Keiretsu. She pointed out that a Western conglomerate "is easily reorganized (with parts being added and sold off) as economic concerns prescribe," whereas the reorganization of a business group is "less likely and thus less frequent" because "the firms in a business group are connected personally as well as economically" (Keister, 2000: 31). Keister's argument reminds us that these two kinds of organizations are not completely the same and there are subtle differences between them.

The first publishing group which used the term "group" in its title was the Shandong Publishing General House (Group) launched by the Shandong provincial government in April 1992. It consisted of all the business entities affiliated to the provincial publishing administration department, including publishing houses, book distributors, printers, and printing materials suppliers. The title of this new grouping, combining the more enterprising title of "group" with the more orthodox title of "publishing general house" (*zongshe*), seemed tentative and signaled a sense of compromise in the sensitive political context when the concept of market economy was still not officially embraced after Deng Xiaoping's speeches in early 1992.[1] The launch of this group received the blessing of both the provincial government and GAPP. The active role of the state apparatus was confirmed by Shi Hongyin, the then director of this publishing group, when he noted that this group had been launched "under the directive of provincial Party Committee and provincial government," and received the "support and encouragement" of GAPP (Shi, 1992). Although GAPP had proposed trialing publishing groups in its meetings with the directors of several provincial Press and Publications Bureaus (PPBs) in April and May 1992 (Wei, 2001), which was just a couple of months after Deng's highly publicized speeches, it was the local Party committee and government who took the initiative. According to Shi (1992: 11), the Shandong Publishing General House originally set out the goal of conglomeration in 1991, which was much earlier than the meetings convened by GAPP. Hence, we can argue that the idea was first officially endorsed by the provincial government and that GAPP acquiesced in its establishment.

After the launch of the Shandong Publishing General House (Group), several other provincial publishing groups followed suit. The Sichuan Publishing Group Company was launched in September 1992 through the ratification of the Sichuan provincial government. However, according to Wei, due to the power struggle between the publishing group and the Sichuan Provincial Press and Publications Bureau, it could not function properly. In response, the Sichuan Provincial Party Propaganda Department issued an official directive to "coordinate the relationship between the group and the provincial administration bureau," which effectively abolished the Sichuan Publishing Group Company as an autonomous entity, though it still existed nominally (Wei, 2001: 12). A third publishing group, the Jiangxi Publishing Group, was set up in February 1993, with the head of the provincial publishing administration department also assuming the position of the director of the group (ibid).

All these early publishing groups were launched by provincial govern-ments, and none of them was officially endorsed by the central party-state. Critics argued that their organization and operation were hardly different from publishing general houses, which will be discussed later in this chapter, or provincial publishing administration bureaus (ibid), which used to directly control major provincial publishers, book distributors, and other publishing-related enterprises. They saw them taking over "the market, resources, human resource and administrative power" of a pro-vincial administrative bureau or publishing general house with only a "change of title" (Lin, 1998: 5). At the level of the transfer of resources this is a tenable argument. On the other hand, at the ideological level it can be argued that the title of "group," which carried connotations of a more business-oriented enterprise, did signal a breakthrough.

It was not until 1998 however that the central government tentatively endorsed the establishment of publishing groups. The plan to establish Guangdong Provincial Publishing Group and Shanghai Century Publishing Group was ratified by GAPP in December 1998. The Shanghai Century Publishing Group was officially launched in February 1999 as the first publishing group ratified by the Central Party Propaganda Department and GAPP, followed by the launch of the Guangdong Provincial Publishing Group in December 1999. A few other publishing groups followed suit. At this stage however, most groups were still under the control of the provincial PPBs and as many provincial PPBs did not hand over all affiliated publishing business to the corresponding provincial publishing groups, many groups comprised only a limited number of member firms and most did not acquire legal status as full business entities. The control of a group over its subsidiaries was usually achieved by "administrative power" inherited from relevant government departments rather than economic ties such as ownership (Wei, 2001: 44).

After several years of trial and observation, the central party-state decided to adopt conglomeration as its official policy for the transforma-tion of book publishing, a move signaled by the launch of the China Publishing Group in April 2002. Its establishment involved a radical reform of GAPP, which gave up its control over nearly all its affiliated publishing and distribution business entities to provide the economic base for the new group.

This move coincided with the central Party starting to treat the cul-tural sector, including the media industries, as a new site for economic growth. The development of the cultural industries was proposed at the 16th Party congress held in November 2002 and as part of the effort to reform the "cultural system (*wenhua tizhi*)," the central government selected a few publishing groups and publishing houses as pilot "cultural units" for the new policy of corporatization. Benefitting from a privileged policy of tax breaks,[2] these pilot "cultural units" were encouraged to transform themselves into business entities rather than staying as "public service units." The China Publishing Group, which was owned by the central government, was transformed into a business entity in March 2004 and the administrative control over its subsidiaries was replaced with ownership control. A parent company was established to exercise owner's rights over the subsidiaries within the group. Following the corporatization of the China Publishing Group, the Shanghai Century Publishing Group took over seven more publishing houses from the Shanghai Municipal Press and Publication Bureau and was transformed into the Shanghai Century Publishing Company Ltd. in November 2005. It became China's first publishing shareholding company, with 70% of its shares being held by the Shanghai Century Publishing Group.

The central government took the lead in this round in the transformation of publishing groups. During this stage, many publishing groups not only expanded by acquiring more business organizations from their provincial PPBs, but also became independent of the PPBs' direct control. The move toward consolidation was rapidly followed by diversification of ownership. A publishing group in Liaoning province, after its transformation into a business entity, was listed on the Shanghai Stock Market in December 2007. This publishing group was hailed as China's first media company to issue shares for all its operations, including the editorial units.

Conglomeration was not a policy clearly pursued by the party-state at the beginning however. A couple of retired leaders of GAPP had expressed skepticism about the possible economic advantages of publishing groups (Shu, 2000) due to the unavoidable need to retain state control over book publishing. The then director of GAPP, Long Xinming, also warned that the "reform (of publishing) does not necessarily mean conglomeration" (Long, 2006). Although these critics of conglomeration could offer defensible arguments from an economic perspective, they completely missed the point that conglomeration is neither a process led by a single force, nor a result of purely economic considerations. Despite the skepticism, further conglomeration was pursued by GAPP. Except for regions (such as Hainan, Qinghai, Xinjiang, and Tibet) with much smaller scale publishing industries, all other provinces have established publishing groups. By the end of 2013, there were a total number of 33 publishing groups in China (see Table 5.2). A couple of them are

Table 5.2 List of publishing groups in China[a]

Name of publishing group	Date of official launch[b]
Shanghai Century Publishing Group	1999.2
Beijing Publishing Group	1999.7
Guangdong Publishing Group	1999.12
Liaoning Publishing Group	2000.3
China Science Publishing Group	2000.6
Hunan Publishing Investment Holding Group	2000.9
Zhejiang Publishing United Group	2000.12
Shandong Publishing Group	2000.12
Jiangsu Phoenix Publishing and Media Group	2001.9
China Publishing Group	2002.4
Jilin Publishing Group	2003.12
Sichuan Publishing Group	2003.12
Henan Publishing Group	2004.3
Hebei Publishing Group	2004.4
Shanghai Literature and Art Publishing Group	2004.6
Hubei Changjiang Publishing Group	2004.10
Jiangxi Publishing Group	2004.12
Yunnan Publishing Group	2005.1
Chongqing Publishing Group	2005.4
Guizhou Publishing Group	2005.9
Anhui Publishing Group	2005.11
Gansu Readers Publishing Group	2006.1
Shanxi Publishing Group	2006.12
Shannxi Publishing Group	2007.12
Heilongjiang Publishing Group	2009.05
Yellow River Publishing Group (Ningxia)	2009.09
Guangxi Publishing and Media Group	2009.12
Tianjin Publishing and Media Group	2009.12
Channel Publishing and Distribution Group (Fujian)	2009.12
Inner Mongolia Publishing Group	2009.12
China Education Publishing and Media Group	2010.12
China Finance and Economics Publishing Group	2013.8
China Industry and Information Technology Publishing Group	2013.12

[a]*Wuhan Publishing Group, Chinese Writers Publishing Group* and *Shenzhen Publishing and Distribution Group* are not included in this list, as they do not quite meet the definition of publishing group in this discussion.

[b]It refers to the official launch date after the endorsement of GAPP. Some groups, such as the Shandong Publishing General House (Group), although approved by their provincial governments, relaunched officially as publishing groups after the endorsement of GAPP at a later stage. Only the launch dates after the official ratification of GAPP were listed here.

considered national publishing groups, such as the Science Publishing Group which is controlled by the Chinese Academy of Sciences, China Publishing Group which is affiliated to the central government, and China Education Publishing and Media Group which is controlled by the Ministry of Education, but most of them are provincial publishing groups with similar structures.

As can be seen from this list, the establishment of publishing groups has been an evolving process stretching over a decade, from 1999 to 2013. During the initial stage, as we noted earlier, regional governments took the initiative to push the process forward while the central government was cautious about the possible repercussion for its political control. The central government tentatively endorsed the establishment of several publishing groups and once trials had shown that it was unlikely to have negative political consequences, the policy was pushed forward. The initially cautious attitude of the central government toward the establishment of publishing groups clearly suggests that the conglomeration of book publishing was not seen by the party-state as a means to enhance its control. Rather, it was concerned with maintaining its existing political control by promoting the "four unchangeables"[3] as the unequivocal prerequisite for the commercialization of book publishing. This meant that political control would remain and that publishing groups had to explore new ways of implementing it. Continuing control was exercised through several channels, most notably personnel and ownership. Many general managers or directors came from Party or government departments and the hierarchical Party system still existed in publishing groups. The key personnel, such as the chair of the board and the director, who are usually also the leaders of the Party committee of the group, have to be appointed by the provincial Party propaganda department. Added to which, even though a publishing group could become a public listed company, the majority of shares would be controlled by state-owned companies. An example is the Liaoning Publishing Group. Although listed on the stock market, over 73% of its shares are controlled by a state-owned company and the party-state retains strong control over it (see Du and Xu, 2008).

The continuing and central role of regional governments is mainly manifested in the economic aspects of publishing conglomeration. Regional governments fostered the conglomeration of their affiliated publishing business, but also tried to block the incursion of nonlocal publishing groups into the local publishing industry. Although GAPP encouraged cross-regional mergers of publishing groups,[4] most publishing groups are still constrained within the administrative boundary of their affiliated governments.

5.2 INSTITUTIONAL ORGANIZATION

Every provincial publishing group has been established by its provincial government, and normally consists of all the publishers, book distributors, and other organizations which were formerly affiliated to the provincial publishing administration department. As the structures of the publishing industry in different provinces are similar, provincial publishing groups display strong resemblances in their structure.

A provincial publishing group may engage in the business of book publishing, magazine publishing, book distribution, printing materials supplying, printing and property management, with book publishing and distribution being its core business. A provincial People's Publishing House, a science and technology publishing house, a children's publishing house, a literature and art publishing house are all normally the members of a provincial publishing group. There is also likely to be an ancient classics publishing house and an electronic audio−video publishing house within a provincial group. Most provincial publishing groups control the provincial Xinhua Bookstore, which might have been transformed into a provincial book distribution group.

The Shandong Publishing Group epitomizes China's provincial publishing groups. After the establishment of Shandong Publishing Group, it reorganized its businesses and formed a new shareholding group, Shandong Publishing and Media Company, in 2011 with itself being turned into just a holding company of the latter. This new shareholding group recently got listed on the domestic stock market in November 2017. It comprises of nine book publishers, one audio and video publisher, three magazine publishers, one digital publishing company, four printers, the Shandong Provincial Xinhua Bookstore Group, the Shandong Printing Materials Company, and some smaller nonpublishing businesses. Within the headquarters of this shareholding group, there is a department responsible for a highly profitable textbooks reprinting business for the local market. By paying a small amount of royalties to other textbook publishers, mainly the People's Education Press in Beijing, this reprinting business provides the economic lifeblood for the shareholding group. Nearly every provincial publishing group owns a textbook reprinting business. Due to the huge student population in most provinces, the market for textbooks is both extensive and constantly being replenished. It is estimated that the profit from textbook reprinting normally accounts for "more than half of the total profit" of a provincial publishing group and this figure could go "up to over 90 percent" for some groups (Chang, 2005). Textbook reprinting, a legacy of the planned economy,[5] has therefore continued to be an important profit source for provincial publishing industries even after the commercialization.

5.2.1 The Administration of China's Publishing Industry

The formation of publishing groups is the result of the separation of the publishing business from government administration. In order to understand how this separation has happened, we need to look at the government administration reforms.

There have been several major government administrative reforms since the onset of economic reform, carried out in 1982, 1988, 1993, and 1998, respectively. One of the key issues has always been the separation of government and business. A few government ministries were transformed into group companies, such as the China National Petroleum Corporation (successor to the Ministry of Petroleum) and the China National Nuclear Corporation (successor to the Ministry of Nuclear Industry) during this process. Administrative reforms also impacted on publishing administration departments. During the 1982 reforms, the National Publishing Administration Bureau was merged into the Ministry of Culture. However, the profit-seeking of the publishing industry and the proliferation of publishers at the beginning of the 1980s started to exert pressure on the ideological control of the party-state. In response, the government felt it necessary to establish the State Press and Publications Administration (*xinwen chuban shu*) in 1987 as a separate government department to enhance its administrative control. This is the most likely reason why the publishing administration department did not follow the reform route of some other industry ministries. After the official endorsement of the market mechanism in 1992, administrative reform started to focus on "reappraising the role of the state in society" (Hassard et al., 2007: 78), leading to the retreat of government departments from business activities. In 1997, at the 15th Party Congress, the Party proposed the reform of the State Council and its government departments. This administrative reform, which was approved by the National People's

Congress in March 1998, was "the largest and most radical since the founding of the People's Republic of China in 1949" (ibid: 80) and provided the impetus for the central government to approve the formation of publishing groups.

The "separation of government and enterprise activities" (ibid: 79) was one of the major efforts of administrative reforms. Since the beginning of the economic reform period, the government had tried a couple of times to forbid government departments and government officials from running businesses.[6] However, the powerful army and judiciary departments[7] had largely been left intact and they engaged extensively in businesses, causing serious corruption problems and huge revenue losses due to rampant smuggling. As part of the government administration reform in 1998, the party-state determined to forbid these powerful organizations from engaging in business activities. The publishing administration department and the Party propaganda department may have sensed that the separation of government and enterprise activities would be unavoidable for the publishing industry, and set out to explore the possibility of establishing publishing groups as a way of separating the publishing business from the government administration departments.

At the local level, the adjustment of the provincial publishing administration usually followed the examples set by the central Party although there were variations between different provinces. However, the focus of provincial publishing administrations was slightly different from that of the central publishing administration. First, the size of the local publishing industry was usually small before the economic reform and the administrative responsibility limited. Second, ideological control was less important for provincial administration departments, as final decisions on many sensitive ideological issues were taken at the central level. Consequently, there was more scope for business operations to be their principal focus, which also explains why publishing groups started in the provinces first.

5.2.2 From Provincial Publishing General Houses to Provincial Publishing Groups

Prior to the rapid expansion of provincial publishing industries in the 1980s, publishing in provinces centered around the provincial People's Publishing Houses, which were sometimes also part of the provincial publishing administration department. For example, the Shandong People's Publishing House had also been the Editorial Section (*bianshen chu*) of the Shandong Provincial Publishing Administration Bureau (*shandong sheng chuban shiye guanliju*) (see Zhang et al., 1993: 48–49), and when the Shandong Publishing Bureau was abolished in 1983 in the administrative reforms, the Shandong People's Publishing House assumed the government administrative responsibility and was renamed the Shandong Publishing General House in 1984.

Between 1978 and 1985, many specialized editorial branches of the provincial People's Publishing House were spun off as separate publishers, such as the provincial Education Publishing House and the Children's Publishing House. In addition, many government departments or social organizations launched their own publishing houses or magazines during this period, and unlike the provincial People's Publishing House, they were not affiliated to provincial publishing administration departments. The number of private booksellers also increased rapidly and de facto private publishers emerged.

The expansion of the provincial publishing industry made a new government administration department necessary. After the State Press and Publications Administration (SPPA) was separated from the Ministry of Culture, provincial governments established local press and publications bureaus and many abolished the provincial publishing general houses in 1986. Although provincial press and publications bureaus were government departments, their budgets mostly came from the financial profits made by their textbook publishing subsidiaries. They assumed the responsibility of administration and, where there was not a separate publishing general house, business operation of provincial publishing.

During the initial process of administration adjustment, provincial publishing general houses gradually became the organizations that assumed responsibility for the business operations of local publishing industries. The title of Publishing General House was introduced in 1983 as a result of the restructuring of government departments. After the state publishing administration department was merged into the Ministry of Culture during the government downsizing program in 1982, most provincial publishing administration departments, except for those in Shanghai, Tianjin, and Hunan province, were merged into local Bureaus of Culture, or transformed into the so-called publishing general houses (see Hu et al., 1991: 133). These new entities not only coordinated business relations among local publishing-related enterprises or organizations, they also assumed responsibility for administrating the local publishing industry. Although they had mixed responsibilities, their operations were tilted in favor of business and enterprise. Hence, when the central government established the State Press and Publications Administration in 1987, provincial governments also launched the local press and publications bureaus accordingly and most of them retained the general publishing house as another title for the local publishing administration department. The practice of "dual titles for one organization" (*yitao banzi, liangkuai paizi*) allowed the provincial publishing administration department to appear as both a government department and a business entity, and to assume both administrative and business responsibilities.

In some provinces, such as Guangdong, the publishing general house was completely scrapped. In a few others, such as Shandong, it was kept as a separate organization to manage the business operations of local publishing houses while the administration task was left to the provincial publishing administration department. These general publishing houses, which gained independence from the provincial publishing administration department, became business entities with the responsibility of managing the business operations of major provincial publishers, book distributors, and printers, and were de facto publishing groups. The title change of the Shandong Publishing General House demonstrated the close relationship between the publishing groups and the publishing general houses. The Shandong Publishing General House (Group) was launched in 1992, but later dropped the title of "general house" after the Shandong Publishing Group was officially endorsed by GAPP in 2000.

The business relationships among provincial publishing houses, book distributors, printers, and printing material suppliers were developed during the period of the planned economy. Provincial publishing administration departments had to control printers, book distributors, and printing material suppliers to avoid dealing with the bureaucracy of another state agency and to facilitate the smooth operation of local publishing industries. The economic relationships among them were also coordinated by the local publishing administration department. These business relationships persisted after the economic reform for a couple of reasons. First, market forces were only gradually introduced into the publishing industry, and the relationships among publishers, book distributors, and printers still required the coordination of government. Second, and more importantly, the publishing administration departments had economic incentives to keep their affiliated publishing businesses tied together in order to facilitate their control and keep all their subsidiaries afloat. This motivation was the reason for the establishment of publishing general houses and later publishing groups.

Jiang di'an, the former Head of the Jiangsu Provincial Press and Publication Bureau, has confirmed this as the primary incentive for the formation of publishing groups. According to him, in a meeting convened by SPPA in April 1992, SPPA proposed the establishment of publishing groups not only because of the encouragement from the "Southern Tour Speech" of Deng Xiaoping to be more enterprising, but also because of the forthcoming restructuring of government in 1993. In order to "avoid an established and complete system (of provincial publishing industry) being broken up again, SPPA wanted to maintain the system by establishing groups in advance" (Jiang, 1996 preface: 12).

To recap, publishing general houses, which were originally established to replace the local publishing administration bureaus during the restructuring of government, gradually evolved into business entities in some provinces and became the predecessor of publishing groups. However, the party-state never intended to release its control over publishing and after the establishment of publishing groups, most of them were controlled directly by their corresponding Party Propaganda Departments, which is a requirement stipulated by the central government for the formation of publishing groups.[8] The so-called separation of state and enterprises is therefore nominal since the Party has now assumed direct control of publishing groups. Although publishing groups are not Party organs, the entangled relationships between the party-state and publishing remain. Hence, the conglomeration of book publishing can be seen as simply the latest stage in the realignment of the relationships between the Party, the government, and the publishing business.

5.2.3 Business Groups

Improving the performance of state-owned enterprises (SOEs) has been a major aim of the economic reforms, because the SOEs not only provided significant fiscal revenue for the government, but also jobs and social services for their employees. In addition, their performance had substantial implications for China's banking system, as they were major borrowers. According to Dowling (2008: 464), the major state-owned commercial banks "served as the financial arm of the SOEs" and this system of "credit allocation to SOEs has created a credit crunch for domestic private firms." As a result, the successful reform of the SOEs has been seen as a key issue for the health of the banking system and for the economic growth as a whole.

Although business groups started to emerge in the mid-1980s (Keister, 2000: 11), the Group Company System only became a major policy for reforming the SOEs in the 1990s (Hassard et al., 2007: 130). In December 1991, the State Council agreed to form some pilot group companies.[9] Further efforts to establish business groups were initiated by the State Council in 1997.[10] The establishment of publishing groups in 1992 and 1998 exactly followed the general reform policy for state-owned enterprises.

5.3 ECONOMIC ADVANTAGES

The assumed economic advantages of conglomerates provided the main justification for the establishment of publishing groups. Commercialization turned the Chinese media into both a mouthpiece and a money-spinner of the party-state (Zhao, 1999). The publishing industry not only gradually became independent of direct government subsidies after commercialization, but also started to generate sizable revenues for the government. The party-state's gradual recognition of the economic potential of the media industries was one of the main impetuses behind the push toward commercialization. But there was also another economic reason underlying its support for the development of media industries. After the initial development of low value-added manufacturing industry, weakening competitive advantages from soaring labor costs, coupled with the continuing deterioration of the environment and energy shortages prompted a widespread consensus that China had to upgrade its industry structure. The cultural industries came to be seen as one of the new industry sectors that would propel future economic growth (see Liu, 2006; Xinhua Net, 2008). However, it was not until 2000 that the concept of "cultural industries" was officially endorsed by the Party in its Fifth Plenary Session of the Fifteenth Party Congress. The Party proposed to "enhance the construction and management of cultural markets and push forward the development of cultural industries" (CCP, 2000) in its report in 2000 as part of the National 10th Five-Year Plan.

Once the concept of "cultural industries" was ideologically endorsed by the Party, the conglomeration of publishing was mainly led by the central party-state, a push marked in a very public way by the establishment of the China Publishing Group in 2002. As part of the effort to develop the cultural industries, a series of directives were issued. One particularly important one was the so-called No. 17 Document[11] issued by the Central Party Committee and the State Council in August 2001, encouraging media groups to operate across different regions and sectors. GAPP also issued a specific document[12] in 2003 on the development of publishing groups in which the formation of publishing groups was presented as an "important strategy to adjust the (industry) structure, optimize the allocation of resources, increase the business concentration, and acquire the advantage of economies of scale" within the publishing industry. As these key phrases made clear, improving economic efficiency was an important goal of the state-led conglomeration of publishing.

The Chinese government saw Western media conglomerates as models for China's media groups. However, the social context is completely different. Media conglomeration in Western countries can be attributed to the rise of neoliberal free market thinking in the 1980s, when public ownership and certain forms of regulation over the media industry were delegitimized. Commercial companies, in search of potentially greater profits put increasing pressure on governments for deregulation. The favorable response to these demands provided emerging opportunities for the growth of larger media conglomerates (Hesmondhalgh, 2007: 113; Croteau and Hoynes, 2006: 91). Media conglomeration in China emerged from a very different social background. As we have seen, the rapid expansion and diversification of the provincial publishing industry after the economic reform, especially from 1978 to 1985, laid down the organizational foundations for the emergence of publishing groups. After the party-state embraced the market economy and endorsed the concept of cultural industries, the old ideology about the role of publishing was gradually outweighed by the acceptance of market mechanisms in the economy and profit seeking in book industry. The development of business groups in other industries provided an exemplar for the reform of the publishing industry. All these developments fostered a favorable environment for the emergence of publishing groups.

As a result of these different trajectories of change there are several key differences between media conglomeration in China and in Western countries.

First, Western media conglomerates have emerged mainly through mergers and acquisitions. This kind of expansion, however, is hardly possible in China, since all publishers and major book distributors are owned by different government departments or regional governments. Chinese publishers are not business entities free to amalgamate or to be amalgamated. The only possible way a takeover can occur in China is through a government administrative order. Consequently, the geographic reach of a provincial publishing group is usually coterminous with the administrative boundary of its affiliated local government.

Second, Western media conglomerates operate across a wide range of media sectors rather than a single one. The conglomeration of book publishing in Western countries is incorporated into wider corporate media structures in which publishing is just a minor part of the overall communications mix (Schiffrin, 2000). China's publishing groups, due to administrative boundaries, are usually confined to book and magazine publishing.

Third, and most importantly, the conglomeration of China's publishing industry has not been driven by market mechanisms but by government interventions designed to achieve certain economic as well as political goals.

5.3.1 The Economic Rationale for Media Conglomeration

Despite the above obvious differences, Western models were highly influential in China. Consequently, the arguments offered in support of media conglomeration in Western countries will be discussed a little further here in order to examine their applicability to China's publishing industry.

Economists have offered a variety of general accounts of the advantages of mergers and acquisitions. Coase (1937), in a particularly influential intervention, presented a theory of transaction costs and argued that firms have an incentive to get bigger until the costs of organizing additional transactions within the firm rise to a point of equating to the transaction costs in the open market. This theory has been extended to explain business groups (Keister, 2000: 41). Other arguments include: the economies that come with an increase in size, aspirations to enter industries with higher profit margins, and the positive role of diversification in reducing exposure to risks (Alberts and Segall, 1966, preface). In addition, a number of commentators have argued that governments in most European countries have "encouraged mergers of domestic companies" in order to "meet the 'American' challenge and that of increased competition from abroad" (Hughes and Singh, 1980: 10).

However, some economists have questioned these rationales for mergers and acquisitions, arguing that many events of corporate growth, whether by mergers or otherwise, can be explained by "ignorance and prejudice" (Dean and Smith, 1966: 4). Mueller (1986: 45) extends this argument by putting corporate manager's motivation back into the discussion, arguing that they "favour size and growth as corporate objectives, since they increase their power to achieve any other more direct personal goal the managers have." He does not oppose mergers and acquisitions altogether, but maintains that mergers, if they are to maximize profit, should "take place only when they produce some increase in market power, when they produce a technological or managerial economy of scale, or when the managers of the acquiring firm possess some special insight into the opportunities for profit in the acquired firm which neither its managers nor its stockholders possess" (Mueller, 1986: 155). However, the actual economic performance of many firms following mergers and acquisitions has often fallen short of expectations (Wallace, 1966: 165; Gaughan, 2007: 46 and 63), leading Mueller to conclude that mergers "have on average not generated extra profits for the acquiring firms" and they "have not resulted in increased economic efficiency" (Mueller, 1986: 217). It seems then that, from the perspective of economists, the theories of mergers' causes and effects "are still in conflict, and will probably always remain so" (ibid: 217).

The arguments offered in favor of media conglomeration hinge on the advantages assumed to accrue to size. Although the difficulties involved in managing vast enterprises have been acknowledged, large-size media players are widely seen to be enjoying some distinct advantages (Croteau and Hoynes, 2006). They can afford expensive projects, especially in expensive media businesses, such as the Hollywood films and national television networks. They can pay huge advances for celebrity authors in the publishing industry, with the enormous profits from successful projects reinforcing their dominance. Media giants have the resources for expensive promotion campaigns required when publishers adopt a "blockbuster strategy," especially for celebrity authors. Economies of scale can be obtained from massive sales of major hits, along with reduced unit production cost. They are also more resilient to short-term losses.

Alongside these possible gains, synergy is often cited as another major justification for conglomeration. The logic of synergy is that a single concept or cultural "property" can be developed and packaged across various media, and promoted via different media controlled by the same media conglomerate. By promoting the same product across a variety of media platforms media conglomeration is seen as a way to boost customer loyalty to the brand name. The first phase of post-war agglomeration in the publishing industry, according to de Bellaigue (2004: 3), occurred in the late 1960s and early 1970s when electronic and broadcasting firms decided to enter book publishing in pursuit of synergies. Risk reduction is another often cited justification for media conglomeration. Media giants can reduce their risks by diversifying their interests. They can also reduce the uncertainty of the business environment through the control over different parts of the value chain by vertical integration. Further, the reduction of market competition as a result of mergers and acquisitions also helps to reduce the risk of media giants.

Operational costs can also be reduced. Media conglomerates could improve efficiency and streamline departments by structural changes, which are usually accompanied by cutting redundant personnel after mergers and acquisitions.

Last, cross-national merger and acquisition may expand the market for media conglomerates. The strategy of globalization not only reduces the risk of media conglomerates in a certain market (Picard, 1996: 29), but also enables them to adapt their products or simply distribute existing products to new markets.

However, arguing solely for the economic advantages of media conglomerates may seem functional and one-sided in explaining the economic impulse toward bigger media giants. After the merger of AOL and Time Warner in January 2001, the value of its stock "declined by more than 75%" (Knowledge@Wharton, 2002) and Time Warner finally spun off AOL at the end of 2009. Although this might be an exceptional case, it has nevertheless stimulated caution about ever-growing media conglomerates. It has been argued that "most acquiring firms failed to generate any additional cash flows in excess of what was needed to recover premiums paid for firms" (Greco, 1999: 166). Book publishing, despite the belief in synergy, "witnessed the dissolution" of some amalgamations in the 1970s and 1980s (de Bellaigue, 1997: 128). As Hesmondhalgh (2007: 168) has argued, integration strategies "are subject to change and there are signs of partial disintegration in some industries and new forms of integration." Media conglomerates, like political empires, "do not last forever" and "they rise and fall" (Picard, 1996: 24).

5.3.2 Economic Advantages of Publishing Groups in China?

As discussed above, although media conglomeration in Western countries may achieve certain economic advantages, the arguments in favor have not persuaded all observers. The assumed advantages, some of which have been much touted for publishing groups, are even harder to realize in China, due to the specific structure of China's publishing industry.

The expansion of size was a major goal of China's publishing administration departments. "Getting bigger, getting stronger" (*zuoda, zuoqiang*) became a much hyped slogan of China's publishing industry. However, the advantage of large size is problematic for China's publishing groups. Book publishing is well-known for its low entry barriers. There are very few projects in book publishing which require the huge investment capacity of a conglomerate. Celebrity authors demanding huge advances are practically nonexistent in China. Marketing and promotion budgets are usually low due to the low profit margins of publishing industry. The much touted economies of scale are also questionable. Since China's publishing groups do not operate on a global scale there is no opportunity to reap the benefit of economies of scale from the extra sale of products in other markets. Although managerial economies of scale could be achieved, the holding companies of publishing groups were normally created as extra management entities rather than extensions of the existing management cohorts of a publishing house, creating an extra management layer above the subsidiary publishing houses. The only possible advantage is that the extended pool of financial resources could help some member firms to overcome short-term loss, but this is not a new practice. Before the formation of publishing groups, local administration departments and publishing general houses already subsidized their publishing houses when necessary.

The concept of synergy hardly applies to publishing groups. As China's media are segregated into different sectors and mutual entry is restricted, it is nearly impossible for publishing groups to branch out into other media sectors, such as television and broadcasting. Although newspapers also fall within the administrative area controlled by GAPP, few publishing groups run general daily newspapers. The only significant instance is the *Changjiang Times* (*changjiang shangbao*), which was launched in 2006 by the Changjiang Publishing Group. Overall though, the advantages of synergy are limited within the publishing conglomerates of China.

The advantage of risk reduction in media conglomeration is also questionable for publishing groups. Since they have limited opportunities to diversify into other media business, there is little risk reduction horizontally. And as we saw earlier, vertical business connections between publishers and book distributors, publishers, and printers, had existed for a long time in provincial publishing industries well before the launch of publishing groups. In addition, vertical business relations are more often than not like a forced marriage. Publishers may have to pay higher prices to the printers within the publishing group than the market price. Booksellers are sometimes under pressure to sell a certain number of books published by their publishing groups despite their quality or likely profitability (Sun, 2005: 12).

Nor does publishing conglomeration help much in cementing the loyalty of consumers to the brand. In book publishing, consumer loyalties are more likely to be attached to authors rather than publishing houses. In addition, building on the brand of a publishing group is problematic since as a new organization they have to work hard to get their brands recognized. In addition, the wide variation in the quality of books published by the members of a group is hardly useful for the branding strategy.

Operating costs have also hardly been reduced in publishing groups. There has been little restructuring of the publishing houses within a group, except for the creation of a new management tier in the holding company. Added to which, concerns about social stability, have made personnel lay-offs a sensitive issue that few publishing groups have the determination to embark on.

Nor has the publishing conglomeration expanded the market for publishers. Not a single publishing group in China has the capability to operate on a global scale, so there has been no concerted move into the global market. In the domestic market, there has been little change in the total number of publishers or in their market shares. The provincial publishing groups tend to reinforce their local market share by establishing trade barriers, which results in the intensification of a segregated domestic market.

The best way to assess the economic consequences of publishing conglomeration is to look at the economic performance of publishing groups. GAPP conducted a survey of 25 publishing groups at the beginning of 2007 (GAPP, 2007), according to which their net asset value increased by 7.45% and their sales revenue by 5.22% but their average pre-tax profit only increased by 0.68% in 2006 over 2005. Eleven of them even reported a more than 10% decrease in profits. As calculations of asset value are more susceptible to manipulation, pre-tax profit is a more accurate barometer of performance and on that basis most publishing groups did not achieve substantial profit increases. However, more recent data revealed that 21 publishing groups reported an increase of over 22% of their total profit in the first half of 2014 over the same period of 2013

(Jin, 2014). But, considering the very modest increase in sales in China's book market, the astonishing profit increase claimed by many publishing groups seemed counterintuitive. The source of the increase may largely come from value-added tax (VAT) refund and indirect subsidies from the government or their investment in other businesses. Jiangsu Phoenix Publishing and Media Group, one of the biggest of its kind in China, actually suffered a decrease of profit in its publishing business from 2012 to 2015, and its income from VAT refund and subsidies from the government was consistently above RMB200 million *yuan* (about US$31.40 million) from 2011 to 2015 (Xueqiu, 2017). This is not a single case. According to its IPO prospectus, Jilin Publishing Group Corporation received government subsidies of 17.6736 million yuan in 2014, 49.1615 million yuan in 2015, and 50.6423 million yuan in 2016, accounting for 13.09%, 34.69%, and 34.89% of its annual total profit in these years, respectively. In addition, as discussed before, GAPP and the Ministry of Education introduced new regulations on the publishing of supplementary learning materials from 2011, which operate like an approval system and have effectively limited the participation of private publishers in this profitable business. Consequently, the increasing market share of state publishers in supplementary learning materials business may explain the other source of increase of profit for some publishing groups. Overall, hardly any solid evidence can be found to justify the economic benefits of publishing conglomeration in China.

5.4 GLOBALIZATION AND PUBLISHING GROUPS

The possible threat from multinational media moguls was a widely cited reason for the move to publishing conglomeration in China. Earlier cross-national mergers and acquisitions in publishing were mainly manifested in the mutual acquisitions between American and British publishers in the English-language market. A wave of mergers and acquisitions started in the mid-1980s, as a result of "the progressive deregulation of currencies and of markets generally" (de Bellaigue, 1995: 7). The players were of many nationalities and activity was mainly centered on the US targets. In the late 1980s and the 1990s, continental European media firms, such as Bertelsmann, Hachette, and Wolters Kluwer, acquired mainly US publishers to gain "access to the world's largest and richest nation" (Clark and Phillips, 2008: 15) and to break into the English language market, because "their domestic markets were too small to satisfy their growth aspirations" (de Bellaigue, 1997: 129). It appears that in this context globalization did provide the opportunity for geographic diversification in an extended global market, and contributed to the latest phase of mergers and acquisitions in the publishing industry.

However, the media industry in China is well protected by the government, and consequently the actual extent of the impact of globalization on publishing conglomeration is not simply a matter of economic calculation.

5.4.1 Globalization and Publishing Conglomeration

Due to the rigid regulation, the potential challenge presented to China's publishing industry by globalization was largely kept at bay. Publishing has officially not been open to the foreign investors, although there have been a couple of joint venture companies such as the Tongqu (or Children's Fun) Publishing Company which was set up in 1992 by Egmont and the People's Posts and Telecommunications House. According to Yu (2001a: 26), the main area of cooperation was in science and technology publishing, which had little impact on "ideology, national cultural tradition and state political security." It was not until China was about to join the World Trade Organization (WTO) that discussions of the potential threats from Western conglomerates gathered momentum. However, China's entry into the WTO in December 2001 only opened book printing and distribution businesses. Book distribution has been completely open to foreign companies after a 5-year transition period, during which restrictions on geographic expansion and operation scale were gradually relaxed (Chu, 2003). Even this modest opening of China's book business however prompted increased concern about the potential impact of foreign capital on the publishing industry.

China started to apply to join the "General Agreement on Tariffs and Trade" (the predecessor of WTO) in July 1986. After China and America finally reached a bilateral agreement on the terms of China's entry into the WTO in November 1999, the final entry became just a matter of time. During this process, the government started to assess the impact of WTO entry on the publishing industry. GAPP commissioned a research project on this topic to the Chinese Institute of Publishing Science in 1997 (see Yu, 2001a, preface). It also revamped relevant regulations to cope with the potential impact. These included: the *Regulation on Publication Administration* (promulgated on 25/Dec/2001), the *Regulation on Printing Industry* (promulgated on 02/Aug/2001), and the *Regulation on Audio-Visual Publications* (promulgated on 25/Dec/2001). Other regulations were required by the government to be promulgated, modified, or canceled to meet the challenge of WTO entry.

The Chinese government had reason to be cautious about the impact of WTO entry on the publishing industry. A dispute between the US and China about China's restriction on the imports of cultural products, including books, DVDs, and music, in 2009 was widely taken as a portent of the impact of WTO entry. The conglomeration of the publishing industry, although it started much earlier than the WTO entry, had been put forward by publishing professionals as a strategy the government could employ to fend off threats from western conglomerates (Yu, 2001b: 2; Chen, 2000). A few people in the industry may have used the impact of WTO entry as an excuse to argue for conglomeration, since the pilot publishing groups had already developed a vested interest in legitimizing their existence and securing their status.[13] Some others may just have wanted to develop their personal power by taking this opportunity to form a publishing group. The government did come to see conglomeration as a strategy of defending and advancing the state-owned publishing industry and according to Yang Muzhi, the then Deputy Director of GAPP, the central party-state encouraged the formation of publishing groups so that they could compete with Western media conglomerates (Yang, 2001).

Although publishing groups, as we discussed earlier, were established much earlier, the prospect of WTO entry exerted extra pressure on the government to push forward the conglomeration of publishing.

5.4.2 The Illusory Wolf

At the beginning of WTO entry, the government worried that foreign investors would control the book distribution business and then exert pressure on book publishing "upstream" along the supply chain. However, this worry did not materialize after the transitional restrictions on foreign investors in the book distribution business were removed in 2006, and WTO entry has had little perceivable impact on the book distribution business. Foreign investors have not rushed into China book retailing business, dissuaded by the sizable investment in retail shops required (Qian, 2006) and by continuing policy and market barriers.

There have however been exceptions, most notably Amazon and Bertelsmann Direct. Amazon acquired a Chinese online book selling company in August 2004 for US$75 million and has been in fierce competition with other Chinese online booksellers. Bertelsmann Direct entered China much earlier. It made substantial investment and showed great persistence with more than 10 years of patience for the materialization of the envisaged profit. However, its final retreat from China in July 2008 is one of the most strikingly cautionary cases for any prospective foreign investors to study, and suggests that Chinese fears of the predatory Western wolf finally turned out to be an illusion.

Bertelsmann's attempt to crack China's media market dated back to 1993, when it joined a high-profile German delegation for a visit to China headed by the then German Chancellor Helmut Kohl. The following year Bertelsmann Direct set up Shanghai Bertelsmann in a joint venture with China Sci & Tech Book, which was a subsidiary of the Shanghai Municipal Press and Publication Bureau (Gu, 2006: 175). It launched a book club business in January 1997 followed by an online book selling business in December 2000. Displaying shrewd business tactics in circumventing policy barriers, Bertelsmann Direct entered China's book distribution business much earlier than the business was officially opened, with restrictions, in 2001, and even became "a de facto publisher in China" (Gu, 2006: 176). Bertelsmann Direct later established a bookstore chain by forming a joint venture with Beijing 21st Century Book Chain in December 2003, and entered the book wholesaling business in a joint venture with Liaoning Publishing Group in May 2005. However, most of its businesses did not achieve satisfactory profits and it finally announced the closure of all its 36 franchised retail chain bookstores in June 2008 and, two weeks later, the termination of its book club business and online book selling business. Its joint venture with the Liaoning Publishing Group was liquidated in June 2008 (Zhou, 2008).

When it first entered China's book market, Bertelsmann Direct was seen as a primary example of a prowling Western wolf. But having become the most prominent foreign presence, after a decade of patience and effort, it was forced to retreat, ironically, just as China officially removed all restrictions on foreign investors in the book distribution business. There are several explanations for the failure of Bertelsmann Direct, including the high operating costs of the book club (Hao, 2008), the persistence of piracy and entrenched state monopolies in publishing (Chen, 2008), and the rise of online book sales and fierce competition from

Chinese online booksellers (Yang, 2008). All these factors provided a partial explanation. Book publishing is widely known as a business with low profit margins (Croteau and Hoynes, 2006: 117) and China is no exception. However, two other important reasons, which have been neglected by many commentators, exacerbated the situation of low profit margin and predetermined the grim prospect of competing with the state-owned Xinhua bookstores in book distribution business. First, textbook distribution is monopolized by Xinhua bookstores and as we discussed earlier in Chapter 2, Mapping Book Publishing in China, textbook publishing and distribution is the most important sector of China's book business, and is crucial for the survival of both state-owned publishers and Xinhua bookstores. It is nearly impossible for foreign investors to enter this most profitable sector of book business. This only leaves a much smaller and highly competitive mass market for foreign investors. Second, many Xinhua bookstores could afford to compete in the mass retailing market with little profit or even to lose money because of the profit or subsidies they accrued from other sources. In many big cities, Xinhua bookstores established super bookstores in prime business locations, normally housed within a magnificent building. The profit from book sales is normally negligible in comparison with the sizable income from renting the rest of the building to other commercial companies. This stark market environment makes it extremely difficult for foreign investors to achieve a reasonable profit from China's seemingly huge book distribution business. Hence the anticipated Western wolf entered the forest of the Chinese book business but eventually retreated without the ready supply of red meat it had hoped for.

Bertelsmann's retreat from China is not an isolated case. Rupert Murdoch's News Corp also retreated from Chinese market after two decades of frustration (Williams, 2014). Western media giants are effectively held back by the double barriers erected by the tight control of the party-state over the media and the monopoly of state-owned media groups.

5.5 SUMMARY

As we have seen, the formation of China's publishing groups started in several provinces some time before the central government officially endorsed this policy in 1998. They are neither a completely new institution nor the natural result of mergers and acquisitions driven by market mechanisms. Rather, their essential form can be traced back at least to the formation of provincial publishing general houses which assumed responsibility for the business operations of their subsidiaries. The formation of publishing groups has achieved the nominal separation of government and publishing, but the Party has retained its control. Although it called for the cross-regional and cross-sectoral operation of publishing groups, most of them are provincially based groups and the book market remains segregated. The ambition to develop China's cultural industries gave the government economic incentives to take Western media conglomerates as a model, while the possible impact of globalization exerted extra pressure. However, few tangible economic advantages have accrued from the formation of publishing groups and the threat from Western media giants has proved to be largely an illusion. Publishing conglomeration is therefore most usefully seen primarily as a realignment of the relationship between the Party, the government, and the publishing industry in a changed social context.

ENDNOTES

1. Deng Xiaoping, the former Chinese leader, although retired at that time, made a series of significant speeches during his famous tour of southern China in January and February of 1992, in which he criticized the stagnation of economic reform and called for the adoption of a predominantly market-led economic mechanism in China. Later that year, the 14th CCP Party congress officially ratified the idea of the market economy in October 1992, and this is generally considered a significant event during China's economic reform.
2. See No. 105 document issued by the General Office of State Council (*guowuyuan bangongting*) in 2003, which is entitled *Notice on Supporting the Development of Cultural Industries and the Transformation of Business-oriented Cultural Organization into Business Entities during the Pilot Reform of Cultural System* (*guanyu yinfa wenhua tizhi gaige shidian zhong zhichi wenhua chanye fazhan he jingyingxing wenhua shiye danwei zhuanzhi wei qiye de liangge guiding de tongzhi*).
3. The "four unchangeables" means that under no circumstances can the core principles of "media as the mouthpiece of the Party and the people, Party's control over the media, Party's control over the media cadres and media's role in correctly guiding the public opinion" be changed.
4. See two documents issued by GAPP in 2006, which were titled *Decisions on the Cross-regional Operation of Publishing Industry* (*guanyu xinwen chubanye kuadiqu jingying de ruogan yijian*) and *Implementation Plan for Deepening the Reform of Publishing and Distribution System* (*guanyu shenhua chuban faxing tizhi gaige gongzuo shishi fangan*).
5. It has been discussed in Chapter 3: From Communization to Commercialization: China's Publishing From 1949 to 1992.
6. The Party Central Committee and the State Council issued two official decrees in 1984 and 1986, respectively, to forbid Party organs, government departments, and officials from running businesses.
7. They included the army, armed police forces, Ministry of Public Security, Ministry of State Security, the Procuratorate, and the Court.

8. The Science Publishing Group is an exception, as it is owned by the Chinese Academy of Sciences. According to the *Guidelines on the Conglomeration of Press and Publishing Industry* (*guanyu xinwen chubanye jituanhua jianshe de ruogan yijian*) issued by the GAPP in 2003, publishing groups launched by central governmental departments should be controlled by the relevant departments (which include the Chinese Academy of Sciences, the Chinese Academy of Social Sciences, etc.), all other publishing groups should be controlled by the central or provincial party propaganda departments.

9. The State Council issued a directive titled *Reply to the Application of Selecting Some Enterprise Groups as Pilot Groups* (*guanyu xuanze yipi daxing qiye jituan jinxing shidian de qingshi*) in December 1991.

10. The State Council issued another directive titled *Notice on Extending the Policy of Large Pilot Enterprise Groups* (*guanyu shenhua daxing qiye jituan shidian gongzuo yijian de tongzhi*) in April 1997.

11. Several months later after the development of cultural industries became part of the 10th Five-Year Plan of the State Council in 2001, the Central Party Propaganda Department, the State Administration of Radio Film and Television, and the General Administration of Press and Publication drafted *Recommendations on the Further Reform of Press, Publication, Broadcasting and Film* (*guanyu shenhua xinwen chuban guangbo yingshi ye gaige de ruogan yijian*). This document was accepted and issued by the Central Party Committee and the State Council in August 2001. It is commonly known as the No. 17 Document.

12. This document issued by GAPP was titled *Guidelines on the Conglomeration of Press and Publishing Industry* (*guanyu xinwen chubanye jituanhua jianshe de ruogan yijian*).

13. According to the No. 591 directive (*guanyu guanche luoshi guanyu shenhua xinwen chuban guangbo yingshiye gaige de ruogan yijian*) issued by GAPP in 2002, which was based on the so-called No. 17 Document, if a pilot publishing group couldn't reach the goal of the reform after a period of operation or was found in breach of regulations, its status as a pilot group could be canceled or the privileged policy granted to it could be terminated.

REFERENCES

Alberts, W., Segall, J. (Eds.), 1966. The Corporate Merger. The University of Chicago Press, Chicago.

Chang, H., 2005. Breaking the ice of monopoly in school textbook publishing and distribution (*zhongxiaoxue jiaocai chuban faxing longduan pobing*). Finance and Economy (caijing) 2005 (19), <http://edu.people.com.cn/GB/44071/3711361.html> (accessed 08.12.08) (in Chinese).

Chen, S., 2008. Bertelsmann backs away from China. <http://www.forbes.com/2008/06/16/bertelsmann-china-bookselling-markets-equity-cx_jc_0616markets03.html> (accessed 28.10.08).

Chen, X., 2000. WTO and China's Publishing (*WTO yu zhongguo chuban*). Guangxi Normal University Press, Guilin (in Chinese).

Chu, X., 2003. 'Crossing the river by feeling the pebbles': WTO membership spurs reforms in Chinese publishing. LOGOS 14 (2), 95–100.

Clark, G., Phillips, A., 2008. Inside Book Publishing, fourth ed. Routledge, London.

Coase, R.H., 1937. The Nature of the Firm. Economica 4 (16), 386–405.

CCP, 2000. Proposals of the Central Committee of the Communist Party of China on drawing up the 10th Five-Year Plan for National Economic and Social Development (*zhonggong zhongyang guanyu zhiding guomin jingji he shehui fazhan di shige wunian jihua de jianyi*). http://cpc.people.com.cn/GB/64162/71380/71382/71386/4837946.html (accessed 10.01.11) (in Chinese).

Croteau, D., Hoynes, W., 2006. The Business of Media: Corporate Media and the Public Interest. Pine Forge Press, Thousands Oak, CA.

de Bellaigue, E., 1995. Mergers, acquisitions and takeovers in publishing: why they go on, and on, and will go on? LOGOS 6 (1), 6−15.

de Bellaigue, E., 1997. Conglomeracy and the book business: where next? LOGOS 8 (3), 127−134.

de Bellaigue, E., 2004. British Book Publishing as a Business Since the 1960s. The British Library, London.

Dean, J., Smith, W., 1966. The relationships between profitability and size. In: Alberts, W., Segall, J. (Eds.), 1966. The Corporate Merger. The University of Chicago Press, Chicago, pp. 3−30.

Dowling, J., 2008. Future Perspectives on the Economic Development of Asia. World Scientific Publishing Company, New Jersey.

Du, J., Xu, W., 2008. The journey of a state-owned cultural enterprise toward getting listed on the stock market (*yige wenhua guoqi de shangshi zhilu*). <http://chinaneast.xinhuanet.com/dbtk/2008-04/18/content_13020115.htm> (accessed 20.08.09) (in Chinese).

GAPP., 2007. Comparison of economic performance of publishing groups in 2005 and 2006 (*chuban jituan 2006 nian yu 2005 nian jingji zhibiao duibi*). <http://www.bkpcn.com/Web/ArticleShow.aspx?artid = 064302&cateid = A01> (accessed 28.10.09) (in Chinese).

Gaughan, P., 2007. Mergers, Acquisitions, and Corporate Restructurings. John Wiley & Sons, New Jersey.

Greco, A., 1999. The impact of horizontal mergers and acquisitions on corporate concentration in the U.S. book publishing industry: 1989−94. Journal of Media Economics 12 (3), 165−180.

Gu, Q., 2006. Bertelsmann in China: low profile, patient growth. LOGOS 17 (4), 173−181.

Hao, T., 2008. Bertelsmann meets Waterloo after 13-year endeavour, ends China book club. <http://www.interfax.cn/news/3747/> (accessed 28.10.08).

Hassard, J., et al., 2007. China's State Enterprise Reform: From Marx to the Market. Routledge, London.

Hesmondhalgh, D., 2007. The Cultural Industries. SAGE, London.

Hu, Z., 2003. The post-WTO restructuring of the Chinese media industries and the consequences of capitalisation. Javnost: The Public 10 (4), 19−36.

Hu, Z., et al., (Eds.), 1991. Archives of Hunan Province, vol. 20: Publishing (*hunan shengzhi xinwen chubanzhi chuban*). Hunan Publishing House, Changsha (in Chinese).

Hughes, A., Singh, A., 1980. Mergers, concentration, and competition in advanced capitalist economies: an international perspective. In: Mueller, D. (Ed.), The Determinants and Effects of Mergers. Oelgeschlager, Gun & Hain, Cambridge, MA, pp. 1−26.

Jiang, D., 1996. Preface two. In: Gao, J., et al., (Eds.), Archives of Jiangsu Province: Publishing (*jiangsu shengzhi chubanzhi*), 1996. Jiangsu People's Publishing House, Nanjing (in Chinese).

Jin, Y., 2014. 40 Publishing and book distribution groups saw over 27% increase in their profits in the first half of the year (*40 jia chuban faxing jituan shangbannian lirun zengsu cao 27%*). China Press and Publishing Journal (zhongguo xinwen chuban bao) 14 October 2014. <https://www.ce.cn/culture/gd/201410/14/t20141014_3696787.shtml> (accessed 20.11.17).

Keister, L., 2000. Chinese Business Groups: The Structure and Impact of Interfirm Relations During Economic Development. Oxford University Press, Oxford.

Keister, L., 2009. Interfirm relations in China: group structure and firm performance in business groups. American Behavioral Scientist 52 (12), 1709−1730.

Knowledge@Wharton, 2002. The mega-media business model: doomed to fail, or just ahead of its time. <http://knowledge.wharton.upenn.edu/article.cfm?articleid = 600> (accessed 14.10.08).

Lee, C.C., He, Z., Huang, Y., 2006. 'Chinese Party Publicity Inc.' conglomerated: the case of the Shenzhen Press Group. Media, Culture and Society 28 (4), 581−602.

Lin, X., 1998. The Development and Impact of Publishing Groups in mainland China (dalu chuban jituan fazhan qushi ji yingxiang). Mainland Committee of State Council, Taiwan (in Chinese).

Liu, B., 2006. Cultural industries are a new sector propelling economic development (wenhua chanye shi zhongguo jingji de xin zengzhang dian). <http://media.people.com.cn/GB/22114/88454/5977181.html> (accessed 20.10.08).

Long, X., 2006. Reform does not equate with conglomeration (gaige bu dengyu jituan hua). People's Daily (renmin ribao), 06 April 2006. <http://politics.people.com.cn/GB/1026/4274467.html> (accessed 27.10.09).

Mueller, D.C., 1986. The Modern Corporation: Profits, Power, Growth and Performance. Wheatsheaf Books, Brighton.

Picard, R.G., 1996. The rise and fall of communication empires. Journal of Media Economics 9 (4), 23−40.

Qian, J., 2006. Embracing the post-WTO transition (yingjie wto hou guoduqi). http://www.bkpcn.com/Web/ArticleShow.aspx?artid = 062347&cateid = B04   (accessed 27.10.09).

Schiffrin, A., 2000. The Business of Books. Verso, London.

Shi, H., 1992. Shandong publishing industry is on the way toward a publishing group (shandong chubanye zoushang jituanhua de daolu). Publishing Research (chuban faxing yanjiu) 1992 (6), 7−13 (in Chinese).

Shu, T., 2000. Retrospection of Publishing Groups (chuban jituan shanglu hou de huigu). Editors' Friend (bianji zhiyou) 2000.4, 2−7 (in Chinese).

Sun, B., 2005. Analysis of publishing group organization models of China (woguo chuban jituan de zujian moshi fenxi). Journal of Hebei University: Philosphy and Social Science Edition (hebei daxue xuebao zhexue shehui kexue ban) 30 (5), 10−15 (in Chinese).

Xueqiu., 2017. Ten years development of Jiangsu Phoenix Publishing and Media Group (Jiangsu fenghuang chuban chuanmei jituan shinian fazhan). <https://xueqiu.com/1626721691/83907777> (accessed 20.11.17).

Wallace, F.D., 1966. Some principles of acquisition. In: Alberts, W., Segall, J.E. (Eds.), The Corporate Merger. The University of Chicago Press, Chicago, pp. 165−182.

Wei, Y., 2001. Study on China's Publishing Groups (woguo chuban jituan yanjiu). In: Yu, M. (Ed.), Research on Publishing Groups (chuban iituan yanjiu). China Books Publishing House, Beijing, pp. 1−55. (in Chinese).

Williams, C., 2014. Rupert Murdoch gives up on China with sale of Star China TV. The Telegraph 02 January 2014. <http://www.telegraph.co.uk/finance/newsbysector/mediatechnologyandtelecoms/media/10547453/Rupert-Murdoch-gives-up-on-China-with-sale-of-Star-China-TV.html> (accessed 20.11.17).

Xinhua Net, 2008. Cultural industries have become a new sector propelling economic growth (wenhua chanye yi chengwei woguo de yige xin de jingjin zengzhang dian). <http://www.gd.xinhua.org/newscenter/ztbd/2008-05/17/content_13291387.htm> (accessed 20.10.08) (in Chinese).

Yang, L., 2008. Bertelsmann chain stores closed across China. <http://www.shanghaidaily. com/sp/article/2008/200806/20080616/article_363412.htm> (accessed 28.10.08).

Yang, M., 2001. Speeches on the fifth national working conference of university presses (*xinwen chuban zongshu yang muzhi fushuzhang zai di wu ci quanguo gaoxiao chubanshe gongzuo huiyi shang de baogao*). <http://sinobook.com.cn/press/newsdetail.cfm? iCntno = 3236> (accessed 27.10.08) (in Chinese).

Yu, M. (Ed.), 2001a. Entry into WTO and the Development of China's Publishing Industry (*jiaru wto yu zhongguo chubanye fazhan*). China Books Publishing House, Beijing (in Chinese).

Yu, M. (Ed.), 2001b. Research on Publishing Groups (*chuban jituan yanjiu*). China Books Publishing House, Beijing (in Chinese).

Zhang, S., et al., (Eds.), 1993. Archives of Shandong Province: Publishing (*shandong shengzhi chubanzhi*). Shandong People's Publishing House, Jinan (in Chinese).

Zhao, B., 1999. Mouthpiece or money-spinner? The double life of Chinese television in the late 1990s. International Journal of Cultural Studies 2 (3), 291−305.

Zhao, Y., 2000. From commercialization to conglomeration: the transformation of Chinese Press within the orbit of the party state. Journal of Communication 50 (2), 3−26.

Zhou, L., 2008. Bertelsmann to revise its global strategy (*Beitasiman mouqiu quanqiu zhanlue zhuanxing*). <http://www.caijing.com.cn/2008-07-18/100075178.html> (accessed 02.08.10) (in Chinese).

Zhu, J., 2005. Study on the Development of China's Publishing Groups (*zhongguo chuban qiye jituan fazhan yanjiu*). Liaoning People's Publishing House, Shenyang (in Chinese).

CHAPTER 6

Corporatization: The Transition to Enterprises

Alongside conglomeration, corporatization, or the so-called "transformation into enterprises" (*zhuanqi gaizhi*), is the other central plank in the party-state's approach to the reform of the publishing industry. The two movements were closely entwined, since at the later stage of the conglomeration process publishing groups were actively encouraged by the government to transform into business entities. According to Liu Binjie, the then deputy Director of General Administration of Press and Publication (GAPP), the establishment of publishing groups was the first step in restructuring the publishing industry, and the next step would be to transform them into corporations and to get some of them listed on the stock market "when the time is ripe" (Liu, 2002). Before corporatization as a policy was adopted, book publishing in China was considered part of the public sector. Most publishing houses were "public service units managed as enterprises" (*shiye danwei, qiyehua guanli*). The term *shiye danwei* referring to organizations delivering public services or providing public goods has been translated in a variety of ways such as "public service units," "public institutions," "institutional units," "nonprofit organizations" (World Bank, 2005: 10), or "cause-oriented undertakings" (Zhao, 2008: 77). The term of "public service unit," which is commonly used by the World Bank (2005) and OECD (Organization for Economic Co-operation and Development) (2005), will be adopted in this discussion. The main consequence of defining publishing houses as public service units was that they were not supposed to be purely profit-seeking and were not entitled to the full legal rights of business entities. Corporatization would change the legal status of publishing houses and, theoretically, endow them with full operational autonomy. This chapter will examine the rationale for the policy of corporatization and illustrate how it was shaped by the bargaining of different interest groups.

China's Publishing Industry
DOI: https://doi.org/10.1016/B978-0-08-100919-2.00006-1

6.1 INTRODUCTION

At the beginning of the economic reform process, book publishing underwent a significant transformation due to the push of the government and the pull of market forces. After the introduction of commercialization the publishing industry was under the hybrid control of the party-state and the market mechanism. The legal status of publishing houses, as "public service units" but "managed as enterprises," manifested exactly this hybrid system. Many state-owned publishing houses, and the state agencies they affiliated to, developed vested interests in this hybrid system and were resistant to further changes. As a result, the pull effect of market forces was gradually blunted and the commercialization reached a bottleneck. After the media was endorsed as part of the "cultural industries," the central party-state started to push forward the commercialization of the media from 2001. Two official directives, the No. 17 Document and the No. 16 Document, were issued by the central party-state in August 2001 and in July 2002, respectively.[1] These two documents cautiously opened the door for publishing houses to receive investments from other state-owned companies. However, publishing houses and groups were requested to separate their editorial sector from their "business sector" (jingying bumen) such as the marketing and distribution departments, and only these latter sectors were open to "outside" investments. In addition, publishing houses or publishing groups were required to retain at least 51% ownership in this kind of cooperation. This tentative and cautious policy signified the party-state's desire to improve the economic sustainability and profitability of the industry. A couple of joint ventures were set up following this policy[2] but these attempts did not work well. Since content creation is the core of the cultural industries it is hardly feasible to separate the editorial department from the other departments of a publishing house.

The party-state introduced a bolder reform policy in 2003 when two new directives were issued on 31 December[3] to support the development of the cultural industries. Some pilot "cultural public service units (wenhua shiye danwei)" were encouraged to transform themselves, including their editorial sectors, into enterprises, a move which officially kicked off the process of corporatization. Unlike the establishment of publishing groups, which had started in several provinces before official endorsement by the central government, the transformation into enterprises only began after this policy was promoted by the central government. The transformation of China Publishing Group into a business enterprise in March 2004 offered an official stimulus to the corporatization of the publishing industry. Once the legal status of China Publishing Group was changed from a public service unit to an enterprise, it had to be restructured in order to meet the requirements of the company law. To this end, GAPP gave up its proprietary right over this group due to the principles of "separation of government and enterprises" and "separation of government and public service units." A new government department, the State-owned Assets Supervision and Administration Commission (*guoziwei*), was set up in 2003 to act as the proprietor of national state-owned enterprises,[4] but China Publishing Group was not handed over to it, probably because the Party wanted to retain its control. The State Council became the owner and authorized the Ministry of Finance to supervise the operation of the state-owned assets of this publishing group, but the group was mainly under the leadership of the central Party Propaganda Department. As a result, although the government was the owner according to the law, effective control was handed over to the Party. This hybrid structure struck a convenient compromise between the ideological control of the Party and the commercialization.

Similar arrangements on ownership were adopted by corporatized provincial publishing groups. For most of them, the Finance Departments of provincial governments supervise the operation of state-owned asset, and ideological issues are controlled by local Party propaganda departments. However, as the finance departments of local governments do not have specialized staff or essential expertise to supervise the business operation of publishing groups (Zhou and Xiao, 2010), publishing groups are mainly under the control of local Party propaganda departments.

The policy of corporatization, however, was not welcomed in many publishing houses and groups. Most of them were transformed into enterprises mainly because of the determination of the central party-state. Impatient with the slow pace of restructuring and the tacit resistance from many publishing houses, GAPP set a deadline in 2008 requiring most publishing houses and publishing groups to be transformed into enterprises within three years (Liu, 2008a). Only a handful of publishing houses would remain as public service units. According to the policy of the central government, all cultural organizations would be divided into two categories: those serving the "public interest" would remain as public service units, while those operating mainly for profit would be transformed into business enterprises. In book publishing, the People's

Publishing House, the Braille Publishing House, minority language publishing houses, and military-owned publishing houses would remain as "cultural public service units for public interests" (*gongyixing wenhua shiye danwei*), for it might be difficult for them to survive in the market. Although these publishers could get some financial subsidies from the government, they were also required to separate the "business sector" and the "public service sector" within their houses.[5] Only those publishing projects for "public service" would receive subsidies, and the "business sector" of these publishing house would, theoretically, still have to compete in the market for profits. All other publishing houses would be defined as "commercial cultural enterprises" (*jingying xing wenhua qiye danwei*) and would have to be transformed into enterprises. The transformation of publishing houses from public service units into state-owned enterprises was, according to the Director of GAPP, just the first stage of this reform (Liu, 2008b). In the next stage, these state-owned publishing enterprises would be transformed into shareholding companies, which he described as the "dominant form of socialist ownership" (ibid). In the book distribution business, most provincial Xinhua bookstores (except for those in Tibet) were transformed into enterprises by the end of 2009.

The People's Publishing House, which serves as a main outlet of propaganda books of the party-state, was initially handed over to China Publishing Group. But as it was defined as a public service unit, this move was incompatible with the status of China Publishing Group as a corporation, so it was handed back to GAPP in May 2006. The central government left the legal status of provincial People's Publishing Houses to be decided by local governments (Chen, 2006). After a short period of indecision, most of them were transformed into enterprises, though provincial governments continued to subsidize specific publishing projects.

Corporatization was not just a change of titles for publishing houses or publishing groups, there were three major substantive tasks to be carried out in the process. The first task was to clarify the ownership of the state-owned assets of publishing houses. As government departments were forbidden to own enterprises, many publishing houses, which used to be affiliated to government departments, had to adjust their ownership. This usually meant the unwilling handover of ownership by a government department to another organization. The second task was to assess the value of the state asset held by a publishing house to arrive at a figure, which would then be used as a benchmark in evaluating its future economic performance. How to deal with the large unsold book stock of publishing houses was at the core of this task. The third task, which was the most difficult, was to change the status of the staff of publishing houses from cadres in the public sector to employees of business enterprises. Although this shift may theoretically lead to more autonomy in personnel management for the directors of publishing houses, it also meant that the income of most staff would become linked to the economic performance of their publishing houses, coupled with the decrease of their pensions and the loss of the guarantee of a life-long job. Some publishing houses and publishing groups were also facing the additional task of getting listed on the stock market, a move which would not only channel more funds into the publishing houses, but also diversify the ownership.

6.2 THE STATUS OF PUBLISHING HOUSES

Many researchers assume that all Chinese media institutions had always been defined as public service units until 2003, before the start of corporatization. This assumption, however, does not apply to the publishing industry. Although most publishing houses were "public service units," most of them had actually been defined legally as enterprises before the economic reform.

As discussed in Chapter 3, From Communization to Commercialization: China's Publishing From 1949 to 1992, the party-controlled publishers were handed over to the government after 1949, and most book publishing houses became enterprises while newspaper publishers became public service units. For publishing houses, however, being defined as public service units or enterprises did not make much difference during the period of the planned economy, as both were strictly controlled by the party-state. Song Muwen, the former Director of SPPA (State Press and Publication Administration), has provided a detailed description of the historical evolution of the status of publishing houses (Song, 2004a). At the beginning of the 1950s, most state-owned publishers were defined in official documents as enterprises[6] and it was only in the 1960s that the Ministry of Culture proposed to transform several national publishers into public service units in a campaign to rectify the "political mistakes in their publications." The purpose of this proposal was to restrict the impact of profit-seeking on ideological control. But the Ministry of Finance refused this proposal on the ground that publishing houses should not enjoy both the better salaries paid in public service units and the extra bonuses paid in state-owned enterprises (Song, 2004b).

Interestingly however, the Shanghai Municipal Publishing Bureau adopted this proposal and transformed several affiliated publishing houses, such as the Shanghai People's Publishing House and the Shanghai Literature and Art Publishing House, into public service units (Song, 2005). Only the editorial departments were retained by these publishers, while the production departments were hived off and merged with a local printing company to form the Shanghai Publishing and Printing Company, which provided production services for these publishers. These publishing houses, with only editorial responsibility, became public service units and were fully financed by the municipal government. This seems to be the earliest instance of an effective separation of the editorial department from other departments in a publishing house, a practice that was proposed again by the central government four decades later. But this was an exception to the general rule that, before the economic reform, "most publishing houses, which were economically self-sustainable, operated as enterprises, a few publishing houses which could not make enough profit operated as public service units" (Song, 2001).

After the start of economic reforms, the central government approved a plan in 1982 to increase the salaries of civil servants in government departments and public service units. To address the "low salary level" in its affiliated national publishers, the Ministry of Culture reclassified those publishing houses as "public service units managed as enterprises" in 1983. Due to this redefinition, the bonus system practiced in enterprises was terminated in those publishing houses, but the salary level was greatly improved and the average total income of their staff increased. All other publishing houses followed suit. Song Muwen, one of the then policy makers, recollected in his memoir that another major goal of redefining publishing houses as public service units was to ensure their political direction when they were becoming increasingly aggressive in their pursuit of profit after the start of economic reforms (Song, 2004a: 17). The bonus system, however, was reintroduced into publishing houses in 1984 when the central government decided to devolve more operational autonomy to state-owned enterprises. Since then, publishing houses had always been defined as "public service units managed as enterprises" before the start of corporatization.

Before most publishing houses were forced to transform into enterprises, there had been debates in professional journals on the question of whether publishing houses should be defined as public service units or enterprises.[7] Although these debates may seem at first sight to be both arcane and technical, they had an important ideological dimension. The key issue was whether they should operate for "economic benefit" (*jingji xiaoyi*) or so-called "social benefit" (*shehui xiaoyi*). Or, to put it another way, whether they should be mainly profit-oriented or not. The party-state has always demanded that publishing houses achieve both "economic benefit" and "social benefit," which was known as "dual benefits" (*shuangxiao*). But the relative importance of these two "benefits" varied. Publishing houses under the planned economy mainly served as the mouthpiece of the Party and were under no economic pressure to generate profits. Although they were defined as enterprises during that period, they enjoyed little autonomy (Song, 2004c). After the start of economic reforms however, profit-seeking was actively encouraged by the party-state and the balance gradually tilted in favor of "economic benefit" when state-owned enterprises greatly increased their operational autonomy and became primarily profit-oriented. As publishing houses were still defined as enterprises however, the party-state faced the dilemma of encouraging profit-seeking while also keeping them within the boundary of the party line. Although the consideration of increasing the income of employees was behind the shift of most publishing houses from enterprises to public service units in 1983, ensuring the "(correct) political direction" (Song, 2004a) was the main ideological reason for the legal status of publishing houses to be redefined as public service units. If publishing houses had still been "defined as enterprises," they would have had to struggle for "continual increase of annual profit" in order to increase the income of their staff, which might lead to "deviation from the (political) direction of publishing" (Song, 2001).

The policy of "public service units managed as enterprises" was the result of the compromise struck between the demands of a "socialist market economy" and the need to maintain a "socialist spiritual civilization" (Song, 2005). The adoption of corporatization by the central government, however, did not mean that the party-state would relinquish its grip on the publishing industry. According to Liu Binjie, the then Director of GAPP, the "social benefit" should still be upheld as "the first priority" in the pursuit of "dual benefits" (Liu, 2004a). At the same time, corporatization also aimed to "achieve a new stage of connecting the publishing houses more closely with the market" under the new context of "socialist market economy" (Song, 2004c).

Although the phrase "social benefit" is mainly used as a euphemism for the ideological interests of the Party, it does also contain a dimension of public interest. Institutionally, the Braille Publishing House and some minority languages publishing houses have been defined as "public service units" so that books for disadvantaged social groups that may not survive in a system governed purely by market competition could still be published. This principle extends more generally to a variety of other books with less commercial potential, such as academic books, ancient classics, and books for other disadvantaged social groups (such as peasants and migrant workers in the cities). In the case of propaganda books however, the party-state intentionally deploys claims to "social interest" to conceal its ideological interests. Interestingly, publishing houses have sometimes also used the ideological concerns of the Party as an excuse to conceal their own pursuit of economic interests, as exemplified by their change of status from enterprises into "public service units" in 1983 in pursuit of increased salaries.

6.3 THE REFORM OF PUBLIC SERVICE UNITS AND THE TRANSFORMATION OF PUBLISHING HOUSES

As "public service units managed as enterprises," publishing houses were granted a certain degree of autonomy. They operated in a similar way to state-owned enterprises except for the lack of certain legal rights, such as the rights in personnel management, disposal of the state-owned asset, merger and acquisition, and financing from other sources. The corporatization of publishing houses needs to be seen as part of a much broader reform of the whole public service units system.

6.3.1 Social Backcloth for the Reform of Public Service Units

In addition to providing a range of basic public services such as health care, schooling, and libraries, public service units (*shiye danwei*) in China also cover a range of other areas, including broadcasting and sports organizations. Unlike their counterparts in Western countries, they are closely intertwined with the government and some even assume administrative responsibilities. Under the planned economy the pervasive power and responsibilities of the state meant that it controlled many services which could have been run commercially or by nongovernment organizations. The elimination of market mechanisms and private businesses also left the state as the only possible provider of many services. As a result, the number of public service units was huge.

According to *Regulation on the Registration and Administration of Public Service Units* issued in 1998,[8] public service units usually have the following characteristics:

- The purpose of their establishment is for the "social public benefit." Even though they may charge for their services their ultimate goal is not commercial profit;
- They are funded by the government or by the state-owned assets of other organizations;
- They provide public services such as education, research, health care, and cultural services.

Although this regulation was promulgated after the start of economic reform, it offers a workable definition of public service units in any period. The party-state, for ideological reasons, wanted publishing houses to operate as public service units promoting "social benefit" rather than as purely profit-seeking enterprises, which fits the first requirement in the above definition. However, as the state was reluctant to subsidize the publishing industry from its already tight financial budget, publishing houses did not meet the second requirement. This discrepancy provided the basis for the debates about the status of publishing houses.

Together with government departments and state-owned enterprises, public service units were one of the most important social organizations in China during the period of planned economy (Wang, 2004: 136; Huang, 2000: 2). After the start of economic reform, as both government departments and state-owned enterprises underwent several rounds of reform, public service units came under increasing pressure to change (Wang, 2004). Their reform was an essential dimension of the general economic reform.

The first reason for the reform of public service units was the huge financial burden they presented. It was estimated that the total number of public service units was over one million, employing nearly 30 million by 2002, 41% of the total number of employees in the public sector[9] (World Bank, 2005: 10). Although only 47.6% of the total expenditure of public service units came from the government budget in 2002, it already accounted for one-third of the total fiscal expenditure of the government (ibid: 12 and 10; Cheng, 2001), which was a huge financial burden for the government. Despite the fact that the government greatly increased its budget to public service units between 2000 and 2002, most of this additional funding was spent on the increased number of employees and the increase of staff salaries (World Bank, 2005). Relieving this burden became the main target of the initial reform of public service units.

The second reason for the reform was the perceived decline in the quality of the services they provided and the negative impact of their business activities on the economy. Public service units were funded in three different ways. They could be fully or partially funded by the government, or be fully self-funded. Since the government could not afford to underwrite the entire budget for all public service units, it had to allow those that were partially funded to charge fees for their services or operate business activities in order to raise extrabudgetary revenues. For those fully self-funded public service units, such as publishing houses, the government offered some preferential economic policies in exchange for services. However, the incentive of profit-seeking in many public service units not only shifted the financial burden to the public, it also led to a decline in service quality, due to the lack of real pressure from market competition and effective supervision from government (Reform of Public Service Units Research Team, 2003; World Bank, 2005). The inefficiency of public service units caused severe social problems for disadvantaged social groups in their access to key social services such as health and education. The profit-seeking activities in public service units also brought about the problem of slush funds and corruption (Xu, 2004). As their accounting systems were not as rigid as government departments, many government departments treated their affiliated public service units as their backyard profit centers (World Bank, 2005: 11). It has also been noted that some public service units transferred nonoperating assets to operating assets in their business activities, a move which resulted in a substantial loss of state-owned assets (Cheng, 2001: 324). In addition, public service units were eager to expand their business activities to increase their profits, but the benefits they enjoyed from preferential economic policies created unfair competition (Gu, 2005). This had negative impact on the nascent market economy that the government was endeavoring to foster (Wang, 2004; Reform of Public Service Units Research Team, 2003). Lastly, public service units continued to tie up enormous economic resources, such as well-educated professionals and very substantial state assets (World Bank, 2005), some of which could have been diverted into economic activities or deployed much more efficiently in the market.

The low levels of efficiency in public service units were another reason for the impetus to reform them. Public service units had a number of features in common with government bodies. Their staff were included in the quota for government bodies (Cheng, 2001: 320) and their employees had ranking positions corresponding to those in government bodies with staff of same rank usually receiving the same level of salary. The relatively generous remuneration coupled with de facto life-long employment attracted people to "flood to the increasingly swollen institutions" (ibid). In addition, many redundant officials in government departments were transferred into their affiliated public service units during the reshuffle of government departments (World Bank, 2005: 11). The bureaucratic style of personnel management was also seen as suppressing "the motivation and innovation of employees" (Cheng, 2001: 320), reinforcing low efficiency. Another reason for their low efficiency was that public service units were segregated and isolated due to their different controlling entities. This made it difficult for them to coordinate and cooperate among themselves, which resulted in the waste of resources as similar services or organizations were duplicated (Reform of Public Service Units Research Team, 2003: 76).

Attempts to address some of these problems began in the mid-1980s. The early reform focused on giving public service units more autonomy at the operational level and allowing them to raise their own revenues in the market (*chuangshou*). Although this policy helped relieve the financial burden on government to some extent, it led to other problems (ibid, 2003: 74) discussed above.

The reform of public service units lagged behind the efforts to restructure state-owned enterprises for several reasons. According to Cheng (2001: 319), this is partly due to the priority given to economic development during the reform, and partly due to the difficulties presented by the huge number of public service units and their employees. In addition, the reform of public service units required comprehensive reforms in other areas, including the relevant legal system (for nongovernment organizations), fiscal procedures, and the social security system (Reform of Public Service Units Research Team, 2003: 77). Without these accompanying reforms, commentators argued, "reform (of public service units) can hardly be pushed forward successfully" (ibid, 2003: 76).

A key issue in the reform of public service units was their intricate relationships with government departments and state-owned enterprises (*guoyou qiye*) (World Bank, 2005: 11). Public service units were usually supervised and controlled by a government department. Some units also assumed administrative power, and many also owned their business entities. The fundamental issue in the reform was to separate these three different organizations by following the guideline of "separation of government and public service units, separation of public service units and enterprises" (*zhengshi fenkai, shiqi fenkai*). Although the policy of "separation of government and public service units" were decided by the government in July 1996,[10] there could be little real progress when the social security system was not well established, and it was not until the 16th National Party Congress of the CCP in 2002,[11] half a decade later, that the reform of public service units began to gather momentum.

A nationwide reform of these units was initiated by the central government in March 2004 (Lin, 2004). It aimed at "commercializing what can be commercialized, and restructuring the rest" (OECD, 2005: 81). To this end, public service units were classified into three categories, administration units, public service units, and profit-seeking units, based on their different functions. A few of them, which had assumed administrative responsibility, would be merged into government departments. Those that mainly ran as businesses for profit were required to be transformed into enterprises. Consequently many cultural organizations, including publishing houses, which had formerly been classified as "public service units managed as enterprises," were redefined as enterprises, laying the basis for the corporatization of publishing houses.

6.3.2 The Transformation of Publishing Houses

Although many publishing houses preferred to remain as public service units, they could hardly resist a reform policy decided by the central party-state. As Fan Hengshan, a branch leader in the NDRC (the government department of the State Council responsible for designing overall reform policies), made abundantly clear, public service units with substantial business activities had to be transformed into enterprises (Fan, 2004). The impact of the broader reform of public service units on publishing houses was also testified to by many other government officials and professionals involved in the publishing industry. According to Song Muwen, the former director of SPPA, for example, "the reform of public service units is inevitable" and "it is getting impossible" for publishing houses to remain as "public service units managed as enterprises" (Song, 2004c).

The promulgation of corporatization by the central government in 2003 was by no means a smooth process. On the contrary, it was met with a considerable amount of tacit resistance from various vested interests. Publishing houses affiliated to universities or to central state agencies were particularly unwilling to be transformed into enterprises. The presidents of a few high-profile universities expressed their objections to the transformation of their affiliated publishing houses in 2004. According to the President of the People's University, "universities-affiliated presses should not be separated from the teaching and research of the universities" and should not "be transformed into commercial presses" together with other publishing houses (Chubanren, 2004). Faced with this opposition GAPP postponed the implementation of the policy and set a new deadline in June 2008 specifying that publishing houses affiliated to central state agencies and universities must be transformed into enterprises within three years. Although the ideological concerns of the party-state had been an important reason for publishing houses to be defined as "public service units managed as enterprises" in the early 1980s, after corporatization was endorsed by the central government, the main barriers to change came from publishing houses and their sponsoring proprietors.

The first resistance came from the sponsoring proprietors of publishing houses. According to the sponsoring system, publishing houses should be sponsored and owned by either a Party/government department or a state-controlled mass organization. Hence, even if GAPP was determined to push forward with corporatization they needed the cooperation of the sponsoring proprietors. Many publishing houses were owned by ministries of the central government or other central state agencies that were usually more powerful than GAPP in the hierarchical system. These ministries treated their affiliated publishing houses as a well-paid "retirement center" for relocating redundant government officials or using them as backyard profit centers.[12] As government departments are not allowed to own any enterprises or business entities, corporatization would force them to give up these benefits.

The intricate relationship between publishing houses and their sponsoring state agencies was the result of the sponsoring system, which requires media organizations to be affiliated to a "sponsor unit" (Zhao, 2008: 80). It, together with "the licensing system," ensured the party-state's continuing control during the process of media commercialization. Although this regulation was only officially promulgated in the 1990s, it had already become a national practice after the elimination of private publishers in mid-1950s. It was reiterated in ideological rectification campaigns after the student movements in 1986 and 1989. Based on the experience of these campaigns the SPPA promulgated a provisional sponsor unit regulation in 1993 (Song, 2003). This regulation was finally endorsed by the State Council in the *Publishing Administration Regulation* promulgated in 1997.

The sponsor unit regulation is "an important policy" for ensuring "the ideological safety and healthy development" of the publishing industry (Song, 2003), but also had the effect of cementing a close relationship between Party organs or government departments and their affiliated publishing businesses. After the economic reform, these publishing houses became the source of slush funds for their sponsoring proprietors, who in turn assisted in the compulsory distribution of titles from their affiliated publishers by using their administrative power. The collusion between them made compulsory distribution a serious problem, particularly for disadvantaged social groups without the political power to resist this exploitation or the economic ability to comply with it. Compulsory distribution became such a rampant social problem that it attracted the attention of the top leaders of the Party in 2003 and the central government started to crack down on it.

Another problem resulting from the sponsor unit regulation was the segregation of the publishing industry during its commercialization. Mergers and acquisitions were impeded by the sponsoring proprietors' unwillingness to lose their control over their affiliated publishing businesses. This, according to the former GAPP Director, was "an important reason that many newspaper and book publishers can hardly grow bigger and stronger" (Shi, 2003). In addition, local governments tried to protect their local publishing industry by setting up trade barriers.

The sponsor unit regulation as a mechanism of securing ideological control was therefore in contradiction with the goal of turning publishing houses into independent business entities in the market. Some officials from the GAPP were well aware of this.[13] As Song Muwen, the former Director of SPPA noted, while ideological considerations required publishers to be affiliated to their sponsoring proprietors, the central government also "required publishers to be separated from sponsoring organizations in order to deepen the reform and foster the development (of publishing industry)" (Song, 2003). One solution to this contradiction put forward by an official from NDRC, was to discontinue the sponsoring system (see Fan, 2004). A modified version of this proposal was pursued by GAPP when they adjusted the sponsor unit regulation. On the one hand, provincial publishers were required to be separated from their previous sponsoring proprietors, which were the provincial Press and Publication Administration Bureaus, during their transformation into enterprises. On the other hand, they had to find a new sponsoring organization according to the sponsor unit regulation. The emerging provincial publishing groups met this need perfectly and became the new sponsoring organization of provincial publishers.

Many publishing houses affiliated to central state agencies (*buwei chubanshe*) were also subject to these competing demands during their process of corporatization, and in some cases the China Publishing Group became the new sponsoring proprietor of a couple of this kind of publishers. The Huawen Publishing House, affiliated to the United Front Work Department of the central Party (*zhongyang tongzhanbu*), and the China Democracy and Law Publishing House (*zhongguo minzhu fazhi chubanshe*), affiliated to the National Congress, both became new subsidiaries of China Publishing Group in 2010 after they were separated from their previous sponsoring organization (Wang, 2010). It seemed then, that the establishment of publishing groups helped to keep publishers within a hierarchical system of ideological control.

Another source of resistance to corporatization came from the publishing houses themselves. Many of them relied heavily on the so-called "system distribution" (*xitong faxing*), which operated compulsory distribution within a hierarchical administration system, for profit (Lin, 2005). The protection provided by the administrative power of their sponsoring proprietors was central to the operation of this system and many publishers were reluctant to relinquish it during the process of corporatization. More importantly, many publishing houses resisted corporatization because of the likely decrease in the income of their employees. Retired employees of publishing houses were used to receiving pensions equivalent to those paid within government departments and other public service units, and those figures were usually much higher than those from state-owned enterprises.[14] Consequently, the transformation of publishing houses into enterprises would mean a considerable drop in pension for most staff. According to the policy of central government, while already retired staff would carry on receiving a higher pension after the transformation, employed staff would have to accept the fact of a decreased pension in the future. Not surprisingly, staff approaching the age of retirement tried to bargain for a better pension settlement. As most of them were senior staff or top leaders in publishing houses or publishing groups, they demanded compensation during the transformation. In meeting these demands publishing houses had to assume a huge financial burden during the process of corporatization. First, in order to hand over the pension arrangements of their employees to the social security system, they had to compensate the latter as many staff had made no contribution to the pension pool held in the social security system. Second, as the social security system for enterprises was only willing to pay the standard amount of pension, publishing houses would have to make good on the income discrepancy for retired staff and also compensate those senior staff approaching the age of retirement.

China's contributory pension scheme, as part of the social security system, was started in 1992 for urban enterprise employees in different provinces, but it was not widely implemented until 1997. However, this system has been under increasing pressure of meeting pension repayments, mainly because of the increasingly aging population and the legacy pensioners who made no contribution to the pension pool before the system was set up (Pozen, 2013). Six provinces already reported deficits in their pension funds in 2015 (Reuters, 2016) and this problem seems to be getting worse. Apparently, taking over the pension arrangement from the public service units for their employees without requiring some compensation to the system would cause deficit problems and also raise questions about the fairness and credibility of the system.

Taking these factors into account it is clear that the costs involved in the corporatization of a publishing house could be substantial. Although tax breaks were given to publishing houses to support their transformation, many still had to seek the financial support from their sponsoring proprietors or even government budgets. In the case of local publishers, local governments often assumed at least part of the cost. For example, the cost of pension compensation during the corporatization of the Liaoning Publishing Group was assumed by the provincial government (Lin, 2005). The Yunnan provincial government paid for the cost of some financial services, such as asset assessment, incurred during the transformation of its provincial publishers (Ren, 2010). The transformation of national publishing houses affiliated to central state agencies tended to be more difficult however. Many senior staff in these publishers used to be government officials, which gave them considerable bargaining power. As most of these publishing houses were overstaffed, the compensation costs were often huge, presenting a major hindrance to their corporatization. If every staff member in a publishing house affiliated to central state agencies was paid about RMB10,000 yuan per year to compensate for the income discrepancy resulting from the different pension systems, then the total cost per year would, according to the estimation of a professional in Beijing,[15] be around RMB50 million yuan (about US $7.85 million) (Lin, 2005). If on average they have to be compensated for 20 years as pensioners, this would be a huge cost.

In addition, as mentioned earlier, the social security system had to be compensated as well. After the pension scheme was established in 1992, many publishing houses and their staff made no contribution to it. The social security system therefore required publishing houses to reimburse the contribution back to 1992 before it would agree to take over the pension arrangements of their staff. This constituted another huge financial burden for publishing houses.

Different publishing houses had to bargain with their sponsoring proprietors and local social security systems before they agreed to be transformed into enterprises.[16] As many publishing houses were affiliated to central state agencies based in Beijing, it became a problem for the Beijing municipal social security system. According to the so-called No. 105 document issued by the State Council in 2003, publishing houses that had been transformed into enterprises would only need to pay the social security system from the date of their transformation. That would place the entire financial burden on the Beijing municipal social security system, which was not willing to assume all the costs. It was estimated by several deputy-directors of publishing houses affiliated to central state agencies that "a middle-sized publishing house would have to reimburse (the social security system) by at least RMB60 million yuan (around US $9.42 million) just for the pensions of its staff" (see Hu et al., 2008). But after some bargaining between GAPP and the Beijing municipal social security system, publishing houses were finally exempted from reimbursing the contributions before 2003, which had the effect of shifting the financial burden onto the public.

By operating as "public service units managed as enterprises," publishing houses concealed the true costs of their pension contributions. In addition, many obtained hidden subsidies from their sponsoring proprietors. Many university-affiliated publishing houses, for example, received university administration services and office buildings for free. All these costs would have to be borne by the publishing houses themselves after their corporatization (Hou, 2005). The loss of hidden subsidies to their business operations was another reason for many publishing houses to resist the transformation.

6.4 ECONOMIC SUSTAINABILITY AND THE CORPORATIZATION OF PUBLISHING HOUSES

In 2003, the publishing industry was rated as one of the most profitable businesses in China (Wei, 2004) and there had never been a bankruptcy in any state-owned publishing house. But as illustrated above, many publishing houses would have been struggling to survive if all the hidden operational costs were taken into account. Although they were subsidized in different ways, many, according to a Deputy Director of GAPP, were "running out of cash flow" and were "facing survival crisis" (Liu, 2006c). The serious economic problems they faced were manifest in the excess inventories they carried. Two factors had at least partially contributed to this situation. First, publishing houses were not willing to reduce their title output or to liquidate their unsold book stock. When directors of publishing houses reported to their sponsoring proprietors, the factors that were taken into account when assessing their performance usually included title output, total list price, profits, and book prizes (usually state-controlled) received (Li, 2005). Consequently, they tended to invest heavily in some books in order to compete for prizes with little regard for their "marketability" and "economic returns" (ibid). The outcome was often excess inventory. More importantly, a stable title output was essential both for keeping the staff of publishing houses employed and for the manipulation of profits. Directors were therefore more concerned with keeping their publishing house running than with earning reasonable economic returns, so that, even though they knew that many publishing projects would hardly be able to break even, they still approved the publishing plans.

Publishing houses were also unwilling to liquidate unsalable book stock. When they were public service units with less strict accounting regulations, they often chose not to devalue their inventories in order to boost their reported profits[17] and the asset value. Although they were authorized to devalue their inventory year by year, "few (publishing houses) have actually implemented (the policy)" (Miao, 2005). If the book inventory was liquidated, it would appear as a financial loss in the accounts. But if it was not liquidated, the increased unsold book stock could be listed as an increased state asset (An, 2006). In addition, if the liquidation of book stock exceeded the amount permitted by the Tax Law, publishing houses would have to pay income tax (Bao, 2005; Liu, 2004b), which also discouraged publishers from liquidating their book stocks.

The second reason contributing to excess inventories was that publishing houses as public service units did not have full operational rights in disposing of asset endowed by the state. Since book inventories were regarded as state assets, publishing houses normally had to follow strict bureaucratic procedures in order to liquidate them. They not only had to acquire the approval of their sponsoring proprietors, but also "the endorsement and agreement of (relevant) finance department" (An, 2006). As a result, even though book inventories incurred extra warehousing costs, the rules governing publishing houses as public service units "encouraged the huge increase of book inventories" (Miao, 2005: 5).

But if the economic situation of many publishing houses was stark, why hadn't there been a single case of a publishing house going bankrupt? This was partly because public service units were legally not allowed to go bankrupt. They could be terminated by government order but all their debts would then have to be borne by their sponsoring proprietors. And it was also partly because publishing houses could rely on additional sources for cash flow or for profit. Bank loans were an obvious option, and it was said that some publishing houses were surviving on them.[18] But it would become difficult to continue to obtain loans if publishing houses could not make any profit.

Another valuable resource held by state-owned publishing houses was their quota of ISBNs, which constitute licenses to publish. Hence although some publishing houses might not be making any profit, they could sell their ISBNs to private publishers. A qualified editor could hold five ISBNs from GAPP. If each of these is sold for 20,000 yuan (around US$3,140),[19] the income a small publishing house could earn from selling ISBNs to private publishers "would be enough for the salary expenses of the whole year" (Liu, 2006a). Although private publishers depend on state-owned publishers to acquire publishing licenses, since they are usually more market-oriented and more flexible in their operations, they have also become strong competitors. According to the estimation of publishing professionals, the annual title output from private publishers was around 20,000, which was about one-tenth of the total national annual title output, and in all kinds of bestseller lists "over 80%" of bestsellers were produced by private publishers (Chubanren, 2006). It was estimated that private publishers also accounted for an over 60% share of the school ancillary books market (ibid). With private publishers taking a sizeable share of the overall market and profits, state-owned publishers found themselves under increasing pressure.

In this situation, the most important source of profit of many publishing houses was their continuing monopoly on textbook publishing. It was estimated by some professionals that the annual total profits from school textbook publishing was RMB30 billion yuan (Yuan, 2007) and that 70% of the total profit of the publishing industry came from the textbook market (Cao and Jiang, 2008). Similarly, most provincial publishing groups or publishing general houses relied on textbook reprinting for over half of their profits (Chang, 2005). Although there was no reliable official data to verify these figures, it was widely acknowledged that textbook publishing was and still is the key profit source not only for publishing houses, but also for Xinhua bookstores. It was reported that over 70% of the profits of most Xinhua bookstores came from the distribution of textbooks with this figure rising up to 90% for many lower-level Xinhua bookstores (ibid).

If the profit from textbook publishing was the cornerstone of the economic sustainability of the state-owned publishing industry, this cornerstone was under threat.

First, due to the one-child policy implemented for decades, the numbers of schools and enrolled students had been declining steadily (see Table 6.1). Compared with 2006, the total number of students in compulsory education in 2011 declined from 166.6948 million to 149.9317 million, a 10.1% decrease. This drop led inevitably to a shrinking market size and profit margin for textbook publishing. China had been relaxing its rigid one-child policy to some extent since the late 1990s, but only scrapped this policy in 2015. It will still be a few years before the student numbers start to increase significantly.

Table 6.1 Numbers of students and schools during the stage of compulsory education (2006–11)

	2006	2007	2008	2009	2010	2011
Primary schools (thousand)	341.6	320.1	300.9	280.2	257.4	241.2
Students enrolled in primary schools (million)	107.1153	105.64	103.3151	100.7147	99.4070	99.2637
Junior middle school (thousand)	60.885	59.4	57.9	56.3	54.9	54.1
Students enrolled in junior middle schools (million)	59.5795	57.3619	55.8497	54.4094	52.7933	50.6680

Source: Ministry of Education.[20]

Secondly, educational reform had also been squeezing the profits of publishers. During the period of the planned economy, the government developed a set of national textbooks, which was published by the People's Education Press in Beijing and distributed to schools by Xinhua bookstores at different hierarchical levels. As discussed before, in order to save on the costs of production and transportation, the publishing of school textbooks followed a practice known as "plate-renting" which allowed provincial publishing administration departments to rent printing plates from the People's Education Press by paying a 3%–4% royalty,[21] and arranging for reprinting and distribution locally. During the period of the centrally planned economy, all profits from the publishing industry were essentially controlled by a more or less monolithic central government and it did not matter too much how the profit cake was split among the different players in this business. After the start of economic reform however, local governments acquired their own interests due to financial decentralization, and book publishers and distributors were turned into profit-oriented business entities. The practice of "plate-renting" carried on after the start of economic reform, and textbook reprinting, without any editorial costs and market uncertainty, became an important profit source for local publishing industries, not only for local publishing administration departments, but also for local printers, paper suppliers, and Xinhua bookstores.[22] However, the central government decided to introduce competition into textbook publishing in order to improve the quality of school education. Since 1999 the Ministry of Education has been promoting a shift from examination-oriented to quality-oriented schooling (*suzhi education*) and it also started to encourage the publishing of different versions of textbooks in 2001. The monopoly of People's Education Press was broken and any publishing house could publish textbooks as long as their versions were approved by the Ministry of Education.

In addition, the central government was also keen on reducing the price of textbooks in order to relieve the financial burden on students, especially those living in rural areas. Because students from poor families could not afford the tuition fees and the textbooks,[23] there was a problem of high drop-out rates from compulsory schooling in rural areas. As a result the price of textbooks became a concern of the central government. An investigation in 2000 found that the cost on textbooks made up around 30% of total financial burden on school students, and concluded that high prices were caused by the monopoly in textbook reprinting and distribution (Chang, 2005). To address this problem the central government decided to introduce the bidding system into the local textbook reprinting and distribution in a couple of pilot provinces in 2002.

Many publishing houses started to enter the textbook publishing business with one account recording 83 publishers producing a wide range of school textbooks.[24] As the market fragmented, the profits from textbook publishing were squeezed. The bidding system also threatened to reduce the cover price and endanger the monopoly of local textbook reprinting centers and local Xinhua bookstores. To avoid this, provincial governments manipulated the bidding procedure in order to maintain the monopolistic profits of local state-owned publishing industries. Consequently, the bidding system implemented in pilot provinces "did not achieve the expected goal" (Chang, 2005) of reducing prices and introducing competition. In order to push forward the reform, the central government instructed the powerful NDRC to extend the textbook bidding system to more provinces. The NDRC, unlike GAPP and the Ministry of Education that had affiliated publishing houses, had no "sectional interest in textbook publishing and distribution" (Chang, 2005) and planned to expand the bidding system nationwide by 2008. However, provincial governments tried to resist the reform in order to protect their affiliated publishing business. According to a leader of NDRC, "some local governments and organizations, out of concern for their own interest, used their administrative power" to "exclude competitors" in the bidding (ibid).

Despite the intention of opening up markets to competition, the manipulated bidding system that emerged from the reforms only served to strengthen the monopoly in textbook publishing and distribution. Before the bidding system was introduced, publishers could promote their textbooks directly to local education departments or schools in other provinces and acquire a reasonable market share. As provincial education departments and publishing administration bureaus were authorized in the bidding system to organize the bidding for textbook printing and distribution for the whole province, they tried to strengthen the monopoly of their provincial publishing groups by forcing nonlocal publishers to license the reprinting rights to local publishing groups. If they refused, the provincial government departments would not include their textbooks in the provincial Catalogue of Approved Textbooks (*jiaoxue yongshu mulu*), effectively excluding them from the whole provincial market, since local schools were only allowed to choose textbooks from this catalogue. The Ministry of Education issued the national catalogue of approved textbooks every year and stipulated that provincial governments were "not allowed to add (any textbooks) to or remove (any textbooks) from" the list (Zhang and Lin, 2008).

The manipulation by provincial governments clearly contradicted this instruction. As a leader of the Ministry of Education commented in an interview in 2008, "it is illegal for provincial governments to use administrative power to force the rent of plates or refuse textbooks listed in national Catalogue of Approved Textbooks to enter local markets" (Zhu, 2008). But he also acknowledged that "there is a rationale for the existence of plate renting practice" (ibid). This recognition of economic necessity suggested that the Ministry of Education had no will to challenge the provincial governments. The normal royalties from licensing the reprinting rights is 3% of the list price. The People's Education Press, which was estimated to have taken about a 50% share of the textbooks market (see Han, 2009), could still afford to "rent plates" to local textbook reprinting centers because it enjoyed economies of scale. Most provincial textbook publishers could at least secure a certain market share in their local market with the support of local governments or swap their market with publishers in other provinces if there was no competition between their textbooks. However, the monopoly of local publishers made it extremely difficult for some national textbook publishers without a local market or for ambitious provincial textbook publishers with just a small local market to compete fairly in the marketplace.

Textbook publishers with a small market share had little chance of making a reasonable return as they had to pay 2% of list price to authors, which would only leave 1% to cover their costs and generate a profit (Zhang and Lin, 2008). As a result, when the NDRC decided to extend the bidding system on a nationwide scale in 2008, this move was opposed by many publishing houses because they worried that the bidding system would be manipulated by provincial governments to strengthen the monopoly of local publishing groups and endanger their survival. Opposition from these publishers was effective, and the extension of the bidding system, which was planned to be implemented in February 2008, had to be halted (ibid) and was finally stopped in November 2008 by the central government (Shandong Publishing and Media Corporation, 2017). At the same time, governments in some rich provinces such as Guangdong and Jiangsu started to provide free textbooks to school students in 2008, although the nationwide provision of free textbooks was not implemented until the spring of 2017.

The bargaining over the implementation of the bidding system in textbook publishing was a manifestation of the conflict between different interests. Although the State Council decided to introduce competition into textbook publishing and distribution in order to improve the quality of textbooks and reduce their cost, it had to take into account the interests of local governments and the local publishing industry, and to tolerate the practice of forced "plates-renting." As an official from the NDRC admitted in 2005, "the reform was not fully implemented" due to the possibility of causing "too many blows to local economic development and social stability," although he affirmed that "the administratively forced plate-renting will be terminated sooner or later" (Chang, 2005). This was destined to be a half-hearted reform since it posed a dilemma for the central government. Although competition in the publishing and distribution of textbook was seen as desirable, the "complete eradication of monopoly in the publishing and distribution of textbooks" would lead to the "sharp decline in the economic income of the whole (state-owned) publishing industry and Xinhua bookstores," which would be a consequence "nobody dares to be responsible for" (Zhang and Lin, 2008). The economic sustainability of the state-owned publishing industry is the prerequisite for the fulfilment of the Party's propaganda task. Publishing houses had always used their profit from textbooks or supplementary learning materials to cross-subsidize the publishing of other books, which is a practice known as *yishu yangshu*. This cross-subsidy seemed to be endangered during the education reform, which started to undermine the economic viability of many publishing houses. In arriving at a response, central government had to balance the Party interest against the economic sustainability of the publishing industry.

Although the attempt to introduce competition into the publishing and distribution of textbooks only achieved limited success, it was generally accepted that it did bring down the price of textbooks to some extent. In provinces which had not introduced the bidding system the government also adopted another measure to achieve this end. According to a directive issued by several central government departments in 2001,[25] the standard price per signature of printed textbooks should be set by central government departments, which included NDRC and GAPP, as a guide price. Provincial governments were then required to use a set formula to calculate the local retail price based on this guide price. Although they could change the standard price per signature according to their particular circumstances, this had to be within the margins allowed by the central government. The central government not only reduced the guide price in 2006 but also set it as a cap price for local governments. There is no official data on the impact of these measures, but according to a report by the Chinese Academy of Social Sciences, the introduction of the bidding system in 2006 led to price falls ranging from 6% to 20% in several provinces (Xu, 2007: 134).

The government also started to promote textbook recycling for some subjects from the spring of 2008 across the country (Sun, 2010). This intervention, although restricted to certain subjects,[26] also reduced demand for textbooks and put a further squeeze on the profits of publishing industry. The declining profits from textbook publishing added to the financial pressures across the whole publishing industry.

GAPP was well aware of the economic problems facing publishing houses. In 2006, Liu Binjie, the then deputy Director of GAPP, acknowledged that many state-owned publishing houses and their business operations were "on the brink of collapse" while private publishers were flourishing. He noted that the private sector was producing about 50,000 titles annually in "cooperation with" state-owned publishers, a fact which he saw as clearly confirming the inability of state-owned publishers to operate alone to "publish books according to the market demand" (Liu, 2006b). Faced with this situation GAPP had been taking steps to maintain the economic sustainability of the state-owned sector.

After the rapid expansion in the early 1980s, the publishing industry gradually entered a stage of stagnation at the beginning of the 1990s. To address this, in an official guideline issued in 1994, GAPP encouraged the industry to shift from a stage "characterized by the increase of scale and amount" (*guimo shuliang zengzhang*) to a stage "characterized by the (increase of) quality and efficiency" (*youzhi gaoxiao*). In pursuit of this aim GAPP controlled both the number of publishing houses and the number of titles they published. The policy of limiting the total ISBNs issued to publishers was implemented in 1994. According to an official of GAPP, this measure was introduced to control both the "blind increase in the total amount of book titles," and the rampant "trading of ISBNs" (*maimai shuhao*) between state-owned and private publishers (BKPCN, 2003). The establishment of publishing groups, by facilitating cross-subsidies across operating divisions also helped to maintain the economic sustainability of some struggling publishing houses, even though this was not its initial purpose. According to Liu Binjie, in an interview conducted by the China Central Television in 2006, for financially struggling publishing houses, the plan was to "ask strong publishing groups to merge, restructure, and acquire them" (Liu, 2006a). The other major plank in the restructuring policy, corporatization, was also regarded by the government as a means of improving the capability of publishing houses to compete in the market and of strengthening the economic sustainability of publishing industry. Liu spoke for many observers of the industry when he noted that the biggest problem facing state publishing houses was the absence of "mechanisms of business operation" and the ability to "participate in the market competition" (Liu, 2006b).

6.5 THE REFORM OF STATE-OWNED ENTERPRISES AND THE COMMERCIALIZATION OF PUBLISHING HOUSES

If the term of "public service units" carried connotations of ideological control in the Chinese context, "managed as enterprises" pointed to the state's commercial ambitions for publishers after the start of the economic reform. Publishing houses, being defined as "public service units managed as enterprises," were not only subject to the impact of the reform of public service units but also the reform of state-owned enterprises (SOEs). As all licensed publishing houses in China are state-owned, their commercialization generally followed the route of the reform of SOEs and so it was not possible to go beyond the boundaries of this process.

Although problems with SOEs are not unique in China, due to their scale and importance, their reform has been of central concern "not only economically but also socially" (Hassard et al., 2007: 3) and remains "at the heart of China's economic reform programme" (ibid: 9). Economists specializing in the restructuring of SOEs have proposed three possible policy interventions; privatization, promoting a competitive market, and improving management at both the state level and the enterprise level (ibid: 21). China's SOE reforms have pursued all three at different times.

The SOEs reforms in China since 1979 can be divided into two stages (Wu, 2005; Brandt et al., 2008). The period between 1979 and 1993 was characterized by expanding autonomy and incentives to enterprise. At the beginning of the reform, profit retention and bonuses were linked to performance in the market after the fulfilment of the state mandatory plan.[27] Profit retention was introduced into Xinhua bookstores from July 1979. Profit remittance to the government was soon replaced by the profit taxes system. From 1987 to early 1990s, the Contract Responsibility System was implemented on a large scale. The main aim of measures introduced during this period was "to change the distribution of power, responsibility, and benefit between the government and the 'insiders' of enterprises (i.e., the managers and workers)" (Wu, 2005: 142).

During the second stage, which started in 1994 and continues into the present, the main aim was to establish a "Modern Enterprise System." Although many enterprises converted themselves into state-owned companies, they were initially only similar to modern corporations "in form" (Wu, 2005: 155). To give some substance to the label, diversification of ownership began to be encouraged from 1999, and large and medium-sized SOEs were required to introduce a shareholding system. This was pursued in several ways including: cross-shareholding among enterprises, the establishment of joint ventures, and restructuring for an initial public offering (IPO).

Although the reform of state-owned publishing houses followed the route taken by the reform of SOEs more generally, it lagged slightly behind due to ideological concerns. When the State Council decided to expand the operational autonomy of SOEs in May 1984, the central Party Propaganda Department and the Ministry of Culture applied this policy to publishing industries a couple of months later (Song, 2006). In a directive issued by the central Party Propaganda Department and SPPA in May 1988,[28] the Contract Responsibility System was encouraged as a pilot reform policy in publishing houses. When the Modern Enterprise System became the guideline for the reform of SOEs, SPPA also instructed publishing houses to explore appropriate ways of implementing this policy in order to improve the management efficiency.

While these reform policies focused on improving management and enhancing competition, changes of ownership required corporatization. As Liu Binjie, the then deputy Director of GAPP, who we quoted earlier, commented, it was legally impossible for publishers to become shareholding companies without corporatization (Liu, 2004b). Remaining as public service units excluded the possibility of diversification of ownership. As noted earlier, the Shanghai Century Publishing Group became the first state-owned shareholding publishing group in November 2005, and the Liaoning Publishing Group managed to get listed on the domestic stock market in December 2007.

The general effectiveness of corporatization in turning state-owned publishers into capable business entities equipped for market competition is questionable however. Take personnel management as an example. Out of concern for social stability, publishing groups and houses were not allowed to lay off extra staff "in principle" during the process of corporatization (Liu, 2004b), which leaves a de facto life-long job for their staff.

More importantly, as the party-state would not relieve its ideological control, publishing houses and groups are still affiliated to agencies of the party-state. They continue to assume propaganda tasks and also, as mentioned in the previous chapter, to receive different kinds of subsidies from the government. As officials of GAPP recognized all too clearly, many publishing houses after corporatization simply changed their title to company but did not become independent business entities in a real sense (Liu, 2009). More cynical observers wryly noted that publishing houses after corporatization should be renamed "enterprises managed as public service units" (*qiye danwei, shiyehua guanli*) (Zhou, 2009).

However, corporatization did open the door for publishing groups to raise funds in the domestic stock market, which would certainly enhance the economic sustainability of the state-owned publishing industry. In 2017, three corporatized publishing groups, China Science Publishing and Media Ltd. (effectively Science Publishing Group), China Publishing and Media Holdings Corporation (effectively China Publishing Group), and Shandong Publishing and Media Corporation (effectively Shandong Publishing Group), managed to get listed on the domestic stock market and others are preparing for it.

6.6 SUMMARY

Corporatization was the second significant policy intervention designed to transform the publishing industry. Although there were ideological concerns over the conversion of publishing houses into independent business entities, as we have seen, the main barriers came from managers and employees working for publishing houses and from the vested interests of their proprietors. However, the general reform of public service units coupled with the growing concern over the economic sustainability of the state-owned publishing industry made the pursuit of corporatization inevitable and laid down the legal foundation for future restructuring.

However, the determination of the party-state to retain its control over the publishing industry renders the effectiveness of corporatization questionable. But how exactly is this control exercised in practical terms? In addition, the rapid adoption of digital technologies may have brought challenges to the existing control mechanism of the party-state. How is the Party managing the challenges while it tries to allow new business models to develop? It is to these questions that we turn now in the next two chapters.

ENDNOTES

1. In August 2001, the General Offices of the Central Party Committee and the State Council issued a document entitled Circular on the Reform of Press, Publishing, Broadcasting and Movie Industries (*guangyu xinwen chuban guangbo yingshiye gaige de tongzhi*), which is commonly known as the *No. 17 Document*. On July 29, 2002, they issued another directive entitled Recommendations of the Propaganda Department and GAPP on Further Strengthening and Improving Publishing Work (*zhongyang xuanchuan bu xinwen chuban zongshu guanyu jinyibu jiaqiang he gaijin chuban gongzuo de ruogan yijian*), which is commonly known as the *No. 16 Document*.
2. Tom.com, a Hong Kong-based company, managed to set up a joint venture with SDX Joint Publishing House in November 2003. Being prohibited from entering the editorial sector, this joint venture focused on noneditorial businesses, such as book distribution and rights trading, of SDX Joint Publishing House.
3. On December 31, 2003, the State Council issued Policy of Supporting the Development of Cultural Industries during the Pilot Reform of Cultural System (Provisional) (*wenhua tizhi gaige shidian zhong zhichi wenhua chanye fazhan de guiding shixing*) and Policy about the Transition of Business-Oriented Cultural Public Service Units into Enterprises during the Pilot Reform of Cultural System (Provisional) (*wenhua tizhi gaige shidian zhong jingyingxing wenhua shiye danwei zhuanzhi wei qiye de guiding shixing*).
4. According to Fan Hengshan, Director General of the Department of Comprehensive Restructuring of Economic System of the National Development and Reform Commission (NDRC), government departments should not directly manage the state-owned assets of publishing houses, and this task should be handled by specialized State-owned Assets Supervision and Administration Commission (*guoziwei*) or something of the kind. He pointed out that, although relevant government departments could still be commissioned to supervise the state-owned assets of publishing houses, this would be just a transitional policy (see Fan, 2004).
5. According Liu Binjie, the then Director of GAPP, "Press and publishing houses with public service responsibilities should deepen their reform and separate their business sector and public service sector" (Liu, 2008c).
6. See Provisional Administrative Decree on Publishing, Printing and Distribution (*guanli shukan chubanye yinshuaye faxingye zanxing tiaoli*), which was promulgated by the State Council on August 16, 1952.
7. See Wang (1999) and Yuan (1999) for an example of earlier debates. See Niu and Yang (2006) for an example of recent debates on the status of university-affiliated publishing houses.
8. This regulation was modified in June 2004 by the State Council, but the definition remained unchanged.
9. According to the report by the World Bank (2005), three other categories of the public sector are the party and government organizations, state-owned enterprises, and other state-sponsored social organizations.
10. In July 1996, the General Office of the CCP Central Committee and the General Office of the State Council promulgated *Several Views on the Reform of Public Service Units*.
11. The 16th National Congress of CCP in November 2002 adopted the policy of "separation of government and public service units" for the reform of public service units. The fifth Plenum of 16th Party Congress in October 2005 adopted the principle of "reform on the basis of different categories" of public service units. Based on this principle, the central Party and the government issued a directive in March 2011 to push forward the reform of public service units, aiming at finishing this process by 2020.

12. According to the deputy director of Guangming Daily Publishing House, most publishing houses owned by ministries had to pay a certain amount of profit, which varied from RMB300 thousand yuan up to RMB1 to 2 million yuan or even more, to their governing ministries (see He, 2005).

13. Wang Tao, an official from GAPP, pointed out that the "sponsor unit regulation" was the institutional cause for a segregated publishing industry (Wang, 2008).

14. The State Council issued a policy in 2008 for five pilot provinces to start the pension reform in public service units. The goal is to bring down the pension level for all public service units to the same level with that of the enterprises. However, little progress was made. The government had to reform the whole pension scheme for all employees in governments and public services units in October 2014.

15. It was an estimated by the Deputy Director of Guangming Daily Press in Beijing (see Lin, 2005).

16. At the time of writing, China has not established a unified national social security system and the local security system has to be responsible for the self-sufficiency of its fund.

17. According to Zhou Liwei, the director of Zhejiang Xinhua Book Distribution Group, "some publishing houses" chose not to devalue their book stock and counted books sent to booksellers as net sales before the end of a financial year despite the fact that many of them were likely to be returned at the beginning of the next financial year, in order to boost their profit in the financial reports (Weng, 2006).

18. This was from an interview with the editorial director of a provincial education publishing house.

19. Estimated by a private publisher (Chubanren, 2008) and based on the exchange rate of 1:6.37.

20. The Ministry of Education publishes an annual Statistical Report on National Education Development (*quanguo jiaoyu shiye fazhan tongji gongbao*).

21. According to a government regulation entitled Further Notice on Strengthening the Administration over the Price of School Texts and Other Issues (*guanyu jinyibu jiaqiang zhongxiaoxue jiaocai jiage guanli deng youguan shixiang de tongzhi*), which was issued by NDRC and GAPP in 2006, the royalties for textbooks in the subjects of fine arts, music, foreign language, and arts are 4%, and for all the rest of the textbooks royalties are 3%.

22. It was usually the publishing general houses or publishing groups that rented the plates from People's Education Press. They sold the textbooks to local Xinhua bookstores at 72% of the list price, and then paid local printers 42% of the list price of the textbooks for production cost and 3%–4% royalty to People's Education Press. For the local publishing general houses or publishing groups, they could easily earn about 27% of the list price of textbooks as their profit with negligible administration cost. This was a sizable amount of income when the huge amount of school students was taken into account (Zhang, 2008).

23. It was only in 2006 that the government announced the policy of free compulsory education to all rural school-age children by the end of 2007.

24. It was said that 2400 textbooks were published for primary schools and 1200 textbooks for middle schools (Zhang and Lin, 2008).

25. This regulation is entitled Administration on the Prices of School Textbooks (*zhongxiaoxue jiaocai jiage guanli banfa*).

26. These subjects are normally considered less important, such as Art, Music, Information Technology, and Physical Education.

27. This is known as the dual-track system.

28. See Several Principles on the Current Reform of Publishing Houses (*guanyu dangqian chubanshe gaige de ruogan yijian*).

REFERENCES

An, M., 2006. Thinking during the process of transformation: views on the prospective industry upheaval and its trend (*biange zhong de sikao—toushi jijiang kaishi de hangye da bianju jiqi weilai zouxiang*). A Vast View on Publishing (*chuban guangjiao*) 2006 (7), 8—13; 2006 (8), 8—13 (in Chinese).

Bao, W., 2005. Different views on book stocks (*guanyu tushu kucun de jidian yiyi*). Information on Publication (*chuban cankao*) 2005 (10). <http://www.heaven-trip.cn/cbck/2005_10xz458/200703/t20070321_361310.htm> (accessed 05.12.08) (in Chinese).

BKPCN, 2003. ISBN number should not be a constraint as long as good books are published (*zhiyao chu haoshu shuhao jiu buying chengwei wenti*). <http://www.bkpcn.com/Web/ArticleShow.aspx?artid = 020180&cateid = A1103>(accessed 19.12.08) (in Chinese).

Brandt, L., et al., 2008. China's industrial development. In: Brandt, L., Rawski, T.G. (Eds.), China's Great Economic Transformation. Cambridge University Press, Cambridge, pp. 569—632.

Cao, L., Jiang, H., 2008. Unbreakable interest chain—textbook recycling: whose cheese is moved (*chebuduan de liyi liantiao jiaocai xunhuan: dong le shuide nailao*). People's Daily (*renmin ribao*), 29 February. <http://news.xinhuanet.com/politics/2008-02/29/content_7690083.htm> (accessed 08.12.08) (in Chinese).

Chang, H., 2005. Breaking the ice of monopoly in school textbook publishing and distribution (*zhongxiaoxue jiaocai chuban faxing longduan pobing*). Finance and Economy (*caijing*) 2005 (19), <http://edu.people.com.cn/GB/44071/3711361.html> (accessed 08.12.08) (in Chinese).

Chen, K., 2006. People's publishing house back to GAPP, questions left for regional people's publishing houses (*renmin chubanshe huagui zongshu, difang renminshe hequ hecong*). <http://www.jcph.com/books/bkview.aspx?bkid=109553&cid=320652> (accessed 20.09.10) (in Chinese).

Cheng, S., 2001. Studies on Economic Reforms and Development in China. Oxford University Press, Oxford.

Chubanren, 2004. The Government Postponing the Schedule of Corporatisation, Full Commercialization of Universities-affiliated Presses Refuted (*guanfang tuihou gaizhi shijian daxue chubanshe quanpan shangyehua zaofouding*). Publishers (*chubanren*) 2004 (11), <http://book.sina.com.cn/news/v/2004-11-19/3/131321.shtml> (accessed 14.11.08) (in Chinese).

Chubanren, 2006. Private publishers facing assimilation (*minying tushu gongzuoshi mianlian shoubian guifan*). Publishers (*chubanren*) 2006 (9), <http://www.5book.com/Class/zxzx/yenei/2006-9/21/09211206271.html> (accessed 07.12.08) (in Chinese).

Chubanren, 2008. Who is going to be the winner in the implementation of title-based book number application system (*shuhao shiminzhi shuishi yingjia*). Publishers (*chubanren*) 2008 (13), <http://www.syjlb.com/read.php?tid=15767&page=e> (accessed 05.12.08) (in Chinese).

Fan, H., 2004. Corporatization is the fundamental goal of reform of publishing houses (*chuban danwei gaige de jiben fangxiang shi qiyehua*). Communication and Media (*chuanmei*) 2004 (6), 13 (in Chinese).

Gu, X., 2005. The reform of public-sector organizations and the transformation of the nonprofit sector in China: towards an enabling role of the state (*nengcuxing guojia de jiaose: sheye danwei de gaige yu feiyingli bumen de zhuanxing*). Hebei Academic Journal (*hebei xuekan*) 2005 (1), 11—17 (in Chinese).

Han, S., 2009. Ten sets of textbooks witnessing the reform and development of China's education system (*shitao jiaocai jianzheng xinzhongguo jiaoyu de gaige yu fazhan*). <http://cips.chuban.cc/chinapublish/hw/cbfxyj/slgc/200911/t20091106_58042.html> (accessed 08.10.10) (in Chinese).

Hassard, J., et al., 2007. China's State Enterprise Reform: from Marx to the Market. Routledge, London.

He, Y., 2005. Juxtaposition of reform and creation: thoughts on the corporatisation of national publishers in Beijing (*gaige tizhi yu chuangxin jizhi bingju: dui beijing diqu zhongyangji chubanshe tizhi gaige de ruogan sikao*). Beijing Observation (beijing guancha) 2005 (6), <http://www.bjzx.gov.cn/pub/lanmus/6/detail_jsp_qid_e595_qsc_lanmuId_e6.htm> (accessed 17.11.08) (in Chinese).

Hou, K., 2005. Key tasks in the corporatisation of universities-affiliated presses (*daxueshe gaizhi guanjiandian*). Information on Publication (*chuban cankao*) 2005 (1). <http://www.pep.com.cn/cbck/2005_1sz429/200703/t20070323_364702.htm> (accessed 29.11.08) (in Chinese).

Hu, C. et al., 2008. Suggestions on the reform of publishers affiliated to central state agencies: three modes of developing the productivity of publishing industry (*dui zhongyang buwei chubanshe gaige de jianyi: sange moshi fazhan chuban shengchanli*). <http://www.waterpub.com.cn/Info/InfoDetail1.ASP?id = 4397&CateID = FB> (accessed 29.11.08) (in Chinese).

Huang, H., 2000. Studies on the Reform of Public Service Units (*woguo shiye danwei guanli tizhi gaige yanjiu*). Heilongjian People's Publishing House, Harbin (in Chinese).

Li, J., 2005. Hopes on the reform of publishing (*guanyu chuban gaige de jidian xiaxiang*). China Reading Weekly (zhonghua dushu bao) 15 June (in Chinese).

Lin, C., 2004. Reform of public service units: the kick-start of a massive transformation involving 29 million people (*shiye danwei gaige: yichang sheji 2900 wan ren biange lakai damu*). <http://business.sohu.com/2004/04/15/10/article219841003.shtml> (accessed 13.11.08) (in Chinese).

Lin, X., 2005. Examining the crux of the corporatization of publishers affiliated to central state agencies (*shenshi buwei chubanshe zhuanzhi nandian*). Information on Publication (*chuban cankao*) 2005 (9), 5–7 (in Chinese).

Liu, B., 2002. More autonomy to publishing industry (*gei xinwen chubanye gengduo zizhuquan*). <http://www.booktide.com/news/20021210/200212100012.html> (accessed 30.10.08) (in Chinese).

Liu, B., 2004a. Three strategic choices for China's publishing industry (*zhongguo chubanye de sanda zhanlue xuanze*). <http://learning.sohu.com/20040906/n221894554.shtml> (accessed 29.08.10) (in Chinese).

Liu, B., 2004b. On six issues during the corporatization of publishing industry (*liu binjie tan chubanye zhuanzhi liuda wenti*). <http://www.gmw.cn/01ds/2004-05/19/content_31765.htm> (accessed 10.01.09) (in Chinese).

Liu, B., 2006a. On the reform of publishing industry (*xinwen chuban zhongshu fushuzhang liu binjie: tan chuban tizhi gage*). <http://news.sina.com.cn/c/2006-05-19/19189911418.shtml> (accessed 05.12.08) (in Chinese).

Liu, B., 2006b. China's publishing business is still a weak market (*zhongguo chubanye haishi ruoshi shichang*). Southern Weekend (*nanfang zhoumo*), 5 May. <http://www.southcn.com/weekend/top/200605250018.htm> (accessed 05.01.09) (in Chinese).

Liu, B., 2006c. Pushing forward the modernisation of publishing by using digitization yong (*shuzihua daidong chubanye xiandaihua*). <http://www.gov.cn/gzdt/2006-10/17/content_415195.htm> (accessed 05.01.09) (in Chinese).

Liu, B., 2008a. Reform of cultural system with route and deadline (*wenhua tizhi gaige, jiyou luxiantu yeyou shijianbiao*). <http://news.xinhuanet.com/newmedia/2008-06/19/content_8397524.htm> (accessed 26.03.09) (in Chinese).

Liu, B., 2008b. On the reform of publishing system and the publishing industry during reform (*liu Binjie tan chuban tizhi gaige yu gaige zhong de chubanye*). <http://www.bkpcn.com/Web/ArticleShow.aspx?artid = 075587&cateid = A02> (accessed 01.11.08) (in Chinese).

Liu, B., 2008c. Implementing the policy of central party and striving for good performance of publishing industry during a special period (*jianjue guanche zhongyang bushu quanli zuohao tebie shiqi de xinwen chuban gongzuo*). <http://www.gapp.gov.cn/cms/html/21/1006/200807/458845.html> (accessed 01.11.08) (in Chinese).

Liu, B., 2009. Restructuration and prospect of China's publishing industry (*zhongguo chubanye de chonggou yu zhanwang*). <http://www.sdxwcb.gov.cn/wxzl/20090831094437.htm> (accessed 08.09.10) (in Chinese).

Miao, L., 2005. Book stock during corporatization (*zhuanzhi zhong de tushu kucun*). Information on Publication (*chuban cankao*) 2005 (9), 5—6 (in Chinese).

Niu, T., Yang, X., 2006. Thoughts on the Reform of Universities-affiliated Press (*daxue chubanshe gaige de sikao*). Publishing Science (chuban kexue) 2006 (1), <http://www.cbkx.com/2006-1/856.shtml> (accessed 03.11.08) (in Chinese).

OECD, 2005. Governance in China. Organisation for Economic Co-operation and Development, Paris.

Pozen, R.C., 2013. Tackling the Chinese Pension System. The Paulson Institute, Chicago.

Ren, W., 2010. Four Breakthroughs during the reform of cultural system in Yunnan (*yunnan wenhua tizhi gaige shixian sida tupo*). Guangming Daily (guangming ribao) 02 March. <http://www.gmw.cn/content/2010-03/03/content_1063665.htm> (accessed 10.09.10) (in Chinese).

Reform of Public Service Units Research Team (*shiye danwei tizhi gaige yanjiu ketizu*), 2003. Several fundamental issues demanding solutions during the reform of public service units (*shiye danwei tizhi gaige zhong xu yanjiu jiejue de jige yuanzexing wenti*). Management World (*guanli shijie*) 2003 (1), 71—77 (in Chinese).

Reuters, 2016. China's pension funds under pressure with rising payments: Xinhua. <https://www.reuters.com/article/us-china-economy-pensions/chinas-pension-funds-under-pressure-with-rising-payments-xinhua-idUSKCN11C137?il = 0> (accessed 01.08.17).

Shandong Publishing and Media Corporation, 2017. Shandong publishing and media corporation IPO prospectus (*shandong chuban shouci gongkai faxing gupiao zhaogu shuoming shu*). <http://stock.qlmoney.com/bulletin/85233866919.html> (accessed 03.12.17) (in Chinese).

Shi, Z., 2003. Further improvement of the sponsoring unit system in press and publication industry (*xinwen chubanshu shuzhang shi zongyuan: yao jinbibu wanshan xinwen chuban de zhuguan zhuban zhidu*). <http://www.fsa.gov.cn/web_db/sdzg2004/internet/person/bgov/cbwzyyl/c2003070002.htm> (accessed 24.11.08) (in Chinese).

Song, M., 2001. Publishing houses are enterprises publishing spiritual products (*chubanshe shi shengchan jingshen chanpin de chuban qiye*). Publishing Science (chuban kexue) 2001 (2), 4—8 (in Chinese).

Song, M., 2003. Investigation into the evolvement and adjustment of sponsoring unit system in book publishing (*chuban danwei zhuguan zhuban zhidu de youlai yu tiaozheng de tansuo*). Publishing Science (chuban kexue) 2003 (4), 4—6 (in Chinese).

Song, M., 2004a. Historical investigation into and current thinking on the issue of corporatisation of publishers (*chuban danwei zhuanzhi wenti de lishi kaocha yu xianshi sikao*). Communication and Media (chuanmei) 2004 (6), 14—22 (in Chinese).

Song, M., 2004b. Letters on the essence of publishing houses as enterprises (*guanyu chubanshe qiye shuxing wenti de tongxin*). Publishing Science (chuban kexue) 2004 (2), 4—7 (in Chinese).

Song, M., 2004c. Necessity and importance of corporatisation of publishing houses (*chubanshe zhuanzhi de biyaoxing jiqi zhongyao yiyi*). Publishing Science (chuban kexue) 2004 (4), 4—8 (in Chinese).

Song, M., 2005. Correspondence between several publishers (*chuban ren liangdi shu*). China Reading Weekly (zhonghua dushu bao) 26 January (in Chinese).

Song, M., 2006. Retrospection over the reform of book publishing: part two (*chuban tizhi gaige de lishi huigu: xia*). China Publishing Journal (zhongguo chuban) 2006 (6), 11—17 (in Chinese).

Sun, Z., 2010. Challengs in the recycling of school textbooks (*jiaokeshu xunhuan shiyong mianlin de tiaozhan*). <http://www.xhyww.com/Article_Show.asp?ArticleID = 4852> (accessed 09.10.10) (in Chinese).

Wang, K., 2010. China publishing group taking over Huawen publishing house and starting to transform it into an enterprise (*zhongguo chuban jituan chongzu huawen chubanshe, quanmian qidong zhuanqi gaizhi*). <http://media.people.com.cn/GB/40606/11739010. html> (accessed 25.09.10) (in Chinese).

Wang, T., 2008. Pushing forward the strategic restructuration of publishing industry (*dali tuijin chuban chanye de zhanlue chongzu*). <http://www.xwcbj.gd.gov.cn/news/html//ldjh/article/1199677931966.html> (accessed 14.11.08) (in Chinese).

Wang, Z., 2004. Study on the reform of public service unit (*shilun shiye danwei tizhi gaige*). Gansu Social Science (gansu shehui kexue) 2004 (6), 136—138 (in Chinese).

Wang, Y., 1999. Public Service Units or Enterprises (*shiye hu qiye hu*). Publishing Research (*chuban faxing yanjiu*) 1999 (1), 1—15 (in Chinese).

Wei, Y., 2004. China's ten most profitable businesses in 2003 (*2003 zhongguo shida baoli hangye zhi chubanye*). <http://news.xinhuanet.com/book/2004-02/19/content_1322157.htm> (accessed 20.08.08) (in Chinese).

Weng, C., 2006. Unreserved reform: Zhejiang United Publishing Group (*buliu huanxiang de gaige: wenhua tizhi gaige shidian baodao zhi zhejiang chuban llianhe jituan*). Publishers (*chubanren*), 2006 (11). <http://blog.sina.com.cn/s/blog_4ae796e3010007m4.html> (accessed 04.12.08) (in Chinese).

World Bank, 2005. Deepening Public Service Unit Reform to Improve Service Delivery (*shenhua shiye danwei gaige, gaishan gonggong fuwu tigong*). <http://www.worldbank.org. cn/Chinese/content/psu_ch1.pdf> (accessed 01.11.08) (in Chinese).

Wu, J., 2005. Understanding and Interpreting Chinese Economic Reform. Thomson Texere, New York.

Xu, J., 2004. Analysis on the routes of public service units reform (*shiye danwei tizhi gaige silu de fenxi*). Social Sciences in Hubei (hubei shehui kexue) 2004 (11), 155—156 (in Chinese).

Xu, S., 2007. Speeding up the development of publishing industry to facilitate the prosperity of cultural industries (*jiakuai fazhan chuban chanye, cujin woguo wenhua chanye de zhenxing*). In: Zhang, X., Hu, H., Zhang, J. (Eds.), Year 2007: Annual Report on the Development of China's Cultural Industries (*2007 nian: zhongguo wenhua chanye fazhan baogao*). Social Sciences Academic Press, Beijing, pp. 131—140. (in Chinese).

Yuan, L., 1999. On the legal status of publishing houses (*tantan chubanshe de xingzhi wenti*). Information on Publication (*chuban cankao*), 1999(6), 6; 1999(7), 9 (in Chinese).

Yuan, T., 2007. Who moved the cheese of textbook publishing: the pain the reform of textbook publishing (*shui dongle keben nailao: jiedu zhongxiaoxue jiaocai chuban gaige zhitong*). Democracy and Law (*minzhu yu zazhi shibao*), 10 December. <http://news.xinhuanet. com/edu/2007-12/11/content_7227486.htm> (accessed 08.12.08) (in Chinese).

Zhang, S., 2008. Overview of the publishing of selected works of Mao Tse—Tung in New China (*xin zhongguo chengli hou mao zedong xuanji chuban gaikuang*). Panorama of Party History (*dangshi bolan*) 2008 (11), 16—17 and 42 (in Chinese).

Zhang, Y., Lin, Y., 2008. Who moved the cheese of textbook publishing: a few publishers united against the bidding system in textbook reprinting introduced by national development and reform commission (*shui dongle jiaocai chuban de nailao: duojia chubanshe lianhe fandui fagaiwei jiaocai zuxing zhaobiao*). Southern Weekend (*nanfang zhoumo*), 5 March. <http://www.infzm.com/content/trs/raw/39380> (accessed 08.12.08) (in Chinese).

Zhao, Y., 2008. Communication in China: Political Economy, Power, and Conflict. Rowman & Littlefield, Lanham, Maryland.

Zhou, A., 2009. Warning against the possible problem of enterprises managed as public service units (*jinfang chuxian 'qiye danwei shiyehua guanli'*). <http://www.sinobook. com.cn/press/newsdetail.cfm?iCntno=9213> (accessed 09.10.10) (in Chinese).

Zhou, B., Xiao, X., 2010. Analysis on publishing groups' management and Countermeasures (*chuban jituan gongsi zhili xianzhuang fenxi ji duice yanjiu*). Publishing Research (chuban faxing yanjiu) 2010 (1), 5−10 (in Chinese).

Zhu, Z., 2008. Hidden interest chain in the distribution of school textbooks: textbook distribution faces regional protection (*zhongxiaoxue jiaocai faxing neicang liyilian: keben faxing zao difang baohu*). Evening Legal News (*fazhi wanbao*). 5 September. <http://news.xinhuanet. com/edu/2008-09/05/content_9802144_1.htm> (accessed 10.12.08) (in Chinese).

CHAPTER 7

Digital Publishing: Challenges and Opportunities

Although the recent institutional transformations of China's publishing industry have largely been led and controlled by the party-state, the impact of digital technologies needs to be explored. Following the wide adoption of digital technologies in China, has there been any disruption to the state control over the publishing industry? How is the industry being shaped by the interplay of the Party control, new technologies, and market forces? Focusing on the trade publishing, this chapter tries to explore the challenges and opportunities brought about by digital technologies.

The possible political impact of the Internet on Chinese society has been well discussed. Although many believed in the liberating nature of information technology at the early stage of its development in China, it has been generally agreed that the party-state has been implementing extensive and sophisticated control of Internet (Brady, 2008; Wacker, 2010). However, the rapid development of information technology is also a crucial source of economic growth, from which the ruling Party derives its legitimacy (Zheng, 2008). Consequently, the party-state holds an ambivalent attitude toward information technology. On the one hand, it has to implement policies to promote the development of information technology, such as the recent Internet Plus plan introduced by the Chinese premier in 2015 to encourage the application of Internet in traditional industries. But on the other hand, it tries to control and minimize the political risks brought about by information technology (ibid). This dilemma is also to be seen in the digital transformation of China's publishing industry.

In the publishing industry, Thompson (2005: 312) has identified four different levels where digital technologies could affect the business, including the operating systems of publishers and book distributors, content management and manipulation, marketing and service provision, and content delivery. My focus here is not on these operational levels, but more on the institutional and regulatory context and its implications for

China's Publishing Industry
DOI: https://doi.org/10.1016/B978-0-08-100919-2.00007-3

the digital transformation in China's trade publishing. As I have argued before, the ideological control from the party-state over the media varies across different media sectors as well as different media organizations within the same sector. Trade publishing is a sector of the publishing business over which the Party has tried rigorously to implement its control. As I shall argue, the strong intervention of the party-state has had a significant impact on the digital transformation of trade publishing. However, this argument should not be interpreted as a deterministic approach, as this chapter is not intended as a full survey of the digital publishing industry in China and only focuses on one dimension of the issue.

7.1 OVERVIEW

7.1.1 Background

Digital technologies, such as the Internet and smart phones, have witnessed an increasing penetration rate among the Chinese population. According to the official statistics from the China Internet Network Information Center (CNNIC), the government agency in charge of the country's domain name registry, China had 772 million Internet users as of December 2017 and the Internet penetration rate has reached 55.8% (CNNIC, 2018). Mobile Internet users accounted for 97.5% of the Internet users, while users connecting to the Internet via desktops, laptops, or tablets accounted for 53%, 35.8%, and 27.1%, respectively. The predominance of mobile phones among the users could have implications for the digital publishing business in China. In terms of age, 30% of the Internet users were between 20 and 29 years old, forming the biggest age group. By education level, 37.9% of the users had a junior high school diploma, and users with a senior high school vocational school education background accounted for 25.4%. Users with a college or higher level education background only accounted for 20.4%. Evaluated by the Network Readiness Index (NRI), China was ranked 59 among 139 nations by the World Economic Forum in 2016 for its overall Internet development (Baller et al., 2016). A few local technology companies have grown into Internet giants. Baidu, Alibaba, and Tencent (known as BAT), which could loosely be described as China's version of Google, Amazon, and Facebook, are the three leading companies in the country. Retail e-commerce in China is growing fast. 69.1% of the Internet users have shopped online, and nearly 68.8% have used online payment.

The developments in digital infrastructure in China have created favorable conditions for the development of digital publishing businesses. Most of the Internet users in China are young and are also active online readers. According to SAPPRFT, nearly 300 million people were reported to have read on a digital device in 2016 (Wang, 2017a). But rampant digital piracy posed a serious challenge to the digital publishing business in China. It was estimated that active e-book piracy websites have reached 14,000 in China (Fu, 2017). But what is odd is that some of the biggest players in the business were not active in fighting the piracy, and were sometimes even involved in the distribution of pirated e-books. It was reported that iReader, a top player in the mobile reading market, provided unlicensed e-books in its reading app to attract users (Li, 2017). Taohua.com, which used to be owned by Alibaba, and Baidu Library (*baidu wenku*) were also involved in the distribution of pirated e-books (Tian, 2010).

7.1.2 Early Developments in Digital Publishing

In order to understand the development of the digital publishing industry, we need to consider at least the following five factors: the content, functionality and the production cost, digital distribution, devices, and the customers. Scholarly journal publishing, with favorable conditions in relation to these factors, was the first sector that underwent digital transformation in China's publishing industry. Scholarly journals are crucial for scientific and technological research, and the additional functionality provided by digital publishing is particularly suitable for journal publishing. University libraries and research institutes, the main customers of journals, are usually well-funded by the government and they adopted digital technologies much earlier than the general households. Starting initially with CD-based database products, scholarly journals have moved on to online products. The major aggregators in China's journal publishing are CNKI (China National Knowledge Infrastructure), Wanfang, and CQVIP, with CNKI being the largest.

Although the party-state holds an ambivalent attitude toward the adoption of information technology, it played a more instrumental role in the digital transformation of China's journal publishing in order to facilitate scientific research (Chu and Richardson, 2016). At the early stage of this transformation, it was essential for the aggregators to secure enough licenses from the journal publishers for their content. However, there were potential problems in this process. Most academic journals in China are run by individual editorial offices as a single journal. It is reported that 4794 science and technology journals were published by about 3000 different organizations (Mo, 2011: 31). In addition, the main source of income for Chinese academic journals is the contribution of authors, and the income from their digital sales is usually insignificant. A survey revealed that in 2014, 68.3% of scholarly journals received less than 10% of their annual revenue from the digital sales (Cheng and Ren, 2017). As a result, most journal publishers would neither have strong momentum nor face enough pressure to negotiate with the aggregators at the early stage of the transformation. The business cost in negotiating with thousands of publishers on the licensing of individual journals would also be high. But as all journal publishers are owned by different state agencies, the support from the party-state would make the negotiations much more efficient. CNKI acknowledged that, when it was launched, it received support from a few important Party and government departments, including the Ministry of Education, the central Party Propaganda Department, and the Ministry of Science and Technology (CNKI, ©2017). The other two players, Wanfang and CQVIP, are also affiliated to the Ministry of Science and Technology and would have received support from it.

The wide adoption of digital technologies among the general population may mean that the time is ripe for the rise of digital publishing in the trade market. However, the government has been much more cautious about the implications of new forms of digital publishing in the trade sector. As new products and business models may fall outside of the scope of regulations, the government has been updating the existing regulations and promulgating new ones to put the digital publishing within its orbit.

7.2 E-BOOKS IN TRADE PUBLISHING

In the publishing industry, different sectors tend to adopt different technologies for their products. In scholarly journal publishing, databases tend to be the norm. In education publishing, online learning platforms, apps, and even CD-based products are the predominant forms in China. The two most important forms of digital products in China's trade publishing are probably e-books and serialized web fiction. Up to now the dominant e-book format and e-book reading devices powered by the E-ink technology are especially suitable for narrative trade books (Hall, 2013: 113). Serialized web fiction is also known by many as "Internet literature" (*wangluo wenxue*) (see Hockx, 2015) and I will refer to it as online fiction. Strictly speaking, Internet literature in China includes other online literary forms such as online poetry. But for most Chinese readers, online fiction is the only form of Internet literature they know about and these two words have become interchangeable for them. Online fiction might not be counted in the publishing industry by many professionals, as the form of its products and its business model are very different from the traditional publishing industry. I only include it in the discussion of this chapter because there appear to be interesting links between the e-book business and the online fiction business in China. As I will argue, these two businesses have experienced contrasting commercial fates in China, and this can be attributed partially to the institutional problems of the publishing industry and the different regulatory contexts these two businesses face.

7.2.1 The e-Book Market

Although it is not easy to measure the size of the e-book market in China, e-books have yet to become a promising business for publishers in China. According to a report from the Chinese Academy of Press and Publication (*zhongguo xinwen chuban yanjiu yuan*), the annual revenue of e-book business was RMB4.5 billion yuan (about US$706 million) in 2014 (Dong et al., 2015). However, it included the sales of the so-called "online original publications" (*wangluo yuanchuang chubanwu*), and we can only guess what that means. In addition, the majority of the figure is from the sales of aggregated e-book collections to libraries, of which the publishers probably do not have a large share.[1] SAPPRFT has started to provide the retail sales of digital publications (including e-books) in its annual report since 2012. Although these figures only include the sales from the state-owned channels, a conclusion can still be drawn from them that e-book sales only account for a minuscule percentage of the income of state-owned publishers (see Table 7.1). The statistics from Beijing OpenBook probably provide a better overview of the market size. According to this data source, the total digital reading market reached

Table 7.1 Sales of digital publications (including e-books): 2012–16

Year	Digital publications (million yuan)	Total book sales (million yuan)	Percentage of digital publications (%)
2012	14	71,258	0.02
2013	327	73,563	0.46
2014	367	77,799	0.47
2015	492	78,142	0.63
2016	566	85,249	0.66

Source: SAPPRFT.

RMB10.8 billion yuan (US$1.7 billion) in 2015, including 9 billion from the online fiction market and 1.8 billion from e-books (Jiang, 2016). Clearly the online fiction business, five times as large as the e-book business, is more glamorous. As Beijing OpenBook recorded a total of RMB62.4 billion yuan for print books sales in 2015, sales of e-books only accounted for about 2.8% of the total retail book market.

In terms of dedicated e-book reading devices, Amazon's Kindle is the top e-book reader in the Chinese market, with similar products from iReader, Dangdang, and Jingdong trailing a long way behind. The price of dedicated e-book reading devices is probably still a bit high for many readers. Mobile phones, which have become increasingly versatile and multifunctional, are the predominant device for most users in their digital reading experiences. The QQ Reader from Tencent is the most popular e-book reading app, accounting for 35.01% of the market by June 2017, followed by iReader from Zhangyue Technology with a share of 23.34% (Sootoo, 2017). Different reading devices, not just because of their inherent differences in functionality, but also because of the different reading environments related to where and how these devices are used, will have implications on the content to be read on them. By and large, mobile phones are more suitable for fragmented reading, and fiction is a perfect form of content for this way of reading.

Unlike their counterparts in Western markets, e-books in China are usually priced significantly lower than their print versions, with some bestsellers being priced at one-seventh or one-eighth of the paperback (Chen, 2017). Online booksellers sometimes provided e-books for free without the permission of the publishers in order to attract more customers, but publishers are now gaining more control over the prices of e-books in the market.

7.2.2 Institutional and Structural Problems

There are three kinds of e-book in the digital publishing industry. The vanilla e-book is the digital conversion of a printed book. Enhanced e-books containing additional multimedia content, and the born-digital e-books are developed specifically for digital devices (Phillips, 2014). The vanilla e-books, by replicating the business model of printed books, have so far been the most successful form in Western markets (ibid). They are also the most common form in China's e-book business, although relatively less successful. Enhanced e-books, probably because they are more suitable for tablets (Hall, 2013: 120) and may also involve issues in the production and distribution, are still not widely adopted by the publishers.

As the market size of e-books is still small, they have not generated satisfactory income for publishers. It was reported that a provincial publishing group in Guangdong only received a "negligible" amount of revenue for all the e-books they licensed (Zhang, 2013). Chinese state-owned publishers are in a dilemma about the digital transformation, as they are at risk of either withering away if they are left behind (*dengsi*) or losing a fortune if they plunge into the business despite the dim prospect (*zhaosi*) (ibid). There are many reasons for the difficulties in the e-book business in China, but it is essential to look beyond the digital publishing business to understand it better. The plague in the e-book business can be attributed at least partially to the institutional and structural problems of China's publishing industry.

First, the state-owned publishers are less capable of innovation in the digital transformation. As discussed before, state-owned publishing houses in China are still not fully market-oriented. Their operation is still more suited to the demand of the state-controlled propaganda system. This is why most bestsellers in China's trade market are produced by private publishers. It is hard to believe that they could come up with innovative business models in the digital transformation if they cannot perform well in the market of print books. In addition, the state-owned publishers are not well-motivated to take digital initiatives. As we know, the state-owned publishers, being the only legal payers in the industry, have enjoyed the monopolistic profit from the school textbooks and supplementary learning materials business. In the schools market, the impact of digital technologies on the publishers is rather limited. Print textbooks are still the most feasible and friendly form for school students in most countries.

Textbook sales are guaranteed by the orders from the government. The business of supplementary learning materials in China, as discussed in Chapter 2, Mapping Book Publishing in China, is now running in a way similar to the textbook business. Although there is a retail market for these materials, schools have to choose some supplementary learning materials approved by the provincial governments, which are usually from the local publishers. Consequently, digital technologies have had little impact on the main business and the profit of state-owned publishers. The so-called *dengsi* or *zhaosi* dilemma faced by the state-owned publishers in the digital publishing business is probably a bit of an exaggeration.

Many state-owned publishers are engaged in both the trade market and the schools market. In addition, the concentration level in China's publishing is low. As a result, book titles suitable for the e-book market from individual publishers or even publishing groups might not be numerous. This weakens the bargaining power of publishers in their negotiations with the e-book retailers or distribution platforms.

Second, the supply of suitable trade book titles for the e-book business is relatively limited. It was argued by Clark and Phillips (2014:17) that genre fiction played an important role in the growth of e-book business in North America, the UK, and Australia, although no further details were given. But some evidence can be found in the US and UK markets to support this view. e-Books in these two markets perform much better than the others, with e-books accounting for 13% of the trade market in the US and 11.5% in the UK in 2012, significantly higher than the 5% in Germany (Wischenbart, 2014). The dominance of the English language may have a part to play in the growth of e-book businesses in these two countries, but the success of e-books in the fiction book market appears to be crucial for their relatively successful e-book businesses. In the UK book retail market, e-books accounted for 50% of the fiction market in 2014, 52% in 2015, and 50% in 2016 (Nielsen, 2017). In the UK nonfiction market, the highest market share of e-books during the period from 2012 to 2016 was only 15% in 2014. e-Books performed even worse in the UK children's market, with their highest market share during the same period standing at only 6% in 2014. e-Books displayed a similar pattern in the US market. In the first quarter of 2017, e-books accounted for 45% of the adult fiction market, 21% of the young adults market, 12% of the adult nonfiction market, and 6% of the children's book market (OpenBook, 2017a). In both countries, e-books accounted for about half of the fiction book market, a much higher percentage than in other sectors. However, we still need to take into account the size of different sectors in the US and the UK trade book markets before we can work out the importance of different sectors for their e-book businesses. In 2016, the market shares of children's books, nonfiction, and fiction in the US trade book market were 36.1%, 42.3%, and 21.7%, respectively, while in the UK market, their market shares were 33%, 40.4%, and 26.6% (OpenBook, 2017b). Although these data from different sources might still be a bit patchy, it can be concluded from them that fiction books are the most important sector for the e-book business in both countries.

If the performance of e-books in the US and the UK markets can be of any reference, then the trade publishing in China may not be supplying enough suitable titles for the e-book business. First, in comparison with the school book business, the trade publishing is a relatively smaller sector in China. As discussed before, according to the annual reports from SAPPRFT, school textbooks and supplementary learning materials consistently account for over 50% of the total sales of China's publishing industry (see Table 2.14). In addition, as these official figures did not include the sales of supplementary learning material sold through the second channel, which were estimated to be at about RMB20 billion yuan, the school books market must be even larger. Consequently, this leaves a smaller market for the trade books. In contrast, trade books in the UK accounted for 63% of the publishers invoiced sales by value in 2014, while school/English language teaching (ELT) books and academic/professional books accounted for 11% and 25%, respectively (Richardson and Taylor, 2016: 2). Second, fiction books only account for a small percentage of the already relatively small trade book market in China. According to the official statistics, the sales of literature and arts books, including fiction, accounted for 6.63% of the total market in 2016 (SAPPRFT, 2017a). Beijing OpenBook also reported that fiction accounted for less than 10% in China's retail market in 2015 (Nielsen, 2016: 8), the lowest share among all the countries reported by Nielsen BookScan, including Brazil and India. This figure is pretty much in line with the official statistics from SAPPRFT. A relatively small trade book sector in China and the small market share of fiction books might have restricted the potential of the e-book business in China.

In addition, the problem of a lack of suitable titles for the e-book business is aggravated by the fact that many published books are not market-oriented titles. As discussed in Chapter 2, Mapping Book Publishing in China, China's publishing industry suffers from the problem of excess inventory and many published titles are unsalable in the market.

This is not very surprising, as the state-owned publishers are not fully market-oriented and are usually required to publish a certain percentage of propaganda books in their publishing plans. This does not mean that propaganda books never sell. According to the official statistics, the annual print runs of a few propaganda titles in 2016 reached over one million copies. One of them even printed 52 million copies in total. Among the top 10 titles with the largest print runs in 2016, at least eight of them are propaganda books (SAPPRFT, 2017b). Although the figure of the print run is not the same as the figure of sold copies, it is reasonable to believe that at least a significant proportion of them would have been sold. In addition, according to the retail market report from Beijing OpenBook, a couple of propaganda books also entered its nonfiction bestseller list (Wang, 2017b). However, as most of these propaganda books would have been sold to the Party or government organizations for organized political indoctrination, e-books are just not a suitable form for this purpose. Although a few propaganda titles might be able to sell well, most other titles are likely to stay in the warehouses. The quality of printed books could also pose a problem for the e-book business. Duokan, a top e-book aggregator in China, complained that the quality of many earlier published print books is "incredibly low" and the problem of missing words or even paragraphs occurred frequently. Duokan had to invest RMB2 million yuan (about US$314,000) every year in proofreading during the digital conversion of print books (Hu, 2013). The availability of plenty of suitable book titles is crucial for the initial development of e-book business, especially for the successful launch of dedicated e-book reading devices. But the lack of suitable and quality book titles hampered the development of the e-book business in China.

If the success of vanilla e-books in Western markets is because they replicate the so far successful economic model of printed books (Phillips, 2014), then the not very successful economic model of the trade publishing in China cannot possibly be replicated in the vanilla e-book form in a successfully way. New and innovative business models have to be found for the digital transformation of China's trade publishing. One possible source of growth is the often self-published born-digital titles.

7.2.3 Regulations and Self-Publishing

There has been an enormous growth in self-published e-books in the United States and other markets (Clark and Phillips, 2014: 4). In the US e-book market, while the share of the big five publishers decreased to 34% in 2015, the share of clearly self-published e-books crept to 12% of the market and when they are combined with the titles from very small publishers, which may also include self-published e-books, their share rose to 42% of the market. In the UK market, the share of self-published titles also rose to 22% of the e-book market in 2015 (Nielsen, 2016).

However, the business of born digital e-books is highly regulated in China by the government. The government was vigilant about the possibility of the e-book business falling into a regulatory lacuna. Well before the e-books became known in the consumer market, the government promulgated the Administrative Provisions on Electronic Publications (*dianzi chubanwu guanli guiding*) in December 1997. This regulation required all business entities engaged in the publishing, production, importation, and distribution of electronic publications, which basically included all players in the supply chain, to be licensed first. Only state-owned publishers with sponsoring organizations can be licensed into the e-book publishing business. Many measures adopted in the control of print book publishing were applied to the e-book business. An e-book has to go through a licensed state-owned publisher before its publication, and an ISBN number designed for the use of electronic publications also has to be issued by the government to it. For the e-book publishers, they have to report their annual e-book publishing plans to the government and seek approval from the government for their titles on sensitive topics. e-Book titles licensed by overseas copyright owners have to be approved by the government as well. In 2008, more details were added to a revised edition of this regulation and e-book publishers are now required to be assessed biennially by the government. Another revision of this regulation was drafted by the government in 2016. Although it has not been promulgated, the government is now planning to ban foreign capital from being invested in the production of electronic publications.

It can be seen that the e-book business in China has been tightly controlled by the government even before it started. In Western markets, mainly due to Amazon's large number of existing customers, the smooth customer experience it provided, and the availability of plenty of e-book titles, the release of the Kindle in 2007 was an enormous success and became one of the key reasons why the e-book market was able to develop than it had been before (Hall, 2013: 111). However, Amazon faced regulatory restrictions when it tried to enter China's e-books market (see Huang, 2012; Chen, 2013). It only managed to launch a tailored e-book store specific for the Chinese market in 2012 and its Kindle e-reader was not available in China until 2013. Restrictions on the big players would make it harder for the e-book business to take off.

For the incumbent state-owned publishers, born-digital e-books are rarely an option for them as the e-book market in China is still small and they also have to go through all the administrative procedure to publish their e-books. Self-publishing is probably the best business option for born-digital e-books. However, the regulations in China required all e-books to be published by a licensed traditional publisher, eliminating the possibility of self-publishing. If disintermediation and globalization are two of the main themes of digital publishing (Phillips, 2014), then due to the government regulations, none of them have materialized in China's e-book business.

7.2.4 Government Support and the e-Book Business

Despite its effort to exercise control, the government did try to encourage the development of digital publishing in China. In order to promote the digital transformation in publishing industry, the central government has set aside a total budget of RMB2.039 billion yuan (US$ 320 million) since 2013 to subsidize 301 digital publishing projects, which was supplemented by another RMB4.8 billion yuan (US$ 754 million) from local governments and publishing companies on these projects (SAPPRFT, 2017c). The other state-led policy was the establishment of national digital publishing bases (or industrial parks). Following its ambition in developing the cultural industries, the central government adopted the Plan on the Reinvigoration of Cultural Industries (*wenhua chanye zhenxing guihua*) in September 2009. In this plan, the government encouraged the launch of cultural industries' business parks, including the publishing industry business parks, to foster business clusters across the country, with preferential policies on land use and tax breaks being offered. Following this guideline, SAPPRFT issued the Decisions on Speeding up the Digital Publishing Industry (*guanyu jiakuai woguo shuzi chuban chanye fazhan de ruogan yijian*) in August 2010, setting the policy of establishing national digital publishing bases. Fourteen such bases have been established in different provincial regions, with the Shanghai Zhangjiang National Digital Publishing Base claiming an annual revenue of RMB33.21 billion yuan in 2015 (see Table 7.2). Many companies in these bases are actually engaged in the business of gaming, animation, or software development rather

Table 7.2 Annual revenue of national digital publishing parks in China in 2015 (billion yuan)

Rank	Industry park	Launch date	Revenue
1	Shanghai Zhangjiang National Digital Publishing Base	02/2009	33.21
2	Jiangsu National Digital Publishing Base	06/2011	26.72
3	Guangdong National Digital Publishing Base	05/2011	19.00
4	Anhui National Digital Publishing Base	12/2012	16.80
5	Xi'an National Digital Publishing Base (in Shaanxi)	06/2012	9.34
6	Hangzhou National Digital Publishing Base (in Zhejiang)	04/2012	9.17
7	Tianjin National Digital Publishing Base	10/2011	7.36
8	Chongqing North New District National Digital Publishing Base	04/2010	6.39
9	Central South National Digital Publishing Base (in Hunan)	11/2011	6.23
10	Jiangxi National Digital Publishing Base	04/2015	4.70
11	Straits National Digital Publishing Base	04/2013	3.28
12	Qingdao National Digital Publishing Base (in Shandong)	03/2014	2.88
13	Central China National Digital Publishing Base (in Hubei)	09/2011	0.18
14	Beijing National Digital Publishing Base	12/2013	0.02

Source: SAPPRFT, 2016. Analysis of the press and publications industry in 2015 (*2015 nian xinwen chuban chanye fenxi baogao*). <http://www.sapprft.gov.cn/upload/files/2016/8/9153448117.pdf> (accessed 21.01.18) (in Chinese).

than the digital publishing as we understand it in the publishing industry, but the local APPRFT or publishing groups often played an important role in them. The establishment of these digital publishing bases was led predominantly by the local governments, and their success also depends to a large extent on the support of local governments. This explains why the revenue in the Beijing National Digital Publishing Base, which was sponsored by a local district government in Beijing rather than the municipal government, is astonishingly the lowest among all bases. However, with the support of local governments, these digital publishing bases are often encouraging the development of the same businesses, including e-books, mobile publishing, digital printing, gaming, animation, e-learning, databases, digital music, and cloud computing, etc., running the risk of creating a homogeneous business structure across these bases (see Bi, 2015).

In order to benefit from the preferential policies and the subsidies from the government, many local publishing groups launched digital publishing operations, such as the China Publishing Group Digital Media Company, the Shandong Digital Publishing Media Company, and the Guangdong Provincial Publishing Group Digital Publishing Company. A few of them launched their own e-book reading devices, such as the China Publishing Group and the Shanghai Century Publishing Group, and embedded their digital content within these devices (see Ren, 2010). They also launched online e-book publishing and selling platforms, such as the Dajianet.com by China Publishing Group, ishuke.com.cn by Shandong Publishing Group, and Iximo.com by Guangdong Provincial Publishing Group. With less consideration for commercial viability, they all wanted to control the whole supply chain of the digital publishing business. As the Shandong Digital Publishing Media Company showcased in its company profile, it is engaged in the publishing, production, and distribution of electronic publications (SDPM, ©2013). Consequently, these operations created a segregated digital publishing industry in China, replicating the same institutional problem in the print book publishing industry. The subsidies provided by the governments to these operations will only disrupt the logic of market and make it harder to build an efficient supply chain for the nascent digital publishing business in China.

7.3 ONLINE FICTION PUBLISHING

While the potential of e-book business in China is restricted, online fiction has become prominent for many Chinese readers. Online fiction, written in an interactive context often by amateur writers and published as original web series, is not uncommon in other parts of the world. However, its overwhelming popularity and commercial success in China "has no real equivalent" in Western countries (Hockx, 2015: 4). According to the statistics from CNNIC (2018), 48.9% of China's Internet users, which amounted to 377.74 million, accessed online fiction in 2017, mostly through their mobile phones. Among Chinese mobile users, 45.6% read online fiction in 2017, which is about 343.52 million users. Due to its immense popularity, many e-book selling platforms now offer online fiction as part of their content supply. Amazon partnered with Migu Reading, an online reading platform owned by the state-owned China Mobile, to release the cobranded Kindle X Migu e-book reader in 2017, which offers users the option to access online fiction from Migu in addition to e-books from Amazon.cn.

The commercial success of online fiction and the underperformance of e-books in China are not a coincidence. According to Ren and Montgomery (2012), China's literature was ideologically oriented. The control of the government over the literary production resulted in limited diversity of fiction and there is a shortage of entertaining fiction to meet the popular demand. They mentioned that this market lacuna helps to explain the rise of online fiction in China. However, this argument needs to be developed further and also take into account the impact of regulations.

7.3.1 Overview of the Online Fiction Business

Chinese online literature was started outside China by overseas Chinese students in the early 1990s through various electronic channels. Although most online literature authors were probably not writing for commercial success, commercial attempts by site owners already started at the early stage of the development of online fiction. The first notable success of online fiction was the First Intimate Contact (*di yici de qinmi jiechu*), a fiction posted by a graduate student in Taiwan on a BBS (Bulletin Board Systems) in 1998. It was published the following year in China and immediately became a bestseller. The success of this book probably signaled the commercial potential of online fiction and attracted more commercial attempts. A website called Rongshuxia (or Under the Banyan Tree) was created as an online literature platform at the end of 1997 in Shanghai. It started to exploit the commercial potential of online fiction in 1999 (Kong, 2005: 179) and was later sold to Bertelsmann in 2002. The early commercial operations for online fiction were mainly to publish prospective fiction in cooperation with traditional publishers.

During the commercialization of online fiction, two important events that set the features of China's online fiction business were the launch of the highly popular website of Qidian (or Starting Point) in 2002 and its later acquisition by Shanda Interactive Entertainment. Qidian tried the freemium business model, which basically means that the readers have to pay for part of the chapters of a novel after reading a few free chapters (Phillips, 2014: 89; Ren and Montgomery, 2012). Readers were required to pay a couple of cents per thousand words in the fee-paying chapters they read. Depending on the subscription level of readers, the price varies slightly, but the medium price is 3 cents per thousand words. The income is then shared between the authors and the website according to a seventy-thirty split. Although the payment is extremely low, novels with millions of words and a vast amount of readers could bring a sizable amount of income. This freemium model has become the norm of the online fiction business. Realizing the potential of online fiction as an important source of content for its game development, Shanda Interactive (a leading online game company in China) acquired Qidian in 2004, becoming the first case of the involvement of large commercial capital in the online fiction business.

The freemium model proved to be working in China, and the copyright licensing of successful online fiction provides another important source of income. According to SAPPRFT, the online fiction market had reached RMB9 billion yuan (US$1.4 billion) by the end of 2016, and 14 million works of online fiction together with daily updates of 150 million words are available from 40 online literature websites. Tang Jia San Shao, the author with the top income in the business, earned RMB122 million yuan (about US$19 million) in 2017 (Zhang, 2017). The entry of IT (information technology) giants into the business meant that the market is now highly concentrated. The top player, China Literature Limited (*yuewen*), was founded in March 2015 through a merger between Tencent Literature and Shanda Literature (or Cloudary). It controls most of the popular online fiction websites and accounts for 43.2% of market share in terms of revenue. The second player, iReader, lagged a long way behind with a 14.9% share in 2016 (China Literature, 2017). China Literature was successfully listed on the Hong Kong Stock Exchange in November 2017. However, with annual revenue of RMB2.57 billion yuan in 2016, its net profit was only RMB30.36 million yuan (about 1.2% of its revenue) and it even recorded financial losses in 2014 and 2015. Piracy has posed a serious problem for the online fiction business. China Literature estimated that the revenue loss due to pirated online literature content doubles the size of the revenue of the business in 2016. For China Literature, the revenue generated from online reading accounted for 77.1% of its total revenue in 2016. The other two main sources of revenue are copyright licensing, accounting for 9.7% of its total revenue, and the publishing of physical books in cooperation with publishers, accounting for 8.8% (ibid).

7.3.2 Rise of Online Literature

The commercial success of online fiction in China is the result of a number of factors. The increasing penetration of digital technologies among the population and the rise of Web 2.0 are essential for the growth of the online fiction business. Social conditions such as the urbanization, improved literacy levels, and the huge population also laid down the crucial foundation for an enormous pool of creative talent and a large consumer base. But here I would like to focus on arguing that the existing problems in the traditional publishing and the earlier regulatory gray area regarding online fiction provided opportunities for the development of the business.

As discussed before, fiction books account for a much smaller share of the retail book market in China than in other countries. Although this could be explained by either a lack of interest from readers or by a shortage of supply from publishers, the commercial success of online fiction appears to point to the latter. One of the reasons for the shortage of supply is the party-controlled literary production system. The Party has always seen literature as an important tool for its ideological propaganda, a principle manifested by Mao's Talks at the Yan'an Forum on Literature and Art in 1942. A "socialist literary system" was established after the Party came into power, and the Chinese Writers Association became the official body organizing the literary production of writers (Kong, 2005). Most Chinese writers, being assimilated into a state patronage system, effectively became state employees. Under the party-controlled literary and publishing system, genre fiction could hardly come to the market. However, the reduction of state support for the Writers Association and the opportunities provided by a commercialized publishing industry led to a shift toward a more market-oriented literary production, especially in the 1990s, leading to some significant commercial successes (ibid). Although the commercialization of publishing led to the emergence of some genre fiction, such as knights-errant and romance, in the market, the ideological censorship meant that some online genre fiction, such as the homosexual love stories, would not be allowed to go through the tightly controlled traditional publishing process. In addition, the control over the total number of ISBN numbers also meant that works from amateur writers could hardly get a chance to be published. The rise of the Internet provided great self-publishing opportunities for authors (Clark and Phillips, 2014: 44). Genre fiction has been particularly successful in self-published e-books in the Western markets (Hall, 2013: 114). It is exactly the prohibition of self-publishing in the e-book form in China that diverted many authors to the online fiction websites.

The other reason for the rise of online fiction is the relatively loose regulations regarding the business. In the digital publishing world, the very term of books and publishers can become blurred. A serialized web fiction, in the form similar to a regularly updated web page, is quite different from the form of a book, which serves as a container for finished content that is ripe for being distributed (Phillips, 2014: xiv). The freemium business model is nothing like selling books in the traditional publishing business. The role of editors is also displaced by the feedback from readers. As the form and the business models of online fiction business are so different from book publishing, the existing regulations on publishing did not apply. This is why the private capital could establish itself in this business. Although some finished online fiction could be sold as e-books, these have hardly been tried by online fiction platforms because of the stricter regulations on e-books.

Although the existing regulations lagged slightly behind the technology advancement and business innovation, the government still tried to regulate online fiction at an early stage of its development. The State Council issued the Regulation on Internet Information Service in 2000, requiring all websites to be licensed by the government. In addition to this general decree, GAPP and the Ministry of Information Industry (*xinxi chanye bu*) promulgated the Interim Regulations on Internet Publishing in 2002, requesting online publishers to be licensed by GAPP first. In this regulation, publishing of content on sensitive topics are required to be approved by the government, and all content has to be censored by the editors. Although this regulation may not appear to be lenient, a key difference between the regulations on the online fiction business and the traditional publishing is that the government did not try to implement the sponsoring system in online publishing, leaving the door open for private capital.

7.3.3 Regulations and Control

Private capital now dominates the online fiction business. However, the government has extensive administrative power to put the online fiction business under its strict control. It appears that the more influential online fiction business becomes, the more rigid the regulations become.

The government promulgated a revised decree, the Regulations on the Administration of Online Publishing Services, in February 2016 to replace the interim regulations issued in 2002. Although private capital is allowed to continue in the business, this updated version has become much stricter. In addition to existing control measures, new requirements have been implemented. SAPPRFT has raised the bar for business entities to apply for an Online Publishing Service License. In order to get the license, the legal representative of the entity now has to be a citizen with a domicile in China. The business entity must employ at least eight full-time editors with professional qualifications endorsed by SAPPRFT, which has basically excluded small companies. A content scrutiny system needs to be established within the business entity and its server has to be located in China. Foreign capital, including joint ventures, is forbidden in the business. Although they can cooperate with licensed Chinese companies on specific online publishing projects, this cooperation has to be approved by SAPPRFT. In addition, the license has to be renewed every five years. Some control measures used in the traditional publishing industry are also adopted in the online publishing business. Local APPRFTs are required to carry out regular scrutiny reading (*shendu*) of the content of local online publishers, and to review their performances annually. SAPPRFT has proposed to adopt an identifier system, presumably similar to the ISBN number, for online publications. It is also planning to implement the so-called golden share system (*teshu guanli gu*) in all online publishing businesses. This would allow the government to take at least 1% stakes in online publishers, and then legally have the ultimate say on important issues in those private companies. How these proposed measures are to be implemented in the online fiction business remains to be seen.

In addition to the regulation mentioned above, other control measures have also been introduced into the business. In January 2015, SAPPRFT required all online fiction authors to register their real names with their online publishing platform before they can post their works. In order to guide the content output of online fiction business, SAPPRFT adopted a provisional points system in June 2017 to assess the "social benefit" (*shehui xiaoyi*) of online publishing organizations, and those rated "unsatisfactory" will receive warnings from the government.

As a response to the government regulations, self-censorship becomes unavoidable. China Literature, the biggest player in the business, has to invest heavily in the self-censorship of its content. In addition to its computerized keywords filtering, it has recruited over 100 employees, accounting for 7% of its total 1470 employees, in manual censorship (China Literature, 2017). This has significantly reduced the advantages of self-publishing and increased the operation cost of the online fiction business.

As argued before, the relatively relaxed control from the government over the online fiction business was crucial for its success. But the government is tightening up its control over the business, which may damage the very conditions for its success.

7.4 SUMMARY

The intervention of the party-state has had significant impact on the digital transformation of China's publishing industry. Although the party-state played an instrumental role in the digital transformation of scholarly journals, its tighter control over the trade publishing has made it harder for the development of the digital publishing business in the sector. Due to the institutional and structural problems in China's trade publishing and strict regulations, the e-book business has been underperforming. However, the rise of new technology did create regulatory lacuna and bring about opportunities for the self-publishing of online fiction. Probably mainly because of the inability of the e-book business to tap into the market opportunity and the earlier relatively relaxed regulations on online fiction, the online fiction business has achieved an unusual commercial success not seen in any other parts of the world.

I have argued elsewhere that the interplay between state control and market forces led to a distinction between the predominantly party-controlled state-owned sector and a more market-oriented private sector (or second channel) in China's publishing industry, with the state-owned sector being subject to greater intervention by the state but also benefiting from its protection or indirect subsidies (Yun, 2013). This pattern appears to apply to the digital transformation of China's trade publishing. The e-book publishing business, monopolized by state-owned publishers, has been underperforming. On the other hand, the online fiction business, dominated by private capital, has been commercially more successful, functioning as a second channel in the digital publishing business. However, as the party-state is tightening up its control, the online fiction business may suffer.

ENDNOTES

1. Take the Superstar Digital Library (or Chaoxing) as an example, many of its titles were actually licensed directly by authors rather than publishers, and some others are out of copyright titles.

REFERENCES

Baller, S., et al., (Eds.), 2016. The Global Information Technology Report 2016: Innovating in the Digital Economy. World Economic Forum, Geneva.

Bi, Y., 2015. Research report on China's digital publishing bases (*zhongguo shuzi chuban chanye jidi yanjiu baogao*). In: Zhang, L., Wang, B. (Eds.), *Annual report on the digital publishing industry in China 2014−15 (2014−15 zhongguo shuzi chuban chanye niandu baogao)*. China Book Press, Beijing, pp. 333−355. (in Chinese).

Brady, A., 2008. Marketing Dictatorship: Propaganda and Thought Work in Contemporary China. Rowman & Littlefield, Lanham, MD.

Chen, M., 2017. E-books move away from the low-price strategy (*dianzi shu zouchu dijia shidai*). <http://media.people.com.cn/n1/2017/0110/c40606-29010763.html> (accessed 12.12.17) (in Chinese).

Chen, X., 2013. Four challenges for Kindle in China (*kindle ruhua mianlin de sida tiaozhan*). <http://tech.sina.com.cn/i/csj/2013-06-13/08298435254.shtml> (accessed 12.01.18) (in Chinese).

Cheng, W., Ren, S., 2017. The digital publishing business model of CAST-affiliated science and technology journals (*zhongguo kexie keji qikan de shuzi chuban shangye moshi*). Science, Technology and Publishing (keji yu chuban) 2017 (1), 47−52 (in Chinese).

China Literature, 2017. China Literature Limited Global Offering. <http://www.hkex-news.hk/listedco/listconews/SEHK/2017/1026/LTN20171026021.pdf> (accessed 12.01.18) (in Chinese).

Chu, X., Richardson, P., 2016. PA Market Report: China Journals. The Publishers Association, London.

Clark, G., Phillips, A., 2014. Inside Book Publishing, fifth ed. Routledge, London.

CNKI, ©2017. CNKI project: concept (CNKI gongcheng). <http://service.cnki.net/project/project.html> (accessed 19.12.17) (in Chinese).

CNNIC, 2018. *The 41st China Statistical Report on the Internet Development (di 41 ci zhongguo hulian wangluo fazhan zhuangkuang tongji baogao)*. China Internet Network Information Centre, Beijing (in Chinese).

Dong, N., et al., 2015. Annual report on China's e-book industry 2014−15 (*2014−15 zhongguo dianzi tushu chuban chanye niandu baogao*). In: Zhang, L., Wang, B. (Eds.), *Annual Report on the Digital Publishing Industry in China 2014−15 (2014−15 zhongguo shuzi chuban chanye niandu baogao)*. China Book Press, Beijing, pp. 39−50. (in Chinese).

Fu, M., 2017. Build a first-class business ecosystem for China's digital content industry (*jianshe yiliu zhongguo shuzi neirong shengtai lian*). <http://t.cj.sina.com.cn/articles/view/1705573893/65a8fe05034001r8o> (accessed 15.11.17) (in Chinese).

Hall, F., 2013. The Business of Digital Publishing: An Introduction to the Digital Book and Journal Industries. Routledge, London.

Hockx, M., 2015. Internet Literature in China. Columbia University Press, New York.

Hu, X., 2013. How to define the role of Zijieshe, Duokan and Douban Reading in the digial publishing business (*zai shuzi chuban fengong zhong, ying ruhe dingyi zijieshe, duokan, douban yuedu de weizhi*). <https://www.zhihu.com/question/21028010/answer/21731906> (accessed 20.12.17) (in Chinese).

Huang, J., 2012. Kindle staggering into China (*kindle panshan ruhua*). <https://cn.nytimes.com/business/20121218/cc18kindle/> (accessed 12.12.17) (in Chinese).

Jiang, F., 2016. The status-quo of e-books market and its development trends (*zhongguo dianzishu shichang de xianzhuan yu zuixin qushi*). <https://site.douban.com/210084/widget/notes/13298573/note/568543520/> (accessed 15.11.17) (in Chinese).

Li, M., 2017. The popularity of Apps and the scourge of e-book piracy (*suizhe App de zouhong, yidong App cheng dianzishu daoban zhong zaiqu*). <http://www.xinhuanet.com/zgjx/2017-04/12/c_136202085.htm> (accessed 15.12.17) (in Chinese).

Kong, S., 2005. Consuming Literature: Best Sellers and the Commercialization of Literary Production in Contemporary China. Stanford University Press, Stanford, CA.

Mo, L., 2011. Discussions on digital publishing strategies for Science and Technology publishers in China (*qiantan woguo keji chuban qiye shuzi chuban fazhan celue de sheji*). China Publishing Journal (zhongguo chuban) 2011 (4), 30–33 (in Chinese).

Nielsen, 2016. Nielsen Book Research: 2015 in review. <https://quantum.londonbookfair.co.uk/RXUK/RXUK_PDMC/documents/9928_Nielsen_Book_Research_In_Review_2015_The_London_Book_Fair_Quantum_Conference_2016_DIGITAL_FINAL.pdf?v = 635995987941118341> (accessed 28.09.17).

Nielsen, 2017. UK Books and Consumers in 2016. <https://quantum.londonbookfair.co.uk/RXUK/RXUK_PDMC/responsive/images/2017/Steve%20Bohme%20-%20The%202016%20Book%20Market%20Highlights%20from%20the%20Books%20and%20Consumers%202016%20Survey.pdf?v = 636257834636180655> (accessed 30.09.17).

OpenBook, 2017a. Analysis of book retail markets across the world: January–June 2017 (*2017 nian shangbannian guoneiwai tushu lingshou shichang baogao fenxi*). <https://kknews.cc/zh-hk/culture/oglrgm5.html> (accessed 25.09.17) (in Chinese).

OpenBook, 2017b. Analysis of book retail in the domestic market and in the international markets (*2016 nian guoneiwai tushu lingshou shichang baogao*). <www.openbook.com.cn/downloadunlogin.aspx?fsid = 96370> (accessed 30.09.17) (in Chinese).

Phillips, A., 2014. Turning the Page: The Evolution of the Book. Routledge, London.

Ren, D., 2010. Publishers entered the e-book reader market (*shuye xi fali dianzishu yueduqi shichang*). <http://www.cnpubg.com/digital/2010/0526/15470.shtml> (accessed 12.01.18.) (in Chinese).

Ren, X., Montgomery, L., 2012. Chinese online literature: creative consumers and evolving business models. Arts Marketing: an International Journal 2 (2), 118–130.

Richardson, P., Taylor, G., 2016. PA Market Report: The United Kingdom. The Publishers Association, London.

SAPPRFT, 2016. Analysis of the press and publications industry in 2015 (*2015 nian xinwen chuban chanye fenxi baogao*). <http://www.sapprft.gov.cn/upload/files/2016/8/9153448117.pdf> (accessed 21.01.18) (in Chinese).

SAPPRFT, 2017a. General information of the national press and publishing industry in 2016 (*2016 nian quanguo xinwen chuban ye jiben qingkuang*). <http://www.sapprft.gov.cn/sapprft/govpublic/6677/1633.shtml> (accessed 05.12.17) (in Chinese).

SAPPRFT, 2017b. Analysis of the press and publications industry in 2017 (*2016 nian xinwen chuban chanye fenxi baogao*). <http://www.chinaxwcb.com/2017-07/25/content_358659.htm> (accessed 25.09.17) (in Chinese).

SAPPRFT, 2017c. Reply to the No. 2265 proposal from the 5th Session of the 12th Chinese People's Political Consultative Conference (*guanyu zhengxie shierjie quanguo weiyuanhui di wuci huiyi di 2265 hao ti'an dafu de han*). <http://www.sapprft.gov.cn/sapprft/govpublic/9831/1707.shtml> (accessed 12.01.18) (in Chinese).

SDPM, ©2013. Company profile (*gongsi jianjie*). <http://www.sdszcb.com/class.php?id = 218> (accessed 19.01.18) (in Chinese).

Sootoo, 2017. Mobile reading market report in the second quarter of 2017 (*2017 nian Q2 yidong yuedu shichang baogao*). <http://www.sohu.com/a/169459829_174789> (accessed 12.12.17) (in Chinese).

Thompson, J.B., 2005. Books in the Digital Age: The Transformation of Academic and Higher Education Publishing in Britain and the United States. Polity, Cambridge.

Tian, Z., 2010. The Copyright infringement in Taohua and Baidu Library (*taohua wang baidu wenku qinquan shimo*). <http://tech.qq.com/a/20101122/000399.htm> (accessed 15.12.17) (in Chinese).

Wacker, G., 2010. Resistance is futile: control and censorship of the Internet in China. In: Brokaw, C., Reed, C.A. (Eds.), From Woodblocks to the Internet: Chinese Publishing and Print Culture in Transition, Circa 1800 to 2000. Brill, Leiden, pp. 353–381.

Wang, J., 2017a. What's reshaping China's reading market. <https://news.cgtn.com/news/3d4d6a4e7963444e/share_p.html> (accessed 15.12.17).

Wang, Y., 2017b. OpenBook's three bestseller lists and new books lists in November 2017 (*2017 nian 11 yue kaijun sanda changxiaoshu bang he xinshu bang xinxian chulu*). <http://www.cptoday.cn/news/detail/4654> (accessed 05.01.18) (in Chinese).

Wischenbart, R., 2014. Global e-Book: A Report on Market Trends and Developments. Ruediger Wischenbart Content and Consulting, Vienna.

Yun, Q., 2013. State versus market: a perspective on China's publishing industry. LOGOS: Journal of the World Book Community 24 (1), 19–29.

Zhang, H., 2013. Digital publishing, a pitfall of self-decimation if done blindly (*shuzi chuban, mangmu zuo caishi zhaosi*). <http://epaper.bjnews.com.cn/html/2013-08/29/content_461299.htm?div = -1> (accessed 15.11.18) (in Chinese).

Zhang, M., 2017. Online literature industry is now in the dividend period: over 300 million users and 9 billion revenue (*wangluo wenxue chanye buru hongli qi: yonghu chao 3 yi shichang guimo 90 yi*). <http://media.people.com.cn/n1/2017/0815/c40606-29469938.html> (accessed 21.01.18) (in Chinese).

Zheng, Y., 2008. Technological Empowerment: The Internet, State, and Society in China. Stanford University Press, Stanford, CA.

CHAPTER 8

Politics, Profit and Digital Prospect: Guangdong Provincial Publishing Group as a Case

In this chapter we will explore how the control of the party-state is incorporated in the everyday operation of publishing houses through a detailed case study of one major provincial publishing group, the Guangdong Provincial Publishing Group (GDPG). The choice of GDPG as the case study site was informed by several considerations.

First, Guangdong province has been at the forefront of China's economic transformation. Shenzhen City in Guangdong Province was the first Special Economic Zone established by the central government in 1980 to spearhead its reform program and is also the most successful one. The enthusiasm for the market economy was also kindled by Deng Xiaoping, the former Chinese leader, during his "southern tour" to this province in 1992. Consequently, the reform of the publishing industry in Guangdong was a step ahead of many other regions as signaled by the fact that GDPG and Shanghai Century Publishing Group were the first two publishing groups endorsed by the government administration department. However, in comparison with Shanghai, which is a municipality, the structure of the publishing industry in Guangdong is more representative of China's provincial publishing groups.

Second, the fact that the province contains powerful municipalities, most notably Shenzhen and Guangzhou, the capital city of the province, provides an opportunity to investigate the interaction of GDPG with both the provincial government and the local publishing industry in these municipalities.

8.1 BACKGROUND

GDPG was launched in December 1999. It was initially affiliated to the provincial publishing administration department, but eventually achieved full independence. Although book publishing remains its core business, it

China's Publishing Industry
DOI: https://doi.org/10.1016/B978-0-08-100919-2.00008-5

221

has interests in other key links in the publishing value chain and has expanded into new areas such as newspaper publishing and digital publishing. According to the company statistics for 2007, its annual title output was about 4000, in addition to about 500 audio—video products. Its annual sales revenue reached RMB3 billion yuan (around US$471 million).[1] According to *Information Bulletin* (*xinxi dongtai*), a monthly corporate publication of the group, GDPG (excluding a shareholding book distribution company it controls) employed 3307 staff by January 2004. Like most state-owned companies, this publishing group and its member firms are generally overstaffed.

GDPG, with a small amount of investment from the *Southern Daily* press group, reinvented itself as a shareholding company named *Southern Publishing and Media Corporation* in December 2009, and got listed on the domestic stock market in February 2016. This chapter however, focuses on its operations before this transformation in order to explore the impact of the major policy initiatives detailed in previous chapters.

GDPG acted as a holding company for its subsidiaries. Operations within the headquarters were divided into a series of departments: the General Office, Human Resource Department, Finance Department, Development Strategy Department, Audit Office, Publishing Resource Department, and Party-cum-Mass Organizations Department. The Publishing Resource Department played a key role since it was responsible for the coordination and ratification of publishing plans of subsidiary publishing houses. Clearly, the holding company was mainly a management organization rather than a production center. Even so it incurred substantial running costs which were covered out of the profits generated by one of its subsidiaries, the Guangdong Textbook Reprinting Center (*guangdong jiaocai chuban zhongxin*).

The core business of GDPG was book publishing. There were eight subsidiary publishing houses within the group: the Guangdong People's Publishing House, the Guangdong Education Publishing House, Guangdong Science and Technology Publishing House, the Flower City (Huacheng) Publishing House (which specializes in literary titles), the New Century (Xinshiji) Publishing House (which publishes childrens books), the Guangdong Economy Publishing House (focusing on economics, business, and management books), the Guangdong Petrel Electronic & Audio—Video Publishing House, and the Guangdong Language Audiovisual & Electronic Publishing House. GDPG was also the holding company of the Guangdong Xinhua Book Distribution Group Company, which originated from the Guangdong Provincial Xinhua Bookstore.

As we have noted in earlier chapters, the economic sustainability of the book publishing business in China is by no means secure. Profit margins are generally low and the market is already saturated. In response to these uncertainties, GDPG made a concerted effort to identify new profit sources. Digital publishing and newspaper publishing, which fell within the administrative boundary of the General Administration of Press and Publication (GAPP), were seen as plausible options. A weekly newspaper, *Time Weekly* (*shidai zhoubao*), and a digital publishing company were launched in 2008 and 2009, respectively. As some subsidiary publishing houses of GDPG engaged in magazine publishing, GDPG operated in all business areas of print media.

In addition to the member firms engaged in publishing and distribution, there were a range of other divisions operating in other publishing related areas (see Table 8.1 for business areas of GDPG and its member firms).

GDPG then, was essentially a conglomeration of all business entities which used to be affiliated to the provincial publishing administration bureau, but it did not have a monopoly within the province. There are also publishing houses affiliated to other provincial government departments, universities, or municipal Party organs/governments and county or municipal level Xinhua bookstores affiliated to local Party organs/governments, some of which are financially buoyant due to the substantial affluent populations in the major urban centers. Guangzhou, the capital city of the province, and Shenzhen, the Special Economic Zone, both have well developed book distribution businesses controlled by the municipal governments.

Before we examine GDPG's operations in more detail however, we need to delve a little deeper into its formation and development.

8.2 THE CONGLOMERATION OF GDPG

8.2.1 The Development of the Provincial Publishing Industry and the Origin of GDPG

Before the economic reform, the Guangdong People's Publishing House was the only publishing house within the province and served as a propaganda "mouthpiece" of the provincial Party and government. At that time, there were parallel controlling bodies over the local publishing industry within both provincial Party organs and government. According to Wu et al. (1997: 335), the main responsibility of the local Party

Table 8.1 Business areas of GDPG and its member firms
GDPG—holding company

Business areas	Member firms
Publishing	Guangdong People's Publishing House, Guangdong Education Publishing House, Guangdong Science and Technology Publishing House, Flower City Publishing House, New Century Publishing House, Guangdong Economy Publishing House, Guangdong Petrel Electronic & Audio–Video Publishing House, Guangdong Language Audiovisual & Electronic Publishing House, and Beijing Lanyang Guangban Cultural Communication Company (a branch in Beijing)
Distribution	Guangdong Xinhua Book Distribution Group Company
Textbook reprinting and promotion	Guangdong Textbook Reprinting Center, Guangdong Xinyue Textbook Research and Development Company
Digital publishing	GDPG Digital Publishing Company
Printing	Guangdong Xinhua Printing Company
Printing materials	Guangdong Publishing and Printing Materials Company
Disc production	Guangdong Weiya Optical Disc Company
Newspaper/magazines	Times Media Company
Import and export	Guangdong Publishing Import and Export Company
Other businesses	Guangdong Xinzhiben Real Estate Management Company, Guangdong Dayanhai Industry and Trade Company (a company engaged in publishing, distribution, rights trading, and software development, etc. but without any core business area)

propaganda department was to provide political guidance and direction, exercise censorship, and crack down on illegal publications, and its main goal was to prevent "the publishing course from deviating from socialist publishing direction." At the same time, the provincial publishing administration department was charged with implementing "the guidance and policy" (ibid: 337) of the Party in the publishing plans of local publishers, and overseeing relevant aspects of economic planning, such as the allocation of paper and other printing materials, and coordinating business between the local publishers and Xinhua book distributors. To facilitate the smooth operation of the local publishing industry, all the key players, the Guangdong People's Publishing House, the Guangdong Provincial Xinhua Bookstore and the Guangdong Xinhua Printing Factory, were subject to the economic control of the provincial publishing administration department.

When the administration department was terminated in the chaotic Cultural Revolution, the Guangdong People's Publishing House took over its responsibilities from 1971, and acquired the provincial printer, the provincial book distributor,[2] and the provincial printing material supplier. The Guangdong People's Publishing House itself was put under the control of the provincial Party propaganda department. Clearly, this enabled the party-state to control the then book industry directly when its legitimate state agent, the government administration department, was no longer functioning.

After the Cultural Revolution, the initial priority was to restore the institutions destroyed by the political turmoil. The government administration department, Guangdong Provincial Publishing Administration Bureau (*guangdongsheng chuban shiye guanliju*) was established in March 1978. The Guangdong People's Publishing House handed its affiliated printer, printing material supplier, and book distributor back to the government administration department and became purely a publishing house (Wu et al., 1997: 278 and 337).

The initiation of economic reform however, gradually provided huge opportunities and incentives for the expansion of the provincial publishing industry. After the central government called for the development of science and technology after the National Science Conference in March 1978, nearly all provinces established a provincial Science and Technology Publishing House. The Guangdong Science and Technology Publishing House, initially the Science and Technology Editorial Office of Guangdong People's Publishing House, was spun off and launched in May 1978. The initial success of the economic reform generated rising incomes among a population whose cultural life had been seriously impoverished during the Cultural Revolution. The subsequent surge in demand for books provided a golden opportunity for the expansion of book publishing. At the same time, commercialization, which was converting provincial publishing houses and their affiliated provincial government administration departments into profit-seeking organizations, encouraged a rapid expansion in provincial publishing as these organizations looked for increased business opportunities. As part of this process, a number of the editorial offices previously housed within the

Guangdong People's Publishing House (GPPH) were spun off into new publishing houses. They were: the Flower City Publishing House (established in 1981 on the basis of the Literature and Arts Editorial Office of GPPH), the Guangdong Education Publishing House (established in 1985 on the basis of Education Editorial Office of GPPH), the New Century Publishing House (established in 1985 on the basis of Juvenile Books Editorial Office and the Childrens Books Editorial Offices of GPPH). Alongside this spinning off of existing divisions, new divisions were established by the provincial publishing administration department in order to enter new markets. They included: the Guangdong Language Audiovisual & Electronic Publishing House (established in 1983), the Guangdong Economy Publishing House (established in 1995 majoring in business and management books), and the Guangdong Petrel Electronic & Audio−Video Publishing House (established in 1996). In addition, other business entities were developed to diversify activities beyond publishing. These included: the Guangdong Second Xinhua Printing Factory, the Guangdong Publishing Import and Export Company, and the Guangdong Weiya Optical Disc Company. This initial spurt of expansion and diversification in the local publishing business, all of them controlled by the provincial publishing administration department, laid down the organizational foundations for the later establishment of GDPG.

As noted in earlier chapters, during the period of the planned economy, the provincial publishing administration department assumed both administrative and economic planning responsibilities for its subsidiaries[3] and under the centralized revenue collection and expenditure system (*tongshou tongzhi*) was obliged to return any profits generated to the government (Shirk, 1993: 199), which provided its core funding. Following the commercialization of the publishing industry, the provincial publishing administration department and its subsidiaries were turned into profit-seeking business entities. As a result, the Guangdong Provincial Publishing Administration Bureau, although still assuming administration responsibilities, was no longer funded out of the budget of the provincial government, but out of the profits it generated itself, especially from textbook reprinting. This arrangement produced a hybrid of government bureau and business entity generating tensions that gradually increased. As more publishing businesses were spun off from the Guangdong People's Publishing House and new ones were set up, the emphasis shifted to the department's business role.

Meanwhile, the rapid expansion of the publishing industry in the 1980s encouraged both other state agencies and universities to establish subsidiary publishing houses. Notable examples included: the Guangdong Tourism Publishing House (established by the Guangdong Provincial Tourism Bureau in 1981), the Guangdong Higher Education Publishing House (established by the Guangdong Provincial Bureau of Higher Education in 1984), the Cartographic Publishing House of Guangdong Province (established by the Guangdong Provincial Bureau of Land in 1980), and the Sun Yat-sen University Press (established by Sun Yat-sen University in 1983). The leading municipal governments also established their own publishing houses. Shenzhen City launched the Sea-sky Publishing House (*haitian chubanshe*) in 1985 with Guangzhou City following two years later with the Guangzhou Culture Publishing House (*guangzhou wenhua chubanshe*).[4] The profit-seeking orientation of these new publishing houses led to increased demands for the provincial publishing administration department to strengthen its administrative role, something it found difficult to do given that it was itself actively involved in pursuing business interests. This tension was addressed in 1983 when due to the governmental reshuffle the Guangdong Provincial Publishing Administration Bureau was replaced by the Guangdong Provincial Publishing General House. Although seemingly a business entity from its title, the Guangdong Provincial Publishing General House continued to assume responsibility for both administration and business. However, the continuation of this hybrid forms and its associated tensions generated increasing concern with the Party that insufficient administrative control was being exercised over a gradually commercialized publishing industry. Accordingly, in April 1986, the Guangdong Publishing General House was abolished and the Guangdong Provincial Publishing Administration Bureau (*guangdong sheng chuban shiye guanli ju*) restored, on the grounds that a general publishing house was "unfavorable for the censorship of publications and unfavorable for the unified management of editing, printing and distribution" (Wu et al., 1997: 338). In the following March the Guangdong Provincial Publishing Administration Bureau was renamed the Guangdong Provincial Administration of Press and Publication (*guangdong sheng xinwen chubanju*). Although using the title of a government department, it was legally a "public service unit managed as enterprises" (ibid: 338), and it was not until 1995 that it became officially a department of the provincial government and its employees were given the status of civil servants (Wu et al., 1997: 46−47). However, it only started to be funded out of the budget of the provincial government from October 2001 (Ding et al., 2004).

As we noted in earlier chapters, one of the key themes of economic reform was to adjust the relationship of the Party to the state and the state to the society. And as we also noted, although the principle of "separation of government and enterprises" had been implemented in many other industries, it was delayed in the publishing industry due to ideological concerns. To resolve the problems presented by its dual roles, the provincial publishing administration department established the Guangdong Provincial Publishing Company (*guangdong sheng chuban gongsi*) in 1980 to manage its core businesses in textbook reprinting and paper supply. The existence of this company was a major reason why the Guangdong Provincial Publishing General House could be abolished in 1986 while many other provincial publishing administration departments retained the title of provincial publishing general house to assume their business responsibility. The Guangdong Provincial Publishing Company set up a joint venture company[5] with Sino United Publishing, a Hong Kong-based publishing group, in 1988. Four years later, in August 1992, the Guangdong Provincial Publishing Company, and the Guangdong Education Publishing House, a profitable school books publisher, merged to form the Guangdong Provincial General Publishing Company (*guangdong sheng chuban zong gongsi*).

This new entity, which controlled most profitable business within the local publishing industry, was the core member firm of the provincial publishing administration department and was also responsible for its financial budget. The ambition behind its establishment, according to one of the then Deputy General Managers,[6] was to "concentrate the financial resources" in order to expand the provincial publishing industry after Deng Xiaoping's "southern tour" in early 1992.

With access to the sizable profits from school textbook publishing and reprinting, this new company was able to move quickly to consolidate and expand its operations. When the printing industry in Guangdong Province began to develop rapidly it merged two printing factories and established the Guangdong Color Printing Company (*guangcai yinwu gongsi*). Investments were also made in the establishment of the Guangdong Petrel Electronic & Audio−Video Publishing House and the Guangdong Weiya Optical Disc Company. A share-holding book distribution company, the Chunfeng Book Company, was also established in 1995. Through these diversifications and expansions the Guangdong Provincial General Publishing Company turned itself into the prototype of the GDPG.

As well as the Guangdong Provincial General Publishing Company, the provincial publishing administration department also controlled a few other provincial publishing houses and business entities, including: the Guangdong People's Publishing House, the Guangdong Science and Technology Publishing House, the Guangdong Provincial Xinhua Bookstore, and the Guangdong Publishing Import and Export Company. These member firms were largely left to be financially self-sufficient.

8.2.2 The Formation of GDPG

When the Guangdong Provincial General Publishing Company was launched in 1992, a draft plan to establish a publishing group had already been submitted to the provincial government for consideration.[7] Enthusiasm for forming a group was revivified when the party-state called for the establishment of business groups at the 15th National Party Congress in September 1997, and according to a former deputy general manager of GDPG, it was against this favorable general background that the provincial publishing administration bureau applied to the central party-state for the establishment of GDPG.[8] This application was approved in 1998 and became the first of its kind endorsed by the central party-state. Initially the Guangdong provincial publishing administration bureau tried to register GDPG as an enterprise group but the central Party propaganda department only agreed to it being constituted as a public service unit. This argument delayed the launch until the end of 1999 when GDPG was officially established on the basis of the Guangdong People's Publishing House and the Guangdong Provincial General Publishing Company.

The power struggle that accompanied the establishment of GDPG is worth considering further. At the time there were a few precedents for provincial publishing general houses and publishing groups gaining or trying to gain independence from provincial publishing administration departments. The Shandong Publishing General House managed to gain independence from the Shandong provincial publishing administration bureau in 1987, but the power struggle between the Sichuan Publishing Group Company and the Sichuan provincial publishing administration bureau at the beginning of 1990s led to the intervention of Sichuan provincial Party propaganda department (Wei, 2001: 10). The formation and expansion of GDPG followed a similar path. Some senior staff within the Guangdong provincial publishing administration department, who were about to assume important positions within GDPG, argued that it should be independent of the administration bureau according to the principle of "separation of government and enterprises." Most leaders of the provincial administration department however, due to their vested economic and power interests, opposed the independence of GDPG on the grounds that it would "weaken the leadership of the Party over publishing" and "endanger the (ideological) guidance" (Ding et al., 2004). This contest produced a compromise. GDPG achieved nominal independence from the provincial publishing administration department and its sponsoring organization (*zhuguan bumen*) became the Guangdong Provincial Government. However, the provincial publishing administration department was authorized by the provincial government as its agent to supervise the operation of "state-owned assets of the group" (Wei, 2001: 21). The Director of the provincial administration department also assumed the position of Chair of The Board of GDPG despite the opposition of some senior managers of the group. As a result, GDPG was still largely controlled by the administration department. In addition, a number of other provincial publishing business entities, including the Guangdong Science and Technology Publishing House, the Guangdong Xinhua Distribution Group, and the Guangdong Xinhua Printing Factory were still affiliated to the provincial publishing administration department. Although according to the original plan approved by the central party-state, the provincial publishing administration department would gradually hand over all other business subsidiaries to GDPG within a couple of years following the establishment of the group,[9] this step was halted by the provincial publishing administration department because of the continuing power struggle.

At the same time, the support of the party-state for the principle of "separation of government and enterprises" coupled with their ambition to develop the cultural industry favored the independence and expansion of GDPG. The central party-state embarked on the "reform of the cultural system" (*wenhua tizhi gaige*) in June 2003 and Guangdong province was chosen as one of the pilot regions for its implementation. The provincial Party committee and government set a target of building a "preeminent cultural province" (*wenhua dasheng*), and made a plan for the establishment or expansion of several provincial cultural groups, including GDPG and the Guangdong Xinhua Distribution Group. The provincial

Party leader visited GDPG in August 2003 and instructed it to "get bigger and stronger" (*zuoda zuoqiang*).[10] With this support from the provincial Party and government, GDPG eventually gained the upper hand in its power struggle against the provincial administration department, a victory symbolized by the director of the provincial publishing administration department being stripped of the position of Chair of the Board of GDPG in September 2003.

The provincial publishing administration department handed over all its business subsidiaries to GDPG in February 2004 retaining only administrative responsibilities. In a key shift in power, the provincial Party propaganda department took over from the Guangdong Provincial Government as GDPG's sponsoring and managing organization.

8.2.3 The Expansion of GDPG and the Local Government

Although the establishment of GDPG, like other media groups, was "fostered by administrative fiat" (Lee et al., 2006: 585) and backed by central government ambitions to create groups with the critical mass to spearhead the development of the cultural industries, its expansion cut across the economic interests of powerful municipalities within the province, generating struggles it was not always able to win. The battle for control on the Xinhua bookstore system provides a good example.

In 2007 Li Changchun, a former provincial Party leader before becoming the leading central Party functionary responsible for ideological and cultural issues, paid particular attention to the development of GDPG. During a visit to the group, he encouraged the merger of all provincial Xinhua bookstores, and the provincial Party leader agreed to implement this proposal. Although progress has been seen in many county level Xinhua bookstores, the overall target did not materialize. The Xinhua bookstores in Guangzhou City and Shenzhen City had both been heavily subsidized by their municipal governments with the result that it would "compromise the economic interests"[11] of different government departments if they were to be merged with the provincial Xinhua bookstore. Both municipal governments, sensing the potential risk of losing their control, merged their municipal publishing house with their municipal Xinhua bookstore to form municipal "publishing groups",[12] which forestalled the possibility of them being incorporated into the provincial distribution group. Theoretically, the hierarchical political structure should give the higher level Party organs the power to restructure the state-owned publishing industries under their administrative control. However, fiscal decentralization has "assigned local governments property rights over increased income" and "created strong incentives for local officials to pursue local economic development" (Oi, 1992: 100). Within Guangdong province, provincial government started fiscal decentralization from 1979 giving county level governments a certain degree of fiscal independence. It is this fiscal decentralization that limited the expansion of GDPG through administrative power. The municipal Xinhua bookstores in Guangzhou City and Shenzhen City have become economically strong due to their affluent urban markets and the financial support of their municipal governments. The net asset value of the Shenzhen Xinhua bookstore alone for example was estimated to be nearly twice that of the Guangdong Provincial Xinhua Distribution Group,[13] which clearly excluded the possibility of acquisition by the latter.

8.3 THE CORPORATIZATION OF GDPG

As enterprises are charged with profit-seeking as their primary goal, the corporatization of book publishing may seem to contradict the long-standing Party doctrine that regarded publishing houses as the mouthpiece of the Party. When the Guangdong provincial publishing administration bureau applied to the Central Party Propaganda Department to launch GDPG as a "group company," a deputy director of the department refused to register it as an enterprise group arguing that this would breach the principle that publishing houses should not be defined as enterprises.[14] However, this objection was swept away when the central party-state decided on a general policy of transforming public service units into enterprises. According to the Chief Editor of an education publishing house, "(the corporatization of publishing houses) was mainly the result of (the policy of) the central government. Guangdong is a pilot province (for the reform of corporatization). Marketization is linked with the macro state policy. Not only publishing houses, all public service units have to be reformed".[15]

The transformation of GDPG into an enterprise was required by the central party-state, who set a deadline for its completion.[16] Although provincial publishing administration departments lost their control over their provincial publishing groups as a result, provincial Party committees and governments continued to own and control their provincial publishing groups. Hence their political and economic interests were protected.

In addition, provincial publishing groups lost neither their monopolistic profits nor the financial support of provincial governments. As a result, their corporatization was easier than for publishers affiliated to central state agencies.

One major aspect of the corporatization process was the evaluation of the state-owned assets of GDPG as the benchmark for assessing its performance future. In an effort to lower the benchmark, GDPG tried to liquidate as much unsold book stock as they could, with the Chair of the Board urging subsidiaries to "grasp the excellent opportunity of reducing unsalable book stock by taking advantage of the preferential policy (of the government)".[17] The real impact of this jockeying for economic position was probably on the employees. As discussed before, employees in publishing houses would receive a reduced pension following the corporatization. In addition, GDPG had introduced a new salary system, in which 70% of the income of employees would come from bonuses related to individual performance. Although higher level management would be hardly affected by this, most employees might be forced to "dance better with shackles on" under the dual pressures of the party line and the bottom line.

Corporatization did not weaken the control of the Party. As mentioned in earlier chapters, the party-state announced "four unchangeables"[18] as its bottom line for the commercialization of book publishing. Although provincial Party organs and governments may resist some central party-state policies in an effort to protect their economic interests, they are still required to stringently implement the principles of ideological control. According to the requirement of the Guangdong provincial Party committee, GDPG must retain the "absolute leadership of the Party over publishing," uphold the Party's control over "important decisions of publishing organizations, ownership structure, final censorship of content and appointment of leading cadres," and explore "new measures" and "new forms" of retaining the "Party's control over ideology".[19] These requirements were enforced by administrative arrangements whereby GDPG's board of directors, management board, and supervisory board, were all controlled by the Party. These boards operated on the principle of "mutual entry and dual positions" (*shuangxiang jinru, jiaocha renzhi*), which meant that leaders in the Party committee of the group hold all the important business positions in the group. The Party secretary of the GDPG assumed the position of Chair of the board of directors. The deputy Party leader of the group, who had been the deputy director of the provincial publishing administration department before joining GDPG, became the managing director. The rest of the board of directors were made up of the deputy managing directors, all of whom were also leaders of the Party committee of GDPG. The Party discipline and inspection secretary (*jiwei shuji*) of the group, who mainly deals with corruption issues, became the Chair of the supervisory board. The division between the different boards however was an illusion as all their members were incorporated into a hierarchical Party system. Clearly, although GDPG tried to imitate modern corporate governance, the resulting structure was just a new bottle for the old wine. In addition, as the Party organs within the group are subject to the control of the provincial Party propaganda department, the legal status of GDPG as an independent business entity was just nominal.

If corporatization was intended by the party-state to create a more market-oriented publishing industry, this aim was not realized in the case of GDPG. Its member firms, ranging from publishers, distributors, paper suppliers, and printers, all developed business relationships during the period of planned economy and despite the change of economic situation and the development of market economy, these relationships persisted. Before it acquired the Guangdong Xinhua Book Distribution Group, GDPG complained that the "distribution channel (of its subsidiary publishing houses) was not smooth".[20] Now that it was controlled by GDPG, it was under pressure to display and distribute more books for its sister companies whether or not they were profitable. Similarly, publishers within GDPG were obliged to buy a certain amount of printing paper or printing services from their sister companies regardless of cost considerations. The Guangdong Publishing and Printing Materials Company for example, supplied printing paper to several publishers within the group for textbook printing at rates much higher than the market price. Its two major customers were the Guangdong Education Publishing House and the Textbook Reprinting Center, which were the two most profitable member firms of GDPG. The Textbook Reprinting Center paid an even higher price than the Guangdong Education Publishing House for the paper of same quality.[21] The Guangdong Xinhua Printing Company survived in a similar way. Its main business was to print textbooks for publishing houses within the group, but it charged a rate higher than the market price. GDPG also required its subsidiary publishing houses to contract a certain amount of printing business to this printer in order to sustain it.

Even without the preferential treatment given to other members of the group the state-owned publishing houses may still not be fully market-oriented. Take the Guangdong Education Publishing House as an example, it set up two subsidiary companies, the Tongwen Publishing Service Company and the Tongwen Colour Design Company, providing proofreading and typesetting services, respectively. Both were shareholding companies owned by the employees of the Guangdong Education Publishing House. In the case of Tongwen Colour Design Company, each employee was allowed to invest RMB10,000 yuan and usually received an annual dividend of around RMB4000 yuan.[22] However, about 60% of this company's business comes from its parent company, the Guangdong Education Publishing House, and it charged a rate higher than the market price for its service. The business model of Tongwen Publishing Service Company was similar. Even though Guangdong Education Publishing House was overstaffed, proofreading was still outsourced to this affiliate. This practice was not uncommon. The Guangdong Science and Technology Publishing House set up a typesetting company which operated in a similar way.

The available evidence then, suggests that corporatization did not succeed in converting GDPG and its member firms into independent business entities responsive to market forces. At the same time, it also underlined ways in which GDPG's activities and priorities were still shaped by the intervention of the party-state at different levels. It is to the practical operation of these persistent powers that we now turn.

8.4 PERSISTENT POWERS: GDPG AND PARTY POLITICS

8.4.1 Data Sources

Many state-owned enterprises in China publish regular internal newsletters. Within GDPG this role is performed by the *Information Bulletin* (*xinxi dongtai*) issued by the General Office, which informs the subsidiaries of GDPG and their employees of the events going on, policies to be implemented, or important publishing projects. There are also articles from employees expressing their views or publicizing their achievements. Although these articles usually did not cover a particular activity of GDPG, they provided useful information about the operation of publishers.

Before we extract a list of activities from the *Information Bulletin* for analysis however, it is worth bearing in mind that since it operates mainly as a propaganda and public relations tool this publication itself is likely to be selective. This raises two potential problems. First, it is unlikely to contain negative or critical information or commentary. Second, the importance of events perceived from the perspective of this publication is different from the perspective of this research. Events attended by high level Party or government officials, such as visits or speeches, are usually heavily covered, while other events such as decisions on new regulations of censorship are just mentioned briefly. To counter this tendency, the analysis of events will not take into account the amount of coverage given to items. Third, the coverage might not be complete and some events might be missing. Despite these limitations however, the material in the bulletin does provide a preliminary point of entry into the various ways the party-state impinged on the group's day to day operations and decision making.

8.4.2 Logging Activities

Because the focus of this analysis is on the operations of GDPG as a group company rather than on its individual member firms the small number of articles which were solely about the activity of particular member firms were excluded. As a general principle, activities attended by directors of GDPG or organized by GDPG or by different departments within the group company[23] will be counted as GDPG activities. If an event of a member firm was attended by one or more directors from the boards of GDPG (except for the Guangdong Xinhua Distribution Group,[24] it would be counted as an activity of GDPG. Some important publishing projects were also publicized in the *Information Bulletin*, but the group company of GDPG is not a licensed publisher and it has to rely on the cooperation of its member firms for any proposed publishing projects. As a guideline, only publishing projects involving participation or intervention of the group company will be counted as an activity of GDPG.

The volumes of the *Information Bulletin* I collected ranged from the end of 2003 to the beginning of 2007. Among these, only the volumes for 2004 and 2005 were complete. However, as GDPG underwent massive restructuring during its expansion and corporatization in 2004, only the events in 2005 were analyzed on the grounds that 2005 was likely to be more representative of operations in a "normal" year. The volumes of the *Information Bulletin* for other years however still provided useful contextual information about particular activities. Following the above principles, a total of 96 activities were collated from the operations of GDPG in 2005 (see Appendix 1).

There are three key research questions underlying the analysis presented here: To what extent was the operation of GDPG subject to the control of the party-state? What was the role of local Party/government in comparison with the central party-state? What was the function of individual activities?

To answer the above questions, the initiator and function of every activity logged was coded. Fitting messy real-life activities into clear-cut categories proved to be a difficult task and raised a couple of problems.

First, the boundaries between the party-state and GDPG as initiators, and between the central party-state and local Party/government, are often blurred. Although the party-state sometimes gave clear instructions relating to certain activities, it often just set a target and left GDPG to decide on appropriate actions. Within the Group, activities eventuating from clear instruction were known as "compulsory activities" (*guiding dongzuo*) and those with only set targets from the party-state as "optional activities" (*zixuan dongzuo*).

Second, there might be two or more initiators of the same activity or it might not be clear who the main initiator was.

Third, as politics and business are often intertwined in the operation of GDPG, the function of any single activity could be multifaceted. For example, a business meeting of GDPG may also convey ideological instructions from the party-state to the whole group, while the political studies or campaigns, required by the party-state, may also touch on the business issues within GDPG.

Last, there might be hidden or unstated motives accompanying the openly claimed purpose of any activity. For example, although the donation of books to poor areas was usually claimed to be part of poverty relief efforts, publishers may also regard it as a way of dumping unsalable books while also achieving favorable publicity for GDPG.

In order to address the above problems and ensure that the classification of activities was consistent, I developed the following guidelines:

a. Hidden or unsaid motives are not taken into account since on the basis of the evidence before us there is no way of discerning what they might be. While activities may be multifaceted, they will be classified by their main function. By "main function," I mean that without it an activity is unlikely to have happened. When it is difficult to discern the main function of an activity from the information provided, the intended direct beneficiaries of an activity will be taken into account. Multiple labels will apply occasionally when it is still difficult to identify the "main function" by following the above guideline, as in the case of meetings covering a wide range of topics. Multiple labels however should be regarded as a way of minimizing possible bias in the process of classification rather than as a way of achieving absolute precision, which is not intended and also unattainable.

b. Initiators of activities will be classified into "central party-state," "provincial Party/government," and "GDPG." The Party and the government are not differentiated, as they are usually entwined and the relationship between them is not our focus. Only the main initiator will be labeled. It is therefore essential to locate the boundary between the central party-state and the provincial Party/government. If an activity was a direct follow-up to an instruction of the central party-state, the initiator will be labeled as central party-state. Similarly, if an activity was implemented nationwide at the same time, even if the article claimed the provincial Party/government to be the source of the instruction, the main initiator will be labeled as the "central party-state." Otherwise, it will be labeled as the "provincial Party/government." In this case, extra background information of an activity might be necessary in order to make an accurate judgement, and this information can be easily acquired on line. If there is no direct instruction from the party-state, the initiator will be labeled as "GDPG." Following these guidelines, the initiator of most "optional activities" of GDPG which aimed at meeting the target of the party-state will be labeled as "GDPG."

c. In order to examine whether the activities of GDPG mainly served the Party or business interest, "Party" and "business" constitute the two main labels in identifying the function of activities. Party activities, such as the so-called Party construction (*dangjian*) activities, and propaganda will be labeled as "Party." Activities related to economic issues, such as the business operation of GDPG or the implementation of new policies of commercialization, will be labeled as "business." However, two other labels, "publicity" and "social intervention," are also adopted in the classification. Increasingly, the party-state has paid attention to publicity as well as propaganda. For the central party-state, the policy of "going out" is seen as a way of enhancing its "soft power" and improving its image. For the Guangdong provincial government, the target of building a "preeminent cultural province" places a premium on promoting a positive image of the province. The function of this kind of activity will be labeled as "publicity."

d. In addition, GDPG was often instructed by the party-state to help address different kinds of social issues. The plight of peasants in rural areas has been a long-standing concern for example. In an effort to address it publishers have been instructed by the party-state to produce books for peasants or migrant workers, normally accessible books on agricultural skills, or have been encouraged to donate books to poor villages, in order to help with poverty relief efforts. GDPG also published books for other contemporary campaigns, such as anti-SARS (severe acute respiratory syndrome) and antidrug campaigns. These activities will be labeled as "social intervention" according to their intended direct beneficiaries. In the occasional cases where the function of an activity is not discernible, it will be labeled as "miscellaneous."

Following the above principles, 96 activities were classified during the operation of GDPG in 2005 (see Appendix 1), of which 50% (48 activities) were solely or partially initiated by the party-state. In addition, the initiators of four further "optional activities," such as the donation of books to poor villages and the promotion of national or provincial image, were labeled as "GDPG" according to the classification guidelines, although they intended to meet the target of the party-state and were unlikely to have happened without its intervention (see activity 24, 26, 69, and 71).

Some business activities initiated by GDPG, such as corporate meetings on content production or meetings of senior editors, were also attended by officials from the provincial publishing administration department (see activity 5, 10, 34, and 88).

On the basis of these findings we can clearly see that GDPG remained strongly marked by the continual monitoring of the party-state supplemented by frequent interventions in pursuit of particular aims and policies.

8.4.3 The Role of the Party-State

When we talk about the central role that the party-state continues to play in shaping the activities of GDPG however, we need to be careful not to subscribe to the all-too-easy assumption that we are looking at a monolithic political force. As commentators have noted, decentralization has played a major role in dispersing Party power, and as we saw in Chapter 6, Corporatization: The Transition to Enterprises, local government interests are not always coterminous with central government aims.

Among the 48 activities classified here as solely or partially initiated by the party-state however, 29 were initiated by the central party-state and 20 by the provincial Party/government.[25] In addition, some activities initiated by the provincial Party/government were intended to meet the targets set by the central party-state on Party construction (e.g., activity 8, 9, 48, 53, 57) or on poverty relief (e.g., activity 39), although they were classified as being initiated by the local Party/government because they were not carried out nationwide at the same time.

These findings suggest that the central party-state remains the primary influence on the operations of GDPG in comparison with the provincial Party/government. Its dominance was exemplified by the visit of a top central Party leader to GDPG mentioned earlier. After Li Changchun, the top Party leader in charge of ideological and cultural issues, visited GDPG in March 2005, there were immediately follow-up visits from both the provincial Party propaganda department (see activity 16) and the central Party propaganda department (see activity 20) in order to ensure that his instructions were followed, not to mention the measures taken by GDPG in implementing his instructions (see activity 17, 21, 25).

The party-state intervened in the operation of GDPG to fulfill a range of functions—political, economic, and social. As mentioned before, the hierarchical Party organization within GDPG played a significant role in maintaining the Party control. There were frequent ideological study events and campaigns involving Party members rather than all staff. These efforts at exercising control through the "Party branch" constituted an important form of intervention.

The party-state intervened frequently in the content production of publishers but the purpose of intervention varies. Political propaganda continued to exist as a task for publishers but it was joined by interventions designed to bolster publicity, social intervention, or moral education, all of which featured frequently in the activities of GDPG. To differentiate propaganda from other kinds of content control, pure propaganda tasks and ideological censorship will be labeled as "propaganda" while other kinds of content control will be classified as "content."

In terms of business intervention, the central party-state tends to be more interested in institutional reform and industry planning. The provincial

Party/government, which owns GDPG directly, retains control over key personnel. It may also provide subsidies to GDPG by commissioning publishing projects. Correspondingly, "institution," "industry planning," "personnel," and "subsidy" will be used in the classification. The party-state may organize trade fairs or encourage GDPG to attend trade fairs in order to promote local publishing industry or to enhance its publicity. Activities with this kind of intervention will be labeled as "trade fair." All other kinds of intervention in the operation of GDPG will not be differentiated and will be labeled as "others." Meetings usually discuss a wide range of issues, and multiple labels will apply. Following these principles, the 48 activities involving the intervention of the party-state are further classified (see Appendix 2).

The ideological role of the publishing industry seems to have declined greatly in comparison with the Maoist period. Among the 48 activities linked to the party-state, 17 solely or partly fulfilled a "Party" function, while 22 fulfilled a "business" function. We should bear in mind however that other kinds of political controls exercised through regulations might not be manifested in these activities, so GDPG might face more control from the party-state than this list indicates. However, as regards the intervention of the party-state in the daily activities of GDPG, economic concerns appear to have become predominant in comparison with political concerns.

Interventions in content production for the purpose of propaganda were not very frequent in the sample under discussion here (only six activities were related to propaganda or ideological control), with more interventions in content production being actually for the purpose of publicity or social intervention (nine activities). This is arguably the result of the evolution of the Party ideology discussed in a previous chapter. Propaganda has become less effective due to the ideological crisis, and the economic performance and the responsiveness to social welfare concerns have emerged as new sources of legitimacy for the party-state. This was reflected in the shift of focus in interventions in content production, with publicity, social intervention, and moral education becoming more prominent.

However, the ideological indoctrination and the Party construction, such as the political campaign of "keeping communists advanced" or anti-corruption campaigns, still happened frequently within the Party organization of GDPG. As all key leaders within GDPG have to be Party members and a significant proportion of its employees are also Party members,[26] constant political indoctrination enables directors and most editors to work out where the ideological boundaries of the Party end, a perception which is essential for the self-censorship required to stave off more concerted external intervention.

Intervention by the party-state in the content production of publishers has repercussions for their business operations. Not all books for propaganda, publicity, or social intervention are money-losing projects. Take for example a publishing project of the Guangdong Petrel Electronic & Audio–Video Publishing House (see activity 9). It was commissioned by the provincial Party in February 2005 to produce a video CD, 120,000 copies of which were purchased by the provincial Party as training materials for Party organizations within the province. Even if the party-state does not provide a direct subsidy, it might resort to its administrative power to boost sales. A book on moral education was commissioned by the provincial Party from the Guangdong People's Publishing House. With the support of the provincial Party and government, sales reached 320,000 within the first year of its publication.[27]

However, most books of this kind are likely to be money-losing projects because the party-state usually just set a general propaganda target and let the publishing houses decide how they would meet it. As a result, many books were actually pitched at the Party rather than the market. Market research was completely irrelevant for these kinds of publishing projects, many of which were produced within a very short period of time in order to keep up with political events. An example was a book published by the Guangdong People's Publishing House shortly after the Indian Ocean tsunami in 2004. As medical volunteers were sent by the central government to disaster-stricken areas, the deputy director of the Guangdong People's Publishing House thought that there might be an opportunity for a publishing project of "dual benefits" (*shuangxiao*), which meant the book might pitch at the party-state and also for the market. Without any market research, a book about the experiences of several medical volunteers and journalists was commissioned and published in only 20 days. It was not a success.

Ideological propaganda tasks mainly came from the central party-state. Interventions in content production by the provincial Party/government were mainly concerned with securing publicity for the province. The provincial Party propaganda department often organized the publishing of books designed to promote local culture or local identity. Some of these projects, however, may slip into regional discrimination. An example was a book titled *Guangdong: Nine Chapters* (*guangdong jiuzhang*). After superficially comparing the "spirit" of people from different provinces, it attributed the economic growth in Guangdong province to the "Guangdong Spirit" (*guangdong jingshen*) and stereotyped "the Inlanders" (*neidi ren*) as unentrepreneurial.

8.4.4 Internal Controls

Given the persistence of the party-state intervention in its operations, GDPG, as an agent of the party-state, is obliged to assume responsibility for exercising political control over its member firms. There are two dimensions to this control—ideological propaganda and censorship.

In relation to the first, GDPG had to "take the initiative" to publish on "the (topics of) core tasks of the Party and the government"[28] and included all the propaganda topics instructed by the party-state in its publishing plans. To ensure this goal is pursued effectively, GDPG established a regular briefing meeting system, which "notifies and deploys the implementation of new guidelines from the higher level (Party/government)".[29] To encourage the publishing of propaganda books, GDPG provided financial subsidies of various kinds.[30] Benefiting from the sizable monopolistic profits derived from textbook reprinting, it set aside an annual amount of RMB3 million yuan (about US$471,000), as direct bursaries to the publishing of important propaganda books. For other propaganda projects, it either provided low interest loans to its subsidiaries or invested directly in the books as joint publishing projects.

In addition to ensuring that it met its propaganda obligations, GDPG also played an important role in the censorship of books published by its subsidiaries. To this end it established a dedicated department, the Publishing Resource Department (*chuban ziyuan bu*), to ratify the publishing plans of its subsidiary publishing houses. Publishing houses used to apply to the government administration department for approval of their publishing plans. They now had to apply both internally, to GDPG, and externally, to the provincial government administration department. To strengthen its in-house censorship, GDPG appropriated funds to recruit an "experts group" for the "scrutiny reading" (*shengdu*) of its publications.[31] All books on sensitive topics, together with a certain percentage of nonsensitive books, had to go through this process of "scrutiny reading." GDPG also stipulated the political responsibility of different departments, editors, and leaders of publishing houses and specified the possible penalty if there was any deviation from the party line in their publications[32].

GDPG, by working as both a key node in the communication flows between the party-state and its subsidiary publishing houses and as a financial sponsor of propaganda tasks, facilitated the continuing control of the party-state over the otherwise decentralized publishing houses following the "separation of government and enterprises."

On the basis of this case study we can argue that conglomeration, as a major policy for advancing the commercialization of publishing, may have led to stricter ideological control over publishers. Before the establishment of publishing groups, the provincial publishing administration department assumed both administrative and business responsibilities over its affiliated publishing houses. As the publishing administration bureaus had economic interest in the prosperity of their affiliates, they tended not to impose too strict a punishment if there was any ideological deviation in publications (Chinese Academy of Press and Publication, 1998: 49). One provincial publishing administration bureau for example, only fined an affiliate a small amount of money for publishing a politically unacceptable book, and even paid the fine themselves (ibid). In contrast, GDPG, having acquired independence from the provincial publishing administration bureau, might face tougher ideological control from the publishing administration department. Since the latter no longer has a direct economic interest in GDPG it may have strong incentive to display its administrative power in any power struggle. As the provincial government administration department had already been exercising censorship in the approval of publishing plans and regular "scrutiny reading" (*shengdu*) of books, the introduction of similar censorship measures by GDPG imposed an extra layer of censorship on publishing houses. As a result, some publishers complained that the establishment of publishing groups created an extra "mother-in-law" (*popo*) to control them. In addition, in pursuit of the group's economic interests, GDPG instructed its member firms to minimize "internal competitions" (*wolidou*) between them,[33] a move which also helped to reduce the possible impact of market competition on ideological control.

8.4.5 Taking Care of Business

Following its corporatization, GDPG has to be assessed regularly on its business performance by the provincial government. After taking over all the business entities formerly controlled by the provincial publishing administration department, the group started to streamline and restructure its business. A printing materials supplier and a paper supplier were merged into the Guangdong Publishing and Printing Materials Company, and two printing firms were merged into the new Guangdong Xinhua Printing Company. In an effort to cut operational costs, the sales and distribution departments of different publishing houses were restructured into a single sales company which provides warehousing and sales services to all subsidiaries. And, as mentioned earlier, it also diversified into digital publishing and newspaper publishing in search of new profit sources.

In addition, GDPG strives to maintain the financial sustainability of its member firms, by providing direct or indirect subsidies to them. For example, the Guangdong Education Publishing House used to be the only member publisher specializing in textbook publishing. In order to redistribute the profits from this sector more evenly across the group GDPG allocated the publishing of different subjects of textbooks to nearly every one of its subsidiary publishing houses. The Guangdong Economy Publishing House, the only publisher without a stake in textbook publishing, was sometimes given direct financial subsidies by GDPG.[34] The printing company and the paper supplier of GDPG, as discussed before, are also cross-subsidized by other publishing houses in the group. These measures had not been envisaged in the initial plans for conglomeration, but they certainly helped in maintaining the financial sustainability of the state publishing industry.

Further consolidation of GDPG was accompanied by tighter economic control over publishers within the group. Before GDPG's establishment, as the administration department of its predecessor, the provincial publishing administration department was not assessed regularly on its business performance and consequently its economic interests were concentrated on a couple of subsidiaries providing direct sources of funds, such as the Guangdong General Publishing Company. Other affiliated publishing houses enjoyed a larger extent of operational autonomy. As GDPG had to be assessed regularly on its business performance and was responsible for the state-owned assets of its subsidiaries, it had a stronger incentive to maintain close supervision over all the subsidiaries. As a result, its component publishing houses faced stronger economic control from the group company. GDPG for example, set up a Payment Center to deal with the cash flows from its subsidiaries, which centralized its supervision. The finance staff of its member firms were also now appointed by the holding company and its human resources department gained control over the staff recruitment of its subsidiaries.

Another important measure taken by GDPG to enhance its control over its subsidiaries was to require all new textbooks published by its member firms to be "invested in by the group (company)".[35] Although this may appear to be a financial subsidy, it has enabled GDPG to legally acquire the copyright of these textbooks. Given that these titles are the economic life-line of its subsidiary publishing houses, it puts them in a vulnerable position. According to the deputy director of a publishing house in the group,[36] although GDPG licensed the publishing of these textbooks to its subsidiaries without any charge, it could terminate the license at any time when it feels necessary. The survival of its subsidiary publishing houses is therefore under the control of GDPG.

Despite its relative economic buoyancy however, GDPG was never intended to be a pure business entity and would be unlikely to survive in open market competition. As a result, another important aspect of its business role is to bargain with the provincial Party and government to maintain the monopolistic profits from textbook publishing and distribution which are crucial for its survival. GDPG relies heavily on the administrative power of the provincial government for its monopoly in the provincial school book market. When its market share of textbooks in Guangdong Province was facing intense competition in 2004, it immediately sought to "win the support of (provincial) government" for protection.[37] In order to relieve the financial burdens on students, the Guangdong provincial government started to provide free textbooks to school children in rural areas from 2007. This annual government procurement amounted to RMB1.2888 billion yuan (about US$202.32 million) (Wei, 2007). GDPG not only won the contract to provide 80% of these textbooks, it was also entrusted by the provincial government with the responsibility for the government procurement of textbooks provided by nonlocal publishers. Publishers from other provinces were forced to sell their textbooks to GDPG at low prices or have their textbooks printed in Guangdong. Although the monopoly enjoyed by GDPG in its local market was criticized by many legal experts as illegal and harmful to the "public interest" (Yao, 2009), it was not weakened at all in the textbook procurements of 2008 and 2009 (Wang, 2009).

Supplementary learning materials are another important profit source for GDPG, and it often petitioned government departments to grant it a monopoly or compulsory distribution. A major government department involved in the market of supplementary learning materials is the provincial Department of Education which can rely on its administrative power to secure its desired outcomes. For example, the provincial Department of Education edited a book which was to be published by the Guangdong Education Publishing House. Although the editor commented in the book proposal that there were "serious faults" with the quality of this book, the book draft was still approved for publishing because the government department could secure a reasonable amount of sales.

8.4.6 GDPG after Corporatization

GDPG launched a shareholding company named the Southern Publishing and Media Company (SPM) by transferring all its core businesses to the latter in December 2009, and SPM was listed on the domestic stock market in February 2016. The transformation of GDPG, which is now effectively SPM, followed exactly the state guideline about the process of corporatization discussed in Chapter 6, Corporatization: The Transition to Enterprises. Although this recent change is not the focus of this discussion, it is worth asking whether SPM, by transforming into a public listed company, has become an independent business entity free from state intervention. The answer, however, remains unchanged.

One example is that SPM, following a directive issued by GAPP in 2012 on the development of publishing groups, established an editorial committee for the whole group company at the beginning of 2013. The main responsibility of this committee, which is composed of the directors of the group company and its subsidiaries, is to supervise the "ideological direction" (*zhengzhi daoxiang*) of its products. SPM also takes part in poverty relief effort organized by the government, and donated RMB2.69 million yuan in 2016 to a rural village that it is responsible for.

With the support of the provincial government, the monopolistic profit from local textbooks and supplementary learning materials market provides a lifeline to SPM, and its monopoly seems to be getting even stronger. SPM influenced the provincial government at the end of 2015 in the price setting of local textbooks, and assisted the government in deciding the provincial catalogue of approved textbooks, which could help the group to exclude the products of its competitors from the local market. When the provincial government raised its procurement budget for school textbooks in 2014, SPM even drafted a document for the government on the budget fluctuation mechanism based on the variation of production costs of textbooks. In addition, as discussed in Chapter 2, Mapping Book Publishing in China, the government started to adopt a series of new policies from 2011 on the publishing of supplementary learning materials, requiring these books to be approved by provincial governments before they can be listed in a catalogue for local schools to choose. These policies effectively turned the profitable business of supplementary learning materials into another area monopolized by the state-owned publishers, giving them a new source of profit. The Guangdong Economy Publishing House, the only publisher without a business in textbooks within SPM, greatly improved its profit by entering the business of supplementary learning materials. This partly explains why the annual revenue and the net profit of SPM have been growing while the whole book market stagnates (see Table 8.2). According to its annual report, SPM made a profit of RMB503 million yuan (US$78.96 million) on its revenue of RMB4920 million yuan in 2016.

Another significant portion of its profit are indeed the result of the preferential policies from the government, including the refund of enterprise income tax and different sorts of government grants, which amounted to RMB123 million yuan in total in 2016, nearly a quarter of its annual profit (SPM, 2017: 150). In addition to providing preferential tax breaks to publishing groups since 2009, the government seems to have increased its grants to SPM over the last few years (see Table 8.2). Consequently, market-oriented books play a much less important role in the business of SPM. SPM set a guideline for its editors to develop new book titles, which is to "pitch for (government) book awards, pitch for (government) grants, and pitch to the market" (*chongjiang, chongjin, chongshi*) (ibid: 28). As one of the SPM editors commented, many editors in the publishing industry tend to focus on Party/government commissioned books or propaganda books. No wonder that to "pitch to the market" is the last and probably least option in SPM's guideline. In the 2015 annual publishing plan of SPM, according to its own assessment, the number of market-oriented book titles only accounted for 54%, not to mention that many of them are likely to be unmarketable.

Table 8.2 Annual revenue and profit of SPM (million yuan)[38]

Year	2014	2013	2012
Revenue	4,414.48	3,800.52	3,178.44
Profit	351.44	295.19	275.65
Government grants	16.03	12.83	4.63

Source: SPM.

8.5 DIGITAL PUBLISHING: NEW TECHNOLOGY, OLD BUSINESS MODEL

With the rise of digital technologies in China, digital publishing business has been widely discussed in the publishing industry. As a response to the challenges and opportunities of digital publishing, GDPG launched the GDPG Digital Publishing Company in January 2009. However, the effort made by GDPG in its digital transformation is not from a purely commercial consideration, and its digital publishing business largely replicated its old business model.

The intervention of the party-state in the digital transformation of publishers is evident. In the case of GDPG, the government played an instrumental role in the establishment of GDPG Digital Publishing Company. As discussed before, many Chinese publishers rely on their monopolistic profit from textbooks and supplementary learning materials to survive, digital technologies have had little tangible impact on them. Although digital transformation is probably more of a buzzword than a real business consideration for many publishers, the Chinese government took strong policy initiatives to encourage the digital transformation in publishing industry. In the National 11th Five Year Plan for the Development of Culture (*guojia shiyiwu shiqi wenhua fazhan guihua gangyao*) promulgated in 2006, the central government called for the digital transformation of cultural industries, including the publishing industry. In order to facilitate this transformation, the government would provide funds for some digital publishing projects and would also launch a few digital publishing industrial parks across the country. Following this policy, GAPP, the government publishing administration department, established a dedicated branch in 2008 to be in charge of the digital publishing businesses. In response to the government initiatives, the China Publishing Group established the China Publishing Group Digital Media Company in 2008 under the "guidance of the Central Party Propaganda Department and GAPP" (China Publishing Group, c2009). GDPG followed suit by launching its New Media Publishing Center in the same year (Ma, 2010). The Guangdong provincial government also announced a few preferential policies in 2008, including government special funds for digital publishing projects, to support the "Digital Guangdong" initiative (Jiang, 2008). It is against the backdrop of these favorable local policies that GDPG turned its New Media Publishing Center into the independent GDPG Digital Publishing Company in 2009.

However, initiatives from the government are not the same thing as a clear and viable business model for publishers. One of the important sources of revenue for the digital publishing projects of GDPG (or SPM) is actually the subsidies from the government. According to the SPM annual corporate report (SPM, 2017: 150), of its ten projects subsidized by the government in 2016, five are about digital publishing or digital transformation, with one being on reorganizing the publishing workflow, one on an online virtual scientific experiments product, one on an educational resources platform, and two on the so-called MPR (Multimedia Print Reader) technology, which is a Chinese multimedia publishing standard similar to but less versatile than the augment reality (AR) technology. SPM received a total of RMB16.7 million yuan from the government (about US$2.62 million) for these projects in 2016. The subsidies from the government are substantial and frequent. One of the special funds from the provincial government granted RMB35 million yuan to seven digital publishing projects in 2009 and RMB40 million yuan to 14 projects in 2010 (GDPG, 2011). A significant proportion of them, if not all, would have gone to SPM. This does not mean GDPG Digital Publishing Company was the only recipient of these subsidies within the group. But it received a total amount of RMB5 million yuan (about US$785,000) in 2016 for the two MPR projects, and since its establishment, it has been granted 13 digital publishing projects subsidized by either the central or the provincial government (GDPG Digital Publishing Company, ca. 2016). The total amount of subsidies it has received must be significant. Recently, it was awarded a joint project subsidized by SAPPRFT in 2017 to establish a technology lab to explore the application of AR in education publishing. Running out of options or genuinely believing in the magic of technology, many subsidized digital publishing projects from Chinese publishers tend to focus on a fashionable digital technology rather than the content. However, focusing too much on technologies may put publishers in a direct competition with high-tech giants with ample resources, which they could never hope to win.

In addition to direct subsidies, digital publishing projects could help publishers to get another important resource from the government—the land. In the case of SPM, one such project is the establishment of the Dongpu Digital Publishing Industrial Park in Guangzhou. In China, all land is officially owned by the state and land sales are usually a crucial financial source for local governments. But the governments sometimes allocate (*huabo*) a piece of land for free to public welfare organizations, including cultural and educational establishments. In line with the polices of the central government, the Guangdong provincial government issued a plan, the Guangdong Provincial Plan on the Development of a Preeminent Cultural Province 2011–2020 (*guangdong sheng jianshe wenhua qiangsheng guihua gangyao 2011–2020*), in 2010 to develop its provincial cultural industries. In this plan, the provincial government decided to launch the Guangdong Digital Publishing Industrial Park (*guangdong shuzi chuban jidi*) and would offer preferential policy on allocating a piece of land for the park. The total gross floor area of this digital publishing park in Dongpu is said to be about 186,000 square meters when it is finished, and most importantly, this park is owned by the SPM. The digital publishing business of SPM certainly would not need that amount of office area, and it is not surprising that this piece of land was later changed from public sector land use to commercial use in 2017, although at a preferential price paid by the SPM. Considering China's heated property market, this piece of land will greatly improve the assets and economic resource of SPM. In addition to this industrial park, two more real estate projects by SPM are also under development. It seems that by taking advantage of the preferential policies offered by the government to the development of cultural industries, the so-called "cultural real estate" (*wenhua dichan*) is becoming another important business of SPM.

The best way to understand the business strategy of GDPG Digital Publishing Company probably is to look at its main projects and products. Its earliest project in digital publishing is the iximo.com platform, a "digital reading" (*shuzi yuedu*) platform supposed to target the trade market. iximo.com was launched in 2010 as an e-book vendor (it also became a self-publishing platform at a later stage), mainly to sell e-books from SPM. Clearly, this is hardly a viable business model as this platform would have to compete with well-established online booksellers such as Dangdang and Amazon. In addition, as iximo.com is a very small vendor, publishers are also unwilling to license their e-books to it. Most of the e-books on this platform are licensed by the member firms of SPM, not willingly though. As a senior manager from a publishing house within SPM commented, SPM as a whole group produces only a limited amount of noneducational titles (3644 titles in 2016 according to its annual report and of them, over 300 are the so-called "theme publishing" propaganda titles). Even if all the books from SPM are licensed to iximo.com, it still cannot become a platform big enough to be attractive to readers. The sales revenue for publishers through this platform would be very limited, not to mention that GDPG Digital Publishing Company takes commissions from the sales.

Understandably, trying to acquire the licenses of e-books from its sister companies has not been an easy task, and assistance from the top management of the group company is essential in this process. Consequently, iximo.com has become more like the bookstore run by a publishing house for direct-to-consumers sales (known as *sheban shudian*), only to be online. Many publishing groups seem to be doing the same direct-to-consumers sales on their own platforms, such as the ibookuu.com launched by Zhejiang Publishing United Group Digital Media Company, and the ishuke.com.cn by the Shandong Publishing and Media Company. Consequently, these online e-book selling platforms launched by Chinese publishing groups seem to be replicating a segregated industry structure in digital publishing.

Digital publishing is not mainly about the digital technology, but more about the publishing of content, and the source of content is crucial. The GDPG Digital Publishing Company, not a book publisher itself, does not have any content to license to other platforms or e-book vendors, and in order to establish its own platform, it needs to acquire as much content as possible. Facing the difficulty in acquiring e-book licenses from publishers, it has tried to turn iximo.com into a self-publishing platform, mainly for online fiction, which could significantly boost the supply of content. However, this effort put itself in competition with other significantly larger and well-established online fiction publishing platforms, and has not been very successful.

For GDPG Digital Publishing Company, the other option is to develop digital products for school students and teachers. After all, education publishing is the main source of profit for China's publishing industry. However, digital products for the education market usually require much more investment than e-books, and selling digital products to schools is not the same as selling textbooks to the provincial government. In addition, there are different versions of textbooks in the local market. Although textbooks published by the subsidiary publishing houses of SPM usually take a certain percentage of the market, those from the People's Education Press (PEP) are the leading ones. To minimize the risk and the investment, GDPG Digital Publishing Company became a sales agency for the digital products from PEP and its sister companies within SPM. The digital products from PEP include a teaching resources product for teachers, an e-learning product for students called PEP e-Learning, a multimedia textbook product, and an English learning mobile app. All these products are designed to supplement the use of textbooks from PEP. Digital Products from its sister companies, including e-textbooks and the Southern Virtual

Experiments (*nanfang xuni shiyan shi*), an online virtual science experiments product, are also intended to supplement the learning of textbooks from these publishers. Of all these products, the PEP e-Learning and the Southern Virtual Experiments are the two most widely used ones (Gao, 2016). However, according to the annual report of SPM, the total sales revenue of PEP e-Learning in Guangdong province, which was hailed by SPM as the top regional sales across the country, only amounted to RMB4.99 million yuan in 2015. The commission of GDPG Digital Publishing Company from these sales would be just a small proportion of it. The other widely used product, the Southern Virtual Experiments, is actually provided as a free additional product to schools who have adopted the science textbooks from SPM. Consequently, with limited income of commissions from these products, GDPG Digital Publishing Company had to try to invest in its own digital products. An important one is an e-learning platform called Smart Learning (*zhi xuexi*), which claims to provide personalized learning experiences for students based on the technology of machine learning and big data. But most of the products from GDPG Digital Publishing Company are meant to supplement the learning of particular textbooks. As the textbook market in China is segregated, the market for digital supplementary learning products centered on textbooks is also segregated, which has significantly reduced the economy of scale for any digital products from GDPG Digital Publishing Company.

But there is another source of revenue. Similar to commissioned book projects, digital publishing projects commissioned by the Party or government provide a source of indirect subsidies. A mobile app named Southern Learning Classroom (*nanfang xuetang*) from GDPG Digital Publishing Company was designed to provide reading materials for the Party members. According to the brief information about this product, it was started in 2010 under the "guidance of Guangdong Provincial Party Propaganda Department," and was designed to be a tool for the "construction of learning Party organizations" (GDPG Digital Publishing Company, ca. 2014-6). It is not difficult to see that it was a commissioned product from the local Party and would have received government funds.

GDPG Digital Publishing Company is still struggling to make a profit.[39] As can be seen, the inherent problems of China's publishing industry greatly impacted on the digital transformation of GDPG. Technology is not a panacea. It may provide solutions for the development of more versatile digital products, but it can hardly solve any institutional problems in China's publishing.

8.6 SUMMARY

As the evidence presented here suggests, GDPG may have gained independence from the provincial publishing administration department, but is still firmly controlled by the Party and far from being an independent business entity. Although regional governments may wish to protect their economic interests by setting up regional barriers, political control from the central party-state is still firmly installed in the publishing industry. Its propaganda role may have declined, but the party-state's ability to maintain its political control has not been weakened, and may have even been strengthened due to the added level of internal censorship instituted within publishing groups.

Although publishing groups have become more concerned with their economic performance, the present situation is some way from full commercialization. Because of their cultural role, publishing groups and their subsidiary publishers were never intended to be pure business entities, and many continue to rely on monopolistic profits or government subsidies for their viability and survival. The digital transformation in the industry can hardly solve the institutional problems and, on the contrary, is heavily shaped and constrained by them.

ENDNOTES

1. Based on the exchange rate of 1:6.37.
2. Guangdong Provincial Xinhua Bookstore became the distribution section of Guangdong People's Publishing House.
3. This was also manifested in the phenomenon of dual positions of government officials in publishing industry. According to Wu et al. (1997), very often the director of Guangdong People's Publishing House was at the same time the director or a deputy director of the government administration department.
4. When the *Guangzhou Culture Publishing House* was terminated by the government in 1990 due to the ideological crackdown following the Tiananmen Square student movement, Guangzhou City launched the *Guangzhou Publishing House* in 1992.
5. This joint venture company was called Farsight (*yuanwang*) Publishing Company Ltd. Although there is no detailed information about its business, it demonstrated the business ambition of the provincial publishing administration department at that time.
6. Interview.
7. Interview.
8. Interview.
9. Interview of a former deputy general manager of GDPG; Guan (2001) also mentioned it.
10. See the monthly corporate publication of *Information Bulletin* (*xinxi dongtai*).
11. Interview.
12. Shenzhen Publishing and Distribution Group was established in November 2007; Guangzhou Xinhua Publishing and Distribution Group was established in December 2008.

13. Interview with the Director of Guangdong Provincial Publishers Association.
14. Interview.
15. Interview.
16. See the corporate publication of *Information Bulletin* (*xinxi dongtai*).
17. See the corporate publication of *Information Bulletin* (*xinxi dongtai*).
18. They were discussed in Chapter 1: Introduction.
19. See the corporate publication of *Information Bulletin* (*xinxi dongtai*).
20. See the corporate publication of *Information Bulletin* (*xinxi dongtai*).
21. Interview.
22. Interview.
23. Labor Union and Youth League are not formal departments of the group and so are excluded.
24. The Chair of the Board of Guangdong Xinhua Distribution Group is also a deputy managing director of GDPG.
25. Activity 3 involved both the central party-state and the provincial Party/government.
26. By the beginning of 2005, about 23% of the employees of GDPG were Party members (see the corporate publication of *Information Bulletin*).
27. See the corporate publication of *Information Bulletin*.
28. See the corporate publication of *Information Bulletin*.
29. See an internal document of GDPG, which is titled Regulation on the Hierarchical Division of (Political) Responsibility of Publishing of GDPG (*guangdong sheng chuban jituan youxian gongsi tushu chuban cengji zeren ji zeren zhuijiu yu chufa banfa*).
30. See GDPG Regulation of Rewarding Content Production (*guangdong sheng chuban jituan youxian gongsi neirong shengchan jiangli banfa*) and GDPG Regulation of Sponsoring Important Projects of Content Production (*guangdong sheng chuban jituan youxian gongsi fuchi neirong shengchan zhongdian xiangmu banfa*).
31. See GDPG Regulation on the Scrutiny Reading of Publications (*Guangdong sheng chuban jituan youxian gongsi chuban wu shenu guanli banfa*).
32. See GDPG Regulation on the Hierarchical Division of (Political) Responsibility of Publishing of GDPG (*guangdong sheng chuban jituan youxian gongsi tushu chuban cengji zeren ji zeren zhuijiu yu chufa banfa*).
33. See the corporate publication of *Information Bulletin* (*xinxi dongtai*).
34. According to an informal interview, *Guangdong Economy Publishing House* once applied to GDPG for bankruptcy, and was given RMB2.5 million yuan (roughly US $392,500) by GDPG to survive.
35. See *Information Bulletin*.
36. Interview.
37. See the corporate publication of *Information Bulletin* (*xinxi dongtai*).
38. SPM IPO Prospectus.
39. Interview.

REFERENCES

China Publishing Group, c2009. China publishing group digital media company (*zhongban jituan shuzi chuanmei youxian gongsi*). <http://www.cnpubg.com/overview/member/2012/1023/5170.shtml> (accessed 15.12.17) (in Chinese).

Chinese Academy of Press and Publication (Ed.), 1998. Research on the Reform and Development Strategy of Publishing Industry (*chuban gaige yu chuban fazhan zhanlue yanjiu*). China Books Publishing House, Beijing (in Chinese).

Ding, G., et al., 2004. Provincial publishing group to be transformed into an enterprise, government department ceased its role of player (*sheng chuban jituan jiang zhuanzhi wei qiye, zhengfu buzai dang yundongyun*). Southern Daily (nanfang ribao) September 3, 2014. <http://www.southcn.com/news/gdnews/hotspot/qhch/tz/200409030098. htm> (accessed 07.04.09) (in Chinese).

Gao, Y., 2016. The Cantonese way of digital transformation of traditional educational publishing (*chuantong jiaoyu chuban de yueshi shuzi hua zhuanxing*). <http://www.chinabookinternational.org/2016/0726/124207.shtml> (accessed 15.12.17) (in Chinese).

GDPG, 2011. National digital publishing base launched in Guangdong (*guojia shuzi chuban jidi zhengshi luohu guangdong*). <http://www.gdpg.com.cn/index.php?g = &m = article&a = index&id = 182&cid = 8> (accessed 12.12.17) (in Chinese).

GDPG Digital Publishing Company, ca. 2016. Company profile (*gongsi jianjie*). <http://www.digigd.com/about.php> (accessed 15.12.17) (in Chinese).

GDPG Digital Publishing Company, ca. 2014-6. Southern learning classroom (*nanfang xuetang*) <http://www.digigd.com/product.php?id = 411db37b6a2a0d9d7c8e29a1c248d942> (accessed 15.12.17) (in Chinese).

Guan, R., 2001. Guangdong provincial publishing group (*guangdong sheng chuban jituan*). In: Yu, M. (Ed.), Study on Publishing Groups (*chuban jituan yanjiu*). China Books Publishing House, Beijing, pp. 112−118. (in Chinese).

Jiang, D., 2008. Industrial output of digital publishing exceeding 10 billion yuan, Guangdong province strives to be an important business centre in 10 years (*guangdong shuzi chuban chanzhi cao baiyi, lizheng shinian cheng zhongyao jidi*). <http://www.china.com.cn/book/txt/2008-09/03/content_16379824.htm> (accessed 15.12.17) (in Chinese).

Lee, C.C., He, Z., Huang, Y., 2006. 'Chinese Party Publicity Inc.' Conglomerated: the case of the Shenzhen Press Group. Media, Culture and Society 28 (4), 581−602.

Ma, T., 2010. The progress of digital transformation in publishing groups (*chuban jituan shuzi hua jinjie*). <http://media.people.com.cn/GB/40628/12606491.html> (accessed 11.11.17) (in Chinese).

Oi, J.C., 1992. Fiscal reform and the economic foundations of local state corporatism in China. World Politics 45 (1), 99−126.

Shirk, S.L., 1993. The Political Logic of Economic Reform in China. University of California Press, Berkeley, CA.

SPM, 2017. SPM annual report 2016. <http://www.sse.com.cn/disclosure/listedinfo/announcement/c/2017-04-06/601900_2016_n.pdf> (accessed 11.11.17) (in Chinese).

Wang, S., 2009. Interpretation: the interest chain behind the plate-renting of school textbooks (*jiedu xuesheng jiaocai zuxing beihou de liyilian*). <http://www.nx.xinhuanet.com/point/2009-04/07/content_16174037.htm> (accessed 24.08.09) (in Chinese).

Wei, X., 2007. Supply of free textbooks for compulsory education in Guangdong (*guangdong yiwu jiaoyu mianfei jiaocai gongying jishi*). China News and Press Journal (*zhongguo xinwen chubanbao*). 12 September, 2007. <http://media.people.com.cn/GB/22114/77961/77962/6250994.html> (accessed 24.04.09) (in Chinese).

Wei, Y., 2001. Study on China's publishing groups (*woguo chuban jituan yanjiu*). In: Yu, M. (Ed.), Research on Publishing Groups (*chuban iituan yanjiu*). China Books Publishing House, Beijing, pp. 1−55. (in Chinese).

Wu, Z., et al., 1997. Archives of Guangdong Province: Publishing (*guangdong shengzhi: chubanzhi*). Guangdong People's Publishing House, Guangzhou (in Chinese).

Yao, F., 2009. Attractive 30 billion market of free texbooks: the monopoly of Guangdong and Guangxi were criticised as illegal (*mianfei jiaocai 300 yi shichang youren liangguang qiangqie dangao bei zhi wefa*). Legal Daily (fazhi ribao) 3 March, 2009 <http://news.xinhuanet.com/edu/2009-03/03/content_10933837.htm> (accessed 24.04.09) (in Chinese).

CONCLUSION

This book has explored the dynamics of institutional change during the commercialization of China's publishing industry. Although the commercialization of Chinese media has been a topic of much research, there is still a lack of literature on how this process is unfolding on the ground. In approaching this task, this study, acknowledging the possible different transformation dynamics in different media sectors, has focused solely on book publishing. Although book publishing has been at the forefront of China's media commercialization, it has largely been neglected in the studies of contemporary Chinese media. This study has been intended as a modest attempt to fill this lacuna.

Professionals in the book trade tend to discuss China's publishing industry from a business perspective. However, applying this perspective to an industry that is not completely driven by business dynamics is destined to reach an impasse in trying to understand the shifting rules of the game. The defining feature that distinguishes China's publishing industry from that of most other countries is the persistent control by the party-state over both individual state-owned players and the game rules of the industry. After the disastrous Cultural Revolution, the party-state was forced to reorient its relationship with the society in order to avoid the collapse of the regime. The resulting reforms have triggered a profound political, economic, and cultural transformation. In the publishing industry, this reorientation has been manifest in the gradual introduction of market forces and the adjustments to the strategies for maintaining the Party control, which led to a hybrid state-and-market system. This study has attempted to investigate how the interplay of the party-state and market forces has been driving the institutional change of China's publishing industry during its commercialization.

It has been argued that the commercialization of the publishing industry cannot be fully understood without taking into account the transformation of the wider political and economic context after the economic reforms. Although the commercialization was initiated by the party-state, it was not completely under its control at the early stage of this process. But after the initial stage of transformation, from a predominantly state-planned system to a hybrid system, the party-state regained predominance over the process of further commercialization. An investigation of two key policies employed to transform the publishing industry, conglomeration and corporatization, revealed that they were mainly processes led by the party-state, though it also revealed the tensions between the central and local levels of the government.

Although the establishment of corporatized publishing conglomerates appears to be a major step toward the commercialization of the publishing industry, it has actually achieved little in improving the economic efficiency of the industry. Empirical evidence, from the case study of the Guangdong Provincial Publishing Group, revealed that the party-state still features prominently in the daily operation of state publishing groups. Although the government administration departments gave up the control over their affiliated publishing houses during the process of conglomeration, the Party propaganda departments have taken direct control of most publishing groups.

Overall, the evidence from this study suggests that the party-state has largely retained its control over the publishing industry in the process of commercialization and that the daily operations of state publishing houses are still heavily oriented toward its requirements and priorities. Although profit-seeking may now feature prominently in the goals of the publishing industry, this can also be considered part of the party-state's efforts to develop the cultural industries. Propaganda tasks may have waned in the operations of the state publishing industry, but this is mainly the result of the ideological renovation of the Party rather than a signal of its weakened ideological control. Since economic growth became the prime task of the party-state, the role of the publishing industry has shifted. This ideological shift has in turn facilitated the commercialization of the publishing industry. However, as the renovation of the Party ideology may have come to an end and there has also been a concentration of power within the Party, the ideological control from the party-state over the media is likely to be intensified.

Decentralization has led to the expansion of local publishing industry, but has not impaired the party-state in exercising its political control. Due to the financial decentralization of the party-state however, local governments have gained greater power over economic issues of local publishing industries and can sometimes resist the policy of the central party-state. However, empirical evidence from the case study showed that the political control of the central party-state continues to be effectively implemented.

Nor has the drive toward commercialization led, in itself, to a greater role for market forces in the operations of the publishing industry. Economically, by relying on monopolistic profit (mainly from school books) and indirect subsidies from the government, publishing groups have helped to maintain the economic sustainability of the publishing industry through cross-subsidies within groups, which cushions and constrains the impact of market competition. In addition, the corporatization of publishing houses has opened a new channel of financing through the diversification of ownership, which also helps to boost the economic sustainability of the industry.

At the same time, the commercialization of China's publishing industry is full of contradictions. As we noted in Chapter 6, Corporatization: The Transition to Enterprises, although the Ministry of Education moved to open up the school textbook market and introduced the bidding system into the textbook distribution business, this was manipulated by provincial governments who acted to protect their local industrial base. The reform initiated by the Ministry of Education had to be halted. The result was a prime instance of how the process of commercialization has been marked by the divergent priorities of central and local government. In addition, although the government encouraged the development of cultural industries, including the publishing industry, market competition has been constrained. Monopoly has become entrenched in the textbook business and also extended to the business of supplementary learning materials. Available financial data from corporatized publishing conglomerates indicate that the government may have increased its indirect subsidies to the state-owned publishing industry, leaving the further commercialization of state publishing industry elusive.

The most significant opening up of the book market has been the emergence of private publishers. As discussed in Chapter 3, From Communization to Commercialization: China's Publishing From 1949 to 1992, private publishers emerged not as a result of central government policies toward publishing but as an unintended consequence of the commercialization. The rise of digital technologies has also opened new business opportunities for private capital. Although e-book publishing business has been restricted to licensed state-owned publishers, private companies have now dominated the online fiction business.

The government has pushed to assimilate private publishers into the state publishing sector in different ways, such as the establishment of joint-ventures between the private and state-owned publishers, and the launch of Beijing Publishing Creative Industry Park where the state-owned Beijing United Publishing Company functions as an agent of the party-state in censoring the manuscripts from private publishers, while at the same time provides certain services to facilitate the operation of private publishers. Here we see that the central government has not only tolerated the existence of private publishers, but also aimed to capitalize on the proven entrepreneurship of the private sector to reinvigorate the state publishing industry.

At the time of writing, the party-state announced its new plan of government reshuffle in March 2018. The press and publishing industry will be put under the direct supervision of the central Party propaganda department. This new development appears to be in line with the trend captured in this study that the Party has intensified its ideological control and has also taken more direct control of publishing groups. How will the role of market forces evolve in China's publishing industry in this situation? Although there might be backlashes in the realignment of state and market relationships in the publishing industry, market forces are likely to carry on playing an important role in this hybrid state-and-market system as long as the economic growth is still the prime goal of the party-state.

APPENDIX 1

GDPG Activities in 2005

Activity number	Events	Description	Initiator	Function
1	Meeting on mobilizing the political movement of "Keeping Communists Advanced"	"Keeping Communists Advanced" is a movement instructed by the central Party from January 2005.	Central party–state	Party
2	Launch ceremony of a book series on the issue of "three-rurals" (peasants, villages and agriculture)	Books dealing with the issue of "three-rurals" are encouraged by the central party-state.	Central party–state	Social intervention
3	Annual meeting on the work plan of the new year	A meeting on implementing the instruction of GAPP and the provincial Party propaganda department. Topics included propaganda and moral education tasks, commercialization and business operation of GDPG.	Central party–state, provincial Party/government, GDPG	Party, business
4	Celebratory meeting about the merger of a printing materials supplier and a paper supplier	The merger of two member firms into one.	GDPG	Business
5	Meeting of senior core staff	A couple of officials from the provincial administration of Press and Publication (APP) also attended the meeting.	GDPG	Business
6	Implementing the political movement of "cadres into rural areas" (*xia jiceng*). A couple of employees were sent to a poverty-relief village	The movement of "cadres into rural areas" was organized by the provincial Party. However, it has been implemented across the country since 1990.	Central party–state	Social intervention

Activity number	Events	Description	Initiator	Function
7	Political study of "Keeping Communists Advanced"	"Keeping Communists Advanced" was a thought work among Party members and was instructed by the central Party.	Central party–state	Party
8	The 7th Publishing Learning Forum (Organized by the provincial APP and GDPG)	This session, entitled "Party's leadership and current economic situation," was claimed to be related to the campaign of "Keeping Communists Advanced."	Provincial Party/ government	Party
9	Publishing of a video CD for the political study of Party members during the campaign of "Keeping Communists Advanced"	This video CD was commissioned by the provincial Party to an audio–video publisher of GDPG.	Provincial Party/ government	Party
10	End of year meeting by the Guangdong Xinhua Distribution Group	Attended by the Managing Director of GDPG and also officials from provincial APP.	GDPG	Business
11	Signing anticorruption commitment agreements in accordance with the Party discipline and anticorruption requirement	Part of the campaign of the central Party against the problem of corruption. All leaders of GDPG and its subsidiaries had to sign it.	Central party–state	Party
12	Visit of officials from the provincial APP to several member firms of GDPG	Purpose of this visit is not discernible.	Provincial Party/ government	Miscellaneous

(Continued)

Activity number	Events	Description	Initiator	Function
13	Recruitment of new staff for the group company		GDPG	Business
14	Celebration of Spring Festival with retired staff		GDPG	Business
15	Visit of Li Changchun, a central Party leader to GDPG	The focus of the visit is on the reform of cultural industry, ideological control and the "going out" policy.	Central party–state	Party, business, publicity
16	Visit of officials from provincial Party propaganda department	Mainly a follow-up meeting on how to implement Li Changchun's Instruction on the reform of publishing industry.	Central party–state	Business
17	Meeting of GDPG on implementing Li Changchun's Instruction	A follow-up meeting on implementing Li Changchun's instruction on the reform of publishing industry.	Central party–state	Business
18	Meeting on the appointment of leaders to the new corporatized GDPG	Appointment was made by the provincial Party.	Provincial Party/government	Business
19	Meeting on the political movement of "Keeping Communists Advanced" (second stage)		Central party–state	Party
20	Visit of officials from the central Party propaganda department and GAPP to GDPG	A follow-up visit on how GDPG would implement the instruction of Li Changchun. GDPG was instructed to push forward its corporatization, implement the policy of "going out," and ensure ideological control.	Central party–state	Party, business, publicity

Activity number	Events	Description	Initiator	Function
21	Visit to Liaoning Publishing Group in order to learn from its reform	Li Changchun instructed GDPG to learn from Liaoning Publishing Group on its reform in his visit.	Central party-state	Business
22	Meeting on the strategy of "going out" and on attending international book fairs	A meeting on implementing the "going out" policy instructed by the central Party propaganda department and GAPP.	Central party-state	Publicity
23	Party's "Democratic Meetings"	Provincial Party required Party committees in governments and SOEs to run open forums in order to receive feedback from employees. But it was a policy implemented from 1990 by the central Party.	Central party-state	Party
24	Donation of books to schools in poverty relief villages and donation of books to a school in Guangzhou	It was claimed to be part of the movement of "Keeping Communists Advanced," but there was no direct instruction from the Party or government.	GDPG	Social intervention
25	Briefing meeting about the visit to Liaoning Publishing Group	A follow-up to Li Changchun's instruction.	Central party-state	Business
26	Salon of the directors of a few publishing houses from Guangdong	The salon, organized by GDPG in Hong Kong, was part of the effort of "going out" and the topic was on the entry into Hong Kong market. It was also attended by the Director of the provincial APP.	GDPG	Publicity

(Continued)

Activity number	Events	Description	Initiator	Function
27	Launch ceremony of a book series on "Lingnan (or Guangdong) Culture"	Book series organized by the provincial Party and government to publicize the local culture.	Provincial Party/ government	Publicity
28	Meeting on the political movement of "Keeping Communists Advanced" (third stage)		Central party–state	Party
29	Visit to a poverty relief county and villages	It was claimed to be part of the "cadres into rural areas" movement.	Central party–state	Social intervention
30	Training course for new staff		GDPG	Business
31	The 20th anniversary celebration of New Century Publishing House		GDPG	Business
32	School textbooks bidding in Yunnan Province		GDPG	Business
33	Invitation to tender of physical examination service to employees		GDPG	Business
34	Meeting about the content production of publishers	The topic was on improving its competitiveness on content production. It was also attended by officials of the provincial APP.	GDPG	Business
35	Visit to Shanghai Century Publishing Group	Learning the experience of Shanghai Century Publishing Group on content production.	GDPG	Business

Activity number	Events	Description	Initiator	Function
36	Board meeting	The meeting approved business plans on the organizational structure, merging of two subsidiaries, human resource management, and the financial report of a member firm.	GDPG	Business
37	Meeting with the provincial government Education Department	The meeting was on the promotion and distribution of supplementary learning materials, and was also attended by the officials from local education departments.	GDPG	Business
38	Awarding ceremony for the successful development of senior high school textbooks	Textbooks were codeveloped with provincial Education Department and South China Normal University. Further tasks, such as teachers training and promotion, were also given.	GDPG	Business
39	Donation of books on the topic "three–rurals" to poverty relief villages	Organized by the provincial APP.	Provincial Party/ government	Social intervention
40	Appointment of managers to a member firm		GDPG	Business
41	Meeting with United Publishing Group (Hong Kong) on possible cooperation	The meeting discussed the possible cooperation on magazine publishing, e-book publishing, online learning, animation production, etc.	GDPG	Business

(Continued)

Activity number	Events	Description	Initiator	Function
42	Entrusting Anhui Provincial Xinhua Distribution Group as the agent for school textbooks bidding in Anhui province		GDPG	Business
43	Cooperating with a local publisher in Shaanxi province for school textbooks bidding in Shaanxi province		GDPG	Business
44	Visit of GAPP officials to Hong Kong Xinhua Bookstore	Hong Kong Xinhua Bookstore was a joint-venture invested by GDPG and a Hong Kong company as a channel of selling books published in mainland China.	Central party–state	Publicity
45	Election of Party Committee of GDPG group company	This kind of election is the requirement of the Party constitution.	Central party–state	Party
46	The publishing of a book on local culture, which is entitled You Don't Really Understand Cantonese People (*qishi ni budong guangdongren*)	The Director of provincial APP and the Chair of Board of GDPG proposed this publishing project.	Provincial Party/ government, GDPG	Publicity
47	Appointment of managers to Guangdong Education Publishing House		GDPG	Business
48	The 9th Publishing Learning Forum (on the topic of anti-corruption)	In response to the provincial Party's movement of "Disciplinary Education Month."	Provincial Party/ government	Party

Activity number	Events	Description	Initiator	Function
49	Visit of Executive MBA training staff to several corporations	Organized by the Human Resource Department of GDPG.	GDPG	Business
50	Meeting on the transformation of subsidiaries into enterprises	Guangdong was chosen by the central party-state as a pilot province for the reform of cultural system.	Central party-state	Business
51	Publishing and donation of a new book on the Antidrug Campaign	Nationwide antidrug education was instructed by the central party-state.	Central party-state	Social intervention
52	Meeting on the editorial administration service	The main topic was on the submission of publishing plans and application for ISBN.	GDPG	Business
53	Mobilization meeting on the movement of "Disciplinary month" and a visit of more than 100 staff to a court trial	Required by the provincial Party disciplinary department.	Provincial Party/government	Party
54	Training for school teachers on the use of textbooks		GDPG	Business
55	Mid-year meeting on the business operation		GDPG	Business
56	Meeting on the political study among leaders of GDPG	The provincial Party instructed this political study in all provincial state-owned enterprises.	Provincial Party/government	Party
57	Meeting on the organization of 2005 South China Book Fair	This book fair is entrusted to GDPG by the provincial Party and government as part of the effort of building a "pre-eminent cultural province"	Provincial Party/government	Publicity

(*Continued*)

Activity number	Events	Description	Initiator	Function
58	Visit to Shanghai Century Publishing Group and Zhejiang Xinhua Bookstore Group	Learning the experience of merging book distribution business of member firms.	GDPG	Business
59	Visit to retired staff who took part in World War Two	Part of the activities in celebration of the end of "Anti Japanese Aggression War." This kind of visit happens in most state-owned enterprises and other state-controlled organizations.	Central party–state	Miscellaneous
60	Visit to subsidiary publishing houses and discussions on their publishing plans		GDPG	Business
61	Meeting on the policy of further reform of state-owned enterprises and enhancing the ability of innovation	Following the visit of the Prime Minister to Guangdong, the provincial Party/government instructed state-owned enterprises to deepen their reform and enhance the ability of innovation.	Central party–state	Business
62	Attending Beijing International Book Fair	Organized by the provincial APP, but GDPG might have attended without its instruction.	Provincial Party/ government, GDPG	Publicity, business
63	Appointment of a deputy manager of Textbook Reprinting Centre		GDPG	Business
64	Organizing the publishing of a book entitled *Annual China Reader*	Effort of GDPG to establish its brand.	GDPG	Business

Activity number	Events	Description	Initiator	Function
65	Graduation Ceremony of Executive MBA training staff	Arranged by the Human Resource Department of GDPG.	GDPG	Business
66	Meeting on the publishing and distribution of supplementary learning materials	Attended also by officials from the provincial government Department of Education.	GDPG	Business
67	Organizing printing exhibition	Organized by the provincial APP and GDPG.	Provincial Party/government, GDPG	Business
68	Celebration of Teacher's Festival	Celebration with about 300 school teachers. It might help with the promotion of books published by GDPG to schools.	GDPG	Business
69	Donation of money and books to a poverty-relief village and other cities		GDPG	Social intervention
70	Meeting on implementing the decisions of the 5th Plenary of 16th National Party Congress	The Party Congress decided the development plan for the next five years. Most state-owned enterprises held such a meeting to implement the guideline of the central party–state. GDPG proposed publishing tasks on ideological propaganda, promotion of local culture, and also planned to finish the corporatization of subsidiary publishers.	Central party–state	Party, business

(*Continued*)

Activity number	Events	Description	Initiator	Function
71	Publishing of a book series entitled *Spirit of Cantonese People* by Guangdong People's Publishing House	The provincial Party/government started a discussion on the so-called spirit of Cantonese people after the SARS epidemic. GDPG then instructed Guangdong People's Publishing House to publish books on this topic.	GDPG	Publicity
72	Opening Ceremony of Guangzhou International Animation Exhibition	Part of the activities of South China Book Fair. The organization of the fair was entrusted by the provincial Party/government to GDPG.	Provincial Party/government	Business, publicity
73	Appointment of managers to member firms		GDPG	Business
74	Anti-corruption meeting on a case happened in GDPG	Organized by the provincial Party disciplinary organ.	Provincial Party/government	Party
75	Pan Pearl River Delta Publishing Forum	Organized by the local APPs of nine provinces including Guangdong.	Provincial Party/government	Business
76	English training for staff attending Frankfurt Book Fair	Organized by the Human Resource Department of GDPG.	GDPG	Business
77	Visit of a deputy Director of GAPP to GDPG	GAPP was collecting feedback in preparing for the development plan of publishing industry.	Central party–state	Business
78	Meeting of staff congress	The reform on human resource management (employment and income has to be approved by the staff congress).	GDPG	Business

Activity number	Events	Description	Initiator	Function
79	South China Book Fair	It was part of the effort of the provincial Party/government in building "a preeminent cultural province."	Provincial Party/government	Publicity, Business
80	Attending the Frankfurt Book Fair	Organized by the Central Party Propaganda Department and GAPP as part of the "going out" effort.	Central party–state, GDPG	Business, publicity
81	The 10th Publishing Learning Forum (Organized by the provincial APP and GDPG)	The speech was given by an industry expert on the publishing business in China.	Provincial Party/government, GDPG	Business
82	Visit to Jieli Publishing House	Learning the business experience of Jieli Publishing House.	GDPG	Business
83	Teaching competition by using a textbook of GDPG	Jointly run by GDPG and the Chinese Society of Education.	GDPG	Business
84	Discussion on the teaching of a textbook of GDPG		GDPG	Business
85	Finishing the transformation of eight subsidiary publishing houses into enterprises	New business licenses were issued by the government.	Central party–state	Business
86	Instruction to subsidiary publishing houses on the publishing plan of next year	Ten topics, which covered a wide range of topics, were listed for publishing houses to focus on. GAPP required publishing houses to report their annual publishing plans.	Central party–state, GDPG	Business, social intervention, Party, publicity

(Continued)

Activity number	Events	Description	Initiator	Function
87	Meeting on the development strategy of magazines published by GDPG	The plan was to merge the magazines published by different member firms into one operation.	GDPG	Business
88	Meeting of senior core staff	Also attended by the Director of provincial APP.	GDPG	Business
89	Board meeting	Discussing the corporate regulations on personnel management, finance and accounting management, censorship, etc.	GDPG	Business, Party
90	Meeting on the implementation of "Three Administrative Reforms"	Discussing the reform of personnel management and remuneration system.	GDPG	Business
91	The implementation of the movement of "cadres into rural areas" (*xia jiceng*)		Central party–state	Social intervention
92	Meeting on the safety measures during the new year's holiday	Implementing the instruction of the provincial government on industrial safety.	Provincial Party/government	Business
93	The 20th anniversary celebration of the Guangdong Education Publishing House		GDPG	Business
94	The 20th anniversary celebration of the magazine of *Great Trade*		GDPG	Business
95	Visit to a member firm about its business operation		GDPG	Business
96	Recruitment of graduates for the member firms of GDPG	Starting from 2006, the recruitment of graduates of member firms would be organized by the Human Resource Department of GDPG.	GDPG	Business

Intervention of the Party-State in the Activities of GDPG (2005)

Serial no.	Activity number	Events	Description	Initiator	Function	Forms of intervention
1	1	Meeting on mobilizing the political movement of "Keeping Communists Advanced"	"Keeping Communists Advanced" is a movement instructed by the central Party from January 2005.	Central party-state	Party	Party branch
2	2	Launch ceremony of a book series on the issue of "three-rurals" (peasants, villages and agriculture)	Books dealing with the issue of "three-rurals" are encouraged by the central party-state.	Central party-state	Social intervention	Content
3	3	Annual meeting on the work plan of the new year	A meeting on implementing the instruction of GAPP and the provincial Party propaganda department. Topics included propaganda and moral education tasks, commercialization and business operation of GDPG.	Central party-state, provincial Party/ government, GDPG	Party, business	Propaganda, content, institution, others
4	6	Implementing the political movement of	The movement of "cadres into rural areas" was organized	Central party-state	Social intervention	Party branch

Serial no.	Activity number	Events	Description	Initiator	Function	Forms of intervention
		"cadres into rural areas" (*xia jiceng*). A couple of employees were sent to a poverty-relief village	by the provincial Party. However, it has been implemented across the country since 1990.			
5	7	Political study of "Keeping Communists Advanced"	"Keeping Communists Advanced" was a thought work among Party members and was instructed by the central Party.	Central party-state	Party	Party branch
6	8	The 7th Publishing Learning Forum (Organized by the provincial APP and GDPG)	This session, entitled "Party"s leadership and current economic situation", was claimed to be related to the campaign of "Keeping Communists Advanced".	Provincial Party/government	Party	Party branch
7	9	Publishing of a video CD for the political study of Party members	This video CD was commissioned by the provincial Party	Provincial Party/government	Party	Propaganda, subsidy

(Continued)

Serial no.	Activity number	Events	Description	Initiator	Function	Forms of intervention
		during the campaign of "Keeping Communists Advanced"	to an audio–video publisher of GDPG.			
8	11	Signing anticorruption commitment agreements in accordance with the Party discipline and anti-corruption requirement	Part of the campaign of the central Party against the problem of corruption. All leaders of GDPG and its subsidiaries had to sign it.	Central party–state	Party	Party branch
9	12	Visit of officials from the provincial APP to several member firms of GDPG	Purpose of this visit is not discernible.	Provincial Party/government	Miscellaneous	Others
10	15	Visit of Li Changchun, a central Party leader to GDPG	The focus of the visit is on the reform of cultural industry, ideological control and the "going out" policy.	Central party–state	Party, business, publicity	Propaganda, Institution, content, others
11	16			Central party–state	Business	Institution

Serial no.	Activity number	Events	Description	Initiator	Function	Forms of intervention
		Visit of officials from provincial Party propaganda department	Mainly a follow-up meeting on how to implement Li Changchun''s Instruction on the reform of publishing industry.			
12	17	Meeting of GDPG on implementing Li Changchun's Instruction	A follow-up meeting on implementing Li Changchun's instruction on the reform of publishing industry.	Central party–state	Business	Institution
13	18	Meeting on the appointment of leaders to the new corporatized GDPG	Appointment was made by the provincial Party.	Provincial Party/government	Business	Personnel
14	19	Meeting on the political movement of "Keeping Communists Advanced" (second stage)		Central party–state	Party	Party branch

(Continued)

Serial no.	Activity number	Events	Description	Initiator	Function	Forms of intervention
15	20	Visit of officials from the central Party propaganda department and GAPP to GDPG	A follow-up visit on how GDPG would implement the instruction of Li Changchun. GDPG was instructed to push forward its corporatization, implement the policy of "going out", and ensure ideological control.	Central party–state	Party, business, publicity	Institution, propaganda, content, others
16	21	Visit to Liaoning Publishing Group in order to learn from its reform	Li Changchun instructed GDPG to learn from Liaoning Publishing Group on its reform in his visit.	Central party–state	Business	Institution
17	22	Meeting on the strategy of "going out" and on attending international book fairs	A meeting on implementing the "going out" policy instructed by the central Party propaganda department and GAPP.	Central party–state	Publicity	Trade fair

Serial no.	Activity number	Events	Description	Initiator	Function	Forms of intervention
18	23	Party's "Democratic Meetings"	Provincial Party required Party committees in governments and SOEs to run open forums in order to receive feedback from employees. But it was a policy implemented from 1990 by the central Party.	Central party–state	Party	Party branch
19	25	Briefing meeting about the visit to Liaoning Publishing Group	A follow-up to Li Changchun's instruction.	Central party–state	Business	Institution
20	27	Launch ceremony of a book series on "Lingnan (or Guangdong) Culture"	Book series organized by the provincial Party and government to publicize the local culture.	Provincial Party/ government	Publicity	Content
21	28	Meeting on the political movement of "Keeping Communists Advanced" (third stage)		Central party–state	Party	Party branch

(Continued)

Serial no.	Activity number	Events	Description	Initiator	Function	Forms of intervention
22	29	Visit to a poverty relief county and villages	It was claimed to be part of the "cadres into rural areas" movement.	Central party-state	Social intervention	Party branch
23	39	Donation of books on the topic "three-rurals" to poverty relief villages	Organized by the provincial APP.	Provincial Party/government	Social intervention	Others
24	44	Visit of GAPP officials to Hong Kong Xinhua Bookstore	Hong Kong Xinhua Bookstore was a joint-venture invested by GDPG and a Hong Kong company as a channel of selling books published in mainland China.	Central party-state	Publicity	Others
25	45	Election of Party Committee of GDPG group company	This kind of election is the requirement of the Party constitution.	Central party-state	Party	Party branch
26	46	The publishing of a book on local culture, which is entitled You Don't Really Understand Cantonese People (qishi ni budong guangdongren)	The Director of provincial APP and the Chair of Board of GDPG proposed this publishing project.	Provincial Party/government, GDPG	Publicity	Content

Serial no.	Activity number	Events	Description	Initiator	Function	Forms of intervention
27	48	The 9th Publishing Learning Forum (on the topic of anticorruption)	In response to the provincial Party's movement of "Disciplinary Education Month"	Provincial Party/government	Party	Party branch
28	50	Meeting on the transformation of subsidiaries into enterprises	Guangdong was chosen by the central party–state as a pilot province for the reform of cultural system.	Central party–state	Business	Institution
29	51	Publishing and donation of a new book on the Antidrug Campaign	Nationwide anti-drug education was instructed by the central party–state.	Central party–state	Social intervention	Content, others
30	53	Mobilization meeting on the movement of "Disciplinary month" and a visit of more than 100 staff to a court trial	Required by the provincial Party disciplinary department.	Provincial Party/government	Party	Party branch
31	56	Meeting on the political study among leaders of GDPG	The provincial Party instructed this political study in all provincial state–owned enterprises.	Provincial Party/government	Party	Party branch

(*Continued*)

Serial no.	Activity number	Events	Description	Initiator	Function	Forms of intervention
32	57	Meeting on the organization of 2005 South China Book Fair	This book fair is entrusted to GDPG by the provincial Party and government as part of the effort of building a "pre-eminent cultural province".	Provincial party/government	Publicity	Trade fair
33	59	Visit to retired staff who took part in World War Two	Part of the activities in celebration of the end of "Anti Japanese Aggression War". This kind of visit happens in most state-owned enterprises and other state-controlled organizations.	Central party–state	Miscellaneous	Others
34	61	Meeting on the policy of further reform of state-owned enterprises and enhancing the ability of innovation	Following the visit of the Prime Minister to Guangdong, the provincial Party/government instructed state-owned enterprises to deepen their reform and enhance the ability of innovation.	Central party–state	Business	Others

Serial no.	Activity number	Events	Description	Initiator	Function	Forms of intervention
35	62	Attending Beijing International Book Fair	Organized by the provincial APP, but GDPG might have attended without its instruction.	Provincial party/government, GDPG	Publicity, business	Trade fair
36	67	Organizing printing exhibition	Organized by the provincial APP and GDPG.	Provincial party/government, GDPG	Business	Trade fair
37	70	Meeting on implementing the decisions of the 5th Plenary of 16th National Party Congress	The Party Congress decided the development plan for the next five years. Most state-owned enterprises held such a meeting to implement the guideline of the central party–state. GDPG proposed publishing tasks on ideological propaganda, promotion of local culture and also planned to finish the corporatization of subsidiary publishers.	Central party–state	Party, business	Propaganda, content, institution, others

(Continued)

Serial no.	Activity number	Events	Description	Initiator	Function	Forms of intervention
38	72	Opening Ceremony of Guangzhou International Animation Exhibition	Part of the activities of South China Book Fair. The organization of the fair was entrusted by the provincial Party/government to GDPG.	Provincial party/government	Business, publicity	Trade fair
39	74	Anticorruption meeting on a case happened in GDPG	Organized by the provincial Party disciplinary organ.	Provincial Party/government	Party	Party branch
40	75	Pan Pearl River Delta Publishing Forum	Organized by the local APPs of nine provinces including Guangdong.	Provincial party/government	Business	Others
41	77	Visit of a deputy Director of GAPP to GDPG	GAPP was collecting feedback in preparing for the development plan of publishing industry.	Central party-state	Business	Others
42	79	South China Book Fair	It was part of the effort of the provincial Party/government in building "a pre-eminent cultural province."	Provincial party/government	Publicity, Business	Trade fair

Serial no.	Activity number	Events	Description	Initiator	Function	Forms of intervention
43	80	Attending the Frankfurt Book Fair	Organized by the Central Party Propaganda Department and GAPP as part of the "going out" effort.	Central party-state, GDPG	Business, publicity	Trade fair
44	81	The 10th Publishing Learning Forum (Organized by the provincial APP and GDPG)	The speech was given by an industry expert on the publishing business in China.	Provincial party/government, GDPG	Business	Others
45	85	Finishing the transformation of eight subsidiary publishing houses into enterprises	New business licenses were issued by the government.	Central party-state	Business	Institution
46	86	Instruction to subsidiary publishing houses on the publishing plan of next year	Ten topics, which covered a wide range of topics, were listed for publishing houses to focus on. GAPP required publishing houses to report their annual publishing plans.	Central party-state, GDPG	Business, social intervention, party, publicity	Propaganda, content, others

(Continued)

Serial no.	Activity number	Events	Description	Initiator	Function	Forms of intervention
47	91	The implementation of the movement of "cadres into rural areas" (*xia jiceng*)		Central party-state	Social intervention	Party branch
48	92	Meeting on the safety measures during the new year's holiday	Implementing the instruction of the provincial government on industrial safety.	Provincial party/ government	Business	Others

INDEX

Note: Page numbers followed by "*f*" and "*t*" refer to figures and tables, respectively.

A

Academic books, 23, 102–103
Academic journals, 199–200
"Accessible books", 84–85
Administration, 24–33
    authority, 24–26
    censorship and self-censorship, 29–30
    of China's publishing industry, 138–139
    sponsoring system, 28–29
Administration of Press, Publication, Radio, Film, and Television (APPRFT), 24–25, 208–209
"Administrative power", 133
Administrative Provisions on Book Publishing, 29–30
Administrative Provisions on Electronic Publications, 207
Administrative reforms, 138–139
Administrative restriction, 78
Amazon, 198, 251–252
Amazon Kindle, 202, 207–208
Annual publishing plan, 29–32, 55–57
"Anti-Rightist Campaign", 69, 115
APPRFT. *See* Administration of Press, Publication, Radio, Film, and Television (APPRFT)
AR technology. *See* Augment reality technology (AR technology)
Asset assessment, 176
Augment reality technology (AR technology), 250
Author payment system, 88, 102–103

B

B2C. *See* Business-to-consumer (B2C)
Baidu, Alibaba, and Tencent (BAT), 198
Baidu Library, 199
Baidu wenku. *See* Baidu Library
BAT. *See* Baidu, Alibaba, and Tencent (BAT)

BBS. *See* Bulletin Board Systems (BBS)
Beijing Motie Book, 45–46
Beijing municipal social security system, 177
Beijing National Digital Publishing Base, 208–209
Beijing OpenBook, 23–24, 35–36, 205
Beijing Republic Publishing, 43
Beijing United Publishing Company, 35–36
Berne Convention and Universal Copyright Convention (1992), 28
Bianji bu. *See* "Editorial branch"
"Blockbuster strategy", 146
Book consumption, 20–23
Book distribution business, 48–51, 73, 152
Book drought, 83–84
Book prices, 102
Book publishers, 31
Book publishing in China, 19–20, 67, 96–97, 221
    commercialization of book publishing, 97–103, 257–258
    communization of publishing, 70–87
    elimination of private publishing businesses, 75–82
    excess inventory, 57–58
        total inventory and total annual sales, 57*t*
    focus and approach, 9–13
    foreign books and capital in, 47–49
        book imports in China, 47*t*
        rights licensing of books, 48*t*
    groups, 131, 145
    ideology and commercialization, 118–120
        China's ideology in flux, 113–115
        China's shaky ideology, 111–113
        ideology, intellectuals, and politics, 120–122

Book publishing in China (*Continued*)
  ideology and publications, 115–118
  industry, 3
  media transformation in China, 3–9
  number of publishers, 75*t*
  operation of planned book publishing,
    87–97
  organization of book, 13–15
  periods of publishing history during
    People's Republic, 68*t*
  problems, 53–58
    of communized book publishing,
      82–87
  reliance on school books, 54–57
  piracy, 53–54
  title output, 82*t*
Book review, 71–72, 81
Books and Periodicals Distribution
  Association of China, 26
Booksellers and supply chain, 50–53, 52*f*
Born-digital e-books, 203, 208
"Bourgeois liberalization", 118
Braille Publishing House, 167–168
Buju. *See* Geographic layout
Bulletin Board Systems (BBS), 211
"Bureaucratic decentralization", 6–8
Bureaucratic style of personnel
  management, 170–171
Business groups, 142–143
Business intervention, 240–241
"Business sector", 162
Business-to-consumer (B2C), 53

C

CAC. *See* Cyberspace Administration of
  China (CAC)
"Capitalist thinking", 119
Catalogue of Approved Textbooks,
  182–183
CCP. *See* Chinese Communist Party
  (CCP)
Censorship, 29–30, 81, 84, 243
  cultural revolution, 115–117
  ideological, 213
  party-endorsed book reviews in, 81
Central Leading Group for Cyberspace
  Affairs, 25

Central Party Press Commission, 70–71
Central Party Propaganda Department,
  25–26
"Central party-state" activity, 238
Central Propaganda Department, 25–26
"Centralized command" system, 6–7
Centralized Xinhua Bookstore system, 89
CEPIEC. *See* China Educational
  Publications Import and Export
  Corporation (CEPIEC)
Changjiang shangbao. *See Changjiang Times*
Changjiang Times, 148
Chanye shuxing. *See* Economic sector
Children's books, 23, 86, 95–96
China
  book market, 20–22
  business groups, 131
  contributory pension scheme, 176
  economic policy, 6–7
  economic reforms, 7–8
  ideology in flux, 113–115
  institutional economic reform, 6
  media, 4, 148
    commercialization, 8
    groups, 131
    system, 4–5
  shaky ideology, 111–113
China Book Business Report, 38–40
China Book Distribution Company, 79
China Book Publishing, 38
China Educational Publications Import and
  Export Corporation (CEPIEC), 47
China Electric Power Press, 35, 42
China Electricity Council, 42
China Internet Network Information
  Center (CNNIC), 198
China Literature, 215
China Literature Limited (*yuewen*), 212
China National Knowledge Infrastructure
  (CNKI), 199–200
China National Nuclear Corporation,
  138–139
China National Petroleum Corporation,
  138–139
China National Publications Import and
  Export Corporation (CNPIEC),
  47, 58–59

China Publishing Governmental Awards, 31–32

China Publishing Group, 58–59, 133–134, 162–163

Chinese Academy of Press and Publication, 22, 201–202

Chinese book publishing. *See* Book publishing in China

Chinese classics, 23, 115–117

Chinese Communist Party (CCP), 3, 25–26, 70–71, 112–113

Chinese media, 1

Chinese publishers, 23

Chinese publishing industry, 71

Chongfu langfei. See "Duplication and waste" of publications

Chongjiang, chongjin, chongshi, 248

Chuban guanli tiaoli. See Regulations on Administration of Publication

Chuban ju. See Publishing Branch of General Bureau of Publications

Chuban ziyuan bu. See Publishing Resource Department

Chuban zongshu. See General Bureau of Publications

Chushu fanwei. See "Subject areas"

Circular on reform of Press, Publishing, Broadcasting and Movie Industries. *See No. 17 Document*

"Class struggle", 97, 115–117

CNKI. *See* China National Knowledge Infrastructure (CNKI)

CNNIC. *See* China Internet Network Information Center (CNNIC)

CNPIEC. *See* China National Publications Import and Export Corporation (CNPIEC)

CNPIEC approval procedure for import of books and periodicals, 47

"Commercial cultural enterprises", 163–164

Commercial Press, 78

Commercialization, 5–6, 9, 225–226, 259. *See also* Decentralization in book publishing
    of book publishing, 4–5, 19–20, 97–103

dismantling monopoly in book distribution, 100–102

expansion of autonomy, 98–100

price controls and author payment, 102–103

of China's media, 8

of online fiction, 211–212

of publishing, 213
    and ideology, 118–120
    houses, 186–188
    industry, 226

Commune bookstore, 89

Communist ideology, 111

Communization of publishing, 70–87, 102
    problems of communized book publishing, 82–87
    unification and specialization, 72–75

"Compulsory activities", 237

Compulsory distribution, 83

Conglomeration of publishing, 14–15, 58–59, 161
    economic advantages, 143–150
    economic rationale for media conglomeration, 145–147
    of publishing groups in China, 147–150
    of GDPG
        business areas of GDPG and member firms, 224t
        expansion of GDPG and local government, 231–232
        formation, 229–231
        provincial publishing industry development and origin of GDPG, 223–229
    of publishing, 129
        economic advantages, 143–150
        globalization and publishing groups, 150–154
        institutional organization, 137–143
        key events, 130t
        publishing groups in China, 135t
        stages, 130–137
        top ten publishing groups, 60t

Consumer books, 23

Content scrutiny system, 214–215

Contract Responsibility System, 186–187

Control
  mapping book publishing in China,
    24—33
    censorship and self-censorship, 29—30
    sponsoring system, 28—29
  measures over publishers, 31—33
  system, 118
Copyright, 212
  law, 28
  protection, 28
Corporatization, 5, 14—15, 59—60, 161.
    See also Globalization
  economic reform process, 162
  of GDPG, 232—235, 247—248
  key events, 130*t*
  publishing houses
    economic sustainability and
      corporatization,
      177—186
    reform of public service units and
      transformation, 168—177
    status, 165—168
  reform of state-owned enterprises,
    186—188
CQVIP, 199
"Criterion of truth", 113
Cultural company, 43
Cultural establishment, 119
"Cultural industries", 120, 143—144, 162
Cultural public service units, 162—163
"Cultural public service units for public
    interests", 163—164
"Cultural real estate", 250—251
Cultural Revolution, 69—70, 91—97,
    115—117, 225
Cultural studio, 43
Cultural system, 133—134
"Cultural system", 119—120
"Cultural units", 119—120, 133—134
Cyberspace Administration of China
    (CAC), 25

D

Dangdang, 251—252
Dangjian. See Party construction
Data sources, 235—236

Decentralization in book publishing, 6—7,
    9, 33—43, 258
  market share of publishers, 35—37
  national and regional publishers, 33—35
  provincial publishing industry, 38—40
"Decentralized command" system, 6—7
Decentralized planned economy, 96—97
Decentralized Xinhua Bookstore system, 89
Decisions on Improving further Scrutiny
    Reading of Books (2004), 28
Decisions on Improving Publishing
    Undertaking by Central Party
    Committee and State Council, 119
Decisions on Speeding up Digital
    Publishing Industry, 208—209
Decisions on the Current Reform of
    Publishing Houses, 118
Decree on Censoring Books and
    Magazines, 28
Dengsi dilemma, 204
Deregulation, 5—6, 144
Di yici de qinmi jiechu. See First Intimate
    Contact
Dianzi chubanwu guanli guiding.
    See Administrative Provisions on
    Electronic Publications
Difang wenyi chubanshe lianhe faxing jituan.
    See United Distribution Group of
    Provincial Arts and Literature
    Publishing Houses
"Digital Guangdong", 249
Digital piracy, 199
Digital publishing, 198—199, 221—223,
    249—253
  business, 249
  e-books in trade publishing, 200—210
  early developments in, 199—200
  online fiction publishing, 210—216
"Digital reading", 251—252
Digital technologies, 198
Digital transformation, 249—250
  of China's journal publishing, 199—200
  of China's publishing industry, 197, 199
  in China's trade publishing, 197—198
  Chinese state-owned publishers and,
    203—204
  promotion, 208—209

Direct-to-consumers sales, 251–252
Disintermediation, 208
Distribution Section of CCP Propaganda
    Department, 70–71
Douzheng celue. See Struggle strategy
"Dual benefits", 166–167, 242
Dual-track system, 186–187
Duokan (e-book aggregator), 205–206
"Duplication and waste" of publications,
    74

E
E-book
    e-book business, government support
        and, 208–210
    annual revenue of national digital
        publishing parks in China, 209*t*
    enhanced, 203
    publishers, 207
    reading devices, 202, 210
    selling platforms, 210–211
    in trade publishing, 200–210
        e-book market, 201–202
        government support and e-book
            business, 208–210
        institutional and structural problems,
            203–206
        regulations and self-publishing,
            206–208
        sales of digital publications, 202*t*
E-ink technology, 200–201
Economic benefit, 166–167
Economic buoyancy, 246
Economic planning, 223–225
Economic reforms, 3, 5–6, 11, 119, 162,
    225–226, 228
Economic returns, 177–178
Economic sector, 119
Economic sustainability and
        corporatization of publishing
        houses, 177–186
    students and schools during stage of
        compulsory education, 180*t*
Economic sustainability and profitability,
    162
Economists, 145–146, 153
"Editorial branch", 77, 98–99

Editorial sector, 162
Editors, 95–96, 248
    in business entity, 214–215
    condescending attitude, 84–85
    publishers and, 31
    qualification, 32
    role, 214
Editors-owned cooperative publishers,
    87–88
"Educated youth", 94
Education/pedagogy, 23
Educational publishing, 23–24, 200–201
English language teaching (ELT), 35–36,
    205
Enhanced e-books, 203
Enterprises, 2, 166–167
"Enterprises managed as public service
    units", 187–188
Enthusiasm for market
        economy, 221
Establishment of publishing groups.
    See Conglomeration of publishing
Expansion of autonomy, 98–100
"Exploiting loopholes", 78

F
Facebook, 198
Farsight, 228
Fengjian yidu. See Poisonous feudal legacy
Fenpei tizhi. See Income distribution system
Financial autonomy, 100
First Intimate Contact, 211
Fiscal decentralization, 231–232
Five Antis Campaign, 80–81
Flower City Publishing
    House, 225–226
Foreign capital, 214–215
Foreign Language Teaching and Research
    Press, 35–36
Foreign policies, 112–113
Four fundamental principles, 11
"Four unchangeables", 11, 136, 233–234
Fragmented market, 41–43
Freemium business model, 211–212, 214
"Fundamental-instrumental discrepancy",
    114–115

G

Gaizao. See Transformation
GAPP. See General Administration of Press and Publication (GAPP)
GDPG. See Guangdong Provincial Publishing Group (GDPG)
GDPG activities (2005), 261–274
GDPG Digital Publishing Company, 252–253
GDPG Regulation of Rewarding Content Production, 243
GDPG Regulation on Scrutiny Reading of Publications, 243
General Administration of Press and Publication (GAPP), 24–25, 28, 133, 161, 214, 223
General Administration of Xinhua Bookstore, 72–73
General Administration of Xinhua Printer, 73
General Bureau of Publications, 70–72, 75–76, 78–79, 81, 84
"General distribution right", 51
General Store of Xinhua Bookstore, 50–51, 70–71, 73, 95
Genre fiction, 204–205, 213
Geographic layout, 27
Globalization, 150–154, 208
    Illusory Wolf, 152–154
    and publishing conglomeration, 151–152
Going out, 49–50
Golden share system, 214–215
Gonghe Liandong. See Beijing Republic Publishing
Gongshe shudian. See Commune bookstore
Gongyixing wenhua shiye danwei. See "Cultural public service units for public interests"
Good political consciousness, 82–83
Google, 198
Government support and e-book business, 208–210
GPPH. See Guangdong People's Publishing House (GPPH)
Great Leap Forward, 69, 87–91, 112

Guangcai yinwu gongsi. See Guangdong Color Printing Company
Guangdong, 232
Guangdong Color Printing Company, 228–229
Guangdong Economy Publishing House, 225–226
Guangdong Education Publishing House, 225–226
Guangdong jiaocai chuban zhongxin. See Guangdong Textbook Reprinting Center
Guangdong jingshen. See "Guangdong Spirit"
Guangdong jiuzhang. See Guangdong: Nine Chapters
Guangdong Language Audiovisual & Electronic Publishing House, 225–226
Guangdong People's Publishing House (GPPH), 225–226
Guangdong Petrel Electronic & Audio–Video Publishing House, 225–226
Guangdong Provincial Administration of Press and Publication, 227–228
Guangdong Provincial General Publishing Company, 228–229
Guangdong Provincial Plan on Development of Preeminent Cultural Province 2011–2020, 250–251
Guangdong Provincial Publishing Administration Bureau, 225–228
Guangdong Provincial Publishing Company, 228
Guangdong Provincial Publishing Group (GDPG), 13, 221–223, 239
    conglomeration of, 223–232
    corporatization of, 232–235
    digital publishing, 249–253
    and party politics, 235–248
Guangdong sheng chuban gongsi. See Guangdong Provincial Publishing Company
Guangdong sheng chuban jituan youxian gongsi chuban wu shenu guanli banfa.

See GDPG Regulation on Scrutiny Reading of Publications

Guangdong sheng chuban jituan youxian gongsi neirong shengchan jiangli banfa. *See* GDPG Regulation of Rewarding Content Production

Guangdong sheng chuban jituan youxian gongsi tushu chuban cengji zeren ji zeren zhuijiu yu chufa banfa. *See* Regulation on Hierarchical Division of (Political) Responsibility of Publishing of GDPG

Guangdong sheng chuban shiye guanli ju. *See* Guangdong Provincial Publishing Administration Bureau

Guangdong sheng chuban zong gongsi. *See* Guangdong Provincial General Publishing Company

Guangdong sheng jianshe wenhua qiangsheng guihua gangyao 2011—2020, 250—251

Guangdong sheng xinwen chubanju. *See* Guangdong Provincial Administration of Press and Publication

"Guangdong Spirit", 242—243

Guangdong Textbook Reprinting Center, 222

Guangdong Xinhua Distribution Group, 236

Guangdong: Nine Chapters, 242—243

Guangdongsheng chuban shiye guanliju. *See* Guangdong Provincial Publishing Administration Bureau

Guangming Daily Publishing House, 173

Guangyu xinwen chuban guangbo yingshiye gaige de tongzhi. See No. 17 Document

Guangzhou Culture Publishing House, 227—228

Guangzhou Daily Group, 131

Guangzhou wenhua chubanshe. *See* Guangzhou Culture Publishing House

Guanli guosi. See "Too inflexible" government

Guanli shukan chubanye yinshuaye faxingye zanxing tiaoli. See Provisional Administrative Decree on Publishing, Printing and Distribution

Guanli tizhi. See Management system

Guanyu dangqian chubanshe gaige de ruogan yijian. See Decisions on the Current Reform of Publishing Houses

Guanyu dui chuban waiguo tushu jinxing hetong dengji de tongzhi. See Notice on Registration of Licensing Contract of Foreign Books

Guanyu jiakuai woguo shuzi chuban chanye fazhan de ruogan yijian. *See* Decisions on Speeding up Digital Publishing Industry

Guanyu jiaqiang tushu shendu gongzuo de tongzhi. See Notice on Strengthening Scrutiny Reading of Books

Guanyu jinyibu jiaqiang tushu shendu gongzuo de yijian (2004). *See* Decisions on Improving further Scrutiny Reading of Books (2004)

Guanyu jinzhi maimai shuhao de tongzhi. *See* Notice on prohibiting trading of ISBN

Guanyu zhongxiaoxue jiaofu cailiao ganli banfa de shishi yijian. See Implementation of Regulation on School Ancillary Study Aids

Guiding dongzuo. See "Compulsory activities"

Guojia shiyiwu shiqi wenhua fazhan guihua gangyao. See National 11th Five Year Plan for Development of Culture

Guomingdang. See Nationalist government

Guoziwei. See State-owned Assets Supervision and Administration Commission

H

Haitian chubanshe. See Sea-sky Publishing
House
Hierarchical political structure, 231−232
High speed rotary letterpress machines,
102−103
Hollywood films, 146
Horizontal piece system. *See* Kuai system
"House distribution", 51−52
Huabo, 250−251
Hunan People's Publishing House, 98−99
Hunan Provincial Publishing
Administration Bureau, 98−99
Hunan sheng chuban shiye guanli ju.
See Hunan Provincial Publishing
Administration Bureau
"Hundred Flowers" movement, 69, 87−88
"Hybrid creations of government and
business", 20

I

"Ideocracy", 111
Ideological arena, 119
Ideological control, 233−234
Ideological crisis, 241
"Ideological direction", 247
Ideological indoctrination, 241−242
Ideological pluralism, 121
Ideological propaganda, 243
Ideological propaganda tasks, 242−243
Ideological rectification process, 118
Ideological variations, 115
Ideology and commercialization,
118−120
China's ideology in flux, 113−115
China's shaky ideology, 111−113
ideology, intellectuals, and politics,
120−122
ideology and publications, 115−118
Illusory Wolf, 152−154
Implementation of Regulation on School
Ancillary Study Aids, 55−57
In-house system of self-censorship, 81
Income distribution system, 118
Informal interview, 245
Information Bulletin, 221−222, 230−235,
246

Information technology (IT), 197, 212
adoption of, 199−200
Initial public offering (IPO), 187
prospectus, 149−150
"Inlanders, The", 242−243
Institutional changes, 118
Institutional organization, 137−143
administration of China's publishing
industry, 138−139
business groups, 142−143
from provincial publishing general
houses to provincial publishing
groups, 139−142
"Institutional units", 161
Intellectual pluralism, 121
Intellectuals, 120−122
"Internal competitions", 244
Internal controls, 243−244
International Standard Book Numbers
(ISBNs), 31
Internationalization, 6
foreign books and capital in China's
publishing, 47−49
going out, 49−50
export of licensed rights by Chinese
publishers, 50*t*
private publishers, 43−47
Internet, 198
"Internet literature", 20−22, 200−201
Internet Plus plan, 197
IPO. *See* Initial public offering (IPO)
iReader, 199, 212
ISBN numbers, 102, 213
ISBNs. *See* International Standard Book
Numbers (ISBNs)
IT. *See* Information technology (IT)
Iximo. com, 210, 251−252

J

Jiangxi Publishing Group, 131−132
Jiaoxue yongshu mulu. See Catalogue of
Approved Textbooks
Jiaqiang tushu shendu gongzuo de tongzhi
(1994). *See* Notice on
Strengthening Scrutiny Reading of
Books
Jidu xuanti. See Quarterly publishing plans

Jiefang she. See Liberation Press
Jingji xiaoyi. See Economic benefit
Jingying bumen. See "Business sector"
Jingying tizhi. See Operation system
*Jingying xing tushu chuban danwei dengji
      pinggu banfa. See* Regulation on
      Grading and Assessing Business-
      oriented Publishing Houses
*Jingying xing wenhua qiye danwei.
      See* "Commercial cultural
      enterprises"
Jizhong guodu. See "Too centralized"
      government

K

Kindle X Migu e-book reader (2017),
      210–211
Kuai system, 33
Learning Publishing House. *See* Xuexi
      Publishing House

L

Legalization, 11–12
"Liberal-pluralist" approach, 10
Liberalization, 5
Liberation Press, 70–71
"Licensing system", 173
Lingdao tizhi. See Control system
Literature and arts books, 23
"*Little Red Book*", The, 93
Liyong. See Utilization
Local APPRFTs, 214–215
Local Party propaganda department,
      223–225
Local people's publishing houses, 73–74
Local Xinhua bookstores, 73
Local Xinhua printers, 73
Logging activities, 236–239

M

Management system, 118
Managing organization, 28–29
*Mao zhuxi zhuzuo chuban bangongshi.
      See* Publishing Office of Chairman
      Mao's Works
Mao's radical approach, 91

Maoist egalitarian principle, 122
Maoist period, 115
Maoist radical model of economic
      development, 112
Mapping book publishing in China
      booksellers and supply chain, 50–53
      decentralization in book publishing,
            33–43
      fragmented
            market, 41–43
      privatization and internationalization,
            43–50
      problems of Chinese book publishing,
            53–58
      publishing as business, 19–24
      recent state policies, 58–61
      regulation, administration, and control,
            24–33
Market, 20
      book consumption, 21*t*
      China's book publishing industry, 21*t*
      economy, 113–114, 221
      share
            annual retail sales, 36*t*
            of book categories, 23–24
            of publishers, 35–37
            top 10 publishers by sales revenue, 37*t*
            top 10 publishing groups, 37*t*
"Market decentralization", 6–7
"Market fragmentation", 6–7
Market-oriented literary production, 213
Market-oriented newspaper publishers, 2
Marketability, 177–178
Marketization, 5
"Masses", 88
Massive piracy, 54
Media, 162
      conglomerates, 147
      and cultural industries, 4
      economic rationale for media
            conglomeration, 145–147
      industry, 2
      marketization, 6
      organizations, 5–6
      transformation in China, 3–9, 13–14
Ministry of Commerce, 77
Ministry of Culture, 28, 88

Ministry of Industry and Information Technology, 25
Ministry of Information Industry, 214
Ministry of Light Industry, 77
Mobile internet, 198
Mobile phones, 202
Monopolized Xinhua Bookstore system, 100–101
Multimedia Print Reader technology (MPR technology), 250
Multiple labels, 237–238
Municipal "publishing groups", 231–232

N

Nanfang xuetang. See Southern Learning Classroom
Nanfang xuni shiyan shi. See Southern Virtual Experiments
National 11th Five Year Plan for Development of Culture, 249
National and regional publishers, 33–35, 34*t*
National Copyright Administration of China (NCAC), 25
National Development and Reform Commission (NDRC), 162–163
National Publishing Administration Bureau, 95, 100
National Reading Promotion Decree (2017), 22
National Reading Survey, 22
National school textbooks, 95–96
National television networks, 146
Nationalist government, 71
Natural sciences and technology books, 23
NCAC. *See* National Copyright Administration of China (NCAC)
NDRC. *See* National Development and Reform Commission (NDRC)
Neidi ren. See "Inlanders, The"
Network Readiness Index (NRI), 198
New Century Publishing House, 225–226
News organizations, 25–26
Newspaper publishing, 221–223
Niandu xuanti. See Annual publishing plan
Nit-picking, 80–81
No. 16 *Document*, 163–164

No. 17 *Document*, 162
Nonconsumer books, 23
Noneditorial sector, 162
Nongjia shuwu. See Village libraries
"Nonprofit organizations", 161
Notice on prohibiting trading of ISBN, 44–45
Notice on Registration of Licensing Contract of Foreign Books, 48
Notice on Strengthening Scrutiny Reading of Books, 28, 30
NRI. *See* Network Readiness Index (NRI)

O

OECD. *See* Organization for Economic Co-operation and Development (OECD)
Online
    booksellers, 251–252
    e-book
        publishing, 210
        selling platforms, 251–252
    genre fiction, 213
    poetry, 200–201
    rising of online literature, 212–214
Online fiction publishing, 200–201, 210–216
    online fiction business, 211–212
    regulations and control, 214–216
    rising of online literature, 212–214
"Online original publications", 201–202
OpenBook, 23–24
Operation system, 118
"Optional activities", 237, 239
Organization for Economic Co-operation and Development (OECD), 161

P

Paper price, 102
Party Committee, 28–29
Party congress, 113–114
Party construction, 238–239, 241–242
Party politics, GDPG and, 235–248
    data sources, 235–236
    GDPG after corporatization, 247–248
    internal controls, 243–244

logging activities, 236–239
party-state role, 239–243
taking care of business, 244–247
Party Propaganda Departments, 25–26, 142
Party-controlled literary and publishing
    system, 213
Party-controlled literary production
    system, 213
Party-endorsed book reviews, 81
Party-state, 76–77, 197
    intervention in activities of GDPG
        (2005), 275–288
    role, 239–243
Party's ideological policy, 121
People's Communes, 69
People's Daily, news organizations, 25–26
People's Education Press (PEP), 74,
    252–253
    e-Learning, 252–253
People's Publishing House, 73, 139–140,
    164
People's Republic of China (PRC),
    120–121
PEP. *See* People's Education Press (PEP)
Periods of relative relaxation, 120–121
Periods of repression, 120–121
Persistent powers
    data sources, 235–236
    GDPG after corporatization, 247–248
    internal controls, 243–244
    logging activities, 236–239
    party-state role, 239–243
    taking care of business, 244–247
Personnel system, 118
Piracy, 53–54, 212
Plan on Reinvigoration of Cultural
    Industries, 208–209
Planned book publishing
    Cultural Revolution and adjustment,
        91–97
    Great Leap Forward and adjustment,
        87–91
    number of publishers, 96t
    operation, 87–97
    output of machine-made paper and
        paperboard, 90t
    title output of China's book publishing, 92t

"Planned distribution" principle, 85
"Plate-renting" practice, 73–74, 181
Poisonous feudal legacy, 83
Political
    ideology, 121
    propaganda, 240
Political studies, 30
Politics, 120–122
Post-Mao era, 70
Post-publication censorship, 30
PPB. *See* Press and Publication Bureau
    (PPB)
PPP. *See* Purchase parity power (PPP)
PRC. *See* People's Republic of China
    (PRC)
Pre-tax profit, 149–150
"Preeminent cultural province", 230–231
Press and Publication Administration
    Bureaus, 28–29
Press and Publication Bureau (PPB), 31, 132
Price control(s), 102–103
    over book production, 103
Printers, 27
Private capital, 214
Private publishers, 43–47, 81–82, 103
Private publishing
    elimination of private publishing
        businesses, 75–82
    sector, 102
Private wholesalers and retailers, 101
Privatization, 5–6
    foreign books and capital in China's
        publishing, 47–49
    going out, 49–50
        export of licensed rights by Chinese
            publishers, 50t
    private publishers, 43–47
Profit margins, 223
Propaganda books, 205–206
Propaganda Department of CPC, 75–76
"Provincial Party/government", 238
Provincial publishing groups, 59
    from provincial publishing general
        houses to, 139–142
Provincial publishing industry, 38–40
    development and origin of GDPG,
        223–229

Provincial publishing industry (*Continued*)
　regional book sales, 41*t*
　title output by regions, 40*t*
　total number of publishing houses, 39*t*
Provincial Xinhua Bookstore, 137
Provisional Administrative Decree on
　　Publishing, Printing and
　　Distribution, 165
"Public institutions", 161
Public interest, 163–164
Public service units, 2, 129, 133–134,
　　161–162, 165, 168
"Public service units managed as
　　enterprises", 119–120, 161, 166
Publications, 115–118
Publicity, 238–239
Publishers, 19–20
　association of China, 26
　control measures over, 31–33
　market share, 35–37
Publishing. *See also* Book publishing in
　　China
　as business, 19–24
　　book consumption, 20–23
　　market overview, 20
　　market share of book categories,
　　　23–24
　conglomerates, 35–36
　conglomeration, 151–152
　groups, 150–154
　　in China, 135*t*
　　economic advantages of publishing
　　　groups in China, 147–150
　　formation, 138
　　globalization and publishing
　　　conglomeration, 151–152
　　Illusory Wolf, 152–154
　industry, 24, 161
　　in China, 1–2
　licensing and price control in
　　　supplementary learning materials,
　　　61
Publishing Branch of General Bureau of
　　Publications, 72–73
Publishing general house, 132, 140–142
Publishing houses, 28–29, 31, 161
　commercialization of, 186–188

　economic sustainability and
　　corporatization, 177–186
　reform of public service units and
　　transformation of, 168–177
　social backcloth for reform of public
　　service units, 168–172
　transformation of publishing houses,
　　172–177
　status, 165–168
Publishing Office of Chairman Mao's
　　Works, 92–93
Publishing Resource Department, 222,
　　243
Purchase parity power (PPP), 20

Q

Qiangpo tanpai. See Compulsory
　　distribution
Qiye. See Enterprises
Qiye danwei, shiyehua guanli.
　　See "Enterprises managed as public
　　service units"
Qiyehua guanli. See "Public service units
　　managed as enterprises"
Quarterly publishing plans, 29–30
Qunzhong. See "Masses"
Quotations from Chairman Mao, 96

R

"Radical-Marxist" approach, 10
Rampant piracy, 53
Real-name registration system, 31
Recommendations of the Propaganda
　　Department and GAPP on Further
　　Strengthening and Improving
　　Publishing Work. *See No.* 16
　　Document
"Rectification" campaign, 91
Reference books, 23, 51–52
Reference books, 95–96
Reform
　of public service units, 168–177
　　social backcloth for, 168–172
　of publishing industry, 221
　of SOEs, 186–188
"Reform of cultural system", 230–231

Regulation
  on administration
    of online publishing services,
      214–215
    of printing industry, 27
  in China publishing, 206–208
  on management of publishing, 28–29
  mapping book publishing in China,
    24–33
    censorship and self-censorship, 29–30
    regulations and laws, 26–28
    sponsoring system, 28–29
Regulation on Grading and Assessing
  Business-oriented Publishing
  Houses, 31–32
Regulation on Hierarchical Division of
  (Political) Responsibility of
  Publishing of GDPG, 243
Regulation on Internet Information
  Service (2000), 214
Regulation on School Ancillary Study
  Aids, 55–57
Regulations on Administration of
  Publication, 27
Reliance on school books, 54–57, 56t
Renmin chubanshe. See People's Publishing
  House
Renming gongshe. See People's Communes
Renshi tizhi. See Personnel system
Restriction, 76–77
"Restriction and transformation" process,
  77
Retail market, 205–206
Rightist attacks, 87–88
Rongshuxia website, 211

S

Sanfan wufan yundong. See Five Antis
  CampaignThree Antis Campaign
"Sannong" problem. *See* "Three-rurals"
  problem
Sanshen. See Scrutiny
SAPPRFT. *See* State Administration of
  Press, Publication, Radio, Film, and
  Television (SAPPRFT)
SARS. *See* Severe acute respiratory
  syndrome (SARS)

Scholarly journal publishing, 199–201
Science Publishing Group, 58–59,
  134–136, 142
Scrutiny, 30
Scrutiny reading, 30, 214–215, 243–244
SDPM Company. *See* Shandong Digital
  Publishing Media Company
  (SDPM Company)
Sea-sky Publishing House, 227–228
Second channel, 101
Selected Works of Mao Zedong, 96
Self-censorship, 29–30, 215
Self-funded public service units, 170
Self-published born-digital titles, 206
Self-publishing, 206–208
Selling platforms, 210
"Sense of political responsibility", 82–83
"Separation of government and
  enterprises" principle, 162–163,
  171–172, 228–231, 243
"Separation of government and public
  service units", 162–163, 171–172
Serialized web fiction, 200–201, 214
Severe acute respiratory syndrome (SARS),
  239
Shanda Interactive (Company), 211–212
Shandong Digital Publishing Media
  Company (SDPM Company), 210
Shandong Publishing General House,
  131–132, 229–230
Shandong Publishing Group, 137–138
Shanghai Publishing and Printing
  Company, 166
Shangwu yinshuguan. See Commercial Press
Shangye hua. See Commercialization
Sheban faxing. See "House distribution"
Sheban shudian. See Direct-to-consumers
  sales
Shehui xiaoyi. See "Social benefit"
Shehui zhuyi gaizao. See Socialist
  transformation
Shendu. See Scrutiny reading
Shengdu. See Scrutiny reading
Shichang hua. See Marketization
Shidai zhoubao. See Time Weekly
Shiming zhi. See Real-name registration
  system

Shiye danwei, qiyehua guanli. See "Public service units managed as enterprises"

Shiye danwei. See Public service units

Shortage economy. *See* Socialist planned economy

Shuangxiao. See "Dual benefits"

Shuhuang. See Book drought

Shuzi yuedu. See "Digital reading"

Sichuan Publishing Group Company, 131–132, 229–230

Sino-Soviet split, 112–113

Smart Learning, 252–253

Smart phones, 198

Social backcloth for reform of public service units, 168–172

"Social benefit", 166–167, 215

Social conditions, 212–213

Social interest, 167–168

"Social intervention", 238–239

Social sciences books, 23

Social security system, 175–176

"Socialist literary system", 213

Socialist market economy, 70, 113–114, 121, 167

Socialist planned economy, 85

Socialist spiritual civilization, 167

Socialist transformation, 69, 75, 79–80

SOEs. *See* State-owned enterprises (SOEs)

Song of Ouyang Hai, The, 115–117

Southern Learning Classroom, 253

Southern Publishing and Media Company (SPM), 222, 247, 250–252

Southern Publishing and Media Corporation. *See* Southern Publishing and Media Company (SPM)

Southern Virtual Experiments, 252–253

Soviet model, disadvantages of, 69

Soviet publishing industry, 71

Soviet Union, 112–113

Specialization, 72–75

Sphere of consensus, 109–110

Sphere of illegitimate controversy, 109–110

Sphere of legitimate controversy, 109–110

Spiritual pollution, 118

SPM. *See* Southern Publishing and Media Company (SPM)

Sponsor unit regulation, 174

Sponsoring organization, 28–29, 74, 229–230

"Sponsoring system", 28–29, 74

SPPA. *See* State Press and Publication Administration (SPPA)

State Administration of Press, Publication, Radio, Film, and Television (SAPPRFT), 22–25, 27, 199, 201–202, 205, 208–209, 212, 214–215

State policies, 58–61
 conglomeration, 58–59
 corporatization, 59–60
 licensing and price control in supplementary learning materials publishing, 61
 village libraries, 60

State Press and Publication Administration (SPPA), 24–25, 140, 165

State-controlled book distributors, 81

State-owned Assets Supervision and Administration Commission, 162–163

State-owned book distributors, 86

State-owned enterprises (SOEs), 142, 186
 reform, 186–188

State-owned enterprises, 235

State-owned publishers, 88, 203–204

STM books, 95–96

Struggle strategy, 77, 79–80

"Subject areas", 12, 31

Supplementary learning materials, 246–247

Supply chain
 booksellers and, 50–53
 copublishing supply chain in China's trade publishing, 52*f*

Synergy, 146–147

System distribution, 93–94, 175–176

T

Taohua.com, 199

Tencent, 202

Teshu guanli gu. See Golden share system

Textbook sales, 203–204
"Theme publishing" propaganda titles,
    251–252
Thinkingdom Media Group, 45–46
Thompson's critical conceptualization of
    ideology, 111
Three Antis Campaign, 80–81
Three Represents, The, 122
"Three-rurals" problem, 60
Tiananmen Square incident, 70
Tiao system, 33
Time Weekly, 223
Tongren chubanshe. See Editors-owned
    cooperative publishers
Tongshou tongzhi, 226
Tongsu duwu. See "Accessible books"
Tongyi. See Unification
"Too centralized" government, 89
"Too inflexible" government, 89
"Totalistic" ideology, 111
"Trade fair", 240–241
Trade publishing, 197–198, 205. *See also*
    Online fiction publishing
    e-books in, 200–210
Trading of ISBNs, 43–44, 185–186
Transformation, 76–77
    of China's book publishing, 19
    of publishing houses, 168–177
"Transformation into enterprises", 161
Tushu chuban guanli guiding.
    See Administrative Provisions on
    Book Publishing
Tushu pinglun. See Book Review
Tushu zazhi shencha banfa. See Decree on
    Censoring Books and Magazines

U
UK book retail market, 204–205
UK nonfiction market, 204–205
Unification, 72–75
United Distribution Group of Provincial
    Arts and Literature Publishing
    Houses, 131
Unlicensed e-books, 199
US e-book market, 206–207
Utilization, 76–77

V
"Valuable but unpopular books", 74–75
Value-added tax (VAT), 149–150
Vanilla e-book, 203
    in Western markets, 206
Vertical line system. *See* Tiao system
Village libraries, 60

W
Wanfang, 199
Wangluo wenxue. See "Internet literature"
Wangluo yuanchuang chuwuban. See "Online
    original publications"
Wenhua chanye zhenxing guihua. See Plan on
    Reinvigoration of Cultural
    Industries
Wenhua dasheng. See "Preeminent cultural
    province"
Wenhua dichan. See "Cultural real estate"
Wenhua gongsi. See Cultural company
Wenhua gongzuoshi. See Cultural studio
Wenhua shiye danwei. See Cultural public
    service units
Wenhua shuxing. See Cultural establishment
Wenhua tizhi. See Cultural system
Wenhua tizhi gaige. See "Reform of cultural
    system"
Western conglomerate, 131
Western markets, 207–208
Wolidou. See "Internal competitions"
Word group, 130–131
World Economic Forum, 198
World Trade Organization (WTO), 28,
    109, 151
Wuhan Publishing House, 28–29

X
Xianzhi. See Restriction
Xinhua Bookstore, 50–52
    General Store, 58–59
    publishing and distribution system,
        70–73
    system, 79
Xinhua Dictionary, 95
Xinhua Monthly Magazine, 71–72

Xinhua News Agency, news organizations, 25–26
Xinhua shudian zong guanlichu. *See* General Administration of Xinhua BookstoreGeneral Administration of Xinhua Printer
Xinhua shudian zongdian. *See* General Store of Xinhua Bookstore
Xinhua yuebao. *See* Xinhua Monthly Magazine
Xinjingdian Wenhua. *See* Thinkingdom Media Group
Xinxi chanye bu. *See* Ministry of Information Industry
Xinxi dongtai. *See* Information Bulletin
Xitong faxing. *See* System distribution
Xuexi Publishing House, 28–29

Y

Yishi xingtai shuxing. *See* Ideological arena
Yuanwang. *See* Farsight

Z

Zhangyue Technology, 202
Zhao mafan. *See* Nit-picking
Zhaosi dilemma, 204
Zhengzhi daoxiang. *See* "Ideological direction"
Zhengzhi xing. *See* "Sense of political responsibility"
Zhengzhi xiuyang hao. *See* Good political consciousness
Zhengzhi xuexi. *See* Political studies
Zhenli biaozhun. *See* "Criterion of truth"
Zhi xuexi. *See* Smart Learning
Zhiqing. *See* "Educated youth"
Zhonggong zhongyang guanyu jiaqiang chuban gongzuo de jueding. *See* Decisions on Improving Publishing Undertaking by Central Party Committee and State Council

Zhongguo dianli qiye lianhehui. *See* China Electricity Council
Zhongguo tushu chuban wang. *See* China Book Publishing
Zhongguo tushu jinchukou zong gongsi jinkou shukan ziliao shenpin guanli guiding. *See* CNPIEC approval procedure for import of books and periodicals
Zhongguo tushu shangbao. *See* China Book Business Report
Zhongguo xinwen chuban yanjiu yuan. *See* Chinese Academy of Press and Publication
Zhonghua Book Company, 78
Zhonghua shuju. *See* Zhonghua Book Company
Zhongxiaoxue jiaofu cailiao guanli banfa. *See* Regulation on School Ancillary Study Aids
Zhongyang dangbao weiyuanhui. *See* Central Party Press Commission
Zhongyang wangxin ban. *See* Central Leading Group for Cyberspace Affairs
Zhongyang xuanchuan bu xinwen chuban zongshu guanyu jinyibu jiaqiang he gaijin chuban gongzuo de ruogan yijian. *See* No. 16 Document
Zhuanqi gaizhi. *See* "Transformation into enterprises"
Zhuanyehua. *See* Specialization
Zhuban bumen. *See* Managing organizationSponsoring organization
Zhuguan zhuban zhidu. *See* "Sponsoring system"
Zixuan dongzuo. *See* "Optional activities"
Zong faxingquan. *See* "General distribution right"
Zongshe. *See* Publishing general house
Zou chuqu. *See* Going out
Zuan kongzi. *See* "Exploiting loopholes"

Printed in Great Britain
by Amazon